For my f[...]
Connie and [...]
Pinkowski,
with all good wishes.
Sincerely,
George Korson

Washington, D.C.
August 26, 1945

AT HIS SIDE

AT HIS SIDE

The Story of

THE AMERICAN RED CROSS

Overseas in World War II

By GEORGE KORSON

COWARD-McCANN, INC.

NEW YORK

This book is published on the same day in the Dominion of Canada by Longmans, Green & Company, Toronto.

MANUFACTURED IN THE UNITED STATES OF AMERICA
VAN REES PRESS . NEW YORK

TO THE MEMORY OF
AMERICAN RED CROSS MEN AND WOMEN
WHO GAVE THEIR LIVES SERVING THE ARMED FORCES IN
WORLD WAR II.

CONTENTS

CONTENTS

FOREWORD

LONG BEFORE PEARL HARBOR, THE AMERICAN RED CROSS SERVED IN World War II. Beginning with the Japanese invasion of China in 1937, it provided relief for the victims of aggression as one country after another was invaded. In the Far East, in Europe, and throughout the Middle East, its foreign war relief operations kept alive millions of civilians, mostly children, with food, clothing, and medical supplies.

The same day that German troops crossed the Polish border, the organization offered help to that stricken country through the International Red Cross Committee at Geneva. Relief, supervised by an American Red Cross staff, was distributed in the Government-General area, supplies being shipped from the United States through Italian ports. With Italy's entry into the war these ports were closed, and the Polish relief program, after available stocks had been exhausted, was discontinued. However, relief was extended to Polish refugees who fled to many countries.

Relief to Great Britain exceeded by far that for any other country. Aid began with a cash grant only a few hours after her declaration of war. Civilians bombed from their homes during the great air raids and refugees from Allied countries received the greater part of American Red Cross assistance. The American Junior Red Cross financed special nurseries for British children orphaned, maimed, or made homeless by German air attacks. The American Red Cross–Harvard University Hospital in England during 1941-1942 was prepared to fight epidemics if they had developed.

An American Red Cross relief mission arrived in Moscow not long after the invasion of Russian soil. From then on, a continuous stream of supplies, most of them purchased with United States Government funds, went to Russia over the winding desert and mountain roads from the Persian Gulf, through the hazardous waters of the Arctic Ocean to Murmansk or across the Siberian steppes from Vladivostok. Russia became the second largest field of American Red Cross foreign relief operations.

The American Red Cross was at work in France before its fall, and subsequently its activities were restricted to the unoccupied area where its workers supervised the distribution among civilians of six shiploads of food, clothing, and medicines. In May and June, 1941, bread made from American flour was distributed in unoccupied France. Later, the organization's efforts were directed toward providing milk for French children and layettes for infants.

Relief of various kinds was extended to many thousands of homeless refugees in Europe and throughout the Middle East.

In nearly every invaded country, relief started immediately after the enemy's attack and was continued as long as the distribution could be supervised by an American Red Cross staff. Norman H. Davis, then chairman of the American Red Cross, insisted upon this policy.

It was a fortuitous circumstance that found Mr. Davis directing the Red Cross in the most crucial period of its history. A man with the rare combination of experience and vision, of warm human traits and executive ability, he enjoyed the confidence of most of the civilized world and the affection and admiration of his fellow countrymen.

Chairman Davis was a roving ambassador for two wartime presidents, Woodrow Wilson and Franklin D. Roosevelt, and in peacetime served under two other presidents, Calvin Coolidge and Herbert Hoover. Most of his diplomatic missions in Europe concerned disarmament and peace, ideals closest to his heart. By nature a gentle, good-humored man, he was willing to fight only for peace. When the cause of world peace seemed lost, he found solace in his appointment by President Roosevelt to head the American Red Cross. That was in 1938. In a letter to Mrs. Roosevelt thanking her for her word of congratulation, Mr. Davis wrote: "I must say there is a humanitarian and spiritual aspect to the Red Cross which makes a particularly strong appeal to me. Having worked earnestly for many years without any appreciable results to bring about disarmament and peace and thus to prevent human suffering, I am glad to devote myself to the alleviation of human suffering which cannot be prevented."

As resolutely as he had fought for peace, Norman H. Davis threw himself into discharging the wartime mission of the Red Cross. Despite poor health, in 1943 he flew all over England, North Africa, and Sicily inspecting Red Cross installations and talking with Red Cross workers and American soldiers and officers. He gave of himself unsparingly until the last day, July 2, 1944, when, a victim of overwork, he died at Hot Springs, Virginia. His death was mourned universally.

To fill the vacancy left by Mr. Davis' death, President Roosevelt, on July 13, 1944, appointed Basil O'Connor, distinguished lawyer and philanthropist, as the organization's tenth chairman. The fol-

x

lowing December, Mr. O'Connor was reappointed, this time to the full term.

Former law partner, trusted friend and advisor, Mr. O'Connor long had been in the President's confidence, and now he was entrusted by him with the chairmanship of an organization that was close to Mr. Roosevelt's heart and to the hearts of countless Americans. To this exalted office, Mr. O'Connor brought personal qualities and experience that had won him distinction as a lawyer and as a national leader in the field of philanthropy, interreligious relations, and brotherhood. A man of vigor and boundless energy, serving as a volunteer, it was characteristic of him that only a few weeks after taking office, he flew across the Atlantic to observe Red Cross activities on European battlefields at first hand and to learn from General Eisenhower and other military leaders how Red Cross services might be improved.

Returning from Europe, Chairman O'Connor traveled thousands of miles visiting Red Cross chapters in various parts of the United States to report on his observations. He was determined to keep in close touch with the "grass roots" of his organization—to report to them and in turn draw inspiration from them. His Red Cross creed is summed up in these words:

"The very first thing that strikes me as Chairman of the Red Cross is the interest the American people have in it—the pride with which they regard it—the support they furnish to it—and the belief they have in its continuing service to mankind.

"The thought that the American Red Cross belongs to all the American people is the cardinal precept in my personal articles of faith in it.

"The Red Cross is great, because it reflects and is sustained by an idea that is lodged in the emotions and in the consciousness of the masses of the people. That idea is the dignity of man, and the responsibility of all society toward its individual members. It is the interdependence of each of us upon his neighbor. It is the bond that unites all men of good will.

"The Red Cross does not exist because of the desire of a few of the people to help the many. It exists because it is the will of all of the people to help themselves. That is the fundamental upon which I think the administration of the affairs of the Red Cross should be based."

Through the many months of uncertainty as the United States was drawn nearer the vortex of war, there was a growing awareness within the Red Cross of an impending crisis. This led to the preparation of plans that were put into effect immediately after the declaration of war. Tremendous demands suddenly were made upon the organization. As an auxiliary of the armed forces, it was called upon to perform a variety of vital services for the Army and Navy on the home front and overseas. Expansion far beyond any point in its history was required.

To finance this tremendous program an appeal for a $50,000,000 war fund was made soon after Pearl Harbor. This amount the people generously oversubscribed. They responded similarly to 1943 and 1944 appeals, bringing the American Red Cross total war fund to more than $420,000,000, the largest amount ever raised by voluntary contributions in this, or any other, country.

Immediately after Pearl Harbor millions of men and women turned to the Red Cross for training to qualify for various civilian defense posts under the Office of Civilian Defense. Six months later three million persons had earned their first-aid certificates. Thousands of nurses were recruited for service in the Army and Navy Nurse Corps. Thousands of trained nurses' aides helped fill the gap by serving in civilian and veterans' hospitals. Face to face with the shortage of doctors and nurses, women by the hundreds of thousands qualified for Red Cross Home Nursing certificates. Dietitian's aides volunteered for civilian hospital work. Thousands of troops, preparing for amphibious warfare, took the Red Cross functional swimming and water-safety training.

Red Cross volunteer production workers made hundreds of millions of surgical dressings, knitted sweaters and other comfort articles requested by the armed forces, sewed millions of relief garments, and sewed and packed millions of kit bags. Volunteer women and girls packed millions of Red Cross standard food packages consigned to the International Red Cross Committee at Geneva for distribution to American prisoners of war and civilian internees in enemy camps and to other United Nations prisoners of war. Other volunteers drove cars, ambulances, and trucks, served many thousands of meals to troops and civilian disaster victims. Home Service workers helped care for the families of servicemen and women in financial or other trouble.

Valuable as were these contributions they could not be compared to the people's giving of blood for the armed forces through the Red Cross. This transcended any other volunteer service on the home front. It was the gift of life itself.

The gigantic effort on the home front—the generous outpouring of time and energy on the part of some 6,500,000 Red Cross volunteers—constituted preparation and implementation for the battles of the nation's fighting forces overseas. Serving with them were more than seven thousand Red Cross men and women who had been put through an intensive course of orientation and training in a "mercy" school at Washington, D. C.

From every state, from the territories, from the insular possessions came an unending procession of enrollees. Selected on the basis of education, experience, and qualities of leadership, without distinction of race, creed, or color, they were as representative a body of earnest Americans as may be found anywhere. Some wore campaign ribbons of World War I. Many had sons, daughters, or husbands in this war, some as prisoners of war. Many of the men were over the draft age or were physically unfit for actual fighting. But all were eager to participate in the war.

Starting with the pioneers who, before Pearl Harbor, were with the United States garrison troops on naval bases leased from the British, and those who accompanied the first task forces to Iceland and Northern Ireland, Red Cross workers went out with many troop transports from the United States. They went with the troops, literally, to the ends of the earth.

Through the activities of these workers, this book endeavors to tell the story of American Red Cross overseas operations in World War II. I am far from unmindful of the importance of the Red Cross home-front program, but that is a big story in itself, demanding a book all its own.

My principal sources for *At His Side* were: returned overseas workers whom I interviewed at National Headquarters; story material submitted from the various war theaters by Red Cross staff correspondents; official narrative reports from overseas workers in various parts of the world; and the *Red Cross Courier*, informative and readable official magazine. To all these men and women, and to the *Red Cross Courier's* able editor, Alwyn W. Knight, my sincere appreciation.

For making accessible to me all pertinent official Red Cross documents, and for making it possible for me to interview returned workers, I am deeply grateful to the following top executives charged with the direction of the gigantic Red Cross overseas program:

National Headquarters, Washington, D. C.: Richard F. Allen, Vice-Chairman in charge of Insular and Foreign Operations; Robert E. Bondy, Administrator, Services to the Armed Forces; Don C. Smith, Deputy Administrator, Services to the Armed Forces; Walter Wesselius, Assistant to the Vice-Chairman, Insular and Foreign Operations; William S. Hepner, Director, Military and Naval Welfare Service; and Thomas M. Dinsmore, Assistant Director, Military and Naval Welfare Service.

War theater heads: Harvey D. Gibson, Commissioner to Great Britain and Western Europe; Charles K. Gamble, Commissioner to the Southwest Pacific; Stanton Griffis, Commisioner to Pacific Ocean Areas; Stirling Tomkins, Delegate to North Africa–Italy; Robert C. Lewis, Director of Operations, China–Burma–India; and Raymond R. Fisher, Director of Operations, Middle East.

I also wish to acknowledge my indebtedness to the following members of the special Red Cross editorial committee who took time off from their busy duties to read the manuscript and to advise me: Mr. Wesselius; G. Stewart Brown, Vice-Chairman in charge of Public Relations; Howard Bonham, Director of Public Relations; and Mrs. Katherine Lewis, Assistant Director of Publicity and Foreign Editor.

To all my National Headquarters' associates, too numerous to list here, who so generously co-operated with me, and who bore so patiently the added burden of having one of their number in the throes of book writing, my sincere thanks.

George Korson

Washington, D. C.
January, 1945

AT HIS SIDE

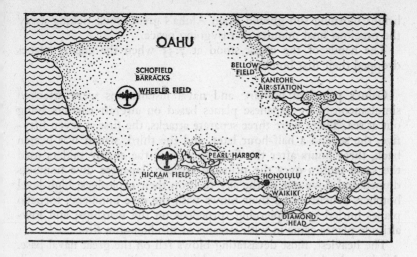

Chapter I

PEARL HARBOR

WITHIN TWO MINUTES FROM THE TIME THE FIRST BOMBS FELL on Pearl Harbor, the American Red Cross was in action.

December 7, 1941, had begun with the usual bright sunshine, giving promise of another quiet Hawaiian Sabbath. Aboard the great warships berthed at the naval piers or lying in the calm inner waters of Pearl Harbor, as well as at the Army's forts, camps, and airfields, signs of life had slackened off.

As the Japanese air armada sped through the clouds, servicemen not on duty were planning to spend a day of leisure. Honolulu's civilian residents were waking to the relaxed and easy tempo of their Sunday mornings. Those who had risen were either at breakfast, in church, in their automobiles getting out to the sunlit beaches, golf courses, tennis courts and baseball grounds, or working in their gardens.

From the elevated balcony of the Aloha tower at the waterfront the city of Honolulu rolled over the broad coastal plain toward the mountain slopes with their sugar-cane and pineapple fields. The

3

bright morning sun glinted upon Aloha's great clock ticking away the precious final minutes of easygoing peace.

The hands of the clock stood at 7:55 when the enemy planes dropped their first bombs.

Oahu's principal military and naval installations were attacked simultaneously by Japanese planes based on aircraft carriers lying out at sea. There were three separate attacks, the first at seven fifty-five, the second a half-hour later, and the third, which was beaten back, three hours after the first. Each time the enemy raiders used the same tactics over the primary targets: Japanese dive bombers dipped and dove out of the sky to drop their explosives; high-level bombers synchronized their blows with the dive bombers'; torpedo planes hurled armor-piercing torpedoes on the warships; and low-altitude planes came in with streams of machine-gun fire.

The heaviest, most devastating blows fell on the great naval base. As the calm harbor waters turned into a cauldron of burning oil, the sky was filled with smoke and flames, and gun crews manned their battle stations on decks buckling with heat.

Bombs also rained down on Hickam Field adjoining Pearl Harbor and the other airfields on Oahu Island. Hangars, and planes concentrated on concrete aprons, offered tempting targets as the Japanese swooped down out of the sky.

While soldiers, sailors, Marines and airmen fought and died, the families of many of them were exposed to the same enemy strafings and bombings. Hundreds of wives and children in the flaming areas around Pearl Harbor and Hickam Field huddled in their island cottages. Those who escaped injury suffered from the effects of the wholesale devastation—lack of food, water, clothing, and in cases, shelter—and were haunted by uncertainty regarding the fate of their heroic husbands and fathers.

Japanese planes were over Honolulu, too, that Sunday morning. They swept in from the sea by way of Diamond Head, thundered and whined over Waikiki Beach and the city. They flew so low that the Rising Sun emblem on their wings was plainly visible from the streets. Rooftop-scraping planes sprayed machine-gun fire on a bewildered, fear-stricken people. Mothers huddled in doorways trying to protect their babies from the fire-spitting enemy. Driving to prearranged emergency tasks, American Red Cross workers saw the shattered bodies of children, and of men and women who had been riddled by enemy bullets or wounded by antiaircraft shell fragments.

4

Hawaii on that tragic day was not merely an outpost of America. It was a symbol representing the honor, dignity, and fiber of Americans. All racial and national differences were quickly merged in the common bond of defense. From that day Hawaiians joined the proud company of the people of London, Chungking, and Stalingrad, who in the testing hour had proved their unity.

And through the darkness of Hawaii's travail, the Red Cross emblem shone as a beacon of hope. To the wounded, the sick, the homeless and hungry—young and old, regardless of race, creed, or color—the Red Cross carried the sympathy and help of the whole American people. Known for its traditional works of mercy, for its miracles of restoration in peacetime disasters, the Red Cross had the people's faith, and its emblem calmed and comforted them.

At Pearl Harbor the American Red Cross was represented by its Hawaii chapter, made up of local volunteer men, women, and children, aided by a few Red Cross workers from National Headquarters. Through a vast network of chapters and branches, the Red Cross covers virtually every part of the United States, its territories and insular possessions. In peace or war, it is always where disaster strikes. There is a saying that the Red Cross does not have to go there; it *is* there.

Plans for a possible enemy air attack were perfected long before December 7. Some 2,000 civilians in the Hawaiian Islands, including doctors and dentists, had received Red Cross first-aid training. Under Mrs. A. V. Molyneux, production chairman, Red Cross women volunteers had put in long hours rolling surgical dressings and sewing hospital garments in quantities far in excess of their quotas. These, together with a great quantity of clothing, food, and medical supplies, had been quietly stored in widely separated sections of Honolulu against the day of their need. The canteen corps and motor corps were well organized and trained, and even the Junior Red Cross was prepared for its part.

Therefore there was confidence, even with disaster all around, as Chairman Alfred L. Castle of the Hawaii chapter met with workers at the city hall to put prearranged plans into effect. Mr. Castle, Hawaiian businessman who had been in Red Cross field service during the First World War, held a firm grip on the many intricate details involved in meeting the needs of this disaster. By his side, dressed in her trim gray uniform and officer's cap, was Mrs. Herman von Holt, director of the chapter's Volunteer Special Services, who mobilized and directed the Red Cross women volunteers. Also present were W. S. Allen, Jr., chapter executive director, and Red Cross

5

Field Director John F. Gray, who doubled as chapter executive secretary.

For civilian defense workers, the canteen corps under the leadership of Mrs. Vernon Tenney and Mrs. Wayne Pflueger set up a canteen in the basement of the Iolani Palace, royal residence of Hawaii's kings before the revolt of 1893 and now Territorial capitol. The Red Cross girls who worked behind the serving table in twelve-hour shifts came from every walk of life. Passing before them in an almost continuous file, hour after hour around the clock, were the hundreds of defenders—sentries off duty, men on vital work in and around the palace grounds, the disaster council and staff who came over from the armory, dispatch riders, ambulance drivers, and emergency-truck drivers.

The story of this canteen was told by Mrs. Tenney in her chapter report.

At ten o'clock, the canteen was called to duty. At one P.M. we were serving sandwiches and hot coffee.

From that time until the 17th of December [when the real emergency was over] we worked in two shifts on twenty-four hour duty.

Two of our canteen committee, Miss Juliet Carpenter and Miss Renee Halbedl, volunteered on the night of the seventh to stay on duty for as long as they were needed.

It seemed doubtful if they could function after dark, but function they did, without stopping—by flashlight—rising above such minor shocks as a gun going off in their midst. Some poor exhausted rookie had trustfully propped his rifle against the wall, probably with the safety off, and a jar had sent a bullet through the roof.

They went for more food and hot coffee in a truck without lights, crawling through black streets—never knowing when some nervous youngster on guard duty might shoot without asking any questions or when enemy raiders might arrive overhead.

The next day permanent space was allotted to us in the basement of one of our government buildings [Iolani Palace]. The menu was increased to include soup, hot cocoa, hot cereal and fruit juices. The number fed increased from 300 in the first twenty-four hours to 1,000 in the same period. With the volunteer aid from four Chinese restaurant cooks, we were able to serve full dinners in the middle of the day.

Our canteen soon became the meeting place at night for every one who could snatch a few minutes from their work for a little

6

sustenance, the rendezvous for the guards when off duty, a haven for patrols who came in chilled and fatigued from lack of sleep, for the Medical Unit and the Emergency Police. We sent meals all over town to people who could not leave their posts—RCA operators, telephone operators, and others.

By the fourth night the natural gaiety of the Hawaiians reasserted itself. The Territorial Guard brought their ukeleles with them, and when off duty relieved the tension with old and new hulas, popular music and school songs.

We could not have carried on without the volunteers who worked as canteen aides—the *lei* women who washed dishes, the Boy Scouts who helped them, and the truck drivers who transported supplies for us at all odd hours.

In Honolulu injured civilians, including many children, were treated at the first-aid stations of the Honolulu County Medical Society. They were staffed by doctors, nurses, and Red Cross volunteers who worked tirelessly for many hours the day of the attacks. On succeeding days and nights they served on twelve-hour shifts while waiting tensely for a renewal of the Japanese air raids.

Many civilian casualties were taken to Honolulu's Queens Hospital, where the surgery and first-floor emergency room were scenes of horror. Some were laid on boards supported by chairs and tables as there were not enough beds for all. At nightfall, owing to the strict blackout, all signal lights were discontinued, flashlights were covered with blue cellophane, and blankets were draped over the windows near seriously ill patients so that dim lights might be used. Many Red Cross nurses were on duty in Queens Hospital.

There were also many volunteer civilian nurses from the Red Cross registry at the Hickam Field station hospital, in the Army's Tripler General Hospital, in the U.S. Naval Hospital at Pearl Harbor and on the Navy's hospital ship, *Solace*. They worked with members of the Army and Navy Nurse Corps, many of whom had been recruited for war service by the American Red Cross.

Nurses gave hypodermics, administered blood plasma, dressed burns, sutured wounds, and helped the hard-pressed surgeons with their frequent operations. Performing these emergency tasks with only the faint blue light of a dimmed flashlight was both difficult and unnerving. Many of the girls worked until they dropped from exhaustion, and they slept in their uniforms so that they would be ready for instant duty when called.

Tripler General Hospital received a constant stream of casualties from Hickam Field, one of the worst of the bombed areas. Walter

7

Wesselius, American Red Cross executive, witnessed the bombings from the rear porch of this hospital and pitched in to help. A patient, he was being treated for malaria contracted in China while serving as director of China Relief.

Red Cross field director at Tripler was Mrs. Margaret H. Lutz, a native of the Hawaiian Islands. Formerly stationed at the Walter Reed Hospital, in Washington, D. C., Mrs. Lutz had come only a few weeks before to inaugurate a Red Cross program for hospitalized soldiers. Her recollections follow:

December 7, 1941. I was awakened about 8 o'clock by a neighbor's radio, and recognized the voice of my friend Webley Edwards of KGMB, one of the two local radio stations. He was saying, "This is no joke! This is the real McCoy! We are being attacked! Stay off the streets and the telephone. Keep calm, keep calm, keep calm!"

I dressed hurriedly and drove down to the hospital with my husband. Everything in the city was in turmoil. At the hospital my husband and I were guided to the parking space outside the military reservation.

The first person we saw was a corpsman, Corporal McLean. "Oh, my God, Mrs. Lutz, ain't it awful!" he said. Ambulances were bringing in casualties from Hickam Field. Blood was everywhere. Bloody clothing that had been cut from wounded bodies lay in piles along the corridors.

When I asked the Adjutant what I could do, he said, "If you have any cigarettes, give them out. The boys have been asking for them."

We broke open the seals of two cases and passed out cigarettes freely. In the halls I met our secretary, Helene Pesante, working on the wards after having made several trips from Honolulu to Pearl Harbor with sailors whose liberty had been cancelled by the Japanese attack. She burst into tears, hung on my neck, and said, "They are bombing our ships."

Patients who could be moved were transferred to a school building about a mile and a half away. The wards were miraculously cleared for casualties. We walked through the wards giving out cigarettes and drinks of water. Several beds held boys who were beyond human help. After each bed had been vacated, we got fresh linen and made it up for the next occupant. And all the time the Jap planes were overhead strafing the hospital. They killed a patient who was helping unload an ambulance, and shot holes in the roof of the surgery and dental offices.

My thoughts went to the Gray Ladies and how I wished we had some who could help us. I knew of one who had been trained as a Gray Lady at the Walter Reed Hospital when I was there. She was Mrs. Frank J. McCarthy (Gladys McCarthy, who was later employed as a Red Cross recreation worker on the professional staff of the mobile unit at Aiea). While her husband, an Army officer, was on duty in Honolulu she was alone at home on the other side of the island [Oahu] where I reached her by long-distance telephone. She promised to join me at the hospital in the morning.

December 8, 1941. This was another terrible day. My husband and I arose at 4:30 A.M. and cooked eggs under small blue lights, the only ones allowed in the blackout. As no cars were allowed to have lights, we drove in total darkness at about ten miles an hour. When we reached School Street, Japs started strafing and my husband pulled the car under a banyan tree. "Lie on the floor," he yelled. I did as I was told. We stayed in this position for half an hour. The strafing suddenly stopped, and we went on, he to his work and I to mine.

When I arrived at the hospital I found Mrs. McCarthy already there. We had between 400 and 500 casualties from Hickam, all of whom had lost their personal belongings in the battle. Mrs. McCarthy with her gray uniform and veil went to work immediately helping me pass out toothbrushes and tooth paste. At one bed I asked a patient if he would care for a toothbrush. His face lit up as if I had offered him a million dollars. "Lady," he said, "would I like a toothbrush!" On succeeding days Mrs. McCarthy and I continued distributing Red Cross toilet articles, cigarettes, pipe tobacco, and reading material to patients and duty personnel, enlisted and commissioned.

Many patients and almost all hospital personnel wished to get word to their families on the mainland that they had survived the raid. As they were all ordered to stay on post and the cable companies were forbidden by the Military Governor to take messages over the telephone, it was the job of the Red Cross to meet this need. Therefore, I assigned Mrs. Ruth Benny, our recreation worker, to this task. It was announced over the loud speaker that the Red Cross was making this service available to anyone who wished it. The line formed down the hall from our office, and that first day we had nearly 200 messages.

About Wednesday cable messages began to pour in from frantic relatives on the mainland who had been notified by the War Department. These messages I attended to myself, first interviewing

9

the doctor in charge of each patient concerned and then the patient. Wires of necessity had to be brief, but I tried my very best to give some word of cheer to those anxious relatives and to let them know that the Red Cross was at the side of their wounded sons, husbands, and sweethearts.

One message I well remember sounded more anxious than all the others. It was impossible to contact the doctor at the moment, so I sought out the patient. He was assisting in the care of other patients on the ward. When I told him that his mother was anxious about him, he became very angry. "Do you mean to tell me that they notified my mother and worried her when all I've got is a broken finger on my left hand?"

I explained that the War Department was most particular to notify their nearest of kin in all battle casualties.

"Well, you can tell my mother there ain't nothing wrong with me, and I'm going out to get me a Jap."

The way the wounded took it on the chin had everyone's respect. There was no moaning nor cries for help. The most frequent request from badly wounded soldiers was, "Let my mom know I'm O.K."

Meanwhile, at the U.S. Naval Hospital, another field director, Miss Nell Ennis, veteran World War I Red Cross worker, was going without sleep and change of clothing to perform emergency duties. Throughout the first day and night, and daily for weeks after, she gave devoted service to hospital patients.

I was having breakfast in my hotel that morning, and immediately hurried down to the Naval Hospital to offer my services to the Commanding Officer.

In a matter of minutes the hospital changed from a quiet, well-organized institution to one of intensive activity.

The Red Cross office was in the basement of one of the wings next to a dressing station. At first I was the only Red Cross worker on duty, and spent much time making beds. As soon as a casualty was taken away to the operating room, I would turn the blood-soaked mattress and put clean, fresh linen on it.

There being a desperate shortage of nurses at the Naval Hospital, I was requested by the Commanding Officer to visit the Queens Hospital in Honolulu and recruit volunteer civilian nurses.

The response was overwhelming. From December 7 to New Year's Day, 144, many of them Red Cross nurses, gave their off days and nights to the Naval Hospital.

Doctors and nurses kept requesting Red Cross toilet gear for their patients. With the aid of my Gray Ladies I was able to distribute comfort articles from our own stock room and additional supplies from the Hawaii chapter. The chapter mushroomed over night with seemingly unlimited supplies and resources.

On Tuesday morning, the 9th, I was trying to make a patient comfortable on the lainae when I suddenly heard airplane motors overhead. The patient, horribly burned and almost lifeless, looked up and murmured, "Don't worry, Red Cross, those are our planes. You can't fool me on their sound." By noon he was dead.

Several days before Christmas, a young sailor said, "What, no Christmas tree?" I sensed that his question reflected the feeling of the rest of the patients, and so decided to arrange for a Christmas party in the hospital. Christmas trees and trimmings obtained from Honolulu stores by our Gray Ladies decorated the wards. One of the medical officers played Santa Claus in a Santa suit borrowed from the Salvation Army. He went from ward to ward using a blue flashlight in the blackout. He also visited the children in their dugout and gave them each a toy, a gift of the Junior Red Cross.

There was a young sailor—we'll call him Bill—who we were sure wasn't more than fifteen years of age. Very ill yet uncomplaining, he was the favorite of all of us. In giving his history to one of the doctors, he said he was "Nineteen, sir."

The doctor asked over and over again the question, "How old are you, Bill?" to get the kid to tell his right age. But the answer was always the same, "Nineteen, sir."

Admiral Chester W. Nimitz, who visited the Naval Hospital when each new load of casualties arrived, was told about Bill. He took the boy's hand and asked, "How old are you, Bill?"

"Nineteen, sir."

The Admiral smiled and said, "Regardless of your age, Bill, you're a good sailor, the bravest and best, and we are proud of you."

Bill, a smile on his lips, died shortly afterwards.

Red Cross workers, nurses, and corpsmen, all working as a team, helped naval doctors write a heroic chapter in American medical history. Directed by Captain Reynolds H. Hayden, then commanding officer of the U.S. Naval Hospital, medical officers cared for nearly 1,000 casualties within the first sixteen hours after the initial air attack—at the rate of a man a minute. For several days the most seriously wounded were operated on in the hospital's amphitheater by surgery teams working in ceaseless relays.

More than sixty per cent of the cases were burns, chiefly "flash" burns that occur when the body has been exposed to the source of injury for as short a time as a second or two.

The use of sulfa drugs marked a revolutionary step in their treatment. Patients suffering from burns were treated by spraying a mixture of mineral oil and sulfanilamide on the burned surfaces with ordinary flit guns; at the same time, large doses of sulfathiazole were given by mouth as a further aid in preventing infection.

Even more dramatic than the revolutionary sulfa drugs was the dried plasma, processed from blood collected by the Red Cross, and used for the first time on a large scale. Many hundreds of casualties were unconscious from shock. Not one of the great healers of the past would have given them a chance to live; by all the former rules of medicine they were doomed to die. But, through the miracle of blood plasma, men who even a few months before would have died of burns, infection, or shock, came back to live, to work, and perhaps, to fight again.

An extraordinary record was made by the Hawaii chapter's motor corps. Its forty members, most of them wives of Army and Navy personnel, were fully prepared for their emergency duties. For many months, under the farsighted leadership of their captain, Mrs. Goodale Moir, they had received first-aid training with emphasis on the emergency delivery of babies. They had practiced military drills and blackout driving; had taken part in gas and chemical warfare demonstrations; and a course in automobile mechanics enabled them to handle a private car, station wagon, truck, or ambulance with equal skill and dexterity.

In prewar days, members of the motor corps took convalescents from naval and Army hospitals on semi-weekly drives. In this way they became well known at the Navy Yard and on the Army posts, while familiarizing themselves with the location of hospitals and emergency centers—an experience that proved invaluable during the emergency period.

Soon after the first Japanese bombs fell, Mrs. Moir began calling in her corpswomen by telephone from all parts of the island. By two o'clock the women, in their trim gray gabardine uniforms with tin helmets and gas masks strapped to their shoulders, were mobilized. Their home for the duration was the Castle kindergarten, an old landmark in downtown Honolulu, which had offices, a large kitchen, and a dormitory. During the first few weeks the entire corps worked every possible hour, with a considerable number remaining on duty continuously for days.

Their first assignment on December 7 was the delivery of Red

Cross surgical dressings and medical supplies to the Army and naval hospitals and civilian emergency hospitals set up in school and government buildings. Their uniform was recognized and respected everywhere. These women were accustomed to driving in wind and storm, and now they were on the firing line, not knowing the fate of their soldier or sailor husbands as they drove through the tumult of machine-gun fire and the splatter of shrapnel.

The corps' biggest single mission was the removal to safety of hundreds of civilians trapped in the bombed areas surrounding Pearl Harbor and Hickam Field. The majority were women and children—the families of Army and Navy personnel and defense workers—whose desperate plight touched their compassion.

Most of the evacuation took place after the sun had set in the blue Pacific, ushering in Hawaii's first total blackout. Honolulu was so completely blacked out that the corpswomen were haunted by fear of head-on collisions. They will never forget the weird black stillness that settled over Honolulu that first night, the stillness of a seemingly dead city. Behind blacked-out windows and doors life was charged with high tension. Rumors of enemy parachutists, mysterious short-wave radio operators, and many fantastic happenings shook the people.

The same nervousness affected some of the youthful Territorial guards who fired aimlessly in the dark. Their stray bullets worried the overworked corpswomen groping through the black streets with precious human lives in their vehicles.

Many trips were made back and forth between Honolulu and the danger zones, the women bringing refugees and immediately returning for more. Each car carried a first-aid kit, splints, blankets, extra clothing, food, and drinking water, all of which were used when necessary. Hour after hour this shuttle service went on uninterruptedly until finally, at three o'clock in the morning, the last group of three thousand refugees had been removed from danger.

Not until then did these angels of mercy, exhausted, their eyes red from lack of sleep, have time to think of themselves.

Evacuees were taken to private homes or housed in hotels, schools, and government buildings previously designated as refugee centers. There, other Red Cross workers took care of them. Those suffering from slight injury or shock received first-aid treatment. Warm garments and blankets were distributed among them; also pencils and paper on which to scribble "all's well" messages to be telegraphed or radioed to anxious relatives on the mainland.

Red Cross workers moved about the restless refugees all through the first night and for many nights after, comforting crying chil-

13

dren, calming their mothers' frayed nerves, and easing pain and discomfort in countless other ways.

The Red Cross information service helped servicemen locate their wives and children from whom they had become separated, and relieved anxious families in Hawaii and on the mainland with reports of the condition of their wounded in the hospitals. And the Red Cross gave financial assistance to the stranded families of Army and Navy personnel.

The canteen corps served three meals a day to 1,500 evacuees until relieved of the responsibility by a government agency.

There were still other opportunities for Red Cross service when a mass evacuation to the mainland was begun in mid-December.

Aboard the first ship carrying civilian refugees from Honolulu were scores of burned and wounded Navy men. Just before the ship weighed anchor the Hawaii chapter received an urgent call from the U.S. Navy for nurses to relieve the critical shortage aboard the vessel. Within two hours chapter officials located fourteen registered nurses who volunteered to serve even though they had no time to go home for personal belongings. They went directly to the ship and reported for duty. When the ship docked in San Francisco on Christmas Day, service cases were taken to military hospitals, civilian injured to city hospitals. Able-bodied civilians were given every assistance by the San Francisco chapter of the American Red Cross. Children in the group were treated to a Christmas party by Red Cross women and received candy and toys.

Many other ships carried civilians to the mainland. To help evacuees bear the cold weather when they debarked in San Francisco or other Pacific coast ports, the Hawaii chapter sent cases of warm clothing, sweaters, and other knitted garments to every ship. These articles, together with toys for children, were distributed by Red Cross workers sailing with the evacuees.

To facilitate the latter's return to their home towns with the least discomfort, the Red Cross operated a shuttle service. Home Service workers sailed to Honolulu to return on the evacuation ships. During the homebound voyage, evacuees were grouped regionally. Workers accompanied them to distribution points in various parts of the United States. From most of these points it was only a short trip to their homes or the homes of relatives.

The chain of Red Cross service was unbroken across land and water, as experienced by Mrs. Daniel Larson, of Mankato, Minnesota. Mrs. Larson and her three children—family of a naval officer—were at their home in the Pearl Harbor area when the Japanese planes first attacked.

Our house was only 150 feet from the battleship *Arizona* when it was sunk. When I realized that an attack was on, my first reaction was anxiety for the children. I made a dash for the basement with them. I had just gotten to the bottom of the basement stairs when a bomb hit the *Arizona*. The explosion broke all the glass in the bedroom from which the children had just been removed. . . . It was through the Red Cross that I got my child to the hospital after he had contracted a severe chest cold. The other children and I were taken to the home of a Red Cross worker who furnished the children with clothes and even toys.

A week after the bombings, Mrs. Larson and the three children were among evacuees taken by a U.S. Navy bomber to San Diego, California, where they were met by local chapter workers.

The Red Cross wired my parents in Mankato. Red Cross workers took me shopping for warm clothing for the children, bought my tickets, took me to the station, helped me with the children and arranged with a train porter to take care of my baggage all the way through. They wired the Los Angeles chapter for someone to help me in making a transfer of trains.

At San Diego, while waiting for the train, I received funds from the Mankato [chapter] Red Cross. When I arrived in Mankato . . . I received additional funds from the Garden City Red Cross chapter.

Chapter II

THE *SS. MACTAN*'S ESCAPE
FROM MANILA

Late in the afternoon of december 31, 1941, army ambulances came clanging down Manila's Pier 1 and halted alongside the American Red Cross hospital ship *Mactan* moored there.

They were followed by others, and for three hours an unending line of stretchers bearing seriously wounded American and Filipino soldiers streamed up the *Mactan*'s gangplank. Men with bandaged heads, with legs in casts, with arms in slings, and with hidden shrapnel wounds were borne aloft by Filipino doctors, nurses, and crew. Their faces pallid and eyes expressionless, they had no idea where they were being taken. They did not seem to care, except that the large red crosses on the ship's sides were a reassuring sign that they were in friendly hands.

There were 224 officers and enlisted men in the group of wounded —young boys of the new Philippine Army, youthful American airmen, grizzled veterans of the Philippine Scouts (an arm of the United States Army), and gray-haired American soldiers with many years' service in the Far East. All had been wounded fighting the Japanese invaders during the bloody weeks preceding the historic stand on Bataan.

These casualties had been left behind in the Sternberg General Hospital when General Douglas MacArthur withdrew his forces to Bataan. Anxious, however, to save them from the rapidly advancing Japanese armies, he had requested the American Red Cross to transport them to Darwin, Australia, in a ship chartered, controlled, staffed, and fully equipped by the Red Cross. The only military personnel aboard, apart from the patients, would be an Army surgeon, Colonel Percy J. Carroll, of St. Louis, Missouri, and an Army nurse, Lieutenant Floramund Ann Fellmeth, of Chicago.

Aboard the *Mactan*, berthed at Manila's only pier to survive constant Japanese air attacks, Irving Williams, of Patchogue, Long Island, lanky Red Cross field director, observed the three-hour procession of wounded up the gangplank. From now on until the ship reached Australia—an estimated ten-day passage if things went well-- responsibility for them was in his hands.

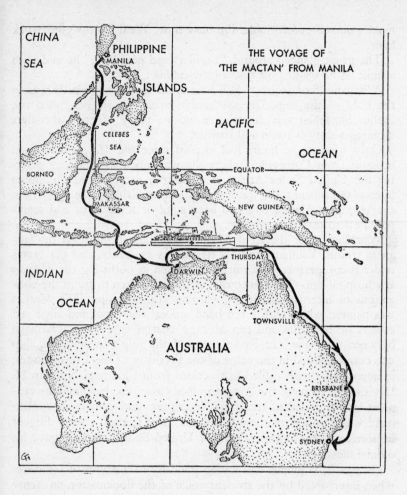

As the patients were being transferred from ambulance to ship, Williams co-ordinated and integrated the many different operations to one end—the *Mactan*'s departure before midnight.

He was supervising deck hands at the winches when a tall man dressed as a priest handed him a letter introducing the Reverend Thomas A. Shanahan, of Waterbury, Connnecticut, an English professor at Ateneo de Manila, the Jesuit university, who was to be the *Mactan*'s chaplain.

"What may I do to help, Mr. Williams?" asked Father Shanahan.

Williams, harassed and worried, who well could have used a strong hand at that moment, said, "Father, please find a cabin and make yourself comfortable. I'm busy now. We'll discuss your work later."

The priest glanced around. "I understand perfectly," he said with a smile, as he walked off toward the cabins.

A half-hour or so later, Williams again saw the priest. It was in the hold of the ship. Dressed in dungarees, his sleeves rolled up, Father Shanahan was directing a fatigue party of crew members cleaning a shower room and latrines.

Only forty-eight hours had elapsed since the *Mactan* had been brought from Corregidor where she was unloading military stores for the United States Army. A 2,000-ton, decrepit old Philippine inter-island steamer, she was the only ship available at the time when everything in Manila Bay had been sunk or scuttled or had scampered off to sea.

Working under threat of Manila's imminent occupation by Japanese troops, Williams and his Red Cross associates, and the crews under them, performed a miracle of speed in outfitting the *Mactan* as a hospital ship. Simultaneously, steps were taken to fulfill the obligations of international law governing hospital ships: The *Mactan* was painted white with a red band around the vessel and large red crosses on her sides and top decks; a charter agreement was made between the American Red Cross and the ship's owners; the ship was commissioned in the name of the President of the United States; in accordance with cabled instructions from Chairman Norman H. Davis in the name of the American Red Cross, the Japanese Government was apprized of the ship's description and course; all contraband was dumped overboard; and the Swiss Consul, after a diligent inspection as the representative of United States interests, gave his official blessings.

On board, Williams was saying good-by to a group of associates when interrupted by the strident voice of the dockmaster, an Army major, bellowing from the pier below: "Will you fellows get the hell out of here? You've had me worried all day. Now get moving."

With the Manila office of the United States Coast and Geodetic Survey bombed out, the *Mactan* would leave the pier without detailed charts for the long passage to Australia.

"Have you located detailed charts, Irving?" asked Charles Forster, manager of the Philippine Red Cross.

"Not yet, but the *Don Estebán* is supposed to bring us a set off the breakwater."

Williams' face twitched nervously. His blue eyes betrayed anxiety. "Any word yet of Japanese clearance?" he asked.

Forster, Thomas J. Wolff, chairman of the Philippine Red Cross, and James W. Cullen, field supervisor, shook their heads.

Williams gripped the handrail and sighed, "We'll sail without it. We must get under way."

A few minutes later the *Mactan* felt the rhythm of its slow-turning engines as it picked its way through the watery graveyard of Manila Bay, its own lights a contrast to the spectral hulks still spewing smoke where Japanese bombs had wrecked them.

Off the breakwater, the *Mactan* dropped anchor to await the *Don Estebán*.

As the hours passed, a little group joined Julian C. Tamayo, the *Mactan*'s skipper, on the bridge for a last look at Manila's skyline. Besides Williams, there were Father Shanahan, Colonel Carroll, and Chief Nurse Ann Fellmeth.

Having been declared an open city, Manila once again was ablaze. The incandescent lights, however, were dimmed by the curtains of bright flame hanging over the city. The Army was dynamiting gasoline storage tanks at its base in Pandacen and its installations on Engineer Island to prevent their use by the enemy. The docks were burning, and over smoldering Cavite Navy Yard, devastated by heavy Japanese air attacks, intermittent flashes of fire reddened the sky.

As if by design, promptly at midnight the last of the Pandacen gasoline tanks blew up with a terrific explosion, throwing up masses of flame which seemed to envelop the whole city.

A new year was ushered in, but the little group on the *Mactan*'s bridge was in no mood for celebration.

The charts brought by the *Don Estebán*'s master were not the ones Captain Tamayo had asked for. They were too general.

"Do you think you can sail without detailed charts?" asked Williams.

"I think so," replied the swarthy, pug-nosed little skipper with characteristic confidence.

Once again, the *Mactan* weighed anchor. The moon was high in the sky as the ship approached Corregidor for a last-minute rendezvous with a United States naval vessel. From the shadow of The Rock sped a corvette, a gray wraith floodlighted by the moon, to lead the *Mactan* through the maze of mine fields. The corvette led the lumbering *Mactan* a merry chase; highly maneuverable, the former made the various turns at sharp angles, while the latter would reach the apex of a triangle and extend beyond it before making a turn. The corvette slowed down and a voice bellowed: "You damn fools! Do you want to blow yourselves to kingdom come? Follow instructions."

Meanwhile the zigzag course had unnerved the excitable Captain Tamayo who swore volubly in English and his native Tagalog.

The corvette finally signaled farewell and good luck and sped back toward Corregidor.

The *Mactan* was now on its own. Out there on the open sea, sharply etched against the track of the moon, it looked small, and terribly lonely.

Irving Williams had arrived in Manila on October 9, 1941, with two associates, to organize American Red Cross field director service for the armed forces in the Philippines. The Philippine Red Cross, a chapter of the American Red Cross though working autonomously under a Philippine Commonwealth charter, had previously confined its activities to civilians.

The three Red Cross men called on General MacArthur at his office, a large room in a rambling wooden building in Intramuros, Manila's ancient walled city. Military campaign trophies and gifts from the various Filipino tribes were everywhere. MacArthur was seated behind his desk smoking a heavy Filipino cigar as the Red Cross workers entered. As soon as the meeting got under way, he rose and paced the floor. In deliberate and colorful language, he described in great detail some of the facilities he hoped the American Red Cross would establish for the Philippine Army then being organized.

"The American Red Cross," concluded MacArthur, "is to the Army and Navy what pepper and salt are to food."

The news of the Japanese attack on Pearl Harbor at first stunned the Filipino people. Ordinarily the din of honking horns in Manila's streets was very disturbing to a newcomer, but on that fateful morning Williams was struck by the pall of silence that seemed to have fallen over the city. Cars were moving rapidly and apparently aimlessly, but the horns were not honking. In the afternoon, however, when news of the bombing of Clark Field had reached Manila, the horns again let loose. From the rooms of the Red Cross building the noise was reminiscent of Times Square on New Year's Eve— shouts, honking horns, trolley bells clanging, and everybody giving vent to outraged feelings.

A Red Cross call for volunteers had brought immediate response. From noon until late afternoon the Red Cross building was crowded with persons offering their services, their automobiles, their homes, and their money. While the volunteers were being registered and classified, a telephone call came from Harold Graybeal, assistant field director at Fort Stotsenburg, about sixty miles from Manila, announcing that adjoining Clark Field had been bombed.

The emergency machinery of the Philippine Red Cross functioned with surprising efficiency. Even though few had expected war to come so soon, the Philippine Red Cross had made extensive preparations for almost any eventuality. Large supplies of food, clothing, surgical dressings, and other medical supplies were stored in *bodegas*, or warehouses, located at strategic points in the city and throughout the provinces. Contracts had been made with transportation companies so that in a flash buses, automobiles, ambulances, and horses could be made available. A large staff of doctors and nurses had been enrolled as volunteers for the ten emergency hospitals operated by the Philippine Red Cross in sections vulnerable to attack from the air, particularly along the waterfront. When the bombings began they worked day and night giving first aid to persons wounded by bomb fragments, flying stones, and other missiles.

The Red Cross building, just beyond the crowded business section, was regarded by many in the streets as a safe haven when the air-raid alarm sounded. The building was of frame construction covered with stucco which gave it an undeserved appearance of solidity. The fact that it was a Red Cross building added to the people's sense of security.

A plan for the evacuation of nonessential men, women, and children from Manila had been developed by the American Red Cross and the Philippine Red Cross in co-operation with the Philippine Government. Before General MacArthur gave the evacuation order, however, many Filipinos took to the road on their own initiative. On a highway north of Manila, Field Director Williams saw every type of conveyance, from dilapidated old buses to *calezos* drawn by tiny horses and bearing six to eight members of a family and their furniture. And from the opposite direction came another exodus. Here one bus was so overcrowded that it could scarcely move, and was holding up a long train of cars, *calezos*, and *carromatas*, a twelve-passenger coach drawn by two tiny horses. And after the Cavite Navy Yard was bombed, hundreds of citizens fled from the town. Most of them traveled on foot, carrying on their backs or in arms whatever household articles they could take with them. Two men carried a hundred-pound sack of rice between them, and a wizened old Filipino bore his most prized possession, a parrot in a cage. Fearing that his people might be stranded on the road without adequate food or shelter, the mayor of Cavite appealed for assistance to Williams who was then in Cavite on an urgent official mission.

After much trouble, Williams reached Red Cross headquarters in Manila by telephone and relayed the mayor's plea. Shortly after two Red Cross trucks loaded with rice, dried fish, and kitchen utensils met the refugees, and kitchens were opened along the road.

When the prearranged evacuation plan was finally carried out at General MacArthur's orders, Field Supervisor James W. Cullen was put in charge. To gather these frightened refugees from their homes, transport them to railroad and bus stations, have them properly tagged, prevent their carrying anything other than articles essential to minimum health and comfort, feed them, and provide medical and nursing care en route; and organize a staff to receive them at evacuation centers in the provinces twenty to sixty miles from Manila and distribute them to designated homes—all this was a task of tremendous proportions. And Cullen and his staff of Filipino assistants thus removed almost 80,000 men, women, and children from Manila.

However, the Japanese closed in on Manila from the provinces instead of making a frontal attack upon the city, thereby imperiling the evacuation centers. To avert an uncontrolled exodus back to the city at the approach of the Japanese forces, causing confusion and road congestion, an organized return to Manila was ordered for all evacuees. Unfortunately the Japanese armies were moving too fast to complete the re-evacuation, and the subsequent occupation of Manila by the Japanese nullified the value of this tremendous effort.

One of the Red Cross heroines was Mrs. Frances Hobbs, of Manila, assistant field director at Fort William McKinley. Her office was in the chaplain's house, a one-story building with a wide porch skirting two sides. One day a crowd of frantic women and crying children, left behind by Philippine Scouts who were suddenly alerted and moved out of the fort at night, jammed her office and porch. Without food or money, they had come to the Red Cross for financial assistance. The women were so nervous and distracted that Frances Hobbs had difficulty calming them even with the promise that the Red Cross would meet their needs.

As women milled about and children whimpered, Mrs. Hobbs, with the aid of a Filipina school girl, made individual loans and recorded them. This work was at its peak when suddenly the air-raid alarm sounded: Japanese planes were bombing Nichols Field and the outskirts of Fort William McKinley. Instantly the women became hysterical and the children cried louder than ever. The women started jostling one another in a mad stampede increasing the danger that some of them, especially the children, might be trampled to death.

With surprising calm, Frances Hobbs climbed on a desk and called upon the women to follow her in the Lord's Prayer. The women immediately dropped to their knees and recited the Lord's Prayer after her, repeating it over and over again during the thirty minutes that the air raid lasted.

From Assistant Field Director Harold Graybeal at Fort Stotsenburg came frequent pleas by telephone for more and more surgical dressings. A six months' supply was consumed in the first two days after Clark Field's bombardment. The Army then rushed two truckloads which were gone in a matter of hours. Graybeal's pleas were heartbreaking. The hospital was out of surgical dressings; the wounded from Clark Field were still pouring in; would not Red Cross headquarters please do something about it right away? Red Cross volunteers, rolling furiously, had stored up a large pile of surgical dressings. Irving Williams loaded them into a station wagon, and after a wild ride in the blackout delivered them at the hospital. The sights in the wards chilled him.

On the morning of December 24, some twenty Red Cross volunteer women were in the official residence of Francis B. Sayre, High Commissioner to the Philippines, packing Christmas gifts for soldiers and sailors in hospitals in and around Manila. Mrs. Sayre was in charge of the group.

Suddenly, at eleven o'clock, Mrs. Sayre looked up from her task at the tables to see her husband standing in the patio doorway beckoning to her. She slipped quietly out of the room and stood in the patio.

"I have an urgent message from General MacArthur," said Mr. Sayre in a low voice. "The city may fall, and we must be ready to leave for Corregidor at one-thirty!"

Mrs. Sayre was stunned. "But we must finish these bags. They're the only Christmas our boys will have."

"Pack as quickly as you can," he said and left hurriedly.

Mrs. Sayre went back to the tables. The women worked quickly, and in silence, to complete their task before the daily noon Japanese air raid over Manila.

The treasure bags, as they were called, made hundreds of American and Filipino soldiers and sailors happier in their hospital wards that dark Christmas Day. Irving Williams helped Gray Ladies make the distribution in the Sternberg General Hospital. The work was under the direction of Miss Catherine L. Nau, of Pittsburgh, assistant field director at the hospital, who later was to distinguish herself for her work among the troops on Bataan and Corregidor, before the Japanese interned her.

23

Of the gift distribution at Sternberg General Hospital, Irving Williams said, "I shall never forget the boys' beaming faces and delighted eyes as we went from ward to ward. The simple comfort articles meant so much to these boys, who had lost all of their possessions on the field of battle."

Not until three days later—December 28—did Williams know that these same boys would be entrusted to his care on one of the most hazardous missions of the war. Major General Basilio Valdes, then commanding general of the Filipino Army, came straight from MacArthur's headquarters on Corregidor with the urgent request that the American Red Cross undertake to transport all serious casualties from the Sternberg General Hospital to Australia. President Manuel Quezon of the Philippine Commonwealth helped the Red Cross locate the *Mactan*.

Failure of the Japanese Government to grant "safe passage" cast a pall of suspense over the *Mactan*'s staff, patients, and crew. On Field Director Williams this suspense fell heaviest. Day after day he had to face one problem after another growing out of this uncertainty. The ship was completely at the mercy of the Japanese, who knew her course and description. At night she stood out like an electric light in a coal mine; in daytime she was conspicuous as a toy sailboat in a pond.

What went on aboard the overloaded *Mactan* as she labored against sea and wind to reach her Australian haven? What of the wounded American and Filipino heroes? What of the brave Filipino doctors, nurses, and crew who had left families behind? Mr. Williams, the *Mactan*'s central figure, gives us some of the highlights of the voyage in the following personal narrative:

January first, 1942, dawned warm and clear. As the sun lifted the veil of night, some of the tenseness of those final hours of the departure from Manila seemed to be drawn off with it. Our spirits rose and we briskly set about the business of organizing the routine of the ship. Colonel Carroll assigned the Filipino doctors to various sections of the ship and reviewed with them the medical histories which he had brought with him from Sternberg Hospital. Ann Fellmeth organized the nurses in locations and shifts, and then went below to unpack and arrange the medical supplies. I was on the bridge, checking with Captain Tamayo and Chief Mate Huerto the course we were to take in accordance with our advice to the Japanese Government.

The next morning, Captain Tamayo reported that we were

entering the Sulu Sea and by nightfall we should be approaching Pearl Reef. He showed me Pearl Reef on the map and said, "Meester Weelyems, I am worried. These chart ees too beeg. Pearl Reef ees very bad."

To my suggestion that he speed up the ship to pass the reef by daylight, the captain shook his head. "The *Mactan*, she now does nine knots and I am worry about the engines. They should have been overhaul before we leave Maneela."

This was a new angle. The ship owners had assured us that the ship was mechanically sound, and here, less than two days out, the captain was worried about the engines.

That afternoon a strong wind came out of the northeast, and the captain informed me we were having difficulty keeping on our course, and the speed of the ship was slackened to seven knots. At that rate we would reach the vicinity of Pearl Reef at midnight.

"Meester Weelyems, you are in charge of sheep. There is much danger at Pearl Reef. What shall I do?"

Now, as never before, I felt the full weight of my responsibility. I had only a novice's knowledge of navigation, yet I was being called upon for a decision that involved the lives of 318 persons [including the crew], many of them too ill to help themselves in an emergency. We knew that the Japanese were in Davao on the island of Mindanao and they were also in northeastern Borneo. Between the two was a string of small islands. We should have to pass through the Japanese lines of communication between Mindanao and Borneo. If we could get past Pearl Reef we could sail through the islands at night with a much better chance to get through than by day. If we got past Pearl Reef!

Captain Tamayo and I went back to the charts and after much manipulation of dividers and parallel rules, we decided that the risk of Pearl Reef was greater than the chance of being seen by the Japanese.

To avoid disturbing the patients, we concluded to sail until an hour after sundown, and then gradually swing around and back-track on our southward course until dawn, at very slow speed.

The boys were hard to fool, however. The wind was blowing briskly and the sea had become rough. Normally we should have been putting on more speed. As the engines were throttled, many of the patients became alarmed. Was there something wrong? Had we sighted something suspicious? Were we off our course? Father Shanahan and I went among the beds placating the men, assuring them that all was well—we were merely ahead of schedule.

During the night while heading northward the wind died down

and the moon came up brightly, swathing the *Mactan* in soft silver. We slipped along, almost silently through the still water for two hours, then the clouds gathered again and a light rain began to fall. Those two hours of tell-tale moonlight gave us away to some of the airmen trained in celestial navigation.

In the morning, after we had passed Pearl Reef and the Japanese-held islands, and were in the Celebes Sea, one of the boys, a navigator on a B-17 before the Japs got his plane—and him—at Clark Field, spoke up. "I thought you said we were going to Darwin? Where were we heading last night?"

I evaded with, "We were following the course we had plotted."

Meanwhile, the men in nearby beds had pricked up their ears. Any deviation from normal aboard a ship is vital news. Questions flew from every direction, and I parried. In one respect, this interest was heartening as it demonstrated the the boys were beginning to stir out of their lethargy.

The B-17 navigator spoke up again. "On our course, huh? Well, it's damned funny that the moon was on the wrong side."

Then I confessed what we had done, and why. The reaction was gratifying. One of the men who had been more jittery than the rest, remarked, "Thank God, somebody around here is using his head."

That January third is memorable not only for the aftermath of tension caused by the Pearl Reef incident but for the drama following news of the capitulation of Manila. Perhaps "capitulate" is the wrong word, as Manila had been without defense since General MacArthur had declared it an open city. The Japanese merely marched in and occupied it.

It was shortly after supper that a musical broadcast from San Francisco coming in over the *Mactan*'s radio was interrupted with, "Repeating the announcement made over this station earlier today—the city of Manila was occupied by Japanese troops at ten o'clock this morning. The Japanese were at the gates of the city yesterday, but delayed entry until they could organize a triumphal march into the ancient capital of the Philippines."

The broadcast was heard only by a few in the vicinity of the radio room. I was just coming down the ladder from the bridge when the radio man rushed up the narrow deck aisle between the rows of cots shouting hysterically, "They have taken Manila! They have taken Manila!"

Tears were streaming down his face as he almost knocked me over in his haste to get up on the bridge. From all parts of the ship, Filipino crew members were converging on the bridge. There

26

was an excited babble of voices as several of the Filipina nurses came up from the lower deck.

One of them, Mrs. Domingo, had left four children with her mother when she volunteered for the *Mactan* mission. "My cheeldren, my babies! Why did I leave them?" she wailed.

As usual, Father Shanahan, sad but calm, saved the day. His clear mellow voice carried a note of sternness. He knew his Filipinos. Did they no longer have faith in the Saviour? Were they to allow this misfortune to swerve them from their avowed objective of forty years—the independence of their homeland? They must, at this very moment, dedicate themselves before Christ, to do their utmost to restore their country to their people. . . .

On a cot just off the foot of the ladder to the bridge an American soldier, his right side padded in bandages where once was an arm, wept softly and then suddenly shrieked, "The ——; the little yellow——! We'll beat them if it is the last thing we do."

I went up to the bridge and found Captain Tamayo standing motionless, tight-lipped, staring out into the emptiness of the sea. Usually highly emotional, now he was grim, silent. I touched his sleeve and he turned, forcing a smile. He had left his wife and five children behind in Manila.

I murmured, "Captain Tamayo, this is just the beginning. America will keep faith with the Philippines."

A sudden gust of wind swept across the bridge and the ship lurched sharply. The captain cast off his gloom and turned sharply to look at the barometer.

"She is dropping, Meester Weelyems. I think we have a storm." Then he sang out above the wind, "Huerto, Huerto!"

The first mate came on the run, and the captain addressed him sharply in his native Tagalog. The mate sounded the ship's bell and two deck hands appeared. More instructions in Tagalog and the deck hands started off on the run.

I came down from the bridge and watched the crew as they lowered the canvas drops to protect the decks from the rain which had begun to beat in on the patients. Some of the beds were already quite wet and the nurses were busy changing the linens.

I returned to my cabin and found Father Shanahan sitting on my cot thoughtfully smoking his pipe. Neither of us spoke for a few minutes. Breaking the silence in a low voice, I said, "Thanks, Father, for the way you handled those Filipinos tonight."

Father Shanahan remained silent, puffing at his pipe with a vigor that showed his mind was working at top speed. He laid the pipe on the table, and, staring across the room, he mused, "The Fili-

27

pinos are a devout, decent, sturdy little people. We can't let them down. Why, I remember . . ."

For a half-hour he reminisced on the Filipinos, their home life, their loves, their politics, their war—observations made after many years' residence in the Philippines as a Jesuit missionary and teacher. And for another hour we shared experiences of those terrible weeks in Manila bfore the *Mactan's* departure.

Suddenly we were interrupted by a pile of cigar boxes crashing to the cabin floor. The ship had risen high on a wave and a cross wind caused her to heel sharply to the starboard. So engrossed were we in our conversation that we had failed to notice the increasing intensity of the storm.

We both went out on deck and viewed a terrifying scene. The canvas drops had provided poor protection against the beating rain, and the doctors, nurses and crew were busy drawing the cots back from the rail. The sudden lurch of the ship had shifted cots all over the deck like an upset jig-saw puzzle. The medical staff were working frantically to restore order out of chaos the while they were trying to maintain their footing on the swaying and bouncing decks. A sudden lunge forward, and there was a wild melee as a huge wave broke over the decks. The drenched patients were grumbling and swearing, and a few had hobbled from their cots into the shelter of the companionway leading to the saloon. As I threaded my way forward to assist them, another mountainous wave broke over the side of the ship and drenched me to the skin. Blinded and gasping from the brine I finally made my way to the top of the companionway where a sorry-looking group of patients stood huddled together. I helped them below one by one and rushed to find blankets for them.

The saloon, converted into the operating room of the ship's hospital, was a scene of utter disorder. Bottles and instruments which had been so orderly arranged on small tables by Nurse Ann Fellmeth were strewn about on the floor. Foul-smelling liquids, broken bottles and piles of dressings littered the room. I directed one of the attendants to straighten up the place, but in view of the ship's violent tossing this was futile.

While in Colonel Carroll's cabin—the Colonel was ill—I was interrupted by Dr. Francisco Roman, one of the Filipino doctors, who excitedly reported that one of the Filipino soldiers with bad shrapnel wounds in arm and shoulder was having a hemorrhage.

With an alacrity that was amazing in view of his own indisposition, Colonel Carroll bounced out of his cot, got into his raincoat and followed Dr. Roman to the wounded soldier's bed. The wind, howling the length of the ship, had the Colonel's raincoat flapping like a sail torn from its halyards. The deck lights being too dim for a satisfactory examination, the Colonel stuffed the wounds with gauze and ordered the boy taken to the saloon-operating room. There a further examination showed the need for immediate amputation of the arm.

While awaiting Nurse Ann Fellmeth, Colonel Carroll tried to assemble the instruments strewn about the floor. Ann soon appeared with two others of the nursing staff, Miss Basilia Hernando, senior Filipina nurse, and Miriam Fowles, Canadian-born wife of an English diplomat evacuated with other British women from Hong Kong. They straightened up the room and prepared the patient for the operation.

Cases of canned goods were stacked at the foot of the operating table to keep it from shifting in the storm.

Seldom was surgery performed under such difficult conditions. With the ship pitching and rolling, Colonel Carroll's dexterous hands worked with lightning speed. Frequently the ship's lurching made it difficult for surgeon and nurses to keep their footing. The weird howling of the wind and the sound of waves crashing on the decks often drowned out the Colonel's orders. The room was hot, stifling, and heavy with the odor of ether. One of the nurses kept daubing away the perspiration as it beaded on the Colonel's face.

I watched the operation from a corner of the room near the bottom of the companionway. A group of patients stood huddled near by. We all were transfixed by the drama of the operating table.

Action at the operating table was suddenly paced up. From behind his operating mask, Colonel Carroll snapped orders, unintelligible to us because of the noise from wind and seas.

The saloon lights seemed to be growing dimmer, and Ann beckoned to me for a flashlight. As I handed it to her I observed Colonel Carroll leaning over the patient as though listening intently. While others around the table prevented me from getting a full view, I sensed that something suddenly had gone wrong.

Colonel Carroll seemed to sag. Ann went to him quickly. Untying his mask, she spoke sharply as if to brace him. But the Colonel made no reply. He wabbled out of the room, passing me without as much as a nod. The others were also moving from the table revealing the inert form of the soldier.

29

Her hands spread in a gesture of despair, Ann Fellmeth came toward me and murmured, "Thrombosis."

It all happened so fast, even though the operation was proceeding well, that there was no time to send for Father Shanahan to give the soldier the last rites of his church.

The next day, as the *Mactan* was passing from the Celebes Sea into the Strait of Makassar, Williams was called into the captain's cabin and told that the ship was dangerously low on oil and water. The news shocked the Red Cross man, who had been given the impression in Manila that there was enough fuel and water to last ten days.

"We have very bad weathers, Meester Weelyems," explained the captain. "The engineer he remarks we need more oil. Also the *Mactan* she never carry so many passengers so we use more water."

Williams wiped the perspiration from his face. Any deviation from the announced course might give the Japanese an excuse to attack and destroy the unarmed ship. Yet to stop somewhere off the course for oil and water appeared unavoidable. But where? It was finally decided to put in at Makassar at the southwestern tip of Celebes Island, Netherlands East Indies. The next day, as the sun was setting, the *Mactan* was piloted into Makassar, a small piece of Holland isolated in the South Seas.

There followed five days of bewilderment and confusion as Williams endeavored to obtain definite information from Darwin and the American Legation at Canberra, Australia's capital, regarding the *Mactan*'s final destination.

The first words to come over the radio-telephone from the American Legation were: "Are you all right? There's a report that you'd been bombed."

This was Williams' first intimation of newspaper reports in Australia and the United States that the *Mactan* had been attacked. He worried about the reports: by inciting the Japanese they might put the hospital ship in further jeopardy.

While awaiting final word from Nelson Johnson, United States Minister to Australia, the *Mactan* took on fuel, water, and provisions. Patients, staff, and crew enjoyed the generous hospitality of the Dutch colony. But there were many patients aboard whose wounds required a type of hospitalization lacking on the *Mactan*. Two men had died, and a third had been saved by blood plasma. Colonel Carroll's concern for the others increased momentarily.

The next day—January 9—Williams received the following instructions from Minister Johnson over the radio-telephone: "Proceed to Darwin. Additional orders will await you there."

From then on, the *Mactan*'s passage, while beset, as before, by storms, enervating heat, and continued suspense regarding Japanese intentions, took on the aura of a triumphal march. Darwin in those dark days of the Japanese blitzkrieg was a haven for United Nations vessels. As the *Mactan*, under escort of an Australian gunboat, sailed into the harbor scores of them gave her a deafening welcome. With Darwin under constant Japanese air attack, the *Mactan* was advised to continue to Sydney. All day long launches and lighters brought supplies given by the Australian Red Cross. Three of its officials, Mrs. A. W. Abbott, president of the Northern Territory Division, L. R. McKenzie, deputy assistant commissioner, and Mrs. Peters of the Darwin chapter brought towels, chocolate, cookies, and comfort articles; and they introduced the boys to Australian "cordials," concentrated fruit syrups which made a delicious drink when mixed with iced water.

On the way from Darwin to Townsville, the next leg of the journey, fire broke out aboard the *Mactan*.

One of the Filipina nurses [recollected Williams] passing by the gangway leading to the engine room discovered smoke coming from below. In a moment there was a dull explosion and smoke and flames shot from the engine room. The ship's bell sounded the alarm and the crew raced to their fire stations. Colonel Carroll, first on the scene, pulled a fire extinguisher from its rack and dashed into the smoke-filled gangway.

He soon backed out gasping, but drawing a handkerchief over his face returned to the engine room followed by one of the Filipino patients also carrying an extinguisher.

The crew's fire-fighting team joined them and worked furiously to get the fire under control. I dashed up to the bridge to tell the wheelman to head toward shore, but Captain Tamayo had already given him this instruction. I then joined Father Shanahan and Ann Fellmeth directing patients into their lifebelts. While there was much excitement a panic was avoided. The fire lasted only a half-hour, but might easily have developed into a catastrophe but for the prompt and heroic work of Colonel Carroll and José H. Senorosa, the patient. The following entry appears in my log for January 15: "7:30 P.M. All clear sounded. Patients took whole situation without undue alarm and did much joking about it. While fire was on, one of the boys started playing his mouth organ and several others in vicinity began to sing. So endeth a brief experience with fire at sea."

When we dropped anchor off Townsville, Mrs. W. J. Heatley of the local Red Cross chapter visited the ship.

From the patients, she brought back a list a yard long of comfort articles needed by them which the Australian Red Cross Society would supply. To my profuse thanks, she replied, "This is the least we can offer in the face of the contribution the United States is making to our security."

We arrived at the mouth of the Brisbane River at three o'clock in the afternoon of January 24. The Brisbane River winds its way inland from the Pacific for a distance of eight miles to the city proper. At the mouth of the river is a broad, flat delta but farther upstream the land rises on either side and the slopes are dotted with the homes of Brisbane suburban dwellers. Having received advance news of our arrival, the good folk of Brisbane were out to give us a royal welcome. As we proceeded slowly toward the city we were cheered from the hillsides. Folks were gathered on their porches waving small United States flags, bedsheets, tablecloths and handkerchiefs. It was a stirring reception and one of the American patients, his eyes wet with tears, remarked, "Gee, it's just as if we were coming home!"

We were greeted at the pier by the American consul, Joseph P. Ragland, Colonel A. L. P. Johnson, commander of the American base at Brisbane, Major George Dietz, the Quartermaster, and Lieutenant Robert H. Odell, assistant military attaché of the United States Legation at Canberra.

From Colonel Johnson I learned that the first United States troops had arrived at Brisbane.

We departed from Brisbane on the morning of January 25. The boys were consuming gallons of milk and ice cream and crate after crate of oranges and bananas which Colonel Johnson had put aboard. Lieutenant Odell, who was accompanying us to Sydney, went from deck to deck teaching the boys the famous Aussie marching song, "Waltzing Matilda," which we planned to sing coming up the harbor to Sydney.

It was Sunday and that evening Father Shanahan conducted his final service. After delivering a fervent prayer of thanks for our safety, he concluded with the Lord's Prayer in which we all joined. The closing hymn was being sung when from the port promenade deck resounded the cry, "Man overboard!"

We rushed to that side of the ship and found the tell-tale empty cot of the missing Filipino soldier. The bridge rang "full speed astern," to the engine crew. The ship trembled and the engines

32

went into reverse. Spotlights were focussed on the seas then running rough. Lookouts were posted along the rails in all parts of the ship as for several hours we cruised about in the turbulent waters without finding a trace of the missing soldier.

Father Shanahan was terribly disturbed by the incident, thinking perhaps that something he had said in his sermon might have caused the soldier to take his life. We finally persuaded him that this could not have been the case as the boy understood no English.

The incident depressed the entire ship and the following day, January 26, their spirits were further lowered by cloudy skies and violent seas. The roughest part of the whole voyage occurred on this final stretch. Captain Tamayo paced the bridge, hour after hour, wringing his hands and moaning, "My sheep; my God, my sheep!" No rain fell but the wind was so strong that it threatened to tear the ship apart. The *Mactan* rose on its stern and slapped down on the angry waves with a crash that sent terror through our hearts.

Lieutenant Odell joined us in calming the patients who, for the first time, began to show signs of panic. With Sydney, the final destination, within reach the possibility of a disaster now was more than they could take. Even Captain Hervey, the pilot, who had sailed these waters for many years, began to show signs of strain by the gruff manner in which he called his instructions to the wheelman.

Throughout the night and into the next day, the *Mactan* ploughed its way through the heavy seas, straining and groaning as it took the battering of the waves. Every member of the crew was on the alert. A group of men was selected to check each bed to be sure that life preservers were ready for instant use.

But our luck held out, and on the morning of January 27, the sun broke through the clouds and the seas gradually calmed. At noon we were steaming through "The Heads," the cliffs that rear so boldly on either side of the narrow entrance to beautiful Sydney Harbor.

The boys were up in their cots chattering almost hysterically as they viewed the colorful landscape that graces the seaward approach to Australia's greatest metropolis. The harbor was full of shipping, and the *Mactan*, like a cocky bantam, proudly passed her larger sister ships while they saluted her with a terrific din of bells and whistles.

From the *Mactan*'s rear deck the strains of "Waltzing Matilda" sounded as one of the boys struck up the tune with his mouth organ. Immediately from all decks voices rose as one, singing the stirring ballad in salute to the proud little nation that was to be our home for so many months.

With a tug almost as big as the *Mactan* herself nosing us in, we slid into the quay at Wooloomooloo, the main dockside of Sydney. On the quay was a string of ambulances and motor cars winding out beyond the warehouses of the dockfront. Australian soldiers in their cocky hats with brim turned up stood in formation, stretchers replacing guns. Women in the uniform of the Australian Red Cross Motor Corps stood at attention at their ambulances and cars. A group of important looking civilians and army officers looked up. And from the *Mactan* came the rousing chorus of "Waltzing Matilda."

The first to come aboard was Ely E. Palmer, United States Consul General for Australia, and his first assistant, William Flake, American consul for Sydney. They were followed by officers of the Australian and United States Armies, Australian Government and officials of the Australian Red Cross Society.

The Australian stretcher bearers came aboard smartly and proceeded at once to transfer our bed patients to the ambulances. Ambulatory patients were led to waiting automobiles and ambulances. In one hour and a half all patients had departed from the ship, and were on their way to the Australian Army General Hospital No. 13.

Thus ended the long voyage of the first United States hospital ship in World War II. It is impossible in this brief account to detail all the dangers and tensions that lurked around the *Mactan* every inch and every minute of the way; or to give adequate recognition to the valuable services on board of Father Shanahan, Colonel Carroll, and Chief Nurse Ann Fellmeth; or to record fully the devotion and courage of the Filipino doctors and nurses who gave up their homes, families, and livelihood for the duration to serve on this hospital ship as Red Cross personnel.

To Irving Williams, the *Mactan* was one of those emergency assignments faced constantly by Red Cross field directors in the line of duty. He overlooked no detail to strengthen the faith of the wounded soldiers in the ability of the Red Cross to transport them to safety, thereby helping to sustain their morale. For his part in the mission he sought no reward but the satisfaction of having brought his heroic charges safely to Australia. He was both surprised and gratified, therefore, to receive the following document from them:

34

S. S. *Mactan*, Red Cross Hospital Ship
At Sea, January 12, 1942

National Headquarters
American Red Cross
Washington, D. C.

We, the undersigned officers and enlisted men of the USAFFE, in grateful appreciation of the services rendered by the Philippine Chapter of the American Red Cross under the supervision of Mr. Irving Williams, Field Director, wish by this letter to express our gratitude.

The evacuation of the wounded soldiers from Manila by the Red Cross prior to its occupation by the enemy was instrumental in preserving the lives and health of the undersigned.

The document bore the signatures, rank, and home addresses of 210 of the *Mactan*'s patients—all of them except those who had died or were too sick even to write their names. The addresses represented almost every state in the Union and every province in the Philippines.

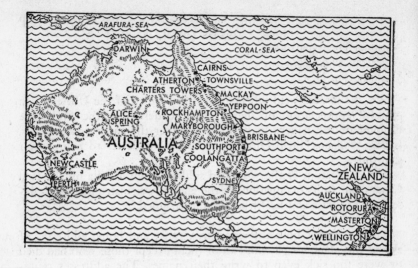

Chapter III

AUSTRALIA AND THE
SOUTHWEST PACIFIC

THE ONLY AMERICAN RED CROSS WORKER IN AUSTRALIA, FIELD Director Irving Williams faced a staggering load. He felt a continuing concern for the *Mactan*'s patients in the hospital. He helped place the ship's Filipino doctors and nurses in Australian hospitals, maintained members of the crew until employment could be found for them, and negotiated the disposal of the *Mactan* to the United States Army.

He also assumed responsibility for American Red Cross traditional services to the small force of United States troops already on Australian soil.

Among the distressed cargo from United Nations' ships hastily diverted to Australian ports at the outbreak of war, Williams found fifty-nine cases of Red Cross supplies consigned to him in Manila. They were the nucleus from which grew the mammoth stores of the American Red Cross in the South and Southwest Pacific. In 1944 there were twelve huge warehouses from which poured a flood of comfort articles, cigarettes, pipe tobacco, and recreation equipment for American soldiers, sailors, Marines, and airmen.

The appointment of dynamic Charles K. Gamble as American Red Cross Delegate on a voluntary basis hastened the organization of the Red Cross program. He was later made Red Cross Commissioner. A former Californian, Gamble was managing director of the Vacuum Oil Company in Australia with fifteen years' experience on the continent.

Mr. Gamble's pioneer headquarters staff consisted of the following: Irving Williams, field supervisor for all services to the armed forces; John S. Gibson, of Washington, D.C., business manager; Albert A. Scott, of Arlington, Massachusetts, liaison with the Australian Red Cross and Comforts Fund; David K. Wood, of Houston, Texas, and Mahlon T. Milburn, of Washington, D.C., accountants; William C. Warren, of New York City, and William J. Wright, of Philadelphia, club directors; Field Directors Stanley L. Sommer, of Washington, D. C., Donald E. Morse, of Webster, New York; and Walter L. Howard, of Austin, Texas, assigned to headquarters to assist Supervisor Williams.

Shortly after General MacArthur's arrival in Australia from the Philippines, Gamble and Williams called on him in Melbourne to discuss the Red Cross program. They found him weary but none the worse for his harrowing experiences on Bataan. In a letter to Chairman Norman H. Davis, Gamble wrote, "There is no doubt that General MacArthur is a great friend of the American Red Cross and is convinced of the potential importance of the American Red Cross to the American armed forces here."

The flow of American Red Cross men and women staff workers to Australia, New Zealand, and the islands of the South and Southwest Pacific started soon after the interview. Loaded down with knapsacks, gas masks, tin helmets, bed rolls, and musette bags, groups of Red Cross workers were aboard many troop transports crossing the Pacific from the United States. Surrounded by the same veil of secrecy that concealed troop movements, they slipped away to their missions of mercy without benefit of gay farewells. On shipboard they entered into the informality of free time, leading group singing, planning deck games, or organizing shows.

Along with the troops, they endured the discomforts and stern discipline necessary on an ocean passage under constant threat of enemy air and submarine attacks. Now and then a shipwreck, floating slag oil, or an empty raft on the water reminded them of their danger.

Australia, in the weeks immediately following Pearl Harbor when Japan was on the loose in the Pacific, mobilized to defend its life.

In a few lightning strokes, boldly conceived and ruthlessly executed, the Japanese amphibious war machine had conquered a vast sea-and-land empire in southeastern Asia and the southwestern Pacific. The Philippines, Netherlands East Indies, Malaya, Thailand, Burma, and Indo-China, with their immense wealth of raw materials and manpower, had fallen. Singapore, guarding Britain's gateway between the Pacific and Indian Oceans, heretofore thought impregnable, had crumbled. The Solomon Islands, New Britain, and a portion of New Guinea had been overrun. And now this land-sea-air juggernaut was knocking at the very gates of Australia.

Australia and her neighbor, New Zealand, were extremely worried. A considerable proportion of their land, air, and naval forces were committed elsewhere, particularly in Malaya and the Middle East. Meanwhile the Japanese almost daily were bombing Port Moresby, last remaining Australian outpost in New Guinea, and Darwin, on Australia's northern coast, which lay directly in the path of the Japanese sweeping down the Netherlands Indies.

In these circumstances, the arrival in Brisbane on December 22, 1941, of two transports bearing 4,500 Yanks gave the depressed Australian people a tremendous lift. These troops were at sea heading for the Philippines when they were hastily rerouted to Australia by the news of the Pearl Harbor attack. They received a heroes' welcome from the grateful Australians. Homes were thrown open to them and housewives struggled with hamburgers, apple pie, and coffee in a noble effort to make the Yanks feel at home. This generosity was to last as long as American troops remained on Australian soil.

The country's military outlook was improved considerably in March by three outstanding events: the arrival of General MacArthur and staff from the Philippines; the coming of the first big convoy directly from the United States with many thousands of fresh troops and large quantities of war supplies; and the return of General Sir Thomas A. Blamey with a large force of veteran Australian troops from the Middle East. Meanwhile United States Army Air Force units and naval reinforcements bolstered the defenses against the anticipated Japanese invasion.

Upon assuming the supreme command of Allied forces in the Southwest Pacific, General MacArthur found the Australian people committed to the so-called "Brisbane defense plan." It represented their realistic approach to what they feared inevitable: a Japanese invasion of unfortified Queensland and adjoining Northern Territory. The area was evacuated and a defense line based at Brisbane was set up.

General MacArthur, however, felt that the Allies should carry the fight to the Japanese aggressors in New Guinea instead of waiting for them to land in Australia. The Battle of the Coral Sea, May 4-8, 1942, in which the United States Navy, assisted by some Australian warships, decisively broke up a formidable Japanese invasion fleet removed an immediate threat. There was no further need for the "Brisbane defense plan."

Under the new plan, Australia and New Zealand were to be built up as major bases for offensive operations in New Guinea and the Solomon Islands through lend-lease from America and increased production of local munition plants. Australia was also to become the invasion training ground for thousands of American and Australian troops.

American contingents in southeastern Australia were moved up into Queensland, and there they were joined by many thousands of their comrades arriving over a period of many months from the United States. In Army camps all along the Queensland coast as far north as Cairns, Yanks learned the principles of jungle warfare. They also practiced debarking from transports, clambering down cargo-netted sides of ships into assault craft, and charging beaches— a training which was to enable them to capture one Japanese stronghold after another along the New Guinea coast on the hard but triumphant march to the Philippines.

This northern region, called Never-Never Land by Australians, was one of the most desolate in the world. Here American troops, side by side with their Australian Allies, endured not only the rigors of simulated battle, but also the most primitive living arrangements and adverse natural conditions imaginable. Mostly it was the heat that bothered them. From there a Red Cross field director wrote:

> The days go on, still oppressively hot. You and your clothing are saturated with Northern Territory cologne. You shower and before you can get your clothes on and your shoes laced, it's running off your face, muddying your glasses and soaking through the back of your shirt. You drink gallons of water and consume salt pills wholesale. But the funny thing is you get used to it.

American Red Cross field directors and recreation specialists were in this wild territory to help the fighting men adapt themselves to the primitive life, and to act as a link between them and their families at home. Their presence was particularly welcome in view of the prevalence of dengue fever and malaria, both extremely depressing.

Most field directors were mature men, some of them veterans of World War I. Selected for their judgment and experience in handling large groups of men, toughened to stand strenuous military life, strong of spirit, fearless and resourceful, they were fully prepared for the trials of the bush. They roughed it with the soldiers in virtually every phase of their training, sleeping and living out in the open.

For them life in the bush was a tough game of ingenuity and perseverance against great odds, as indicated by Field Director C. W. Ashley, of Baltimore, Maryland:

> Dust—clouds of it—in red, white and gray, eating your face; mosquitoes, flies that bite like ants, centipedes, spiders, and many strange bugs; temperatures of 130 degrees and rains of three or four inches—these are some of the things that a field director in Northern Territory has to contend with in his daily routine.
>
> After a drive of 300 miles over washboard roads in an army jeep you arrive at your headquarters to find a batch of mail to be answered. After clearing your desk it is midnight, and as a cool breeze blows through your tent you relax at the very thought of obtaining a good night's sleep on your army cot. Then about 3 A.M. the alert sounds. That was every night; you could set your watch by Jap raids. You jump from under your mosquito netting, stub your toe in the dark as you search for your helmet, and then dive for the nearest slit-trench. When the "all clear" sounds you cannot sleep again, even after counting thousands of sheep.

The American Red Cross recreation program in the bush, and throughout the Southwest Pacific, was divided into two parts: one for hospitalized men, the other for able-bodied troops. In the former case, the Red Cross provided a recreational specialist, usually a woman, on the staff of each hospital. The able-bodied program in camps was carried on by an assistant field director for recreation working under the Red Cross field director. The Red Cross furnished large quantities of recreational articles for able-bodied troops as distinguished from comfort articles such as razor blades, cigarettes, soap, comb, etc., furnished to hospitalized men. Recreational supplies ranged from pocket-sized books, playing cards, checkers, and cribbage boards to portable phonographs, horseshoes, table-tennis sets, harmonicas, pocket knives, baseball equipment, second-hand pianos, and band instruments.

40

Besides providing motion pictures, band concerts, and an active sports program, Red Cross field men took advantage of the primitive environment to create novel diversions for the men. They arranged and conducted visits to aboriginal villages where soldiers could witness the corroboree, a festival held on moonlight nights, in which native men danced to music played by their women.

They also promoted fishing and hunting trips in the bush. If lucky, a soldier might shoot wild geese, a 1,500-pound water buffalo, flying fox, wild pig, kangaroo, wallaby, or even a crocodile.

The men were encouraged to cultivate hobbies. One of the most popular was the catching and training of pets. Field Director William R. Fluharty said that many a cockatoo was trained to beg for food, shell and eat peanuts, shadow-box, take a shower bath, and even drink beer. Kangaroos and wallabies were equally good as pets. It was no uncommon sight, added Fluharty, to see a doughboy leading a kangaroo on a leash as he walked down to the mess tent. Mealtime at camp was heralded by a parade of birds and animals that seemed to have adjusted their feeding hours to those of United States soldiers. At breakfast wild cockatoos flew up from the surrounding gulleys; at lunch flocks of wild turkeys appeared; and at dinner a herd of wild goats made their call.

In addition to being a training ground for the invasion of Japanese-held territory, Australia became a leave area for officers and men of the United States Army and Navy as well as for Army nurses. At first this created a serious social problem. Australia, equal in area to the United States but with a population of less than nine million people, had only limited facilities to satisfy the needs of servicemen on leave. Crowded conditions brought about by the war prevailed in all cities. Moreover, the country's strict blue laws kept all shops, restaurants, and amusement places closed on Sundays, a serious problem for those with week-end leaves.

How grave the situation was from the Americans' standpoint was demonstrated by an incident in Brisbane, characterized by Australians as "a city the Yanks have taken over." Brisbane was a lusty overcrowded town redolent of the colorful days of the American frontier. Its narrow streets were jammed with fighting men—husky Aussies in their wide, upturned sombreros and bronzed Yanks in khaki shorts and pith helmets or in jungle-green coveralls—soldiers, sailors, Marines, and airmen stationed within the city or in surrounding camps, or on leave from the bush, or just in from the jungle war to the north.

Into this military boom town late one afternoon came three thousand Marines, fresh from months of jungle fighting on Guadalcanal, for a seventy-two-hour leave before proceeding to a rest camp farther south. Many of them were infected with malaria. The club was not large enough to accommodate more than a small proportion of the Marines in town, and due to unavoidable delays, Army cots had not arrived.

Moved by the Marines' plight, Miss Mary K. Browne, director of the Red Cross club, routed high-ranking Army officers from their quarters and brought them to the club. Their response was immediate. They went out themselves and dug up cots and blankets for five hundred men, and arranged for the transportation of the remainder to an Army camp outside the city.

For services like this, Mary K. Browne won the respect and affection of many American officers and enlisted men who passed through her club to and from the combat zones. To all of them she was simply "Mary K."

Middle-aged, her black hair streaked with gray, she was as energetic and intense as in the golden days of tennis when she was women's national champion for three consecutive years, and played in mixed doubles with Big Bill Tilden.

Arriving early in June, 1942, she was one of the first two American Red Cross women club workers in Australia. A routine introduction to General MacArthur inspired her "to make a home for the boys away from home," in Brisbane. Recognizing her instantly, the General said, "Young woman, the last time I saw you was at Forest Hills. You were fighting for your life with Helen Wills Moody, and I remember how you kept hitting the ball."

Undeterred by lack of professional training as a club worker, she simply kept "hitting the ball" until she succeeded in building a Red Cross service club that was the pride of Australia. Her attitude was expressed in a sign on the wall:

> The extremely difficult
> We do immediately;
> The impossible
> Takes a while longer.

She faced almost insurmountable odds because of terribly overcrowded conditions. The only space available was some rooms occupied by a small women's club on the top floor of a five-story building in the center of the business district. This was the beginning of the Red Cross club in Brisbane. General MacArthur moved his headquarters from Melbourne to Brisbane; so did the Army Services of Supply. Use by United States Navy of the Brisbane River channel brought sailors into town. With every substantial increase of

42

American military and naval personnel, Mary K. Browne took over more space in the building, tearing out walls here, throwing up a new partition there, installing hot showers and dormitories first for 120 men, then for 150, and finally for 300 men, until the entire building passed into Red Cross possession.

She established an eighteen-hour restaurant serving up to 2,000 full meals and 2,500 short orders a day, a watch-repairing station, and a night club featuring a milkshake bar. She instructed Australian carpenters how to build a lunch counter Los Angeles style, and Australian sausage makers how to make authentic hot dogs. A laundry and pressing service, a private lounge serving as downtown headquarters for United States Army nurses, and a first-aid station with a trained nurse always in attendance, were some of the club's amenities. Through the information and hospitality bureau she arranged for week-end entertaining of American servicemen by Australian families.

Her work was not without its minor, as well as major, crises, however. On a certain Sunday evening, for instance, a new recreation room was to have been opened with a carefully rehearsed soldier show. Several hours prior to curtain time, she suddenly discovered that through faulty wiring the recreation room could not be lighted without throwing the rest of the club into darkness. A modest, quiet-spoken Australian soldier offered his services. Miss Browne watched him work diligently all afternoon, and then, his task apparently completed, she went to her hotel for a rest. Presently the telephone rang. It was the Aussie reporting that the lights had fused, and where was the fuse box located?

Mary K. was annoyed. Recalling the incident, she said:

I knew where it was, but I was afraid to tell him for fear all the lights in the kitchen would also be shot. I rushed back to the club and found everyone worried. My assistant got me aside and said, "I'm afraid this Australian doesn't know too much about electricity."

Anyway I took him to the main switch box and as he started to look the fuses over, I timidly asked, "Do you know enough about electricity to do this?"

The youngster calmly located the faulty fuses and replaced them. Then he turned to me and grinned, "Well, Miss Browne, I wired the tunnels at Tobruk."

To meet this need of American servicemen and women on leave, the American Red Cross operated a chain of clubs. As Vice-Chairman Richard F. Allen pointed out in a letter to Mr. Gamble, the Red Cross had a "traditional policy against charging men in the service for the things the Red Cross does for them." The Red Cross, then, was prepared to furnish beds and meals free, but Australian and New Zealand agencies operating similar clubs for their own men and women protested that this policy would embarrass them. Lacking large financial resources, they maintained their clubs at cost and requested the American Red Cross to do likewise.

The same problem had arisen in Great Britain where the American Red Cross representatives were as reluctant to charge for meals and lodging as those in Australia. There followed a series of negotiations in Washington between the War Department and the Red Cross at which the latter fought for the principle of placing meals and lodging—the only items at issue—on the same free basis as other Red Cross services to the armed forces.

Secretary of War Henry L. Stimson finally laid down the War Department's worldwide policy on this matter. In a letter dated May 20, 1942, to Chairman Norman H. Davis, he wrote: "The War Department appreciates the motive of the Red Cross with respect to this matter and its established policy of free service, but under the circumstances it is believed impractical, unnecessary, and undesirable that food and lodging be furnished free. It is understood that all similar clubs in the British Isles make suitable charges for this particular service. It is believed advisable that American soldiers be required to pay at least the actual cost of meals and lodging furnished for their convenience and benefit while on furlough. Such procedure is considered a sound business arrangement and conforms to local practise. It is therefore believed that such procedure should be adopted because of its merit rather than because the local military commander requests that charges be made for the proposed services."

The charges were nominal and did not exceed the cost of the raw food. For example, in one Australian city, doughboys on leave paid twelve cents for a bed for one night, and an additional twelve cents for a breakfast of ham and eggs, toast, and coffee. The porterhouse steak dinner they had dreamed about in their foxholes cost them only twenty-five cents each. Charges varied in the different theaters according to the currency value of the country in which the facility was operating. No charge was made for refreshments when served on special occasions, nor were charges made at any time for doughnuts, coffee, and other accessories served by clubmobiles.

The first American Red Cross club in Australia was opened in Melbourne in June, 1942, with the official blessings of General Sir Thomas Blamey, Commander in Chief of Allied Land Forces in

44

Australia. It was made ready and equipped by American business-men with funds provided by the Red Cross. Housed in a five-story building with a capicity of 500 beds and a canteen capable of serv-ing 6,000 meals daily, this developed into the largest of the Aus-tralian clubs.

The club program as a whole was launched under the inspiring leadership of Miss Helen Hall, on a year's leave of absence from the Henry Street Settlement in New York, soon after her arrival in August, 1942. To this assignment Miss Hall brought a rich experi-ence as director of American Red Cross activities in base hospitals in France during World War I, and as organizer (1920-22) of serv-ice clubs in China and the Philippines.

On her supervisory staff were Stanley L. Sommer, of Washington, D.C., a former newspaperman, and Grey M. Lusty, of Salt Lake City, former State Supervisor of Recreation for California.

Their problems were numerous. The American Red Cross, enter-ing the market three years after the Australian Comfort Fund and the New Zealand Patriotic Fund, found few buildings available for club purposes. Stringent restrictions against wartime construction precluded building clubs from the ground up. Every city and dis-trict where United States troops were stationed or allowed on leave underwent careful scrutiny for buildings that might be converted into Red Cross service clubs. Acquisition was not easy, but through the Australian Hiring Authority possession was obtained of private hotels, a small department store, a labor union hall, a sanitarium, a guest house, race track sites, and other buildings.

At Perth, a U.S. Navy base on Australia's west coast, a two-story boathouse standing on piles over the water was rebuilt to look like a ship, and a flat barge attached to it was converted into a dance hall. The Red Cross operated a Marine air officers' rest home near Auck-land, New Zealand, in a mansion of a Melbourne millionaire depart-ment-store owner, a former American.

In the South Sea Islands, Red Cross clubs generally were housed in native-type huts with thatched roofs. The largest, 60 by 130 feet, was on New Caledonia. It was built of bamboo, its supporting posts being festooned with tree ferns and growing orchids.

Clubs contended with varying conditions of climate and environ-ment. One club director wrote: "Our problems are still the same— too little of this, too little of that, but customers, God bless them, plenty of customers."

One of the serious shortages in some areas was of water for drink-ing, bathing, and dishwashing. Too much water, on the other hand, afflicted an officers' rest home that had weathered a typhoon. When the club was finally bailed out, ducks were found floating in a bedroom, and a baby squab was rocking in the mosquito netting over a Red Cross girl's bed.

Red Cross clubs were a modern miracle to the Marines from Guadalcanal. What the average Marine had dreamed about and wanted so much in Australia were a good bed with clean white sheets, a hot shower, a good meal, and plenty of recreation. It was not long before these American heroes learned that the Red Cross was the place to find all of them. After months of eating chow from tin mess gear at the edge of a foxhole, it seemed almost unreal to sit down at a table covered with a white tablecloth and be served a home-cooked dinner in regular china dishes by a woman volunteer worker.

In New Guinea, Negro GI's, in anticipation of the arrival of eight Negro Red Cross girls for their "Club Papuan," built them the best living quarters on the island. They selected a site on a hilltop overlooking the sea and constructed a twelve-room house, including a large reception hall, parlor, and a private bedroom for each girl—and something hitherto unheard of in New Guinea—a bathroom with flush toilets. And to bring water to the house, the men piped it for a quarter of a mile.

At the height of the program there were more than 100 Red Cross clubs and rest homes in the South and Southwest Pacific, staffed by approximately 500 Red Cross staff workers from the United States, aided by some 20,000 local volunteers. On the map, these installations formed an ellipse whose circumference was nearly 6,500 miles, extending along Australia's 2,000-mile eastern coast, across the Torres Straits into Papua, eastern Guinea, then 1,500 miles across the Coral Sea into New Caledonia, and down to New Zealand. They were separated from one another by submarine-infested waters; towering mountains; and vast distances of undeveloped territory, scrubby desert lands, and immense sheep and cattle stations.

In New Zealand, Mrs. Tillman Durdin, wife of the *New York Times* war correspondent, assumed direction of an enlisted men's hostel. Mrs. James F. Clymer, long resident in Australia, formerly of Syracuse, New York, ran a seaside resort rest home for battle-weary Marines. Mrs. E. L. Moser, of Melbourne, formerly of New York City, flew 1,800 miles to northern Australia to establish a rest home for officers on leave from New Guinea; Lenore Lucas, only American woman correspondent accredited to General MacArthur's command, and wife of Walter Lucas, English war correspondent, transformed an old stone hotel in an isolated farming settlement

46

into a homelike service club for troops stationed near a secret air base in Queensland.

Miss Coletta Ryan, former apartment-house and tea room manager of Washington, D.C. became widely known for her outstanding work in behalf of servicemen in the South Pacific. She accompanied Mrs. Franklin D. Roosevelt on her inspection tour of Red Cross installations in 1943. Seeing how devoted Miss Ryan was to "her boys," Mrs. Roosevelt said, "You do carry each one of them in your heart." Miss Ryan, together with three girl assistants, came to New Caledonia in the early days of the war when the island was still very primitive. Her work later won her a promotion to supervisor of club service with a staff of 125 Red Cross girls.

On New Caledonia in 1944 served Mrs. Alice Bowring, a two-hundred-pound, rollicking, yet deeply understanding Australian woman, known to thousands of American servicemen as "Mom." Before the war she lived in feudal luxury at Wau, New Guinea, where she operated her own gold mine. The Japanese were stopped only three miles from her place, and then long enough for her to pack up and flee. In Sydney the American Red Cross employed her to supervise a club kitchen because she had "experience in handling natives." Proving herself capable of more responsible duties, she was assigned as Red Cross club director on New Caledonia. One of the most wonderful things about her was her unrestrained laughter. Her hearty expressions might raise the hair on your head, yet she could recite Shakespeare at any given cue. Walking through the club she would slap a Marine on the shoulder, pause to put her arm around a teen-age sailor, or address a couple of Seabees in dungarees. "She expresses in her personality what democracy means," said one GI. "She's equally nice to us all, from the stars to the stripes." One Australian newspaper featured her as the GI's "No. 1 pin-up girl," rating a salute of eleven guns. The members of a Seabee outfit immediately wrote asking for her picture. "You're the First Lady of the South Pacific," was the toast of an Australian newspaper correspondent—anyway, next to Admiral Halsey, "Mom" Bowring was probably the best-known personality in the South Pacific from the equator to the tip of New Zealand.

Red Cross club and program directors received valuable aid from local volunteers. Early fears of a scarcity of women and girl volunteers proved groundless. The youthfulness, exemplary behavior, and dash of the American troops moved women and girls to compete for the privilege of working at the American Red Cross service clubs.

At one club alone 600 women were on the weekly roster, waiting on tables, handling laundry, dry cleaning, sewing, looking after checkrooms, and making billeting reservations. Some served on the hospitality committees that obtained theater passes for servicemen and women, and arranged week-end excursions into the Australian bush and overnight stays with Australian and New Zealand families.

All the clubs held dances, the number depending upon the size of the club and the ability of the community to supply dancing partners. The larger clubs had between 500 and 1,200 girls on their dance rosters, and additional hundreds on waiting lists: college coeds, society debs, business girls, and stenographers. To be accepted as a dancing partner, a girl had to be approved by a committee who determined her eligibility by her dancing, personality, and character references.

Supplying clubs with food posed an extremely difficult problem of transportation, accentuated by Australia's anachronistic railway system, which altered its gauges at every state border. Food was obtained within Australia, but much club equipment, utensils, and other necessities had to come from the United States. For many months shipping from America was a serious bottleneck. Most Red Cross supplies were carried by air transport, especially to remote installations. Traveling by Red Cross personnel often was in Army and Navy planes. Miss Hall, Sommer, and Lusty estimated that in a year they traveled about 120,000 miles by air. The supply problem primarily was the concern of Albert A. Scott, of Arlington, Massachusetts, in charge of purchasing, and his staff of Australians, New Zealanders, Englishmen, and Free Frenchmen, as well as of Dow Sweeny, of Akron, Red Cross expediter. This staff somehow managed to get results. Its accomplishments were due to skill and ingenuity, to the good old Army game of bartering, and to extraofficial sympathy and co-operation from military and civilian leaders all the way down the line.

Red Cross clubs were intended to be "a little bit of America" for United States servicemen and women and merchant seamen, but Allied troops were also welcome.

While most clubs were for enlisted personnel, Army and Navy officers were not overlooked. For them the Red Cross operated clubs in Sydney, Mackay, New Zealand, and on New Caledonia. Officers on leave otherwise might have been compelled to live in camps.

Red Cross clubs in places having large concentrations of Negro troops were staffed by professional Negro Red Cross men and women workers.

Distinct from service clubs were rest homes, or rest areas, operated by the Red Cross. These establishments were for enlisted men and officers convalescing from wounds or tropical diseases; Air Force personnel in need of a change from combat flying; and nurses on leave from long months of work in forward hospitals. Heroes of the first assault on Tulagi and Tanambogo in the Solomons—many of them malaria victims—convalesced at one of these rest areas, a large country estate with surfing facilities, golf, and horseback riding. Some veterans of the 32nd Division back from the Buna campaign rested at Coolangatta, a popular winter resort not far from Brisbane. Nurses, exhausted by the tropic heat and grime of New Guinea, toned up their health and mental outlook at their own rest homes in Sydney, Brisbane, and Townsville. An atmosphere of pleasant, friendly informality prevailed. After months of wearing their uniforms nurses were relieved to find that they could take their meals in their wrappers if they wished. A comfortable bed, hot-water showers, and good food were a welcome contrast to the discomforts of the jungle. Each club ran a beauty parlor where the girls could get their hair done and their nails manicured, a service unheard of in the advanced areas.

There were several rest areas in the South-Southwest Pacific theater. One of them was the Kia Ora, perched high on a hilltop overlooking the beautiful harbor of Auckland, New Zealand. An interesting departure from the routine for its officer guests was a buffet supper from ten to eleven P.M. when guests raided the ice box of cold chicken, ham, pickles, and other delicatessen. To each registrant was given a small silver Maori charm, called a *tiki*, which officers cherished on combat missions as a token of good luck. From Kia Ora, as from Auckland and Wellington, the Red Cross organized trips to Rotorua, New Zealand's own version of the Yellowstone National Park, home of the Maoris. The Red Cross hospitality center in Rotorua made all the local arrangements for the visiting Americans. Built around a huge cone of bubbling hot-water springs, the town has been developed into a commercial resort of international renown. The boys were amused to see Maoris cooking over steam holes between rocks, each family having staked out its own outdoor kitchen. The climax of the entertainment program was Maori folk dances done by natives in picturesque costumes.

The largest rest area, consisting of fourteen buildings within two city blocks, was located at Mackay on Australia's northeastern coast. Built at the request of Lieutenant General George C. Kenney for his Fifth Air Force personnel, it was opened by Red Cross Supervisor Grey M. Lusty on April 1, 1943. Many thousands of American servicemen went through this resort in 1943 and 1944, the guest list averaging about eight hundred daily.

There were no bugle calls at Mackay, the men going to bed and getting up when they pleased. The Army took care of their pay, clothing, and health, including dental service, and the American Red Cross provided food, billeting, and recreation.

This undertaking was a good example of the tremendous amount of work and ingenuity that often went into Red Cross facilities overseas. Supervisor Lusty was at the Townsville club early in March, 1943, when a telephone call by Miss Helen Hall summoned him to the airport. Between planes, she outlined some of General Kenney's ideas regarding a rest home for his fatigued fliers. Lusty hadn't the least idea where he could find a suitable site in a country already overrun with military and naval installations. At Townsville he got on a train with a ticket which permitted stopovers at each station. After inspecting several towns along the railroad, Lusty finally came to Mackay, a town of 15,000 people, the center of an agricultural region, and built with broad streets and beautiful shade trees like those of American country towns. In its favor was the fact that it lay outside the malaria belt. Lusty lost no time calling on the mayor and the town's leading citizens. Within twenty-four hours he had thirteen buildings centered around a large hotel, and through the Australian Hiring Authority leased them for the Red Cross.

Within three days after his initial visit, Lusty brought Douglass Malin, of Glendale, California, who was to become the rest area's first director. Malin, a former construction man, engaged a local contractor to renovate the buildings. Laborers followed the Australian custom of "boiling the billey," or stopping for morning and afternoon tea, and monsoon rains delayed equipment by washing out railroad tracks, but the job was completed within a month.

Though the first group of weary airmen arrived on April 1, there were still some details to be worked out before the resort was acceptable. Local farmers, potential producers of the rest area's milk, vegetables, meat, and poultry, were found to be far behind the times in sanitation and health standards. Pasteurization, refrigeration, and tuberculin tests of dairy herds were unheard of, and for a time the Red Cross and the Army faced a serious problem with farmers protesting innovations entailing expense. But diplomacy, patience, free Army veterinarian service, and premium prices combined to bring about a victory for progress. More than 2,000 head of cattle were vaccinated. The Red Cross rented and operated the local ice plant and advanced funds to the local creamery to install a modern pasteurization plant. To insure a steady supply of fresh eggs and poultry, the Red Cross took over and modernized a poultry farm near Mackay, and within two weeks stocked it with 1,500 poultry—chickens, ducks, turkeys, and geese.

Groups of men were flown in from New Guinea on a ten-day leave. Each day three large Army transport planes taxied down the field and stopped close to an Army bus. Out piled the Yanks, some dressed in regulation khaki, some in fatigue coveralls. Without exception they had that jungle look—faces pallid, drawn, and thin, and eyes somewhat apathetic. In a minute or two they were headed for town. As their bus passed through Mackay's shaded streets with well-kept lawns and attractive houses, their interest quickened.

The bus stopped at a hotel with a large red sign across the front bearing the legend, "American Red Cross." Picking up their flight bags, they piled out of the bus and were greeted with a friendly, "Hello, gang, how about some good fresh ice-cold milk and cake?"

The greeting was extended by Catherine Steltz, of Harrisburg, Pennsylvania, assistant club director, called "Kay" by everybody. She directed the men to a table upon which stood a milk can and plates piled high with frosted cake. For the next ten minutes, amid an exchange of banter, she poured milk, gallons of it, into the large paper cups held tightly by men tasting fresh milk for the first time in more than a year.

The milk and cake, combined with Kay's friendly smile, broke down their reserve as they gathered around her. They wanted to get a good look at her. She didn't mind the special attention. In fact, she rather enjoyed it. Anyway, she explained the routine followed by guests at Mackay, and told of the meals, laundry service, barber shop, free mending service, and the recreation program. "And now," she concluded, "pick up your bags, and Danny will show you where you're going to sleep. You've just enough time for a hot shower and a change before the first call for dinner."

Danny, the Australian employee, led his charges to their quarters, where they picked up an unmistakable aroma of frying steaks and potatoes coming from the kitchen.

The cost of meals to enlisted men was as follows: breakfast and lunch, 25 cents; dinner, 32 cents. Officers paid slightly more. Dining tables were covered with clean white tablecloths. The waitresses were pretty young Australian girls. In addition to two dining rooms, the Red Cross operated three snack bars, or soda fountain lunch counters, two in town and the third at a near-by beach resort, all dispensing ice cream, sodas, banana splits, soft drinks, hamburgers, and chicken sandwiches. In all, these soldiers consumed three hundred gallons of milk daily.

On Club Director Douglass Malin's original staff were Dwight H. Hunter, of Macon, Georgia, program director; Robert H. Brumett, of Rockford, Illinois, recreation supervisor; Marcille Gunther, of Los Angeles, assistant program director; Esther Morgan, of Columbia, Missouri, personal service director; and Miss Steltz. Three months after the opening, Herbert L. Patrick, of Portland, Maine, succeeded Malin as club director, and during a tenure of many months developed the resort to the highest point of efficiency.

Miss Gunther organized a volunteer group of five hundred Australian girls to help entertain the soldier guests. Known as the Air Force Victorettes, the girls participated in nightly dances, beach parties, horseback riding, deep-sea fishing trips, ping-pong, tennis, cycling, and skating parties. When Mrs. Roosevelt visited Mackay in 1943 she was warmly greeted by these Victorettes, who made her an honorary member.

Mrs. Verna Brittain, Red Cross staff assistant, a former Ziegfeld Follies girl, the wife of an Englishman, was living in Singapore when the war began. Always a few hours ahead of the onrushing Japanese forces, she flew first to Borneo, then to Java, from there to Darwin, and finally to Melbourne where she joined the American Red Cross. An attractive blond, she drew upon her theatrical experience to organize and train a chorus of Australian girls, called the Brittainettes, who danced and sang for the men Sunday evenings. Later she resigned from the Red Cross to rejoin her husband in India. While in the Indian Ocean, the ship on which she was a passenger was attacked by Japanese surface craft and she was taken prisoner.

Mrs. Eleanor Seavers, of Pittsburgh, beat out the rhythm for the jam sessions, held whenever a half-dozen men gathered around the piano.

Esther Morgan was the "Mother Cross" of the staff, who advised the boys on problems of the heart and purse.

Twice a week Mary Sullivan, of St. Louis, and Jane Randolph, of Millwood, Virginia, mounted their favorite steeds and rode with forty to fifty GI's to Dumbleton Beach for a swim and a picnic.

As part of its recreation program, the Red Cross leased Eimeo Beach, ten miles from Mackay, with a hotel perched on a promontory overlooking the blue Pacific. Each morning Army buses brought soldiers and Victorettes to this resort, and each evening took them back to Mackay.

Ten days of this unmilitary life of ease and fun rejuvenated the fighting men. They averaged a gain of seven pounds for the leave period. Color returned to their cheeks. And the memories were a continuing strength to their spirits when they returned to the drab life in the jungles.

Success of the Mackay idea led the Army to start a mass furlough program for ground troops on New Guinea and other islands in December, 1943. Each unit furnished a proportionate number of its men to this vacation pool, selections being based on the length of service of a year or more in the Southwest Pacific. Tired GI's by the thousands from all the forward areas were assembled periodically at various concentration points along the New Guinea coast, and from there were shipped by the Army Transport Service to Sydney. Aboard the transports were Red Cross workers serving the officers and men as usual. At the height of the leave program in 1944, six ships ran on a regular schedule, transporting vacation-bound Army personnel to Sydney and returning with those who had completed their leave.

Upon their arrival in Sydney, officers and men became guests of the American Red Cross. Its six large Sydney clubs—three for officers, three for enlisted personnel—and the Red Cross nurses' rest home for Army nurses on leave were filled to capacity; the Army took care of the overflow in temporary facilities, or in Brisbane.

The Red Cross assumed responsibility for a planned recreation program. Glorious memories were stored up by the boys to take back to their jungle foxholes. The Red Cross took over Bondi Beach, Sydney's largest municipal bathing pavilion and one of Australia's most beautiful resorts, and operated it solely for the vacationing Yanks and their guests. This resort was the focal point of all Red Cross entertainment and recreation for the boys. Sydney's most glamorous bathing beauties gave bathing exhibitions. They were part of some ten thousand Australian volunteers who helped the overworked Red Cross staff, led by Hinson L. Trites, of Des Moines, area director, provide parties, dances, excursions, sightseeing trips, motion pictures, and live shows, and home hospitality.

The American Red Cross in this theater also served the sick and wounded. Red Cross workers were in the collecting stations through which casualties were cleared, and on hospital ships.

On the Australian mainland, all transport facilities for the wounded were attended by Red Cross workers. One of them wrote: "We service all hospital trains—either by passing through or by making up supplies for destinations beyond. During one month we serviced about 1,100 patients on hospital trains." Patients were given soft drinks, cigarettes, matches, gum, candy, a newspaper. Slippers, socks, sweaters, and comfort articles were distributed to those needing them.

The Red Cross furnished traditional services to the six U.S. Naval hospitals in the Southwest Pacific. Expeditions by boats and barges for swimming, fishing, and picnics were popular in the recreation program of these hospitals.

The Harvard Unit in Australia—an Army general hospital—offered unusual incentives for the highest type of Red Cross work. The Red Cross recreation building contained a lounge, a reading room pleasantly furnished with brown and green leather chesterfields, a library, and a large game room with ping-pong, pool, and card tables, a piano, and many brightly colored beach chairs. The Red Cross staff had a well-developed program for social service and recreation. Patient-built glass showcases exhibited articles from the arts and skills class.

In another hospital patients made an old-fashioned bar complete with rail. But it served only lemonade and coffee. Carrying out the Western frontier motif in the recreation room, a Negro artist painted a Western mural on the knotty-pine walls, while cutout maps of Western states were placed in blackout windows. Dart and ring-toss alleys were set up in a sort of double-horse stall in one corner of the room, and a modified bowling alley in the other.

In the fall of 1944 there were 475 Red Cross hospital workers in the Pacific areas.

By the time of General MacArthur's landing on Leyte in the Philippines, Australia and New Zealand had been left far to the rear of military operations. As the Red Cross advanced with MacArthur's forward echelons, many of its facilities in rear areas were gradually discontinued. In New Zealand only one hospital unit and one field director remained, while on some of the smaller islands installations were dismantled and staffs sent forward. Clubs in Australian and New Zealand cities were also being closed down as the need for them diminished.

And on November 1, 1944, Red Cross Southwest Pacific headquarters were moved from Brisbane to Hollandia, New Guinea, with Nyles I. Christensen, of San Francisco, as director of operations.

In New Guinea Red Cross workers missed the thousands of Australian volunteers who had given them such valuable assistance. Missed also were the genuine hospitality and neighborliness of the Australian and New Zealand people, whose friendship for homesick Yanks will remain a treasured memory. The Australian Red Cross and the Australian Comforts Fund gave valuable assistance to the

American Red Cross, especially in the early days. American citizens permanently resident on the continent were similarly helpful.

Out of this wartime experience has grown a movement centering around the "Australian-American Association" which has for its main objective the promotion of permanent good will between the two peoples.

Chapter IV

THE BUNA CAMPAIGN

Iɴ ᴛʜᴇ ᴅᴜsᴋ ᴏғ ᴀ ᴛʀᴏᴘɪᴄ ᴇᴠᴇɴɪɴɢ sᴇᴠᴇʀᴀʟ ʜᴜɴᴅʀᴇᴅ ᴀᴍᴇʀɪᴄᴀɴ fighting men, dressed in green coveralls and jungle caps, were seated on logs nailed to stumps in a jungle clearing. Their eyes were riveted on a portable screen, made out of bamboo poles, showing *The Vanishing Virginian*. The blue New Guinea sky was their ceiling, the dense jungle growth about them the acoustic walls. No more notice was taken of the cacaphony of weird jungle noises than of the sound of gunfire which came intermittently from the front lines not far away.... Thunder and lightning, and a shower poured down on them. The parakeets overhead that had been dashing from tree to tree took flight, and so did the mosquitoes. But the soldiers remained in their seats to the end of the picture. "Jungle Jim" Stewart, Red Cross field director, operating the 16-mm. projector, asked whether they were in a mood to see another picture, and the response was overwhelming. So, in spite of the rain, Stewart went ahead with the projecting of *The Kid Glove Killer*.... The rain stopped, the parakeets returned, and the mosquitoes came back to raise more welts on the soldiers' arms and legs.... Suddenly the alert sounded and accomplished what the rain had failed to do. The boys dived into their slit-trenches, but as soon as the Japanese bombers left, they hopped out and went on with the show.

Incidents such as this, illustrating the hunger of front-line troops for entertainment, were common during the Buna campaign of 1942. Among his other Red Cross services, Stewart showed American films. His career in Papua was a continuation of exciting war experiences. Back in 1941 he had enlisted as a driver for the American Field Service on the Libyan desert. While en route, his ship, the Egyptian liner *Zamzam*, was torpedoed by a German surface raider and he was taken prisoner. On his way through occupied France to a German internment camp he escaped, made his way to the American embassy at Vichy, and subsequently was repatriated.

Back in his home town of Oneonta, New York, Jimmy Stewart, still restless, decided to volunteer for General Claire L. Chennault's Flying Tigers. He was on the Pacific en route to Burma when his ship received a flash announcing the Pearl Harbor attack. Changing its course, the ship put in at Melbourne, Australia, where Stewart applied for active service with the American Red Cross.

He drew the hottest assignment in the Southwest Pacific—Port Moresby, Allied outpost on New Guinea's southern coast. In the desperate days of April, May, and June, 1942, Port Moresby, never more than a frontier town, was hurriedly converted into an armed camp without a vestige of civilian life. The town was pitted with bomb craters, and its makeshift roads had been churned into mire by heavy-wheeled military traffic. The first American troops landed in a depressing atmosphere of malaria, enervating heat, and a monotonous diet of corned willy, hardtack, and canned fruit.

It was "Jungle Jim" Stewart's responsibility to help soften the rigors of this life for the American troops. Riding in an Army jeep, he covered a vast territory from the beaches deep into the dark jungles. Since, in the early days, only essentials—ammunition and minimum food rations—received priority on the air transports, he distributed few Red Cross supplies. His 16-mm. projector, generator, portable screen, and American films proved a godsend. With the assistance of doughboys, he hacked outdoor movie theaters out of the jungle and rode the circuit nightly in his jeep. Intermissions, caused by Japanese air raids, came often. His office was a shack turned over to him by the RAAF. The clearing in front of the shack was promptly named "Dogface Avenue," and his slit-trench, "Poobah Palace." With Port Moresby under day-and-night air attacks, communications between the Red Cross office and Poobah Palace were excellent, according to Stewart.

In the spring of 1942 Japan set out to nail down the empire she had overrun with such ease during the first three months after Pearl Harbor. Her plan was to seize certain key points in the Pacific outside the rim of her initial conquests. With landings in the Solomon Islands and along the northeastern coast of New Guinea, and with the concentration at Rabaul, New Britain, of strong invasion forces, she revealed her strategy to invade Australia by a pincers movement. One wing would take the islands of New Hebrides and New Caledonia, severing the vital supply line from the United States to Australia, and bringing Japanese forces within striking distance of Australia's populous southeastern coast.

The other wing of the pincers was aimed at Port Moresby, from where an attack on northern Australia could be launched. Late in July a strong Japanese invasion force landed at Buna, on New Guinea's northern coast, to begin a powerful and determined drive across the Owen Stanley Range to Port Moresby by way of Kokoda. While a Japanese force was pushing across the mountains, another landed along the swampy shores of Milne Bay threatening the Allied positions on the peninsula. This invasion was short-lived. The Japanese, caught in a trap laid for them by General MacArthur, were soon wiped out.

Fighting along the steep and densely forested Kokoda Trail, on the other hand, was savage and bloody. Not until they had driven to a point forty miles from Port Moresby were the Japanese finally turned back. Once the 14,000-foot Owen Stanley Range had been crossed by Australian and American troops, the battle for Buna, Japanese base on the north coast, picked up momentum. Heartbreaking difficulites of terrain and climate, fanatic resistance, and every conceivable transportation obstacle plagued the Allies. Using unarmed transport planes, the Fifth Army Air Force, under command of Lieutenant General George C. Kenney, ferried an Allied ground force of thousands of troops and their equipment over the range, supplied them daily with ammunition, food, and medicines, and flew back the wounded. Before Buna the Japanese had an almost perfect defensive position: shielded in front by an impassable sago swamp, behind by the ocean, and on the flanks by a narrow defile held in depth by fortresses built out of giant coconut logs and sand. The final Allied assault to break through these defenses developed in November under the personal direction of General MacArthur.

The American Red Cross, like the Army, depended largely on native labor for ground transportation during the campaign. Red Cross blood plasma, surgical dressings, and many comfort and recreational supplies, dropped by parachute, were carried to the front lines by the fuzzy-haired Papuans whom the soldiers called "boongs."

American troops came in contact with the sturdy black Christian Melanesians along the north coast, with those of a lighter shade in the east, and seldom with the Negro pygmies of the deep interior. Descendants of head-hunters, these peaceful natives before the war had labored on copra plantations or in the gold mines at Wau, or had lived by farming and fishing. When the Japanese seized Buna, they forced many of them to work as pack animals on their overland drive toward Port Moresby. Torn from their native villages and families, and beaten unmercifully, the natives hated the Japanese and hailed the Allies as saviors. Yanks and Aussies alike were instructed to treat them like human beings and to respect their native customs and superstitions. To kindness, the boongs responded with loyalty and enthusiastic work, which contributed to the ultimate success of the Buna campaign.

Native assistance was vital particularly during the initial, secret stages of the campaign when Allied troops were being landed on improvised air strips encircling Japanese positions. Though the "bamboo telegraph" spread the news far and wide among natives, the Japanese were kept in the dark until the actual assault had begun. Meantime United States Army engineers, assisted by hundreds of natives, had carved out landing fields, located and improved the best jeep trails, and otherwise blazed the way for the Allied assault troops.

As the campaign developed with more or less fixed lines of communication and supplies, contracts were made by the Army with the various village chiefs for labor under the supervision of the ANGAU (Australia-New Guinea Administrative Unit) composed of government officials long resident in New Guinea who spoke the Motuan language fluently. The American Red Cross obtained native labor through the Army. The Allies could not have bought the loyalty of these sturdy, lithe natives. They were happy in Allied employ. Marching in almost continuous procession to and from the front lines, they grinned jovially every time they met a white man along the trail, singing out a friendly "good day," with an occasional "hokay," or "hokay, Joe" thrown in.

The Papuans started out wearing loin cloths, but as the Buna campaign progressed some picked up odd bits of discarded American and Japanese uniforms, which they wore with ludicrous effect. Occasionally they wrapped themselves in a white cloth stamped with a red cross. To the white man's *kai-kai*, or food, they took

59

with ease, and considered themselves lucky when they received a stick of chewing gum from a Red Cross comfort kit.

In the absence of money, natives and Americans carried on a barter trade. For a razor blade a native would do a man's washing. A cigarette bought a green coconut. For jungle souvenirs the boys from Brooklyn, Paducah, Springfield, and Sugar Notch gave the natives colored beads and bangles, and tall combs. The boongs taught the Americans some of their jungle tricks, such as lighting a fire without the aid of matches, a particularly useful device in the humid Papuan climate: a thin stick about a foot long was rubbed up and down a groove in a log until the friction on the fine wood dust brought a spark and then a flame. Sometimes they lit a native cigarette with the flame, their cigarette, incidentally, being a foot long made of licorice-black native tobacco rolled in newspaper.

In the Buna campaign the American fighting man faced two dangerous enemies: the jungle and the Japanese. The enervating drain upon the system of the one reduced his effectiveness against the other. Habits of sanitation helped in the jungle. The men dressed in green coveralls as a protection against mosquitoes and bush cuts which might lead to infection. Latrines were carefully covered. At the end of the mess line in every outpost camp were big tins of boiling water used by the men to wash and scald their mess gear before and after chow. They bathed in jungle streams, and when the latter were polluted, they used improvised outdoor showers, or their helmets. Quinine and atabrine tablets were taken regularly.

These precautions, while cutting down the number of infections, could not eliminate them altogether under combat conditions. To give prompt relief to the victims of malaria, dengue, dysentery and other tropical diseases, as well as to the wounded, the Army Medical Corps sent portable hospitals into the forward areas with sufficient supplies, tents, and cots to handle the flow of casualties. As Allied lines advanced through the jungle, these portable hospitals pulled stakes and moved with them.

Native teams took over the sick and wounded at portable hospitals. Often the same natives who had brought the precious Red Cross blood plasma which saved a man's life carried the patient over the most difficult part of his journey out of the jungle. The natives might trudge for days through weird and difficult terrain before coming to the jeep trail. At this junction the stretchers were placed crosswise on jeeps which were to transport the patients to an air strip. They were then flown over the Owen Stanley Range to evacuation hospitals along the coastal strip in the Port Moresby area.

The gentleness of these jungle natives was a never-ending surprise

to the Americans. They fashioned comfortable stretchers out of sap-
lings and covered the patients with palm leaves to keep the hot sun
out of their eyes. When it rained they stopped only long enough to
cover the stretcher with its waterproof ground sheet. They took no
more notice of torrential rains than of the sound of artillery and
machine-gun fire. And so, through the quagmire mud of jungle
tracks, where white men floundered and stumbled and cursed, the
duck-like feet of the Papuans kept a steady, even pace. Their continual chatter, with its undercurrent of gurgling laughter and intermittent "sing-sings" was broken now and then by the sharp
commands of the Boss Boy. When the shift of a team was over,
the bamboo struts of the sick white man's stretcher changed hands,
and the relief team carried on with a minimum of discomfort to the
patient. Hour after hour, along dark, clammy passageways tunneled
through jungle undergrowth, along narrow footways above a sheer
thousand-foot drop of jungle-clad cliff, through fast-running mountain creeks and over slippery log bridges, the procession went on.

Upon arrival at Port Moresby the patients were met at the airports by Army nurses and Red Cross girls offering a cigarette, a
cool drink, a smile and word of encouragement. In the Port Moresby
area in those days there were the 153rd Station Hospital, and the
10th and 171st Evacuation Hospitals. The three Red Cross girls who
arrived during the Buna campaign were stationed at the 171st, commanded by Lieutenant C. T. Wilkinson, of Wake Forest, North
Carolina; and they also served patients in the other two hospitals.
The unit was comprised of Miss Susan Tate, of Washington, D.C.;
Mrs. Ethel Knapp, of Lewisburg, Pennsylvania; and Miss Helen
Marie Carroll, of South Dartmouth, Massachusetts. Dressed in GI
shoes, woolen socks, and khaki culottes, Miss Tate, former Capital
stenographer, devoted mornings to tramping muddy paths between
wards collecting and taking dictated messages, the afternoons to
writing and transmitting them. Mrs. Ethel Knapp, recreation
worker, won the affection of a host of American doughboys,
who called her "Knappie." She took the same warm personal interest in them as in students at Bucknell University where she once
was a fraternity housemother.

Miss Carroll, a social worker, in the following account describes
the rugged pioneering life led by herself and her two associates at
that remote outpost:

The grim, merciless battle for Buna was at its height when
Ethel Knapp, Susan Tate, and I arrived in New Guinea with the
10th Hospital Unit. It was with some misgivings but no little an-

ticipation that we set up our Red Cross tent somewhere along the road out of Port Moresby, leading to the Kokoda Trail.

As soon as we arrived at the site of our hospital encampment, the work of clearing away scrub got under way. We were assigned to the nurses' quarters—two rows of pyramidal tents, each holding three "residents."

We had no electricity. Ice was only a tantalizing memory. Laundry service was something you talked about as ancient history. Our nearest water supply was five miles from camp and had to be brought in 250-gallon capacity water carts, pulled by trucks, and spaced over the different areas. Drinking water had to be chlorinated in Lister-bags. Until the Red Cross flew a couple of ice-making machines over from the Australian mainland, lukewarm chlorinated water was the "national drink" of New Guinea.

Naturally, showers were non-existent, and washing ourselves of dust molded into mud by perspiration, presented a very real problem in personal sanitation. Each nurse and Red Cross worker was supplied with an ordinary bucket. This we filled with water at the water cart, trudged back with it to our tent, and, putting one foot at a time into the bucket, struggled through the nearest approach we could make to a bath.

Later on, however, we enjoyed real luxury. A wall-tent was set up near the water cart, and in it was installed three galvanized-iron wash tubs in which we could stand with both feet, and splash ourselves to our heart's content. But after a hard day's work in the enervating heat most of us were much too tired to fill the tub with the three or four pails full of water, and reverted to our original, though less luxurious, method.

The experience of the unit during its preliminary six months in Australia gave us good preparation for New Guinea. In the Aussie bush we were stationed at a small hospital, meagerly equipped. Here improvisation or "doing without" things considered essential at home was not the exception. Consequently, when our New Guinea hospital was serving patients far beyond its designated capacity, lack of facilities in themselves did not create excessive hardship. Here we had no "goldbricks" or "bed-warmers."

When those battle-seasoned doughboys, garbed in their hideous camouflage-green jungle uniforms, sat or stood around the admitting-tents, it was hard to recognize in them the young, clean-cut American lads we had known in Australia and in the States. They were so thin, almost emaciated, their clothes, filthy and ragged. None was clean-shaven; their face growth varied from a short stubble to a full-grown beard. Their hair was long and shaggy.

But nothing could keep down the spirit of these boys for long. After they had been cleaned up and their wounds attended to, they came back to normal.

Everyone of those boys had a story to tell. One had lain in a mudhole surrounded by Japs and "played dead" for three days. When asked why he had even tried to hold out after the first day, he said he honestly did not know, but that something made him want to stay alive and "hit back at those Japs" just as soon as he could.

Another boy was bayoneted seven times by a Japanese soldier who then took his rations and ate them while sitting on him. The bayonet wounds were not serious, probably because the Jap was too weak from hunger.

Just as it does in the front lines, comradeship flourishes in the hospital wards. Not a day passed but that I wasn't deeply touched and impressed by the concern these lads expressed—some with a New England twang, others with a Southern drawl, a few with a Bronx vociferation, and a great number whose roots were in the Middle West—for their bedfellows. If some boy was having a particularly bad time, we'd be informed of it by no less than two or three solicitous whispers. If a newcomer was in need of Red Cross supplies, you could be sure we'd learn about it the moment we'd enter the tent.

We made a point of visiting each boy as soon as he came to the hospital, and out of the Red Cross storage tent we were able to distribute razor blades, tooth brushes, talcum powder, dental cream, shaving cream, combs, handkerchiefs, cigarettes, soap, slippers, corncob pipes, ditty bags, etc., with the minimum of red tape or time-lag.

After they had settled down with these primary requirements, we would see them about their other problems. Money belts, wallets, irreplaceable photographs, and pay-books, lost at the front, were traced; friends or relatives, believed nearby, were located; letters and packages were ferreted out and delivered; inquiries about their family's welfare were made through the Home Service of their hometown Red Cross chapters; haircuts and EFM [Expeditionary Force Message; canned messages available to troops overseas at reduced rates] cables were paid for from Red Cross funds.

In her native-built recreation hut, Mrs. Ethel Knapp really provided her boys with diversion from their nightmarish front-line experiences. Here she managed to assemble a ping-pong table, a piano (a piano seems to be a very essential instrument for morale

63

wherever you go out here) a short-wave radio set on which we got programs from San Francisco, a number of table games, a couple of writing tables and a library of some 300 volumes. Books were in very great demand; seldom were there more than fifty left on the shelves at one time.

Twice a week we screened Hollywood films under the mango and coconut trees. Some of these films were of pretty ancient vintage, but that did not matter to these fighting men who had not seen American girls, or for that matter, any white women, in months. I'd often see the same faces sitting through two consecutive showings of the same picture.

One is constantly frustrated by telephones that don't work, with struggles to get transportation to visit neighboring units for information and supplies. The heat and mud, the shortage of water and the sameness of food wear you down. But knowing how much your efforts mean to these boys is compensation enough for anyone. I'd do it again, and jump at the chance.

In mid-December, shortly after the Australians had entered Gona to the north, American troops under General MacArthur captured Buna, the objective of one of the most sanguinary battles in the Pacific. Thus was finished the job begun in the Battle of the Coral Sea. The Japanese threat to Australia from the north was now at an end.

This victory was sweet indeed to General MacArthur's men. But, facing a relentless foe, they could not rest on their laurels. With the approach of Christmas, however, their thoughts turned homeward. For many it was their first overseas Christmas, and they could not help feeling homesick and low in spirit.

Imagine their reaction, then, to the appearance of the American Red Cross in the role of Santa Claus! Through the personal intervention of General MacArthur the Red Cross spread Chrismas cheer all along the front, from the rear base at Port Moresby to the remotest foxhole in the forward area.

The Port Moresby phase of that memorable Christmas observance is best told by the woman who arranged it—Helen Hall, director of American Red Cross service clubs and rest areas in the South and Southwest Pacific. Miss Hall's account, quoted from her article in *The Survey Graphic*, follows:

In the words of the old carol, "Christmas comes but once a year." But this winter, as last, tens of thousands of American families whose sons are soldiers or sailors, Marines or airmen, must have made the discovery that it really comes twice. That sixteenth century axiom does not hold if it runs, for example, to the South and Southwest Pacific. Christmas falls in midsummer in New Guinea and we celebrated it there last year in a huge grass hut the day before it came at home. All because the earth tilts a bit and spins in its path around the sun.

At Army headquarters on the mainland, General MacArthur had forecast early in November that within six weeks the Australians and Americans would have pushed the Japanese back far enough across the Stanley Range for me to bring women into New Guinea to start American Red Cross service clubs. . . .

My hope was that we could get something going by the holidays. In the interval, General MacArthur himself had gone to Port Moresby, the landing stage for the New Guinea operations. Less than two weeks before Christmas, I took off to report and see if he were ready for us.

Our seaplane alighted in a tropical downpour, an open boat ferried us to the dock, and I climbed out soggy and dripping. My companion was a Red Cross medical social service worker assigned to a hospital. There was a telephone in a small shed and a startled voice at the other end of the line switched nervously from "Yes, sir" to "Yes, ma'am," and then back again to "sir," in the conviction that a woman's voice must have been a mistake.

In my early months in the Southwest Pacific I often met this sort of surprise and incredulity. Once I was able to prove I wasn't a trick of the eye or ear, the welcome was always heartwarming enough to make up for rugged traveling.

Army nurses had preceded us to Moresby and would afford shelter. That evening two Red Cross men drove us over, cautiously, by a rocky, roundabout way through the hills, some miles longer than the shore road. Their concern, it proved, was to protect womankind from passing even in the dark any un-uniformed forces—stripped for a cool swim. We reached our destination about nine o'clock and were given a charming welcome by a head nurse with sparkling eyes who made things look easy as she put at our disposal such comforts as were available in New Guinea at the time. In my case, these consisted of a khaki tent shared with two nurses, a bed with a khaki mosquito bar, a khaki coverall to slide into quickly in case of an air raid, a helmet and—what I needed most of all—a "bully beef" sandwich. My recollection is of a big hunk of bread and canned meat which could scarcely have been called tasty, yet I shall never forget how glad I was to get it.

We were put to bed soon after. I was about to sink in with

gratitude under my netting, when an alert sounded. Every light went off. It had seemed strange, after the browned-out night cities of Australia, to get comparatively near the front and find it brightly lighted. There was no blackout in the Moresby area such as we practiced in New York. A single switch, I was told, put every bulb out of commission at once. With the steel helmet wobbling on my head, I took the friendly hand of a nurse who piloted me to a slit trench in front of our tent. Other nurses joined us there and we sat in the wet in our coveralls, feet dangling in the trench, as we fought the mosquitoes together. As the real attack got nearer, the ack-ack made Fourth of July of the southern sky, hunting for Nip planes. We had watched the searchlights disclose these like reluctant flies before I was dragged into the trench. This was my first raid, I was keyed up, and hated to be hauled down under the sandbags.

It must have been two hours before the "all clear" sounded and I could crawl back under my mosquito bar and take on the night's business again. An hour later came another alert and this time it brought no sense of adventure. I had seen an air raid and did not feel the need of another that night. As I staggered to the trench again, the thought came over me how much more devastating fatigue must be than danger to men and women who have had to do this sort of thing months on end.

The Army mail carried me into Port Moresby after breakfast. General MacArthur's timetable had worked and I was to bring over two Red Cross women at once and open our first service club on the island. But first, accommodations had to be found for it and that in a district overwhelmed by the military. Lieutenant General George C. Kenney, head of the Australian and American Air Forces in the Southwest Pacific, took me on his rounds.

The only place not pre-empted was the huge grass hut, eighty feet long by thirty-two wide, handiwork of an army sergeant who had built it for a mess hall. He had tried to improve on native craftsmanship but, alas, the roof was not steep enough to shed the rain. His failure gave our club work its first foothold in New Guinea.

Now, the great advantage of a grass hut in the tropics is that it is one of the coolest forms of architecture ever devised. Its great disadvantage is that it cannot easily be screened. As a result, two schools of thought had developed on the island, dividing on the issue of bugs vs. heat. General Kenney was of the corrugated iron or tin roof school, but that day thatch and bugs won. The hut was all there was to be had and as much a refuge from the tropical sun as the Nepa shacks I had known in the Philippines in the twenties.

Early the next morning, I flew back to Australia and four days before Christmas we had travel orders to return. The companions I had picked for this foray into a man's war were Leota Kelly, a beguiling executive, regional supervisor in the days of the WPA, and Helen Schoeni who for two years had directed our Henry Street Playhouse in New York. We set off with a special allowance of six hundred pounds of luggage between us. By great good luck we had procured the only purchasable amplifying system in northern Australia, but this engrossed much of our precious quota of weight. Then there were musical instruments, games and magazines, songs, play scripts, Christmas decorations, and other things that seemed essential to get going. We knew only too well that what went with you, you had; what didn't, some day you might have.

Our hopes that the plane might be traveling light were dashed at the airport where there was strict counting of pounds, and in choosing what to take, we envied Solomon's ingenuity with that baby. Some of the packages that we had to leave behind were to show up later, carried by soldiers or officers whose sympathy for our predicament had been enlisted.

There were less than three days left after we landed, to get up our Christmas party. To help us we were assigned a soldier and, also, two natives with wonderful headdresses and very little else. A bright red sarong around the one named "Somewally" and the bright blue shorts sported by "Decanter" were in brilliant contrast to their shiny dark skins. They were practically presented to us by the corporal who brought them, with "You do what the ladies say." Speaking loudly to make up for the difference in language, he added, "And wash much." They looked pleased, but speculative. We were a rarity and hoped they would consider it an honor to be with us rather than a step down from the masculine world. We need not have worried, for the next day when the silver tinsel was unpacked for Christmas decorations it was only a short while before our boys were adorned with it head and foot—a bow round the ankle and much wound about the head—primitive, yes, but their kind have counted courageously in military operations and in saving lives throughout the entire New Guinea campaign.

Outfits for miles around soon turned out to help open up for the occasion. Miss Schoeni was busy "scaring up talent" for an impromptu show. Some gathered small palm trees and decorated them with tinsel. Others improvised much of our equipment—benches from boards and packing cases, even a ping-pong table. One missing package was our bundle of magazines, so we made a start with three *New Yorkers* from my personal belongings, spreading them out to look as much like a library as possible. A platform, electric lights, and a piano all came bumping up to our door—or to the opening where a door would have been. These were soon in place with ease, good temper, and humor. At home, men usually look pretty grim about moving a piano, but in the army it is a matter for jokes and a good deal of good humored personal slander directed at each other as they push and pull.

Christmas night we were ready when our audience spread themselves out on the hillside facing the platform we had placed in front of the club. Lights were strung so that a civilian orchestra brought over from the mainland could see their scores. Unfortunately the lights also lit up the orchestra perfectly for the mosquitoes and its members played between angry slaps and scratches.

To climax things, an alert sounded, that switch was turned off again, and we were in sudden darkness. The music stopped short—but almost as swiftly resumed. I climbed on the platform with a flashlight to find that our civilian talent had made for a slit trench and in their place was a wholly new band. Eager musicians from among the soldiers had scuttled down from the hillside and sprung to the instruments. Seemingly without losing a beat, there they were in the dark, carrying on as lively as you please.

Next came a downpour of rain and it took the fear of spoiling the strings to stop our volunteers long enough for the piano to be heaved inside to the one dry spot in the exact center of the hut. Then we started up once more indoors and in the dark, until the all-clear sounded and lights went on to the tune of Christmas carols.

Availability of the canned EFM service at low rates offered the troops an opportunity to cable Christmas greetings to their families. But the men in the foxholes along the Buna front had neither cash nor the required EFM forms. Thereupon three American Red Cross representatives— "Jungle Jim" Stewart, field director; Harry Poague, staff photographer; and George Moorad, director of public information service in the South and Southwest Pacific area—toured the battle sectors offering to take the men's messages on credit. The three Red Cross girls did the same in the hospitals. In this way thousands of cabled greetings direct from the foxholes of New Guinea reached American homes on Christmas Day.

And from the American Red Cross, representing the folks at home, there arrived at the front thousands of Christmas boxes containing cigarettes, dried fruit, chewing gum, candy, V-mail forms, and other items. Though Christmas that year came at a critical time when each ounce of plane space was precious, General MacArthur ordered first priority for tons of these Red Cross packaged gifts, and Lieutenant General Robert L. Eichelberger personally toured the front to oversee distribution by Red Cross representatives and native porters.

George Moorad, who assisted in the distribution, made the following report of the event:

We took off from Port Moresby at dawn, our unarmed transport loaded with four tons of Red Cross packages, a medical officer and a lanky sergeant carrying maps and messages for divisional headquarters. Friends said the dawn flight was best—too early for the Zeros and with a fair chance of piercing the blanket of clouds which almost perpetually swathes the range.

Generally the transports circle to gain height. Our pilot took it on the run, his engines straining to 15,000 feet as we rushed tree-high over the matted jungle. We peered out at the razor ridges rising ahead and on each side, the vegetation so dense it resembled an endless plot of dark green cauliflower. The sergeant nudged me: "What a hell of a nice place to throw old razor blades," he said.

In twenty anxious minutes we had cleared the range and were flying thousands of feet above another world—a land of lush green sloping hills, broken here and there by grassy clearings, rimmed by the bright blue sea. The sergeant pointed to the left. "That's Buna," he said. "See the smoke?" Pretty soon we landed on what seemed a lonely field. We climbed out and shook hands all around.

Strip No. 1—our landing field—was one of dozens of grass plots burned off and tramped down overnight as General MacArthur launched his air-borne invasion. From the air it was a harmless desolate spot, but within a second after we landed, crews of sturdy Papuans were unloading the ship and a caravan of jeeps appeared from nowhere to carry off the cargo. Under the trees at one end of the field a crew of grimy, sweating Americans were assembling a steamroller which had been flown, piece by piece, more than 2,000 miles from southern Australia. There were half a dozen "cats" and scrapers and great piles of flexible steel mats which could be used for a semi-permanent runway. "You won't know this place in a month," one of the engineers told us. "We'll be clearing more ships than San Francisco Airport."

69

We thumbed a jeep ride to divisional headquarters—the fastest miles outside Indianapolis Speedway if you're riding with an Aussie driver, and the slowest miles in the world if you hike through the sweltering fields of *kunai* grass. The travel rule in Papua is "thumb or hike" for natives, officers and enlisted men alike. Only supplies and the wounded have priority. The commanding general was expected to, and did, share his muddy jeep with as many hitch hikers as could hang on.

An affection for the peripatetic jeep reached remarkable heights in this lowland jungle country. The jeeps go everywhere, in any weather, whistling through fields of knife-like *kunai*, through creeks hood-high, and even breast the black bogs using six rear wheels instead of two. They were used as caissons, as ammunition carriers, as staff cars—and on Christmas Day they supplemented the legendary reindeer to carry Red Cross boxes and precious mail from home to troops in the front lines.

To these boys in the jungle foxholes—bearded and filthy—the idea of Christmas must have seemed an ironic travesty. The air seemed filled with the rush of shells pounding on Japanese pillboxes along the beach; there was the spasmodic nervous chatter of machine-gun fire. On clear nights Japanese bombers would sometimes come over five and six times. The days were feverishly hot, but somehow their morale was high.

On direct orders from General MacArthur, Christmas packages were distributed to every man in the combat area, with priority for the front lines. Caravans of jeeps and hundreds of natives were diverted to the job by Colonel George DeGraff, who had also undertaken the herculean task of distributing the latest mail from home.

The commanding general, Lieutenant General Robert L. Eichelberger, who earned the respect of all ranks by going day after day into the hottest action, took it as a personal duty to spread the news that Christmas mail and packages had arrived. There were few men all along the treacherous jungle front who could say that they had not seen the general, if not spoken to him.

I must admit I wondered how the men would react to the Christmas boxes. It is, after all, a comparatively small thing to be distributing Christmas gifts when men were dying in the slime . . . and I wondered how men under such conditions could care. But I found that to them it was still Christmas—something that neither war nor suffering could erase. Almost like children under the Yule tree at home, they opened their boxes and exclaimed over the cigarettes, dried fruit, and the somewhat soggy candy.

Chapter V

GUADALCANAL

WHEN THE MARINES MADE THEIR LANDINGS ON GUADALCANAL and neighboring islands on August 7, 1942, American Red Cross Field Director David S. Oman, of Carrollton, Ohio, went ashore with his unit on Gavutu. In his official report of the invasion, Oman described what he saw and did during the first fateful days:

Our unit entered Guadalcanal Harbor on the morning of August 6. No opposition was met upon landing, and unloading operations continued until 10 A.M. when General Quarters was sounded and we prepared for our first baptism of fire. This came from Japanese four-motored bombers in four waves of seven each. Every Japanese bomber was lost during this raid, with very slight damage to our fleet. At 1:45 P.M. General Quarters sounded again and about forty Zero fighters came in to bomb at low alti-

71

tudes. Our own fighters intercepted them, and the official count from this raid was thirty-eight Zero planes.

We remained in Guadalcanal Harbor until 3 A.M. the next day when we were ordered to occupy the Tulagi group at 6:30 A.M. At 6 A.M. the Third Battalion aboard the U.S.S. *President Adams* was assigned to attack Gavutu, a very small island between Tulagi and Florida where the Japanese were reported in force.

Landing operations commenced at 6:15 A.M. with all men and officers wearing green dungarees and steel helmets and carrying arms, some food rations, a rubber poncho and a heavy pack of ammunition. The only exceptions were the medical groups to which I was attached, and we were issued Red Cross armbands.

I carried a first-aid kit especially prepared by the Red Cross organization connected with the Office of Civilian Defense in San Diego. This kit contained only battle dressings, burn ointment, sulfanilamide powder and morphine suretes. I also carried ashore 100 packages of cigarettes which proved to be nearly as useful as medicine.

During the actual landing at Gavutu we were caught in a cross fire of rifle and machine-gun bullets from Gavutu beach and from Japanese entrenched in pill boxes on the adjoining island of Tanambogo. A first-aid station was established in the only remaining building on the island. The balcony of this building was being utilized by our own machine-gun and sniper units. Half of the roof and one side of the house had been blown away, but it had a concrete floor and offered some protection from the rain, which had increased as the day wore on.

During the day I kept busy giving morphine to the wounded and preparing them for treatment by the doctors. Casualties increased at dusk when we attempted to secure Tanambogo, and it became necessary for me to act as a stretcher bearer. On my second trip out, my partner was killed as we crossed the causeway [connecting Gavutu with Tanambogo]. On the third trip my new partner was wounded, and upon returning to the first-aid station I was informed that eight corpsmen were casualties.

Fighting continued that night, and the rain increased. Water had gotten six inches deep on the concrete floor and we used rocks and boards to elevate the stretchers. The cigarettes I had brought ashore were kept dry and we gave them out one at a time as the casualties were brought in. The next morning we moved the first-aid station to a safer location.

On the fourth day fighting subsided and we had our first opportunity to clear up the battlefield....

After the first few days, when the Marines were too busy fighting to consider any discomforts, they suffered most of all from the lack of comfort articles, cigarettes, soap, razors, and toothbrushes. Having nothing of their own they made out for two weeks with captured Japanese supplies until the first ship arrived with the Regimental Command. This was on August 22. This ship brought thirty-two cases of Red Cross cigarettes, and enough comfort kits for each two men in the entire regiment to share one kit. These kits had been prepared in San Diego, Dayton, Pittsburgh, Cincinnati and a number of towns in Indiana....

The Allied offensive against the Solomon Islands had followed American air reconnaissance showing the Japanese building a flying field on Guadalcanal. The runways were almost finished and supplies and equipment for a strong advance base were being shipped into the island. As soon as this base could be established—a matter of weeks, according to Allied calculations—the Japanese could launch an amphibious drive against New Hebrides and New Caledonia, island outposts guarding the approaches to New Zealand and the southeastern coast of Australia.

The Marine troop landings of August 7, therefore, beat the Japanese to the punch. Within the first forty-eight hours the Marines captured all their objectives, including the nearly completed airfield, immediately renamed Henderson Field.

Thereafter, however, the battle for Guadalcanal went into many rounds in which the Marines repeatedly fought off violent attempts by the Japanese to drive them back into the sea. The first major engagement after D-day occurred on August 21 when 750 Japanese troops landed at night on Guadalcanal's northern shore and moved to the banks of the Tenaru River in an attempt, apparently, to break through the Americans' defenses and recapture Henderson Field. With tanks and artillery the Marines virtually annihilated the enemy at a cost of twenty-eight dead and seventy-two wounded.

Early in November the Japanese landed fifteen hundred troops east of the Americans' positions on Guadalcanal; half the number were killed, and the rest were driven into the jungles.

In a series of naval and air battles, in which both sides lost heavily, United States warships and planes turned back a number of large-scale attempts at reinforcements; but Japanese landings of troops and supplies nevertheless continued to be made periodically through the fall.

Heavy reinforcemets of American troops and supplies, protected by surface ships and air cover, met minor opposition. In mid-

73

October, units of the United States Army for the first time were fighting alongside the Marines. In December, the Marines who had established the beachhead on Guadalcanal and who had fought so long and so well to hold it, were withdrawn for a well-deserved rest in New Zealand and Australia, and Major General Alexander M. Patch, U.S. Army, succeeded Major General Alexander A. Vandergrift to the Solomons command.

On January 3, 1943, the Sixth Marine Division arrived at Guadalcanal to take part in the final drive against the Japanese. Their landing, protected by destroyers and an air cover, was accomplished without incident. Working to unload the ship speedily, hundreds of men jostled one another on the small dock.

Standing out in this crowd of sweating, grimy, and swearing Marines was a khaki-clad giant—Red Cross Director Thomas S. Montgomery, of Berkeley, California, assembling his eighty Red Cross crates scattered among the great piles of military stores. On the advice of Marine veterans from the Solomons whom he met in New Zealand, Montgomery had packed quantities of fishing tackle, musical instruments, radios; and sets of carpenter's, cobbler's, and barber's tools, along with the usual Red Cross comfort articles. Here is a partial list of the articles he brought: 4,000 books; 2,000 sewing kits; 2,500 cakes of soap; 1,000 cigars; 500 cans of snuff; 250 packs of chewing tobacco; 600 tins of pipe tobacco; 2,500 toothbrushes; 40,000 sheets of stationery; 15,000 envelopes; 1,000 decks of cards; 5,000 packs of gum; 500 pounds of candy; $1,000 worth of games; $700 worth of fishing tackle; $400 worth of athletic gear; $200 worth of musical instruments (harmonicas, banjos, ukuleles, etc.); three portable phonographs with $300 worth of records; two short wave radios, a sewing machine, a washing machine, and a piano.

Montgomery, whom the Marines and doughboys had nicknamed "Tiny" because of his unusual height, became an American Red Cross field director by a process of elimination. A graduate of Stanford University ('38) where he was a consistent point winner in intercollegiate shot-put, discus, and weight-lifting events, he had tried to enlist in the Marine Corps, Army, and Navy. None would accept him because his height—6 feet 8½ inches—exceeded all military standards. As he was in perfect physical condition, the Red Cross sent him first to Quantico, Virginia, where he practiced invasion tactics with the Marines, then to Camp Pickett to learn Red Cross field technique, and finally on overseas duty. Upon arrival in New Zealand he requested transfer to the first outfit ordered to a combat zone. This is how he came to Guadalcanal with the Sixth Marine Division.

He pitched his camp about half a mile from the beach, in a coconut grove midway between Henderson Field and a smaller fighter field. Allowed only one tent, he and Sergeant Joe McMurren, of San Diego, California, assigned to him, scrounged two other tents. One served as a storehouse and workshop, another as office and library, and the third as a recreation center. Outside his office tent hung this sign: "The American Red Cross is in this area to assist men of the United States forces in any way possible. Please do not hesitate to call."

The workshop, with its wood-carving tools, two emery wheels, a brace and bit, tin shears, files, and hammers, proved a busy place. Here men off duty made souvenirs—ash trays out of Japanese shells, and pistol grips, bracelets, rings, and other articles from the remnants of shot-down Zeros and Mitsubishis.

Montgomery's short-wave set always drew a crowd, especially when programs from home were on the air. Propaganda broadcasts from Radio Tokyo added to the amusement. Once, however, a lanky corporal from North Carolina tried to kick the radio to pieces when a Japanese vocalist sang "Old Black Joe."

The men would also huddle around a piano to sing their favorite tunes. This was the first piano on Guadalcanal. Montgomery chuckled when he told how he happened to bring it. The piano belonged to the Sixth Marines who used it in their camp at Wellington, New Zealand. They abandoned it as too bulky and an unnecessary luxury when they broke camp to leave for Guadalcanal. Montgomery's sense of thrift could not bear to see it go to waste, and anyway he wanted it for the Red Cross club tent he was going to set up on the island. Without a word to anyone, he crated it and painted this legend on the outside of the box: "American Red Cross. Health and Comfort Supplies." And with the help of a sympathetic Marine sergeant and squad got it past the loading officer and aboard the ship.

Montgomery's barber clippers "left most of my customers worse off than when I began," but the men preferred them to shaggy hair and beards. Bringing a cobbler's last, the only one on Guadalcanal, proved a real inspiration, as the island terrain was rough on shoe leather.

Now and then men showing the effects of excessive strain would be sent to Montgomery's workshop by their officers. "One boy was practically wild when he came to me," said Montgomery. "The night before he had been in the front lines when a shell killed his best friend. He helped me with my chores, distributed supplies, checked out books, fooled around with tools, and played the radio, and within two weeks he was back to normal."

Without his athletic background and good physical condition, Montgomery might have experienced great difficulty keeping up with the youthful fighting men. With the help of Marine Corps and Army Special Service officers, a coconut grove was cleared for a softball diamond. A building previously used as Japanese officers' quarters was turned into a basketball court, and a tournament went on between bombing raids.

Swimming was a favorite sport, particularly with contingents returning from the front. Actually more than a sport, it was the easiest and most pleasant way of removing grime accumulated during days and nights spent in foxholes. Sharks offshore interfered with ocean bathing, but the Tenaru and Lunga Rivers proved good swimmin' holes.

Coconuts were plentiful; often soldiers and Marines were conked on the head by the falling fruit, particularly on windy days. Bananas and limes grew in a section controlled by the Japanese, and so were out of reach.

The Guadalcanal natives, short, wiry, with big flat feet, worked along the beach, on the airfields, and around the Red Cross tents. Those who had attended missionary school at Cape Esperance, on the northwestern tip of the island, spoke good English. Friendly and hard-working, they got along well with the Yanks, saluting them at the least provocation. They acquired the habit of smoking corncob pipes, and would have given an eyetooth for a pipe.

Montgomery made a rule to reach every American fighting man on Guadalcanal, no matter how remote his outpost. Three times a week he loaded his jeep to capacity with Red Cross supplies, and drove as far as it would go. Then, with a bulging knapsack across his broad shoulders, he would proceed to the front-line foxholes on foot, chanting, "Chewing gum, candy, popcorn, soda pop. What'll you have, boys?" "Porgy-bait," or candy, and chewing tobacco were most in demand, the chewing tobacco because smoking in the dark might give away a position. If a man worried about his family, Montgomery took back a message and had the Australian headquarters of the American Red Cross cable to the soldier's home-town Red Cross chapter for an investigation.

Front lines were difficult to determine in jungle warfare—a tree-top sniper here, a lone foxhole gunner there, perhaps four or five men sharing a shell hole on the side of a ridge. On one occasion, Montgomery was following what he thought was a continuous line of American positions when he met a group of Marines walking through a coconut grove. He asked how close he was to the front line.

They looked at him oddly and grinned. "Hell," drawled one of them, "the front line's half a mile behind us. This is a patrol."

The woods were full of Japanese snipers, which prevented his turning back. So he went along with the patrol, dodging bullets on the way.

Once, in the dusk, this bearded young giant, while bouncing along in his overloaded jeep, found himself in the midst of a battle. Bursting bombs shook the ground under him, and the air was filled with the rumble and flashes of gunfire on the ground, in the air, and offshore. Signs of machine guns and rifles hidden behind foliage and coconut trees were not necessary to convince him that he was a target for enemy bullets. Nor was he comforted by the gruesome sight of crumpled, lifeless bodies—many yellow, some white—strewn on the steaming sand. He kept bouncing along in his jeep, nevertheless, until halted by a tall, slender, graying man who, like everyone else in the jungle, wore undistinguished khaki-green fatigues. From a distance he had seen the man receiving reports and giving orders. Now he was face to face with him. Two silver stars on the man's shoulders confirmed Montgomery in recognizing this was Major General Alexander M. Patch, the commanding officer of the Solomons campaign.

General Patch reconnoitered first the jeep piled high with bulging packages and knapsacks, and then the bearded young giant who was its driver. "And what are you doing here, my friend?"

"Oh, just taking some Red Cross stuff up to the boys," grinned Montgomery, as if this were the most appropriate thing for him to do at the moment.

"Hmmm. That's good ... very good. But you want to be careful ... you'd be a hard target to miss."

Montgomery, though, led a charmed life. There was the time he was driving along the beach with a load of supplies and several passengers when bullets started kicking up the sand all around them. Caught between the cross fire of two Japanese machine-gun nests, they couldn't see their assailants yet discerned a movement of leaves in the trees overhead. A patrol silenced the nests with grenades and rifles, but returned less one man.

During one night air raid, Montgomery was crouching in his foxhole—large enough to accommodate a jeep—when "Washing Machine Charlie" droned away overhead dodging ack-ack fire. Suddenly Tiny's booming voice was heard above the noise of the plane.

"Hey, fellows," boomed Tiny to the Marines in their foxholes, "I've been waiting four months to get a letter and finally I got one from the States today. It was from the home office and you know what it said? 'In order to help us win the war those of us in the United States who are not actually fighting will have five per cent of their salaries deducted for the Victory Tax.' Now ain't that one hell of a note?"

Montgomery was within earshot of gunfire all the time he was on Guadalcanal, for that was the period of the final American drive to crush Japanese organized resistance on the island. Between January 15 and February 9, when the battle was over, 6,066 Japanese were killed and 127 captured.

On February 20, Montgomery returned with his Marine unit to New Zealand for a rest. Before leaving Guadalcanal he paid a visit to an ice house erected by the Japanese. To the Yanks it was known as "Tojo's Ice Plant." On it someone had painted the satisfactory sign: "Under New Management."

In a way, this sign symbolized Allied control of Guadalcanal. Veterans of the original landings would hardly recognize Guadalcanal today. Tenaru, Matanikau, Lunga Point—the signposts are there, and on the slopes of Bloody Ridge barbed-wire entanglements of Japanese positions now rust in the undergrowth. From the sea the cloud-shrouded mountains have the same somber appearance they offered the Marines approaching on the morning of August 7, 1942. And along the beach the palms still form an unbroken pattern from Koli Point to Cape Esperance.

However, the endless coconut groves now shelter rows upon rows of tents and prefabricated huts. Where Marines once splashed ashore, today are busy warehouses, wharves, and supply dumps. On the island also are hospitals, Red Cross canteens and on-post clubs, and pretty Red Cross girls, who arrived April, 1944, serving hot coffee, sandwiches, doughnuts, and fruit juices to flight crews, ground crews, enlisted men and officers at Guadalcanal's air strips. At Henderson Field a Red Cross clubmobile is on constant duty.

Guadalcanal has become a forward command post of American Red Cross activity throughout the Solomon Islands. In striking contrast to the early days of Field Directors Oman and Montgomery, when Red Cross supplies and personnel were at a premium largely because of the lack of shipping space, today there are about one hundred Red Cross men and women workers on duty in the Solomons group.

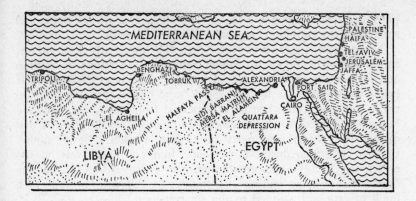

Chapter VI

EL ALAMEIN TO TRIPOLI

IN — COMPANY'S MESS TENT IN THE LIBYAN DESERT A CRUDE SIGN
read: "Two good places to eat—here and home."

The soldiers believed that sign. To them their mess sergeant was
the best in the whole Ninth Air Force. An Alabama boy, his name
was—well, let's call him Bill.

A mess sergeant grew in stature in the desert, where fighting men
ate only when the supply truck caught up with their unit, and
where water had to be hauled long distances from wells and water
holes. A mess sergeant not only planned meals, but often, like Bill,
cooked them himself. For him it was a daily battle with short rations,
sand, and water shortages. When supplies were low he had to barter
and scrounge—make things appear from nowhere.

Bill was adept at both games. In addition he used a profitable
device of his own—crap shooting. One of the best crap shooters in
the Ninth Air Force, he was never more cheerful than when the
bones rattled on the ground. When he needed an extra mess of flour
to make pancakes for the boys, he generally won it from other mess
sergeants in a crap game. And the British Tommies paid dearly in
Egyptian pounds, piasters, and Scotch whisky for the privilege of
learning the game from this Yank master.

With a resourceful mess sergeant like Bill, the boys of — Company had little to grumble about. The chow was always there, and sometimes the cooking even tasted like Mom's.

There came a day, however, when Bill apparently lost interest in his job. The bones no longer rattled. He shunned fellowship and brooded hour after hour in his tent. The boys, shaking their heads sadly, said that Bill had gone "sand-happy" from seeing too many mirages. And when he disappeared from camp, they guessed he had wandered off in the desert after one of his illusions. A day or two later a searching party found him, a solitary figure among the barren dunes, dusty, thirsty, and hungry. There was no use sentencing him to the guardhouse for going A.W.O.L., as the desert itself was an endless guardhouse. So Bill was "busted" to a buck private and ordered to dig slit-trenches.

Bill's punishment may have satisfied the ends of Army discipline, but it did not help company spirit. The boys set up a howl that reached the Colonel's ear. They missed his cooking.

At length the Colonel approached American Red Cross Field Director Orville E. "Bob" Roberts, of Greenbelt, Maryland.

"Bob," he said, "I wish you would talk to — Company's mess sergeant and see if there isn't something we can do to bring him back to himself."

"Colonel," replied Roberts, "Bill is that stubborn that if I went to him and tried to talk to him, I wouldn't get anywhere."

"I know. What would you suggest?"

"If he could be steered into my tent casually, maybe I could find out what's eating him."

Through a ruse, then, Bill found himself in the Red Cross tent talking with Field Director Roberts, a ruddy-cheeked, heavy-set man with graying temples, who was old enough to be his father. A shrewd judge of human nature, Roberts had sensed that the Alabama boy had an early background not unlike his own. So he began by relating the highlights of his own career: He was born and raised on a Kentucky farm; while still a boy he ran away from home to work for a year as a cabin boy on an Ohio River steamboat; at eighteen he was a cook in a logger's camp in the Canadian woods; he played football first at Hiram College, Ohio, and later at West Virginia Wesleyan College; and during the First World War he saw active service in France.

Slowly, haltingly, Bill revealed the few milestones of his career. "When I was so big," he said, "my mother died, and from then on my dad was both father and mother to me."

His father had taught him hunting and fishing—

80

"And cooking?"

"Damn right. My dad could cook food that a man could eat. I didn't learn cooking in this man's army. I learned from my dad."

The boy suddenly grew bitter. He snarled. "My dad—I loved him until he let me down. When your own father lets you down the way mine did—well, how can a guy have faith in anybody or anything in this world?"

"What makes you say a thing like that, Bill?"

"He hasn't written me, has he? Five months, and not a damn line from him. . . ."

As soon as the boy left the tent, Roberts sat down and wrote to Bill's home-town Red Cross chapter in Alabama. After giving the case history, he advised that a Home Service worker see the boy's father and urge him to write at once.

Weeks went by. Bill continued digging slit-trenches, and his company kept asking how soon he would return to the mess truck.

Then one evening a beaming, excited Bill broke into Field Director Roberts' tent shouting, "Look here, Bob, I've got it at last—a letter from Dad."

In paraphrase, the letter opened as follows:

"Dear Son: If you live through this war and come home, I'm going to lick hell out of you. Don't ever set one of them Red Cross gals on me again. I'm on a sheep ranch in Montana, a hundred miles from nowhere. This Red Cross gal came 175 miles to find me. She rode fifty. Her car broke down, and so she hitchhiked to within seven miles of this ranch, and walked the last seven. She sat me down on this rock, gave me a pencil and paper, and said, 'Now write, darn you, write!' And by the devil, I'm writing."

The father went on to explain that having moved from Alabama, Bill's letters hadn't caught up with him. On the other hand, he couldn't write his son because he had lost his APO number. The letter concluded with a promise to write regularly in the future.

The next morning, Roberts, letter in hand, approached the commanding officer. "Colonel," he smiled, "how'd you like to have the old mess sergeant back?"

"What do *you* think?"

Roberts then showed him the letter. Within twenty-four hours Bill was wearing sergeant's chevrons again, and — Company was happy. In fact, everybody was happy.

"Thanks, Bob, for a fine morale job," said the Colonel.

"Don't thank me, Colonel," replied Field Director Roberts. "Thank that little Red Cross girl in Montana. Thank the Home Service Corps of every Red Cross chapter in the United States, who are working for the armed forces and their families every day in the year."

Field Director Roberts was in the desert to bring American Red Cross supplies and services to the United States Ninth Army Air Force, then assisting the British Eighth Army in driving the Axis out of North Africa. Axis global strategy had called for the joining of the European Axis partners with the Japanese in India. To achieve this strategic union—a disastrous prospect for the Allies if consummated—Hitler and Mussolini first had to win control of the Suez Canal, crucial waterway leading into the Indian Ocean. With the Suez Canal in their hands, they could pursue other ambitions, such as the conquest of the Middle East and Africa. The Germans could seize the oil wells of Iraq and Iran and march eastward on the overland route to India, while the Italians could follow up their Ethiopian conquest with further aggressions in East Africa.

Barring the way to the Suez Canal was a desert stretching from the Nile River to the Tunisian border—a distance of approximately fifteen hundred miles—embracing Egypt and Libya. This Western Desert was a wedge separating the European Axis partners from the Japanese, and a land bridge linking Russia with the supply lines from Great Britain and the United States. It was for the mastery of this sandy wilderness, then, with its prize, the Suez Canal, that the great desert drama was played from 1940 to 1943.

With the collapse of France in June, 1940, the whole North African coastland from the Atlantic to the Egyptian border passed into the hands of Mussolini and Hitler. In September, 1940, Mussolini made his first challenge of British power in Egypt by throwing a large army in command of Marshal Rodolfo Graziani into the desert. The Italians quickly overran about fifty miles of Egyptian territory as an outnumbered British force fell back to the Mersa Matruh railhead. But instead of fighting through to take full advantage of his offensive, Marshal Graziani rested at Sidi Barrani.

This pause gave the British their hoped-for opportunity to build up their strength. On December 9, 1940, General Wavell struck a powerful blow, surprising and overwhelming the Italians, who reeled back in disorder. In two months a large number of prisoners and enormous booty were yielded by the invaders. It was during this campaign that the British first took Tobruk. General Wavell chased the Italians as far as the salt marshes of El Agheila, on the Gulf of Sidra between Benghazi and Tripoli, and paused for fresh troops and supplies.

To check the British advance, with its threat to the Axis domination of the Mediterranean, Hitler, amid great secrecy, sent his motorized Afrika Korps into North Africa. Commanded by General Erwin Rommel, the "Desert Fox," this crack army, specially trained and equipped for desert warfare, in March, 1941, smashed through General Wavell's defenses. A depleted British army was sent hurtling back to Egypt, and the Afrika Korps reached Halfaya Pass inside the Egyptian border. Tobruk, however, remained in British hands.

About the same time, the Germans, who had taken over Rumania and Bulgaria through underground agents disguised as "tourists," now blitzkrieged through Yugoslavia and Greece to extricate the hapless Italians. The British had depleted their desert army to reinforce the heroic Greek defenders, but the former's inadequate, ill-equipped divisions—the most that could be spared at that critical time—were no match for the Nazi hordes clanking across the mountains and echoing through the valleys. Greece and Crete fell.

Thus, in May, 1941, the Suez Canal was menaced by Rommel's Afrika Korps on the west, and by the Luftwaffe from newly seized Mediterranean bases along the Balkan shores on the north.

Hitler's diversionary Balkan campaign delayed his invasion of Russia, giving the Russians additional time to prepare their defenses. Its effect on the desert campaign was that reinforcements and supplies which might have gone to Rommel were diverted to the Russian front.

Before resuming his march to Suez, Rommel tried to reduce Tobruk, mighty desert citadel, to prevent the garrison's breaking out of its perimeter and attacking from the rear.

For seven long months, amid incredible hardships and privations, the courageous Tobruk garrison withstood the might and fury of the enemy. By their heroic stand they saved Egypt and the Suez Canal that year and won immortal glory for themselves.

In November, 1941, the British launched their second desert offensive, this time under General Claude Auchinleck. Reinforced by tanks and planes rushed from England and the United States, they chased the Desert Fox back as far as El Agheila. There they halted on January 8, 1942.

Two weeks later Rommel, greatly strengthened by reinforcements and newly arrived fuel and matériel, broke out of his lair, pushing the British back to a defense line running south from the coast at El Gazala near Tobruk. Their defensive tactics, however, proved costly and almost led to complete disaster. Rommel resumed the initiative on May 26 and pierced the British defensive system at El Gazala. On June 12-13 he trapped 300 British- and American-made tanks near Tobruk and smashed 230 of them. Tobruk fell quickly, and the

British infantry, and what remained of their tank forces, fled to the last strong defensive position before Alexandria, at El Alamein.

One fact stood out crystal clear from the surges, now eastward, now westward, of the Axis and British armies across the desert: neither side could muster the necessary punch for a knockout. Each failure was due to overextended supply lines. Supply, the ability to get there with enough stuff on time, was the key to success in modern mechanized warfare. This was even more true in the desert, which, except for occasional oases, was without any resources of its own. Everything required by a mobile mechanized army had to be brought in from the ouside. With only a single two-lane motor highway along the coast, and only camel caravan trails and native tracks in the interior, transportation was extremely difficult.

In this respect the Axis enjoyed a distinct advantage over the Allies. Troops, fuel, and matériel, mostly originating in Germany and transported by rail, were shipped across the narrow Sicilian straits to Tripoli, principal Axis supply base in North Africa. Each time Rommel retreated, he shortened his supply lines, thereby gathering strength and power for stiffened resistance. Conversely, Allied shipping was bombed and torpedoed from one end of the Mediterranean to the other. Supplies from Great Britain and lend-lease goods from the United States took the long water route of more than ten thousand miles around the Cape of Good Hope and up the Red Sea, or were flown from the United States and ferried across central Africa by way of Brazil.

Therefore, to win final, decisive victory in the desert, it became necessary for the Allies to wrest mastery of the Mediterranean from Germany and Italy.

The mission of the United States Ninth Army Air Force, the nucleus of which was activated on June 28, 1942, as the Middle East Air Force, fitted into this picture. During the four months preceding the decisive El Alamein battle this unit was developed as a keen, swift-striking force rather than as a ponderous, crushing power. While British submarines stalked the enemy in the Mediterranean, American planes attacked his docks, ports, and shipping. They were credited with stopping at least twenty per cent, and eventually fifty per cent, of enemy shipping bound for North Africa.

It was in the Battle of El Alamein and in the pursuit of Rommel that the Ninth Air Force scored its most spectacular successes. The El Alamein line, consisting of a chain of pillboxes reinforced by mines, barbed-wire entanglements, and trenches, ran from the coast to the salt marshes known as the Qattara Depression, a natural anti-tank barrier. This bottleneck, only forty miles wide, kept Rommel at arm's length, so to speak. While he rested his troops and received reinforcements and supplies, the British were fast building up their strength for the third and final offensive. Planes were flown across Africa from the United States by the AAF Ferry Command, while ships carried men and matériel—jeeps, trucks, artillery, self-propelled antitank guns, and the superb monster Sherman tanks with their 75's in revolving turrets—to Egyptian ports.

When he had achieved his surprise concentration of troops and matériel, welded together into a mighty force of steel and men, General Bernard L. Montgomery launched his offensive with a terrific artillery barrage. There followed eleven days of the bloodiest kind of hand-to-hand fighting in which Anzacs, Indians, and British Tommies engaged the crack German troops. At the first sign of enemy armor concentrations, which might have indicated a counterattack, American planes smashed the formations. In the first fourteen days of the offensive these American planes made 1,366 sorties, according to official records. On November 4 the Axis lines crumbled. Rommel's vaunted Afrika Korps turned its back on Suez for good and fled headlong across the hot desert sands. Montgomery's Eighth Army pressed irresistibly on, toppling one stronghold after another, in its race to overtake the enemy.

The Ninth Air Force, which formally absorbed the Middle East Air Force on November 12, kept up a steady and relentless pressure on the retreating Axis columns. When the Germans dug in for a stand at El Agheila, where the two previous British drives had been turned back, the Ninth Air Force hit troop concentrations and motor transports, contributing to the destruction which forced Rommel to resume his flight to Tripoli.

The Ninth's troop carrier command kept open the long lines of Allied supply. As soon as the enemy evacuated an airfield, troop carrier planes arrived with gasoline, ammunition, and other priority supplies needed in battle. This speedy service enabled the fighter and bomber groups to stay on top of the German retreat. Troop carrier planes also evacuated the wounded from the front and flew them to hospitals in the rear. The service command also shared in the Ninth's accomplishments by keeping the planes in the air.

As the drive toward Tripoli continued, the Ninth Air Force bombed the enemy's airports, harbors, communication lines, motor transports, and troop concentrations.

And on this historic drive across the desert, from El Alamein to Cap Bon, the American Red Cross was at the side of the Ninth Air Force.

Actually, Red Cross operations in the Middle East began on August 16, 1942, when four field directors arrived with the Ninth's ground crews at Port Tewfik, Egypt. These pioneers, all World War I veterans, were: John M. King, Clinton, Mississippi; Paul Ross, Binghamton, New York; Orville E. Roberts, Greenbelt, Maryland; and Ray L. Goodridge, Rochester, New York.

Later they were joined by other Red Cross workers, men and women, most of whom came on convoys the long way around the Cape of Good Hope, as the Mediterranean was still unsafe for Allied merchant shipping. By June, 1943, there were 173 of them.

American Red Cross operations were dictated by geography, climate and military strategy. Under Director Ralph Bain, Bentonville, Arkansas, the staff of Red Cross workers acclimated itself to face the unique conditions thrust upon American armed forces in the Middle East. Since the Ninth Air Force was on a mobile basis, Red Cross field directors stationed with them were, of necessity, equally mobile. They had to be ready to make convoys across the Western Desert, past the ruins of Sidi Barrani, Halfaya Pass, Tobruk, Benghazi, Tripoli, and other bases to the very portals of Tunis, where they joined Red Cross men stationed in Tunis. They advanced in convoy as their units advanced, and frequently made long, tedious trips in Red Cross trucks over bombed roads and tracks to Cairo, where they assembled athletic equipment and other recreational supplies for the men at the front.

For the youths of the Ninth Air Force the desert was a strange experience. Day after day they saw nothing but blue sky and endless miles of sand glistening in the sunlight. The force often was dispersed and tents were scattered. They were lonely. Their daily diet consisted of British tinned "bully beef," biscuits, and marmalade. The daily water ration was only one quart per man for all purposes. They breathed sand, ate it, and slept with it.

One moment the undulating sand lay smooth and still; the next moment, whipped by a wind, it whirled as if aroused by the wrath of God. Near Tripoli on February 10, 1943, the Ninth's 57th Fighter Group was scourged by a *khamsin*, Arab term for sandstorms that blow continuously for days. This one lasted seven days. American Red Cross Field Director Ray L. Goodridge, who was there at the time, described the scene as follows:

For the entire seven days we were marooned. All planes were grounded. Military operations and Red Cross services were at a standstill. No reports went out to Ninth headquarters in Cairo, and none came in. There was no incoming or outgoing mail of any kind. The whirling, blinding dust stung as if each particle of sand were a pin point. The murk was so thick you couldn't see more than a few feet ahead of you. Out in the open we couldn't stand it for more than a few minutes, so we kept to our tents. At night we could hardly sleep for the steady pounding on the tent canvas and the violent shaking of the tent pole. When we got up in the morning we considered ourselves lucky if we had a roof over our heads. Many tents were carried away during the night, never to be found. Though my tent was closed, I awoke one morning to find myself buried under sand that somehow had found its way inside and had piled up over my cot. Only my head was showing. We couldn't breathe the stuff, and being without respirators, we wore gas masks twenty-four hours of the day. During the seven days we didn't have any solid food, only soups and other liquids.

Mirages were not uncommon on the Western Desert. It was when the Yanks saw too many of these illusory appearances that they were likely to become victims of what was called "sand-happiness." When this state of mind was combined with homesickness, loneliness, battle tensions, and personal worries, the effect upon a man could be devastating.

While they were available for traditional welfare services, Red Cross field directors concentrated on the greatest need—recreation. This is what Field Director Goodridge did while attached to the Ninth's famous 57th Fighter Group. He joined this unit in the staging area preceding the Battle of El Alamein, and remained until the end of the Ninth's desert mission in August, 1943. The most forward and most mobile echelon of the whole Ninth Air Force, the 57th Fighter Group moved close behind the tank and infantry divisions. For obvious reasons, its squadrons often were dispersed fifteen to twenty miles apart. Driving a one-and-a-half-ton Ford truck, Goodridge alternated between airfields, spending a day on each. He would meet fighter crews returning from missions and serve them hot coffee and cookies. In his truck he carried an Army chaplain's tent, capable of enclosing three hundred men and officers, which he used for the showing of 16-mm. motion pictures provided by Special Services.

At each airfield two EPI (Egypt-Palestine-India model) tents were joined to make a fair-sized recreation tent. For atmosphere, the boys filled the inside canvas with their favorite pin-up girls. Goodridge provided chairs, tables, benches, checkers and chess, phonographs and records, books and magazines, which enabled the boys to snatch a few minutes of fun. As an added service he got out a mimeographed newspaper, *Sco-Coc-Pen News*. It was full of desert gossip and little features, including cartoons, with pilots acting as roving reporters. As Brigadier General Auby C. Strickland, the 57th Group's commanding officer, pointed out in one of its editorials, the paper "was actually published while you were in battle and under fire."

Of his experiences with the 57th Fighter Group, Field Director Goodridge recalled:

Considerable travel was necessary in order to put up a program of service while the group traveled forward. From the time I joined the unit until I left, I spent 127½ hours in travel by air, and drove 43,00 miles on the ground.

Frequent interruptions by Jerry, who seemed to take particular delight in retaliating on this group of fighters, made the life more exciting for all of us. Naturally, we came in for our share of shelling, bombing and strafing.

An interesting feature of the whole thing to me was that at one time during the push up the coast we discovered that the Red Cross representative was the oldest man in the Group [age, 52], and the C.O., Colonel Arthur G. Salisbury, was just half his age.

Living with the 57th Fighter Group was everything that a Red Cross man looks forward to in the way of excitement, service and comradeship with the military. There was never any time to think of personal needs. You were too busy. Every moment was full of trying to perform the service you were there to do, a service very hard to perform under mobile conditions. No matter how much you did, it was never enough.

A less hurried and more comprehensive program of recreation was carried out among the Ninth's rear echelons—the bomber and service groups. Working in close co-operation with Major Leroy C. Hinchcliffe, the Ninth Air Force Special Services officer, and with the Special Services officer in each group, Red Cross Field Director Orville E. Roberts, whom everybody called "Bob," was one of the busiest men on the Western Desert during the big push. Flying, or driving a truck or jeep, he seemed to be all over the place at once despite his fifty-one years. His fertile mind worked constantly adding to the recreational program, improvising new methods of entertainment.

When in full flower, the American Red Cross Army recreation program met the needs, and appealed to the taste and interest, of every man in the force. The Ninth's circulating library of 8,500 volumes was carried up the desert in gun boxes, the books being loaned on cards as in any public library. Each group developed its own orchestra from musical instruments scrounged in Cairo and Alexandria. One piano, transported on a truck, covered fifteen thousand miles traveling back and forth on the desert; this was the same piano used by Jack Benny and his party when they entertained at a Red Cross club which Roberts had set up in an oasis outside Tripoli. And there were minstrel shows.

In the handicraft clubs, discarded munition boxes were used for wood carving, and goatskins picked up in Cairo were turned into wallets and cigarette holders. There were also drawing and painting clubs, photography clubs, short-story sessions, discussion groups, and even a poetry-writing club. To keep in good standing in the latter club, GI's had to submit one acceptable poem a week, manuscripts being judged by a colonel, a noncom, and a private. The three best poems were nailed on the bulletin board. In the Ninth Air Force, no flower blushed unseen nor wasted "its sweetness on the desert air." The poetry club saw to that!

Competitive softball, baseball, table tennis, and badminton leagues flourished on the desert. So did track tournaments and horseshoe matches.

But to Field Director Bob Roberts, himself a former college football star and coach, the source of greatest pride was his "Wog Football Association." This was a football league made up of six teams of rear echelon airmen, nearly every one of whom had once played college football. The schedule, interrupted only by sandstorms and operational demands, was maintained across more than a thousand miles of desert.

The opening game was played on a landing field near El Alamein in November, 1942. With Roberts and Special Service officers acting as referees, subsequent games took place on fields behind the lines after spectators had cleared the ground of loose sand. Intercollegiate rules were observed, except that tackling was barred. This was "touch" football to save the players for the more exacting duties against the Axis.

In the passing weeks a keen competitive spirit developed among players and fans. And the Sand Bowl classic between the two winning teams was the most discussed event on the desert, next to the war itself. Played on a field between Benghazi and Tripoli in February, 1943, the game drew more than 2,500 enlisted men and officers. When, in keeping with football tradition, soldier-fans carried away the goal posts, they found them eighteen inches shorter than at the beginning of the schedule; the bottoms had been broken off in successive sandstorms. A silver loving cup for the team and a carton of American cigarettes for each player on the squad were the championship prizes.

At the close of the desert football season Field Director Roberts lay awake nights thinking of new ways of maintaining the Ninth's spirit. One day he conceived the idea of hunting gazelles in Army jeeps. Chasing those delicate, swift desert creatures with a sandy coloration would appeal to the sporting instincts of fliers and ground crews, he believed. When he proposed the idea to Colonel Paul A. Cunyus, commanding officer of the 315th Service Group, the latter said that before giving his official approval he would have to investigate himself. At the Colonel's request, Roberts made the arrangements for the hunt, which proved so successful that, subsequently, gazelle hunts became a popular sporting event on the desert.

In a flush of enthusiasm Field Director Roberts wrote the following report to National Headquarters, American Red Cross, in Washington:

In a recent letter I mentioned that I was going to take a group of officers on a gazelle hunt in a jeep on the Western Desert. Well, I've just returned from that hunt bruised, tired to death, but happy. It was a complete success—so much so, that I must tell you about it.

The party was made up of Colonel Paul A. Cunyus, commanding officer of the 315th Service Group, Ninth Army Air Force, and nine other officers of the command, together with our native guide, Roberto Pare Entis, and myself. The night before the hunt we stayed at a hotel in Jefron located on a sheer cliff between two rugged mountain ranges.

We left the hotel at 4:20 A.M. in three jeeps and trailers, four men to a jeep. In my jeep were Captain Terhune, Lieutenant Frizee, the driver, and Lieutenant Meek. Our spirits were mighty high, I'll tell you, as we took off on that winding road to the south for the thirty-mile jaunt to the gazelle happy-hunting ground.

The desert was rolling, with valleys of a quarter to half a mile between mountain ridges. Vegetation, mostly dry and sun-scorched, was almost knee-deep in some of the valleys. Our guide led us to the highest point where we could see for miles around. Here we unhooked our trailers. The sun, rose-tipped and misty blue-black in the far distance, was just taking a look-see over the eastern mountains. To keep warm we beat and rubbed our hands together and flapped our arms.

We laid our windshields flat over the hoods of the jeeps to give us a shooting clearance all around, made sure our rifles and .45's were loaded to capacity, set our safeties, and set out with the guide's jeep leading, the Colonel's next, and my jeep in the rear.

The leading jeep had scarcely crossed the valley between the point where we had left the trailers and the next ridge when we saw fifteen to twenty gazelles hitting the high spots toward the ridge beyond, and we let out a yell that echoed through the valley. We deployed and soon were hurtling over that rough desert abreast at forty miles an hour. Near the crest of the ridge, the herd split, some gazelles taking to the right and some to the left. My jeep was on the left flank and we raced after those nearest to us. Unsuccessful after shooting at eight or ten of them from about 300 yards, we decided to pick out the largest one and give him a chase. Almost as soon as we had decided that a certain ram gazelle was to be our meat, he scampered off by himself. Never before did I know that a living thing could travel so fast on land!

Where there are ridges, there is erosion. Where there is erosion, there are ditches, and at their bases in the valley, deep sandy and rocky deposits. Now I know that to be a fact. The jeep also knew and told us so. The ram gazelle didn't seem to know it— or maybe he did, and took his own way of letting us know it, too.

Anyway, we found out. I was in the rear seat, right. As we crossed the first ditch I wasn't; neither was Captain Terhune. We were on the spare tire fighting like thunder to get back to our seat. Then we hit deep sand and I was on Lieutenant Meek's back, and he was where the windshield should have been, but luckily wasn't. Then we hit a fairly smooth stretch of about a half mile of desert valley. We drew up to within seventy-five yards of the fleet-footed gazelle. Meek's, Terhune's and my rifles were shooting like machine guns with the St. Vitus dance. Lieutenant Frizee was driving with one hand and pecking away with his .45 in the other hand. Then the flying critter took for the ridge, and we went after him, yelling like Comanche Indians. That gray poetry in motion was moving diagonally down toward the next valley when we crossed the ridge. The lieutenant stepped on it and hit another ditch—about the four-hundredth.

As we neared the valley, the ram gave a long leap over a ditch ten feet deep and wide enough for two jeeps to be buried in at once. My soul took flight on the back of the critter ahead. But Lieutenant Frizee can drive in my chase anytime! Our jeep tumbled stones and sand into that chasm, but we headed up along it for some distance on two wheels, or one or none, for all I know, and succeeded in spanning it at its narrowest point. But this maneuver made us lose our gazelle, now five to six hundred yards ahead of us. I honestly think some men would have quit, but not we.

Finally, we got his range and one of our .45's shot him, breaking his neck. He was running so fast that after falling he rolled fifteen yards in the sand before coming to a dead stop.

We leaped out of the jeep, and, like men at the end of a vital football game, we yelled, slapped each other on the back, took turns lifting each other off our feet, and hugged one another. I had never seen excitement run so high.

"Quel Grand Spécimen!" the guide said of the gazelle, as we tied him to the front of the jeep and drove back to our trailers.

After the chase I know that my heart and liver are all right. My health is all right. I'm tough—me, and that glorious jeep. Brother, can those things take it!

The Ninth Air Force continued to participate in Allied operations to the end of Axis resistance in North Africa. Lieutenant General Lewis H. Brereton, the Ninth's commanding officer, officially commended Red Cross Field Directors Ray L. Goodridge, Orville E. Roberts, and John M. King for their work on the desert. To the three men General Brereton wrote:

I would like to commend you officially for the outstanding and meritorious service which you have so consistently rendered as Red Cross field representatives. ... With Air Force groups from the Battle of El Alamein to the expulsion of the enemy from Africa your duties were performed with an initiative and co-operativeness that has been invaluable in maintaining high morale and operational efficiency. Living in the desert at advanced stations directly behind the front lines of the advancing army forces, despite great personal hardship and danger, you have rendered outstanding service to our armed forces in the furtherance of our war effort.

It was a red-letter day on the Western Desert when the first two American Red Cross girls arrived to open a club. Seeing them for the first time, a sergeant, emerging from his plane, said, "I think I'll go on the wagon; first it's spots, now it's girls in front of my eyes." A tingle of excitement passed through the collective spine of the Ninth Air Force when the news spread. And the two girls themselves were thrilled at the prospect of dispensing American Red Cross hospitality in this remote corner of the world.

It was no picnic, however, transforming a bomb-shattered villa in an oasis into a club fit for an American desert warrior, as one of the girls, Miss Margaret Cotter, of Washington, D.C., soon learned:

We are the first American Red Cross club workers in the desert. After six weeks of the hubbub of Cairo, two of us girls were sent here, along with a director and an assistant director, to establish a club for our soldiers who have been in the blue so long they have forgotten what it is like to have a roof over their heads.

We had little more than a roof to start with in the building which was to be our club. A one-time magnificent villa, it looked sadly shattered and torn at our first glance. Remains of the wall which surrounded the garden lay in pieces along the roadside. The building is typical Italian colonial style, a low rambling affair, tinted in a pale pink color.

The flooring throughout is of tile. The staircase is of white marble supported by a wrought-iron banister.

The building was a desolate sight when we arrived. Inches of dirt covered the floor, and the ceilings were completely hidden by cobwebs. The doors and windows had been bombed off. There was no electricity, no water, not a stick of furniture.

Our club director, William Katzenbach, New Canaan, Connecticut, suggested we stay at the hospital until our place was in shape to house ladies, but we wouldn't hear of it. We wanted to "get in on the ground floor," so we waded through the filth, chose a room, set up our Army cots and made ourselves at home. We had our first experience that night with sand fleas, flies, mosquitoes, etc., and woke up completely covered with bites.

For a week we did nothing but scrub, dust, paint, whitewash, and generally get the place into some semblance of order. Then we furnished it in our best "beg, borrow or steal," method. And, finally, when we had hung a sign which read, "American Red Cross Club—Open Soon," on that one piece of wall left standing at our entrance, we were tired, proud and happy.

I think we must have put that sign up too soon however. The very next day while I was on my hands and knees, still scrubbing, I heard a car approaching. We had company! And there was I in my GI pants, an old shirt, and my hair piled up on top of my head!

My co-worker, Madge Smith, Metropolis, Illinois, had fortunately changed into her uniform, so she did the "receiving." I figured it was probably a couple of soldiers or maybe a lieutenant or two. Then suddenly I heard voices and footsteps approaching. As I looked up, expecting to see Johnny Doughboy, who should be standing there but Lieutenant General Lewis H. Brereton, the commanding officer of the whole Ninth Air Force! And with him were Brigadier General U. G. Ent, Colonel Louis Hobbs, General Brereton's Aide, and countless Majors and Lieutenants!

Speaking of embarrassing moments, I could have gone through the floor, scrub brush and all.

Our callers, however, were very gracious. No one batted an eyelash as I rose from my hands and knees, literally dripping soap and water, and went to greet them.

We took them all over the building, showing off our recreation room, grill room, and lounge. We strolled through the garden and the large pavilion where we intend to hold dances. We even showed them the dog pen which Sergeant Paul Wilman had built for our mascot, a seven weeks' old dachshund puppy given me as a farewell present when I left Cairo.

Before we made our good-byes to the generals I had recovered completely from my confusion and requested General Brereton's autograph. I received the following: "To Margaret Cotter with kindest personal regards, and thanks for her good work."

I guess he must have thought I did a good job on the floor.

The club opened on schedule, and General Ent cut the ribbon. More than 2,500 Yanks, eager for the sight of American girls, and hungry for good old American doughnuts, cake, sandwiches, candy, coffee, and lemonade, overran the premises. All took part in the dance under a tropical moon and swaying palm trees. Popular American dance tunes were played by the —th Bomber Group orchestra. There were only fifteen girls present—six American Red Cross staff assistants and six from the USO camp show then playing in the vicinity, and the remainder from British headquarters. Fifteen girls dancing with 2,500 men!

To say that we were rushed off our feet would be a gross understatement [said Margaret Cotter]. We were mobbed. We danced until we could hardly stand up. Naturally, no girl could get farther than a few steps without being "cut in on." Most of the boys told us they had not danced with an American girl for a year or more.

To reach fliers and ground crews whose airfields were too far from the club, a mobile club service was inaugurated. Using a jeep with trailer attached, called a "jeepmobile," four staff assistants and the assistant club director, William Kormann, of Pittsfield, Massachusetts, left early in the morning with cups and saucers, doughnuts, coffee, cream and sugar. To returning missions they served doughnuts and coffee just as they emerged from their planes. They would stay all day, and sometimes far into the night until the last returning plane had glided into the runway and taxied into position. The pioneer jeepmobile girls were: Misses Cotter and Smith, already mentioned; Beth Helas, Cleveland, Ohio, and Mary Mills Hatch, San Francisco, California. Later the jeepmobile was succeeded by the clubmobile used by the American Red Cross in every war theater.

In addition to the desert clubs, the American Red Cross operated a chain of leave-area clubs throughout the Middle East for servicemen on leave. The largest and most popular, formerly the Grand Hotel, was the Red Cross–Army club in Cairo. The club's bed capacity was about three hundred, but cots in the halls and lounges took care of late arrivals from the desert. Clean white sheets, hot showers, wholesome, appetizing food cooked American style, movies, dances, sightseeing tours—everything dreamed of in the desert was within reach at the Cairo club. There were even lectures on Egyptian culture, as reported in the *Red Cross Courier:*

At first it was an experiment. With some misgivings Program Director George Grenholm of Marquette, Michigan, set about to supply the academic touch, mindful perhaps of the soporific effect of classroom lectures in college days.

When the scholarly professor with the iron gray hair, a goatee and a dignified manner began his opening remarks, the Red Cross staff held its collective breath.

"Gentlemen," he said, "we will consider the history of the First Dynasty and its influences upon the development of Egypt to the time of *Rameses II.*"

The Red Cross staff breathed easier. There was no concerted rush for the door. No one looked bored. On the contrary this audience of young Americans, matured now beyond their years, listened attentively and shifted about to make room for late comers who wanted to hear, too.

Fortified with this intellectual brush-up, the neat construction jobs of the Pyramids and the Sphinx took on added meaning.

Yes, the GI's were curious about Egypt and Palestine. They were eager to see the sacred shrines they had first heard about in Sunday school. For them the American Red Cross conducted a comprehensive tour program all over the Middle East. Most tours were free to soldiers, and when a charge was made to cover transportation, guides, and admittance fees to ancient sites, it was below cost. Red Cross staff assistants acted as hostesses on all tours.

From the Cairo club there were tours to the old city with its mosques, the citadel, and bazaars, and to ancient Memphis and Sakkara. Every Monday, soldiers were taken by motor launch up the Nile to the Delta Barrage. On Tuesday nights there was a moonlight cruise on the Nile; Red Cross staff assistants and local girls invited by the club accompanied the soldiers. The most popular of all the tours from the Cairo club was the one to the Pyramids and the Sphinx. The boys liked to have their pictures taken riding a camel with the Pyramids and Sphinx in the background. Invariably they exclaimed with surprise that the Pyramids weren't a bit like what they had imagined. One iconoclast said, "They should have gotten Kaiser over here. He'd have done a much better job."

On the Alexandria tour, the Yanks observed the water front and Ras-el-Tin Palace, the bombed areas, Pompey's Pillar, the ancient Catacombs, the downtown section with its Nebi Daniel Mosque, the Stadium, large modern hospitals, the residential section, the Nouzha Gardens, and the Zoo.

Perhaps the most interesting of all the tours were those conducted by the American Red Cross club in Tel Aviv. After miles of barren desert, the soldier-tourists came to green country, tired villages in the hills which were old when Christ was born; ancient Roman ruins; walled cities known to the Crusaders, with the sea still washing against their battlements; fields of daisies, orange groves and olive orchards, herds of goats with goatherds looking just like Bible illustrations, and those nomadic Arabs, the Bedouins, with their black tents and crouching camels. And not many Yanks were prepared for Tel Aviv, a completely Jewish community, as modern and attractive as any progressive city in Florida or California, built in the midst of this Biblical setting. The boys were taken through the city with its wide, clean streets, and showed the shopping center, the factory section, the modern school buildings, and the Hebrew Theater. They went to ancient Jaffa, adjoining Tel Aviv, where they observed the native Arab markets and bazaars and many sites having Biblical associations.

From the Tel Aviv club each day, American soldiers left on one-, two-, or three-day tours through the Holy Land. The one-day tour took them to Jerusalem and Bethlehem; the two-day tour to Jerusalem, Bethlehem, the Dead Sea, Jericho, the river Jordan, and Transjordania; and the three-day tour embraced all these and, in

96

addition, Haifa, Capernaum, Tiberias, Nazareth, the Sea of Galilee, and a visit to one of the Jewish co-operative settlements.

The boys got their first sight of the ancient city of Jerusalem from the heights of the Hebrew University. Across the plains they saw the Dead Sea, lowest body of water in the world. Later they went swimming there, and found that because of the salt content they could not dive below the surface. Passing the Well of the Magi and the Tomb of Rachel in the Fields, they came to Bethlehem, where they saw the birthplace of Christ and the Church of the Nativity.

The Garden of Gethsemane, full of flowers and noble old trees, left the Americans awe-struck. Here stood the Church of Nations—also known as the Church of Agony—built on the rock where Christ prayed and was betrayed. The church was built by the faithful of fourteen nations whose emblems are emblazoned on the ceiling.

The next morning the American soldiers crossed the Allenby Bridge spanning the Jordan on their way to view the ruins of Jericho.

On one of these tours Assistant Field Director James E. Ravich, former Hartford, Connecticut, lawyer, was sitting in the bus next to a private who was born in Oklahoma and had spent all his life on a farm. While extremely interested in everything he saw, the boy kept talking on one subject over and over again. "There's just one thing this tour needs to make it perfect—a glass of milk," he said. "Boy, I'd give anything for a glass of milk. I haven't had one for a year and a half."

The tour stopped at one of the many modern co-operative agricultural colonies settled by European Jews throughout Palestine. This one happened to be populated by Rumanian and Czech Jews. When the Oklahoma boy saw the farm, his eyes lit up.

"This is right down my alley!" he exclaimed. He made the rounds of the farm, examined the farm machinery, rode on a tractor, and milked the cows. "Why, these people are doing the same thing my ancestors did. Out in Oklahoma they made farm land out of wasteland too."

When he saw the vineyards and the orange groves he was almost speechless with delight. But the best was yet to come. After the soldiers had gone all through the farm, they were ushered into the community dining hall, where they were given tall glasses of ice-cold milk—milk that had been pasteurized by modern methods.

When the boy saw that glass of milk he winked at Ravich, and down went the milk in one gulp. After drinking three more glasses he sat back in complete happiness.

97

"This trip has been swell," he murmured, "but that first glass of milk in eighteen months is something I'll never forget!"

An interesting commentary on these American Red Cross tours was reported by Turner Catledge, *New York Times* correspondent, in a dispatch from Alexandria, Egypt, January 30, 1944. He wirelessed:

A young flying officer in a mess tent in the desert near Tripoli was describing his trip to the Holy Land. In his own Texas idiom —some of which was not too biblical, he told the story of the Nativity in terms of what he had seen on one of the Red Cross tours. He ended with a flourish:

"And when that outfit comes around for dough next time, they're gonna get some from me."

"Who?" someone asked.

"The American Red Cross, the best blank blank outfit overseas," he said.

Red Cross clubs also offered an informal service which received little publicity; the opportunity for soldiers to get things off their chests. When they came off the desert on leave they liked to talk, and Red Cross staff assistants, carefully selected and trained young women, proved sympathetic listeners. What did they talk about? In the following account, Miss Katherine Blake, New York City, a former *Vogue* editor, reveals the secret:

Most of the soldiers we saw were Air Corps men—bombardiers and combat crews down on leave from "The Blue," or passing through to unknown destinations from thousands of miles away. They were the boys who had been pounding the Axis in the Sicilian and Italian raids, in the giant Bari and Ploesti missions.

They'd pile out of their planes, hot and tired and dusty. Most of them hadn't had a bath for months. They hadn't slept in a real bed for many, many weeks. Sand was ground into their eyes and hair and skin.

Some soldiers would stagger in loaded down with their guns and heavy equipment, passing through on long convoy treks that had brought them through many countries. The [Red Cross] club lobby was always packed with service men in a great, shouting, pressing mass.

They'd talk to you by the hour of what they'd done and seen. And they'd pull out finger-worn snapshots to show you—hundreds of pictures of wives and mothers and sweethearts and babies.

They'd describe their homes to you—down to the last detail. They'd ask you eagerly if you knew their home town. They'd grin happily telling you the exact place on the wall a certain picture hung, what the sitting room looked like, in just what corner the green armchair stood. They wanted it all to stay exactly that way until they came back to it. It was the only real security or feeling of permanence they had.

For a long time the mail came through very slowly. A four months' old *Life* would be grabbed immediately—it seemed new. We'd all share our letters from home. The men would pass them round among each other and read and re-read little details about life back in America, until the much-fingered pages were falling apart. A clipping, an advertisement from a shop you knew, even a familiar postmark on an envelope could make your heart give a funny little jump.

It wasn't that you were homesick. You were too busy, your days were too full, for that. It was just that you liked thinking of things being the same back home, and unchanged in all the strangeness and impermanence about you.

We tried to make the clubs as much like home as possible—places to which the men could come for comfort and relaxation and fun. Places in which they could find real beds and baths and dances and games and people from home to talk to and answer their questions.

They'd ask thousands of questions—where could they buy a puppy, what places in town had the best band, when the bus left for the desert, what would be a good present for a new baby, whom could they talk to about a loan.

They all had a curious detachment, which seemed a little strange at first until you found you'd learned it yourself, a matter-of-fact acceptance of things as they are.

I remember one of the boys describing the Jerrys he'd seen sitting straight and charred in a tank, burned to death. He'd gotten some good photos. I think I gasped a little, and he smiled at me.

"Hell, honey," he said. "That's the way it is. It isn't sad or bad or funny—it just is."

The combat crews had the same point of view. After sweating out long tense hours on a mission, they'd tell you what swell jazz they'd got on their radio coming home.

They all want someone to talk to. They don't talk to you as an individual, really. You know them as little as they know you. Many of them you will probably never see again. But the need

99

for companionship is very strong in war-torn days—the contact with someone from home.

There was the boy who had a hunch he was going to die. He just didn't feel right about things any more. It didn't bother him, dying. "Hell," he said, "I've had a good life. I've had a lot more fun than a lot of guys I know in the last twenty-five years."

But he was worried about his dog. That bothered him. He pulled out some snapshots of her—taken in front of a little white clapboard house with a tree and a bit of grass, somewhere in Connecticut. His face lit up talking about her. "That pooch hasn't been the same since I left," he said with reluctant pride. "Gee, but I'd like to see her again!"

He was killed by ack-ack two weeks later.

Then there was the pilot who was killed a few months ago. He'd always said he'd never be taken prisoner—and he wasn't boasting. His plane got lost behind enemy lines, and his gasoline ran out. He landed the plane and fired it. He and his crew waited for the Germans to come up. And as the Germans came, he blasted away at them with a forty-five. They took the other men prisoners. They buried him there in the sand where he died, and they wrote on his cross, "A brave American transport pilot is buried here."

Coming down to the Red Cross club on leave after a tough mission, they'll slip right back into the boys they used to be at home. "Is there a steak for dinner tonight? Oh, boy! Will you get me a girl for the dance? Put us all in the same room, can you? We're all on the same crew."

They stick together, these crews, bound by a tie stronger than any family tie could ever be. They've lived and fought together, faced dying together on every mission. And, on leave, they refused to be separated.

A boy from one of these crews hobbled into the club on crutches one day. When he was last down, his crew had been with him. Now he'd come in from the hospital. They were sending him home.

"Where are the others, Bill?" we asked him. It always seemed strange not to see a crew together.

"They're all gone," he said simply. "We got shot up with ack-ack over Naples and everyone was killed in the plane except Dan and Joe and me."

Dan, he said, had taken over the plane although he was shot in the head and stomach. Joe had been hit in the arm and head. He, himself, had a leg wound and his thumb had been blown off.

"Funny," he said, "I looked down and it wasn't there. Never felt a thing."

One of their engines had been shot up and they'd had to drop out of formation. Somehow they got across the Mediterranean and made a crash landing in the desert.

They'd crawled out of the plane. None of them could walk. They'd decided to try and make their base, figuring it wasn't far.

"We'd crawl a little way and then stop and then crawl some more," Bill said. At night it was very cold—they'd burrow into the sand.

The second day Dan was dead when they started off. The other two crawled on alone.

"I guess it was about five that afternoon," Bill continued slowly. "Joe said he couldn't go any farther. I lay down beside him and he asked me to get his mother's picture out of his pocket. He lay looking at it and talking about her for about an hour before he died. He asked me to look her up if I ever made it out alive."

After that, Bill crawled on alone.

"I didn't have any water left," he said. "Funny, it was so hot I couldn't think very straight any more. I'd keep seeing the Squadron all lined up and the boys were passing buckets of water back and forth, back and forth. After that I was unconscious I guess. The British picked me up two days later and I ended up down here. . . .

"It seems funny going home."

He didn't want to go home. He wanted to keep on flying.

You heard so many stories like that. And when you heard them you felt that nothing you could do would ever, ever be enough.

As in other theaters, the Red Cross interest went beyond the welfare of the able-bodied troops. In hospitals throughout the Middle East, Red Cross workers saw to it that the wounded and sick received the little additional attention they would get at home—those extra little things that helped a fighting man to quick recovery.

The first American Red Cross hospital recreation and medical social workers to arrive in the Middle East were the following Pennsylvanians: Emile McKenna, Landsdown; Elizabeth Tanner, Abington; Edna Tarr, Pittsburgh; and Florence Keck, Reading.

One incident will illustrate the type of work performed by Red Cross hospital workers in this theater:

A boy who had been shot up with ack-ack on a mission was sent down to a general hospital outside Cairo. He was so badly injured that for a long time he wasn't told that he would be blind permanently.

When he was told, he took it hard. He was only twenty-one, and had been strong and active—an athlete—all his life.

In this hospital, doctors and nurses did not have much time to give a patient extra attention—there was so much for them to do. One of the Red Cross girls filled the gap. Daily she visited the boy, sat and talked to him, explaining the sounds and smells, and describing the ward and the people whose voices he heard.

She brought him a radio set. She wrote his letters to his wife and read her letters to him. He didn't want his wife to know he would not see again.

The Red Cross girl did everything she could do to help him adjust himself to his blindness. And it was difficult because he was bitter—and afraid. She explained how the Red Cross would help him when he got home, how Red Cross people could teach him braille and how to use his hands.

The boy grew to depend very much on that Red Cross girl. The first time he was able to shave himself alone he waited impatiently for her to come so that he could tell her about it.

And one day, weeks later, on one of her regular visits to his room, she asked him what he needed, what she could bring him.

"Matches," he said.

"But I brought you matches only yesterday," she smiled. "What do you do with them—eat them?"

"Hell, no," replied the boy. "People come in to see me and go off with my matches."

He laughed. "Things have come to a new low when people will steal from a blind man!"

And because he was able to laugh, the girl knew that at length he had adjusted himself to his blindness.

Soon after Tripoli had been occupied by the British Eighth Army, four truckloads of American Red Cross relief supplies for Tripolitania's civilian population arrived in the city from Cairo. The incident was described in the *Red Cross Courier* by Robert E. Lewis, then Red Cross public information director in the Middle East: *

The shawled women stood in groups about the truck with the American Red Cross sign on its sides. They eyed with passive apprehension the two Americans who stepped out of the cab, and stayed a respectful distance from them.

* Mr. Lewis was killed in an airplane crash while in duty at Port Moresby, New Guinea, November 26, 1943.

One crept nearer, peered at the small chevrons carrying the words, "United States" the men wore on their shoulders. She smiled, talked eagerly to the women, and her smiles spread rapidly through the group.

Then the interpreter spoke. The truck contained milk sent to the women and children of Tripoli by the American people through the American Red Cross. The milk was there, he said, and more would come to strengthen the bodies of their children and invalids.

The smiles gave way to cheers, and the American Red Cross program of emergency relief for the thousands of Jews, Arabs and Italian refugees of Tripolitania commenced at once.

It was the first civilian relief given to the citizens of the occupied territory of Libya following the advance of General Montgomery's victorious British Eighth Army across the desert from El Alamein to the border of Tunisia. It demonstrated better than words and phrases the meaning of the ideals of the United Nations.

Requested by the British authorities, the supplies, including 115,000 pints of milk and other emergency rations, were brought to the city by the Red Cross in an army convoy over the 1,500 miles long supply route from Cairo to Tripoli.

They were administered under the direction of Ralph Bain, Red Cross director of operations in the Middle East, and conveyed to Tripoli by Charles E. Bailey, Red Cross director of civilian relief.

The Red Cross was on the job in Tripoli itself almost as soon as the retreating gunners of Rommel's forces had blasted at the British advancing forces at the approaches of the city, and it enabled the spirit of America to advance with the troops of the United Nations.

Over roads shelled and mined, the Red Cross convoy followed the fighting army to bring mercy to a population which had suffered the ravages of warfare and which received the evidences of American humanitarianism with a gratefulness verging upon worship.

Everywhere we went, we were cheered by the Italians as well as the other elements of the population. Many of them wanted to know how they could send messages to friends and relatives in the United States.

It was among the Arabs that the Red Cross supplies were needed the most. According to the Red Cross survey of food needs in the occupied territory, made in almost every section of the inhabited coastal regions of the land, many Arabs are eating locusts and grass to survive.

In many communities the flocks and livestock of the communities have been depleted by as much as 90 per cent. The Red Cross emergency supplies are being distributed through these areas.

British authorities expect near famine conditions in parts of Libya before the crops are harvested in April. But due to competent administration of the conquered territory, many of the Italian colonial farmers who abandoned their farms when they heard of the retreat of the Axis forces, are returning to their acres to save the crops they had planted before the retreat of Rommel's desert fighters.

In most cases the returning Italian farmers are accepting the occupation with good grace, verging in some cases upon enthusiasm.

The work of distributing the emergency relief supplies throughout Tripolitania was undertaken by a committee established under the cooperation of the British occupying authorities and the American Red Cross. It contained representatives of the British, Arabs, Jews and Italians.

The fact that the British and Americans were determined to stave off starvation among the civilians of the occupied territory has done much to restore the confidence of the population in the new government.

The remnants of Rommel's battered forces took refuge behind the Mareth Line in Tunisia, merging themselves with Axis troops recently arrived from the continent. There the Ninth Air Force joined the successful Allied effort to smash the line.

The Ninth remained in the desert several months beyond the final collapse of the German and Italian armies in North Africa. On August 1 it carried out a spectacular mission against the Ploesti oil fields in Rumania, and on the fourteenth, bombed Wiener Neustadt, Austria.

Late in October, 1943, on the completion of its desert assignment, the Ninth moved its headquarters from Cairo to England.

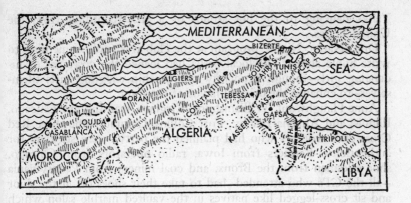

Chapter VII

THE NORTH AFRICAN CAMPAIGN

WHAT AMAZING CONTRASTS GLOBAL WARFARE WROUGHT IN MAR-rakech, mellow oasis city in French Morocco!

Within its palm-fringed boundaries converged camel caravans from distant points in the desert, even as caravans had done for centuries. And at its doorstep was a transatlantic airline terminal where President Roosevelt alighted on his way to the historic Casablanca Conference.

In the *medina*, or native quarter, the bazaar, steaming with a hundred and one strange smells, showed a cool disdain of the war raging about it. Trade went on with the same haggling, raucous shouts and oriental gesticulations. Jostling one another in the crowded, narrow lanes were swarthy Berbers from the mountains in striped robes, silver daggers caught in their girdles; artisans from the desert tribes astride basket-laden mules; bearded sheiks, jugglers, snake charmers, dancers, armorers, leather workers, raconteurs, and musicians playing delicate folk tunes redolent of the desert. Here and there in front of a little shop squatted an old Arab imperturbably drawing tobacco smoke from his narghile.

This was Marrakech's native quarter, and not far from it, hidden among palm trees, with sacred white ibis flying overhead, gleamed the pink walls of a princely palace now turned into an American Red Cross club for American soldiers. Its terrace swarmed with

Yanks dancing to the hot strains of a jazz recording from the United States.

One "Native Night" program at the club was really something to write home about. The local pasha had loaned the costumes of his dancing girls—though prudently not the hip-wiggling girls themselves—to enhance the oriental flavor of the stunt.

Anne Haughwout, Williamsburg, Virginia; Jean Ingram, Chicago, Illinois; and Almena Pashby, Fort Collins, Colorado—the three Red Cross club workers who had planned the party—were sticklers for authenticity. Farmers from Iowa, radio operators from Chicago, shoe salesmen from the Bronx, and coal miners from Pennsylvania —all the GI's who attended—had to take their shoes off at the door and sit cross-legged like natives in the vaulted marble salon which the girls had temporarily transformed into a harem atmosphere. And as the GI's blinked their eyes in amazed delight, native male dancers, tumblers, and fire eaters (the lights were turned out for this act) went through their routines.

Such was the fabulous American Red Cross club in Marrakech— a place where snake charmers and fire-eaters in the salon and camel races in the courtyard were some of the props ingenious Red Cross girls dished up for club entertainment.

It was during the North African campaign that the Red Cross girl first caught the eyes, and typewriters, of American war correspondents. The latter cabled paeans of praise about her—her charm, good sportsmanship, ingenuity, endurance, courage under fire, and above all, her tonic effect on the doughboys. Quentin Reynolds wrote that the Red Cross girl was one of the three greatest discoveries of World War II, the other two being Ernie Pyle and the jeep.

One afternoon two clubmobile girls were driving by a lonely antiaircraft gun post when they observed three Yanks—a sergeant, a corporal, and a private—napping.

"Hi, there, how'd you like some doughnuts and coffee?" called one of the girls.

The poor GI dogfaces woke up startled. They had heard many tales about the African sun and the weird images it created in the desert. Was this, then, a mirage? The sergeant pinched the corporal, the corporal pinched the private, and the private pinched the sergeant. No, they agreed, the two pretty images before them were really Red Cross girls.

"Gee," commented the private, "I didn't know foxholes were so close to heaven."

American soldiers in North Africa were so surprised at seeing

Red Cross girls, and so hungry for the sound of the home twang, that they would stop them on the street just to hear them talk. "Say, lady, are you really an American girl?" they would ask.

In Red Cross clubs the commonest expression was, "Gee, she talks American." A close second: "Say something, lady; anything at all just so long as you go on talking American." And a third: "What part of the States do you come from?"

Early in their career, Red Cross girls learned to take raillery from the men with dignity and good humor. Their first experience came in the Army posts at home when they were on their practice assignments. The mess hall invariably was some distance from the Red Cross office. On the way they would ride to the accompaniment of rising whistles from appreciative soldiers. "Hey, Red Cross! Hiya, babe!" were stock greetings. When a novice felt embarrassed, an older Red Cross woman might say to her, "You know, honey, you'd think you were slipping if they didn't whistle."

Aboard troop transports taking them to their overseas stations they would distribute Red Cross ditty bags; filled by volunteer women in Red Cross chapters, these were Santa Claus, birthday present, Easter gift, and May basket all tied up in one small khaki-colored bag. Article after article came tumbling out—a pencil, writing paper, housewife (sewing kit), detective story, gum, cigarettes, playing cards, shaving cream, toothbrush—about twenty different items. As the girls went through the mob giving out these ditty bags, they heard remarks like these: "Say, girls, are you going to be around when we get there?" "Does Red Cross do things like this all the time?" "Are you going along with us?" and "Say, fellows, this isn't going to be such a bad war, after all."

By the time they landed on the other side, the girls had acquired a technique for handling bantering questions. The soldiers, even the toughest, enforced an unwritten rule that frowned upon discourteous remarks to Red Cross girls. On those rare occasions when a man forgot himself, the girls themselves handled him gingerly before throwing him to the wrath of his comrades.

Red Cross girls were selected not only for character, educational background, and experience, but also for their ability to improvise and adapt themselves to primitive conditions. Their ingenuity won the admiration of all the military from the highest general to the humblest GI. One day General Sir Henry Maitland Wilson, Supreme Allied Commander of the Mediterranean Theater, was inspecting American Red Cross clubs in Algiers. At the club for Allied servicewomen he observed the shower and dressing-room facilities available to enlisted girls of the British, French, and American

Armies. His keen eyes had caught the club's improvisations, and, tongue in cheek, he asked, "Do you have any difficulty getting fuel?"

Katherine Schelbe, of Detroit, Michigan, the club director, smiled. "Yes, sir. We can't produce hot showers and run the kitchen stove at the same time, so we juggle the schedule."

Red Cross girls performed a great variety of tasks, only a few of which were in the book. They planned recreation programs in clubs and hospitals, and danced and sang themselves. They would change tires on a clubmobile or get up at dawn to fry doughnuts. At any moment they might be called upon to do a neat piece of mending on a soldier's blouse, or do a fancy stitching job in chevrons. They bowled, played ping-pong and darts. They could discuss baseball, football, and basketball and pitch horseshoes. They were good conversationalists, and even better listeners, and they wrote interesting letter for hospital patients.

In countless little ways, soldiers tried to show their appreciation. One thoughtful mess sergeant who had been a fancy pastry cook in civilian life would bring a lemon meringue pie or chocolate cake every time he visited the Red Cross club in Constantine. Soldiers driving into town from the airfields could not resist the Arabs selling "eggas" along the road. They would arrive at a club with eggs carried precariously in their pockets. The Red Cross girls cooked the eggs for the men or accepted them as a flattering tribute. Country boys would buy fresh green vegetables from roadside Arab vendors and bring them to the club. Often a girl found herself carrying home a snow-white cauliflower, an armful of fresh artichokes, or even a bunch of leeks to cook over her gas plate at her billet. And flowers in North Africa were so profuse and so irresistible to a soldier with his pockets full of money that many a Red Cross club looked like a star's dressing room.

Sometimes there were unexpected experiences such as the one that came to Rita Hume, of Seattle, Washington, a Red Cross staff assistant:

> One of my greatest thrills was to be present at a broadcast by General Eisenhower to the States on the eve of the [1943] Red Cross War Fund drive.
>
> General Eisenhower was as dynamic as I had pictured him. He entered the small broadcasting room with two aides, Major Lee of Texas and Lieutenant Commander Harry Butcher of Washington, D.C., who were the only others present besides the radio announcers and myself.

After a stirring appeal in which he stressed the tremendous need for the continuance of the Red Cross program, the General turned to me and said:

"This is the occasion of my second broadcast since the start of the war, and my first from North Africa. The Red Cross has a great program. We've got to keep it going."

And I nearly popped every one of the buttons on my trim gray uniform!

The North African campaign represented one-half of a gigantic Allied nutcracker crushing the Axis armies. General Montgomery's British Eighth Army was the other half.

Early Sunday morning, November 8, 1942—the day Mersa Matruh in Egypt fell to the advancing British columns—American and British troops landed on several beaches on North Africa's Atlantic and Mediterranean coasts, principally at Casablanca, Oran, and Algiers. This formidable invasion force had been carried across the Atlantic in the mightiest convoy in history: about 500 troop transports and cargo vessels escorted by 350 warships of the United States and Royal Navies. There were three task forces. One, from the United States, got under way about the same time as the skirl of Scottish bagpipes signaled the launching of General Montgomery's great offensive at El Alamein. The other two left British bases twenty-four hours later. All ships arrived at their designated positions on time except one, which limped in behind schedule because it had been torpedoed. Of the ground forces landed, sixty per cent were American, forty per cent British, but in the air the proportion between the USAAF and the RAF was half and half.

French token resistance ended at Admiral Darlan's order thirty-six hours after the initial landings. Whereupon the British First Army, together with a small American mobile unit and French troops under General Giraud, raced into Tunisia in an attempt to capture Tunis and Bizerte and cut off Rommel's retreat to the sea. Heavy rains which turned roads and advance airfields into quagmires, and difficult problems of supply, robbed the Allies of a quick decision over German and Italian forces being supplied by air and sea from near-by Italian bases.

Before the end of the year, the Allies had stabilized the Tunisian front in the north and continued to spar with the enemy farther south. The final drive to liberate North Africa was postponed until early in spring. The intervening months were put to good use. Reinforcements and matériel were rushed in from the United States and England for the big push that would open the way for the invasion of Sicily and Italy, and at the same time remove for all time the threat of a union between the Germans and the Japanese in India through seizure by the former of the Suez Canal.

The American Red Cross was in the North African campaign from the beginning, when eighteen field directors arrived from England in the wake of the first landings. On the beachheads they assisted Army chaplains and the Medical Corps. Later they accompanied their units on the long and tedious motor convoys from French Morocco and Algeria into positions along the Tunisian front. En route there was little they could do for the soldiers except during stops, when they hooked up their radio sets and invited them to listen in, or promoted informal soccer and touch football games. In the early hectic days at the front they concentrated on visits to evacuation tent hospitals, where they distributed Red Cross comfort articles. Their reward was an appreciative grin now and then from a patient who would exclaim, "Say, boy, this is on the beam!"

Though harassed by tremendous supply and transportation difficulties, the whole program of the American Red Cross developed with the ever-growing needs of the United States armed forces. Many ships bringing in reinforcements carried some Red Cross personnel aboard—field, club, and program directors, hospital workers, recreation workers, staff assistants and secretaries. By June 30, 1942 (prior to the invasion of Sicily), there were 627 Red Cross men and women on duty in North Africa.

Ships bearing matériel for the American troops generally reserved space for Red Cross supplies and equipment. Early in the invasion one shipment, unloaded at several Allied ports, contained hundreds of cases of phonograph records, radio sets, reading matter, and comfort articles. Typical of the supplies which the Red Cross rushed to the forward areas as fast as transportation permitted were one million razor blades and two million packages of cigarettes.

The American Red Cross service network spread over the length and breadth of French North Africa and was directed by William E. Stevenson, of Stamford, Connecticut, and New York, American Red Cross delegate to North Africa. From clubs in base cities it fanned out to cover rear and forward hospitals, scores of recreation rooms at advanced airfields and docks, and, by clubmobile, to serve the remotest outposts. No American fighting man, however isolated his post, was overlooked.

The field service was divided into three great areas, one centering at Casablanca, another at Oran, and the third at Algiers. From Algiers eastward to the Tunisian border a mobile program was adapted to the demands of a fluid front where lines and troop areas shifted constantly. The Algiers area was subdivided into supply bases centering at Constantine, Souk-Ahras, and Tebessa. From these bases, supplies went out to numerous day centers, evacuation hospital units, and club operations fanning out in all directions as close to the actual fighting as the Army permitted. Regional headquarters were at Constantine. Field supervisor there was George "Red" Munson, of Cincinnati, Ohio, former catcher for the St. Louis Cardinals.

One of the Red Cross field directors' teams at the front were: Allen W. Fincke, Tenafly, New Jersey; Herbert Sifford, Greensburg, Pennsylvania; and James Snyder, Reading, Pennsylvania. Working out of Tebessa, they drove their clubmobiles all over the American positions. They ate where they could, leaped into the nearest slit trench upon the approach of enemy planes, and at night they spread their bedrolls on the ground and got their hard-earned sleep under the stars; sometimes they were lucky to sleep under a pup tent.

Once Red Munson and Jim Snyder in a forward area had spent the night sleeping out in the open. Upon awakening they were startled to find two twelve-German gliders resting virtually at the foot of their bedrolls. They never did find out what had become of the Germans.

"Hiya, soldiers! Red Cross coming up! Need any cigarettes, soap, razor blades?"

The big bass voice of Field Director Jim Snyder booming out among the foxholes became a familiar and welcome sound along the Tunisian front. A machine-gun sergeant in France during the First World War (he was decorated several times for bravery under fire), Snyder readily adjusted himself to the rugged life—the rain, the mud, K rations, the loss of sleep, and the thunder of battle. The fear of enemy shells was not in him, though he took the usual precautions against injury. He would park his clubmobile, and then, his arms full of Red Cross gifts, he would make the rounds of the foxholes, calling like a country auctioneer in his native Pennsylvania Dutch region. He served hot coffee and doughnuts and routed personal messages to Red Cross Home Service workers all over the United States. When his supplies were exhausted, he would drive back to Tebessa for perhaps a hundred and fifty miles over muddy, winding roads. All this he did with a good-natured grin, a joke, and a song, which conveyed the suggestion that he was on a lark. "Quite a guy, that Jim," commented Munson, his supervisor.

In the following account of a sixteen-day exploratory tour of the Tunisian front, quoted by Lora Kelly in the *Red Cross Courier*, Red Munson gives a glimpse of Red Cross field operations:

Our purpose was to bring the field service of the American Red Cross as close to the men as was practical. We wanted to see how close to the front we could operate with a maximum of benefit to the troops.

Too close to the fighting men would mean transportation difficulties and inability to establish communications with American Red Cross headquarters in Algiers and consequently to the people of the United States. Too far behind the lines would obviously not be feasible.

We traveled eastward from Algiers for three days, stopping to chat with men camped along the roads. A real friendliness and warmth exist on these North African highways—there's a tin of gasoline for your car when you're running low, a battered can of oil for your boiling, pounding motor just for the asking.

The second night out, at sundown, we ran into an American convoy stopping for their evening rations, which consisted of bologna sausage without bread. In digging through our clubmobile we found some crackers. Putting the two together made cooperation on the highway to the nth degree.

On the evening of the third day we pulled into a small town some 400 miles east of Algiers. After scouting a bit we found a battalion of American infantry, a small army postoffice and a finance office. After conference with the Army officers we were convinced *this was it!*

We bought out a local cafe—lock, stock and barrel—for the sum of $53, but we did permit the proprietor to keep his stock.

Our club was furnished with a piano, a phonograph and a radio. About twelve writing tables were installed, together with a reading room and a small lending library of one hundred books. These were loaned out in the first hour of business. A waiting list was formed as fast as the books were returned. One soldier followed the men to the check-out desk and asked for a book—any book. He didn't care anything about the author, the title or the contents. He just wanted to read English.

It wasn't long until about 800 men were using the club facilities. The men were so enthusiastic they pitched right in and helped. One lad in particular proved a real find. He had been a baker in the States, so I turned over all my doughnut flour to him and he really went to town. You should have seen the smiles of satisfaction of the men when he yelled, "Come and get 'em!" over his first great heaping batch of crisp, golden doughnuts like mother used to make.

Sniping was still going on in the streets of Oran when Red Cross Field Director Fincke hoisted the United States and Red Cross flags over an empty, barnlike automobile showroom and set up the first Red Cross club in North Africa.

Before there was a chair on the checkerboard stone floor, soldiers began to saunter in singly and in pairs. "That's all right," they said. "We just want a place to talk and smoke."

By nightfall there were a dozen small tables, twenty chairs, and a piano, all obtained through the kindly offices of M. Louis Roy, head of the French Red Cross in North Africa. That first evening doughboys gathered round the piano and satisfied their homesickness by singing old American tunes. At the piano was Lucie Lee Kinsolving, New York City, Red Cross hospital recreation worker, who had come off a troop transport only a few hours before. "Gee, this sure is like home," sighed one of the Yanks, and Miss Kinsolving and her colleagues felt rewarded for all their trouble.

From this humble beginning the American Red Cross club program spread across French North Africa. Five clubs with eighteen Red Cross staff workers were in operation in Algiers, Casablanca, Oran, and Constantine only a few weeks after the initial landings. By July 1, 1943, there were thirty-three units—enlisted men's clubs, officers' clubs, on-post clubs, Navy fleet clubs in the ports, rest homes, and movie theaters—staffed by 140 Red Cross club workers. To keep house at the Algiers club for thousands of men daily required a staff of twelve Red Crossers and nearly a hundred civilian employees. The clubs were complete with hotel, restaurant, snack bar, and comprehensive recreation facilities.

Early in the invasion, the Red Cross met the need of the troops for live-talent shows by organizing an entertainment division as part of its club program. One of its most successful enterprises was a vaudeville troupe, "Show-on-Wheels," directed by Frank Goodell, New York City. This mobile troupe consisted of refugee French artists and theatrical stars stranded in Algiers. It played to more than 100,000 troops in camps, hospitals, leave centers, airports and in mountain and desert bivouac areas.

Also popular were the musical revues produced in the Red Cross Empire Club in Oran by Martin Jones, Broadway producer. The club, formerly the old Empire Theater, was packed daily with thousands of American soldiers back from the Tunisian front after their great victory over the Axis forces. Out of the uniformed ranks of the Red Cross there materialized such surprising personalities as Rosemary Ames, former stage and motion picture actress; Evelyn Vaughn, former hat-check girl from New York who had danced through several Warner Brothers shorts; Star Chandler, North Carolina aviatrix and one-time NBC solo pianist; and a florid 250-pound Red Cross field director, Marvin Lewis, former Florida businessman, whose aptitude for mimicry made him the surprise hit of the show. The Army yielded a snake-charming Boston trumpeter, Walter McKenna, formerly of Ruby Newman's band; Irving Bernstein, New York City, former half-pint comedian of the Murray Burns vaudeville team; and others. The cast was finally completed with seven Red Cross workers, six soldiers, and six professional French dancers. Producer Jones staged a series of five musical revues before the Army Special Services decided to arrange its own live-talent shows for the troops.

Probably the most unusual and colorful of the Red Cross clubs in North Africa was the Allied Club in Oran, housed in the same automobile showroom where the first invasion troops were entertained. When the regal Empire Club was opened, the Red Cross decided to continue the Allied Club as an experiment in international relations.

For while it was predominantly an Anglo-American show, the North African campaign was fought by representatives of many nations. On the ground, under General Alexander, were Americans, British, French, Australians, New Zealanders, Indians, South Africans, Poles, Czechs, Dutch, Norwegians, Palestine Jews, Senegalese, French Goumiers (fierce Moroccan warriors), and Indo-Chinese. Admiral Andrew Cunningham's Allied fleet included Norwegian, Greek, and Polish warships. Greek, Polish, and Yugoslav fliers flew with other national groups comprising the Northwest African Air Forces under command of Air Chief Marshal Sir Arthur Tedder. A Free French brigade under the legendary General Jaques Le Clerc assisted General Montgomery in driving the Afrika Korps from its strongly fortified positions behind the Mareth Line after making a three-thousand-mile advance across the Sahara Desert. Another picturesque unit was the *Corps Franc d' Afrique*, the Free Corps of Africa, who fought under General Giraud, though not as a part of the regular French Army. This unit represented a cross section of Europe's despoiled populations. All of its soldiers were refugees, including exiled Germans and Austrians, who had joined the French Foreign Legion before France's collapse in June, 1940. The Allies found them slaving in North African coal mines and on the trans-Saharan railway—betrayed to the Nazis by Vichy after the armistice.

And it was this cosmopolitan army which made the Red Cross Allied Club their headquarters. On any typical night an observer might have seen men in olive drab, blue and brown, garrison and overseas caps, ecru turbans, and tall bright-red fezzes; white, blue, and red-tasseled sailors' caps—all grouped around a grinning Yank pounding away at the piano, the voices in mixed tongues raised in tribute to Dinah.

The club was equipped with a short-wave radio set, a phonograph with many records and needles, a library of 750 books and 250 magazines, tables, chairs, checkroom racks, and the original piano. One of the popular features was the snack bar for sandwiches, fruit juices, and ice cream. The elation on the face of an Arab soldier as he dipped his tin spoon into a dish of ice cream—perhaps his second or third in a lifetime—was something worth seeing.

It was not the props, however, that made the Red Cross Allied Club such a gratifying success, but the friendly international atmosphere maintained by the three Red Cross club workers. The hostess was Mrs. Verna Johnson, Washington, D.C., who, when not arranging flowers, working on interior decorations, sewing on buttons for soldiers, or dancing with the boys, would be conversing with a homesick French trooper in his native tongue. Her capable assistants were Fannye F. "Tex" Beaty, Orange, Texas, former WPA recreation supervisor, and Vivian Acord, Los Angeles, California, former radio performer.

These club workers enjoyed themselves as much as the Allied soldiers, sailors, and merchant seamen. Said Vivian Acord:

> The Allied Club is probably the best answer to the oft-repeated question of why we are here. Recently the success of our enterprise was attested in a manner which made us feel both proud and humble. An American soldier told us how much he thought we were helping create a feeling of friendship between the United States and her Allies. And he backed up his conviction with a sizeable contribution to assist us in our work.

Another significant development was the Town Hall program sponsored by the American Red Cross.

Based on the traditional New England type of forum, the Red Cross Town Hall met the distinct need among intelligent United States Army officers and enlisted men for the kind of thinking stimulated by free discussions. For those men who had little or no conception of what the United States was fighting for, this project opened new horizons. It made them far less susceptible to enemy propaganda broadcasts at the front, and lent significançe to their sacrifices.

While novel among American forces, this type of program was well established among the British Army in North Africa. It was carried on by the British Army Education Corps, whose chief purpose was to stimulate clear thinking by means of informal talks and group discussions. The British appeared keenly aware that the postwar world would be shaped largely by the men who were doing the fighting, and the B.A.E.C. speakers' program was aimed at informing British soldiers.

Red Cross Town Hall hoped to do the same for American soldiers.

The idea was conceived by Dr. Ferdinand M. Isserman, rabbi of Temple Israel, St. Louis, Missouri, in the spring of 1943. Dr. Isserman, who had come to North Africa as a volunteer special American Red Cross representative, spent four weeks of the final phase of the Tunisian campaign at the front. There he noticed how eagerly the American soldiers awaited the daily seven-o'clock broadcast of the British Broadcasting Company. This confirmed his belief that many fighting men, however much their talk and wishes were concerned with physical comforts, also were keenly interested in the world about them.

Upon his return from the front Dr. Isserman persuaded Red Cross club leaders to sponsor a Town Hall program as part of their recreational program in the North African theater. After Army clearance, the club leaders were willing to experiment.

Eager to make an auspicious start, the St. Louis rabbi scoured Algiers for a good speaker. At a rest camp he first approached Ernie Pyle. While entirely sympathetic, Ernie begged off with the statement that for him speaking in public was an unendurable ordeal. Fred Painton of the *Reader's Digest* launched Town Hall with a lecture on "Why Battles Are Boring" based on his experiences in the Tunisian campaign. The lecture, given at the Red Cross officers' club in Algiers on June 7, 1943, won Painton an ovation from the two hundred officers present. The experiment was a success.

The next morning Captain Robert Neville, editor of *Stars and Stripes*, received a letter from a sergeant inquiring why this type of program was given to officers only, and not to enlisted men. This letter led to Town Hall's being extended to the Red Cross enlisted men's club in Algiers. The first speaker there was Relman Morin, former head of the Associated Press bureau in Tokyo, who spoke on "What Led Japan on the Road to War." The following week Colonel Elliott Roosevelt, the President's son, addressed a capacity audience on "Photo Reconnaissance, the Eyes of the Army." When he finished, he was overwhelmed by some two hundred GI's demanding his autograph. He signed American dollar bills, French bank notes, and an assortment of paper scraps.

With Dr. Isserman as moderator, Town Hall became a regular weekly feature on Monday evenings at the Red Cross officers' club and on Friday evenings at the Red Cross enlisted men's club. Subsequently, under Town Hall auspices, groups of officers and men gathered at theaters, lecture halls, overseas clubs, airfields, rest camps, bivouac areas, and hospitals in French North Africa.

One thing Town Hall always insisted upon was complete freedom of speech, and lively discussions developed at every meeting. The Army protected itself by ruling out operational subjects.

A significant development early in Town Hall history was the exchange of speakers with the British Army Education Corps and the *Comité de la Libération*. This led to a notable improvement in mutual understanding among the three chief allies in North Africa —Americans, British, and French.

Town Hall audiences regularly heard well-known war correspondents, authors, historians, diplomats, and Allied Army officers. Some of the speakers were: Robert Murphy, President Roosevelt's personal representative in North Africa, who spoke on "Some Phases of Our French Policy"; Harold Macmillan, M.P., British Minister Resident in North Africa; M. Henri Bonnet, Minister of Information of the French National Committee of Liberation; André Maurois, Captain Leon Torrou, ace G-man who tracked down Nazi spies in America before the war, Major Melvin Purvis, another FBI agent, and Captain Robert Neville, editor of *Stars and Stripes*.

Also the following British and American war correspondents: Gerald Norman, London *Times;* Demaree Bess, *Saturday Evening Post;* Helen Kirkpatrick, *Chicago Daily News;* Drew Middleton, *New York Times;* Cy Peterman, *Philadelphia Inquirer;* Quentin Reynolds, *Collier's;* Roland Stead, *Christian Science Monitor;* Merrill "Red" Mueller, NBC and *Newsweek;* H. R. Knickerbocker, Chicago *Sun* and Pierre Huss, International News Service.

Upon Dr. Isserman's return to the United States in the summer of 1943, Professor A. Buel Trowbridge, on leave of absence from Rollins College, Winter Park, Florida, was appointed by the Red Cross to take over direction of Town Hall.

Under Professor Trowbridge's direction, the program attained its greatest development. With good judgment and taste he chose the most interesting and significant subjects. He showed great skill as a moderator. Being warm and human, he kept the discussions on an intellectual level without sacrificing humor and entertainment values. The boys were diverted as well as entertained, a formula which spelled audience interest. In May, 1944, almost a year after its start, Professor Trowbridge moved the Red Cross Town Hall from North Africa to Italy where it went on winning new successes.

With the approach of spring, 1943, the Tunisian campaign picked up. The Allies occupied positions which threatened the Axis line of communication running from north to south. To extricate himself, Rommel, on February 14, launched an unexpected attack against the American troops west of Faid Pass in the direction of Gafsa. The Americans fought back, but lacking combat experience, they failed to make their counterattacks stick. Forced to give up Gafsa and Kasserine Pass, they established a new base at Tebessa just over the border in Algeria. Rommel's advance reached its high-water mark on February 22. His double-pronged assaults aimed at Thala and Tebessa were stopped cold by American infantry and artillery combined with British tanks and infantry. Here the U.S. Twelfth Air Force, flying in United Nations formations, contributed substantially to Rommel's defeat.

This was the turning point in the Tunisian campaign. The next day, February 23, Rommel was back in his familiar role of the pursued Desert Fox with Allied planes, like enraged eagles, pouncing upon his retreating columns.

General George S. Patton's reorganized Second Corps was soon to avenge Kasserine Pass. On March 17 the Americans recaptured Gafsa, and within a few days possession of El Guettar, Maknassy, and the Kasserine Pass passed into their hands.

The long-expected spring offensive got under way during the moonless night of March 20-21 when General Montgomery threw thunderbolts on Rommel's strong hill defenses in the Mareth Line. At the same time General Patton's American troops, the British First Army, and French contingents opened up from the other side. Five days later Lieutenant General Freyberg's New Zealanders made a brilliant flanking movement which finally forced Rommel to abandon the Mareth Line altogether.

On April 7, American and British Eighth Army patrols made contact on the Gafsa road a few miles southeast of El Guettar. This led to the co-ordination of all the Allied forces in North Africa. Montgomery no longer had to depend for his supplies upon the long and uncertain route around the Cape to Egypt and across the

Libyan desert; his needs now could be met much more expeditiously from North African bases. Also, now it was possible to shift Allied troops from one sector to another to meet specific demands of the campaign.

By the end of April the Allies had won complete mastery of the situation. The initiative was entirely in their hands. Their co-ordinated attacks by land, sea, and air forced the enemy back inexorably to be squeezed into the Tunis–Bizerte–Cap Bon triangle.

One of the decisive factors in this tremendous success was the Northwest African Air Forces. Formed on February 18, 1943, this organization integrated the whole of the United Nations' air strength in North Africa. Notwithstanding its immense size, it flew as one team, closely co-ordinating its activities with the movement of Allied ground forces. Its planes screened Allied maneuvers or spread a protective umbrella over attacking troops, and time and again saved Allied forces from savage enemy thrusts. They protected Allied shipping and bases, while attacking the shipping and bases of the enemy. They blasted Axis airfields and ports not only in Tunisia but in Sicily, Sardinia, and southern Italy. Ultimately they drove the enemy's air support from the skies, exposing Axis troops on the ground to merciless punishment from Allied artillery, mortar, armor, dive bombers, and fighters.

The American unit of this invincible air power was the Twelfth Air Force in command of Lieutenant General Carl Spaatz, who had succeeded Lieutenant General James H. Doolittle. In every major movement of the Tunisian campaign, American flyers contributed substantially toward victory.

American Red Cross doughnuts rolled into the Tunisian campaign late in March, about the time that the great spring offensive was beginning. The first doughnuts in North Africa were served to a surprised and pleased group of soldiers at Fifth Army headquarters in Oujda. Hot coffee and doughnuts were distributed from a Red Cross clubmobile by two Red Cross staff assistants, Mary Ross Moen, of Onawa, Iowa, former secretary to Isadore Lubin, economic advisor to President Roosevelt; and Lois Berney, of Fallon, Nevada, former White House secretary to Harry Hopkins. Their regular assignment was to meet troop trains. At that time there were heavy troop movements to the Tunisian front. Misses Moen and Berney met two trains a day, one in the afternoon, the other at midnight. To keep this schedule, the young women sometimes went without food or sleep, but they felt rewarded once they arrived at the station. The men were tired, dirty, and hungry, and sometimes had just come off a boat. When their officers announced, "Doughnuts and hot coffee; come and get 'em," they poured out of the train and literally danced on the platform.

General Montgomery had prohibited American or British women from going beyond Constantine. This ruled out Red Cross doughnuts to ground forces in Tunisia, except those served by Red Cross field directors.

General Spaatz, on the other hand, requested the Red Cross clubmobile program for his Twelfth Air Force personnel. He became so enthusiastic over the combination of hot coffee, doughnuts, and Red Cross girls as a morale booster that his own daughter, Katharine, became a clubmobile girl in England and later served in France.

Misses Moen and Berney were part of a pioneer ten-girl unit who staffed the first five Red Cross clubmobiles in North Africa. While they met the troop trains, their associates covered advanced air bases of the Twelfth Air Force. The latter, working in teams of two, were: Margaret Roblee, Providence, Rhode Island; Selma Norbeck, Washington, D. C., daughter of the late Senator from South Dakota; Betty Hitchcock, St. Louis, Missouri; Sue Macpherson, Saginaw, Michigan; Elsa Frame, Rydal, Pennsylvania; Margaret Ritchie Risdale, Spring Lake, New Jersey; Eleanor Preble, Bryn Mawr, Pennsylvania; and Lydia Sherwood, New York City, niece of Robert Sherwood, the playwright.

Each pair of clubmobiles operated out of one or the other of two large Air Force headquarters to service the airfields composing each wing. The girls were able to make at least one visit a week to every squadron and gun crew camp spread over many miles of the African countryside.

But bomber and fighter squadrons rated a visit every day they returned from a mission. The girls were told in code by military intelligence when a mission was expected to return. General Spaatz had arranged for this priority. It required the full time of two clubmobiles, one meeting bombers, the other the fighter escorts.

Serving airmen gave Red Cross clubmobile girls a conviction of being useful. The fliers had just been through a terrific ordeal and were pretty well worn down. They may have flown in sub-zero weather, and, perhaps, had not eaten for many hours. Some of their crew mates may not have come back, or had been brought home seriously wounded. One can well imagine what it meant to them to be greeted, as they climbed out of their planes, by attractive, wholesome American girls who laughed and kidded as they poured out hot coffee and dished out crisp doughnuts. The boys' tension was eased. They felt better and were able to give a more intelligent report of their mission in the briefing tent.

Nor were the antiaircraft crews and observation post details overlooked in their lonely, isolated outposts.

The clubmobile program was installed by the American Red Cross in all the war theaters to meet the demands of mobile warfare. In England, India, the Middle East, North Africa, Australia, New Guinea and elsewhere, U.S. troops were scattered over wide areas. The fixed Red Cross clubs did not fill their needs for leisure-time recreation. The problem was solved by the clubmobile which, essentially, was a club on wheels. Clubmobiles varied in size from the large convertible city transportation bus type to small trucks and station wagons, depending on the area and purposes to which they were assigned. Their equipment varied too. Usually a clubmobile had a doughnut machine and facilities to make enough coffee to keep up with the capacity of the doughnut machine. It also carried a circulating library of books and magazines, chewing tobacco, American cigarettes, writing paper, and a phonograph with a loud speaker.

While the first five clubmobiles in North Africa were staffed by teams of two girls, the normal complement was three girls, one of whom was designated the captain.

Soldiers regarded the presence of a man in a clubmobile as a reflection on their chivalry, and so only in areas of danger or where unusual conditions prevailed did a field director or assistant field director accompany a clubmobile unit.

The girls wore regulation overseas uniforms supplemented by heavy driving gloves, sturdy boots, practical raincoats, to say nothing of coveralls for that emergency repair job. The men preferred them in skirts rather than slacks. They were called "doughgirls," "doughnuteers," and "Rover girls."

A close-up of a clubmobile unit in action in North Africa is given in the following report by Eleanor Yinger, of Lansing, Michigan, a Red Cross staff assistant, who accompanied three "doughnuteers" to a lonely oupost:

"Don't bother to put any sugar in my coffee; just stick your finger in it, honey."

I laughed as the remark was new to me, but Rose Marie, ladling cream from a large can, whispered that I would be hearing it many times.

"Hey, where's that smile? A smile with every doughnut, we were told."

So absorbed was I in thinking of a clever rejoinder that I had forgotten to smile. I soon discovered that this long line of helmeted boys emerging from their camouflaged camp into the dusk of the clearing had come for our smiles as for our doughnuts and coffee.

That morning I had watched 2500 golden brown rings pop from their sizzling pan. Now I was to see an equal weight in smiles spread along that line of 800 men. In honor of our visit the lonely outpost had called out its band which played as we served.

I did not really belong there, but went along for the experience with the "three little sisters" of this Division. George Sperry, Glendale, California, clubmobile director, had also come to get things lined up for the evening.

Our clubmobile bore on its side the legend that its maintenance was provided for by the "American Legion Auxiliary, U.S.A." We were bringing an American institution—the doughnut—to the sons, brothers, and husbands of members of a great organization of American women back home, and serving them in their name.

"Hey, Bill, how many times are you going through that line?"

"Don't worry, you guys; I'm not after more doughnuts. I'm collecting smiles!"

Voices ring out above the band music, and occasionally we catch a remark from the group gathered behind us to those who are "sweating the line."

"You never liked coffee before, Mike."

"We never had KP's that looked like this," Mike retorts.

Five fingers are spread—five pegs for doughnuts. Ruth Bondy, Red Cross clubmobiler from Washington, D. C., deposits one on the forefinger and one on the thumb.

"I have a sick buddy back in the tent," he grins. "I don't expect you to believe me." Ruth slips a doughnut on the little finger.

"And I want one for my brother-in-law." Everyone laughs.

The joshing is no longer strained, and laughs reverberate throughout the little hillside clearing. The North African pines no longer seem strange, and the flaming rays of sun dropping to rest over the Atlas foothills, casting their bright reflections in the waters of the Mediterranean below us, speak benediction on this bit of America away from home. "Golly, but it's good to hear you girls laughing around here."

"Where do you live?" I am asked as the scoop of sugar drops into the cup. It is hard to see the two eyes that peer out from the shadows of the helmet.

"Michigan," I reply. "Where are you from?"

His canteen cup of coffee takes a rapid hazardous journey to his left hand as his right one grips mine, sugar scoop and all. "Illinois.

Golly, it's good to see someone from near home. And it sure is a treat to talk to an American girl."

Doughnuts, smiles, talk—that's what it takes to be sister to a whole division; and here I was, sharing the thrill of it all, and seeing just how three Red Cross girls carried doughnuts with smiles to thousands of men.

Ruth Bondy, Esther Crow, St. Louis, Missouri, and Rose Marie De Cotis, Watervliet, New York, carry full cargoes of charm and friendliness. I watched this Red Cross clubmobile unit during the day's operations and felt the contagion and warmth of their smiles.

"Did you make these doughnuts yourself, really?" the boys would ask as they passed along the line. The answer was yes, even to mixing and kneading the dough.

The line dwindles and attention is focused on the band. I can't tell exactly how it happened, but a space was cleared and we girls found ourselves dancing with the most jive-conscious of the boys, with a large hand-clapping audience surrounding us. It's quite an experience to jitterbug on a hillside with vines and twigs decorating your oxfords. Just as you begin wishing one leg were shorter than the other, you find that now you are towering on a higher plane than your partner, looking over his head at a laughing group of amused GIs. Then comes the exciting moment. Your partner swings you out, and you find yourself on a rapid descent down the hill, jerked out of reach of the line of observers by the strong arm of your partner.

Ruth, who is the jitterbug specialist, having raised more dust on the hillsides of North Africa than any other dancing daughter, tells of one sad experience. Her partner failed to retrieve her on that downward swing and she landed underneath a truck. Rescued, she was swung into another round of rugcutting and has survived with a story to tell her grandchildren.

Bill Holt, New York City, the division's Red Cross field director, has a good voice. He sang "Star Dust" and "Night and Day" and soon it was so quiet you could hear the lump in your throat. But this was no time for homesickness. Bill soon had us all singing. How the hills rang, until "Goodnight, Ladies" proclaimed that the clubmobile was ready to convey its little unit back to headquarters. Shouts of "Thanks for coming," and "Come again soon," followed us down the road.

The lonely figure of a guard distinguished itself from the surrounding shadows. "Did you get a doughnut?" called one of the girls. Several had been saved for these sentinels along the way. Their faces looked happy as they stood at the car door.

"Good night," called the Red Cross girls. "See you later."

This evening the officers told us how much that "see you later" means to the men.

Why? I wondered about this as our little clubmobile made its way homeward. Why do soldiers sometimes find themselves speechless when they try to talk to us girls? Why does it all mean so much to them?

Another glance at Ruth, Esther, and Rose Marie gave me the answer. They represent everything these boys admire in American womanhood—vivacity, grace, charm, virtue, beauty, enthusiasm, intelligence, and that wholesome friendliness and interest that reminds them of sister and wife, girl friend and mother.

The final phase of the Tunisian campaign was swift and devastating. On May 1, units of the U.S. Second Corps captured Hill 609 (Djebel Tahent), key to Bizerte. This battle became famous for the skirmish of the stone walls, which took place in an olive grove high up on the hill. Two American platoons faced a unit of Germans across a stone-bordered path only fifteen yards wide and defeated the enemy in a skirmish fought at point-blank range.

On May 7 the U.S. Second Corps blasted its way into Bizerte, while British armored forces rolled into Tunis. Organized Axis resistance folded up along the entire front. Three days later, Axis units who had fled into Cap Bon for an attempted Dunkirk (frustrated by a combined Allied air and naval blockade) gave up to the British and French. On May 13 the enemy surrendered unconditionally. The North African show was over. In the final days the Allies captured more than a quarter of a million Axis prisoners, half of them Germans from crack Panzer units, and the booty in planes, tanks, and other equipment was enormous.

About a week after the victory, the crack U.S. Ninth Artillery Division, whose shells had helped check the Germans at Thala and who were in the vanguard of American troops entering Bizerte, received an unusual and unexpected reward: ice cream from the American Red Cross. Rita Hume, Red Cross clubmobile worker, former Seattle newspaper woman, who helped serve the ice cream, described the event in a report from Algiers. Her narrative follows:

"Ice cream?" bellowed the general.

"Look, Miss, we've been living in fox holes and eating canned rations for four months. We've been fighting Germans at Thala. We shelled hell out of them at Bizerte. We've almost forgotten what an American girl looks like. And now, four of you suddenly pop up in this god-forsaken field and tell us there's ice cream."

"Ice cream! Holy smoke—where is it?"

Those words gave four American girls their biggest thrill in North Africa. It all began when Joe Mason, American Red Cross field director and former Miami physical education executive, arrived at the American Red Cross club in Algiers with news that one of the famous artillery divisions that took Bizerte was on its way back from the front. "Little Joe," as the gang in his division call him, was one of our Red Cross field men at the front. He came in with his helmet, his dirty G.I. clothes and a big grin. His boys had been right in the thick of the fighting for three months. Why couldn't we meet them at their bivouac with ice cream?

It meant a four-hour drive through the Atlas Mountains to do it. It meant disrupting the whole club program for the day. But Marge Bomberger, of Chicago and Larry Cadwell, of Urbana, Illinois, two of our club directors, said, "Sure." So they canceled the afternoon quiz program and the unit dance that night. Our famous ice cream factory was scraped to the last freezer. At 1:30 that afternoon we started off, two cars and a truck.

We met the convoy on the road, after we had driven for three hours. Mile after mile of dusty khaki-toned jeeps, trucks, command cars strung out along the narrow winding road. Perched beside gun mounts, bouncing along in jeeps, peering out of trucks, there they were, the victorious American soldiers. We'd wave and yell at every truck and jeep. Suddenly, as we went by, the khaki clan would wake up to the fact that an American girl had just shouted "hello" and they'd go simply crazy. The whole column would wave and yell and honk. What would they have done if they had known then that the truck following us was loaded with ice cream?

They were a grand sight, healthy and brown. Some of them had poppies strung through the green camouflage netting on their helmets. Bouquets of flowers hung from their jeeps. Most of the men had painted names on their cars. The bright yellow letterings proclaimed such characteristic American corn as "Perk 'n Putt" or "Gypsy Lee."

We finally came to a little French village where the whole populace had turned out to meet the victorious American Ninth Artillery Division. A French guard stopped us, checked our credentials and motioned us on to the bivouac area a few miles beyond the town.

The bivouac area was located in miles of flat field which stretched out on either side of the road. The convoy had already begun to turn off, cars spreading out over the fields in all directions. We ploughed across the rutted, grassy hummocks as far as we could go in our car. Then, afraid of challenging our tired sedan any further, we struck out for the general's headquarters. It proved to be nothing more than the field on which he was standing, one khaki-colored sedan marked by his yellow star, and a small pup tent half heartedly swaying in the breeze. The convoy was moving busily in around him.

Many of the soldiers were already setting up camp. Each group clustered around their own vehicles. Some, stripped to the waist, were busy washing up in their helmets. White lathered faces conspicuously announced the fact that shaving formalities were still observed in this traveling army. "We've been doing this for months," said one of the fellows with whom we stopped to talk. "And this is nothing," chimed in a pal. "Most of the time there's been rain and mud. Boy! Remember how cold it was up there at Thala?"

"We never expected to see you way out here," said the general when he recovered from his first surprise. "But these boys certainly deserve it. They've done a magnificent job. They're the ones, you know, who held the Germans at Thala after the Kasserine break-through. And we were the first ones into Bizerte. We've been fighting constantly since February 15. We've moved this whole division from Bizerte. Tomorrow morning at 5:30 we'll be on our way again. But, say, what about that ice cream?"

The next thing we knew we were bouncing along in a jeep with Captain Harry O. Ellis from Jonesboro, Tennessee. We headed over to the ice cream truck where a crowd of soldiers had collected. The word went out and soon jeeps were tearing madly across the rutted fields, nearly running down the Arabs who were already on the spot bargaining with their eggs.

When the jeeps converged upon us, we discovered they were driven by agents from the several units bivouacked on the field. With three thousand men to serve, it looked like we'd have to do the serving mess by mess.

"The agent from the 34th has arrived," Captain Ellis announced.

Gwen Barrows, a tall brunette from Boston, piled into the jeep between two grinning soldiers and bounced off across the African meadow with an ice cream container jiggling precariously in the back seat. Gwen was on the editorial staff of the *Christian Science Monitor* before she became a Red Cross girl last winter.

126

"Agents from the 27th reporting, sir," said another soldier as he rushed up. "Jeepers, are we really going to have ice cream?"

"Honey, you sure are," drawled red headed Cheshire Cox of Washington, D. C., in the dulcet accent of the South, and off went Cheshire in another jeep between two completely bewitched soldiers. Marge Bomberger, who was managing the show, set off in another jeep. I drew a roving assignment with Sergeant Arthur Daniel, of Hollywood, a recent arrival from a photographic assignment with the British fleet at Malta. He had his camera ready for action.

By now, the whole field had heard the news. The effect as we drove from one mess line to another was like wind blowing through a field of wheat. Everyone would wave like mad. There were still a few doubting souls. One captain insisted he was being kidded as we drove by to announce the ice cream's arrival. He never did show up at his mess. At another field, five soldiers, stripped to the waist, were batting a ball around. One of the girls called out "foul ball" just as an unknowing fellow was about to catch a fly. Last we saw of him he was still staring at the feminine apparition, mouth wide open, the ball scudding off into the bushes.

We continued on our ice cream rounds. The minute a jeep would arrive with girl and ice cream, it would be overwhelmed with shouting soldiers brandishing mess kits.

"Hey, are you from Brooklyn?" someone was sure to yell, or "Ice cream? It's a mirage."

Half the time we'd just give up and dish the ice cream right from the jeep, feeling like something out of Hollywood. Then we'd tear onto the next mess. Everyone wanted to talk.

It was after eight o'clock when we finally got back to the headquarters mess where the general and his aides were waiting for us. The general, a sandy-haired man who wears GI togs and a helmet like his men, sat down to the table on a chair picked up at Ferryville. I drew a canned tomato box.

Nearby, the long aerial attached to a radio-equipped jeep jittered in the breeze. The faint strains of modern songs drifted over to us. A big red full moon had risen over the California-like countryside. Stretched out in bedding rolls spread on the ground beside their trucks were some artillery men, already in for the night. But most of them were very much on hand when we passed out cigarettes, matches and yes, even chewing tobacco, later.

Along about ten o'clock it suddenly dawned on us that we had a four hour drive back through the mountains. We hated to go—

it was so much fun talking to the men. As Larry Cadwell said later, every bit of the work involved was well worth it.

Driving home presented unexpected problems. Ten thousand German prisoners were interned along the route. Two of them had escaped. So the three Red Cross cars maneuvered the dark winding roads in a tight little convoy, stopped frequently by French guards.

So ended our visit to the returning heroes of the American Ninth Artillery Division.

It was not all ice cream, however, for America's conquering heroes. It had been a hard-fought bloody campaign, exacting a terrific toll, though the Axis armies suffered five times as many casualties as the Allies. The grand total of all Allied casualties was less than 70,000. United States losses since the initial landings were 18,558, of whom 2,184 were killed, 9,437 wounded, and 6,937 missing or prisoners of war, according to Secretary of War Stimson. British casualties totaled 35,000.

Serving the nearly 10,000 American wounded was a responsibility of the American Red Cross. Twelve Red Cross hospital workers arriving with their units provided these services to the first casualties. Their number was steadily increased until by October 1, 1943, there were 185 workers in fifty-five American hospitals in North Africa. A Red Cross hospital team consisted of a field director, a social worker, a recreation worker, a staff assistant, and a secretary—all women.

During the campaign the large American general hospitals were all located west from Algiers to Casablanca; here Red Cross girls were on duty. The evacuation tent hospitals at the front were covered only by male field directors, due to General Montgomery's rule barring women from the forward areas. From Algiers east to the Tunisian border were the British general hospitals. There were many American patients in their wards. But they were not overlooked. American Red Cross hospital visiting units called on them on a regular schedule, bringing boxes filled with cigarettes, reading and writing material, and toilet articles. Visiting these American boys, homesick for families and the sight of an American face, was one of the most satisfying and moving experiences imaginable.

At the conclusion of the campaign a number of general hospitals, some in tents, were set up in Tunisia, chiefly in the Bizerte area.

Red Cross hospital workers served the sick and wounded in the same way as Red Cross men did able-bodied soldiers—with additions. Experienced social workers handled family welfare cases involving

Home Service, procured medical and social histories from home to aid the doctors when a man's condition was unsatisfactory. Recreation for hospital patients was solely the job of the Red Cross girls. They, too, pitched a tent and corraled magazines, games, music, and boondoggling materials for patients well enough to walk around but whose long weeks in the hospital were interminably monotonous. They operated movies in the wards. They wrapped Purple Hearts to mail home. They did shopping errands. They wrote letters for men too ill or too bandaged to write their own. They kept the library books circulating, and played the radio. They gave Private Joe a pencil and paper so he might try his hand at sketching. They took a whole ambulance load of crutch patients to the movies in a near-by town. They—but let Carolyn Chapin, Mt. Vernon, New York, Red Cross correspondent, take you to the 12th General Hospital in North Africa, where you can observe Red Cross hospital workers in action: *

"Is this madhouse always like this?" asked a paratrooper as he entered the Red Cross office at the 12th General Hospital.

The Red Cross girls in the office looked up, mildly surprised at his remark. After seven months' evolution they thought things were pretty well organized, and they were used to the kaleidoscope of humanity that flickered in and out of their office. To them it was a normal afternoon, but to anyone watching Red Cross at work in an army hospital behind the fighting lines for the first time, the shifting pattern might easily be bewildering.

Jen and Fran were in the office. "Jen," Genevieve Friedenthal from Sacramento, California, is the assistant field director of the Red Cross unit and "Fran," Frances Bernhard, from Bayside, Long Island, New York, is her fellow social worker. The "office" is a small room near the door of a cement "villa" which has been turned over to Red Cross for their part of the hospital work. The hospital is a collection of such villas, spread over the cliff of a Mediterranean summer resort.

It was hot and Fran had pushed up the sleeves of her gray seersucker uniform. Jen said she looked like a laundress. That set Fran dreaming. She had a vivid picture of the Red Cross girls going into the laundry business and making millions of dollars and being able to charter a ship on which they'd transport thousands and thousands of radios, magazines, ditty bags and cokes—enough for every single American boy lying in a hospital in Africa. When

* Miss Chapin was killed in an airplane crash while on duty in Italy, May 10, 1944.

Red Cross hospital girls dream, they always dream in terms of more supplies.

A patient crawling under the desk to chase a wayward ping-pong ball brought Fran back to reality.

It came from the adjoining recreation room. There the radio was blaring and a perspiration-soaked Negro boy was squeezing hot boogie from the piano. The balls pinged on the ping-pong tables, and a group of patients, huddled over a map, were planning the Italian campaign.

Joe and Mike, two patients looking as alike as Bobbsey twins in sailor hats and chest casts, came in to discuss loans to tide them over until they were invalided home. They filled out application blanks, with the girls' help, and went off to get their ward officer's approval.

One patient requested British air-mail forms; a Brooklyn twang demanded phonograph needles. They were referred to the Library, in the next room, where an enlisted man of the hospital staff, loaned to the Red Cross, presided over books and supplies. A patient came in to exhibit the posters he was making for a variety show.

A medical officer stuck his head in, wanting to borrow a copy of *Stars and Stripes*, Army newspaper, to read while he sat in the barber's chair. "I know you people are only supposed to give them to patients, but..." The girls lent him a copy with their blessing.

A ward man reported that a patient in Ward 13 thought his WAC cousin might be stationed nearby. The ward was all excited. The girls promised to find out.

While Fran wrote a letter to his mother for Howard, a patient with a broken neck, Jen's low voice was heard soothing another patient who couldn't understand why his baby hadn't been born yet. The cabled inquiry had gone out to Red Cross in the States.

An emotionally upset patient came in to chat, but left in a huff because there were so many people in the office, and Fran made a mental note to visit him in his ward.

Two nurses came in, one to request the Red Cross to write for a missing barracks bag, and one to request a case history be obtained for the medical officer from a patient's former company.

An artillery lieutenant popped in to invite all the girls to a dance.

Out in the patio someone was demanding a French newspaper; the girls abstractedly shoved a copy through the window.

Mildred "Milly" Leinback, Reading, Pennsylvania, recreation

worker on the Red Cross team, entered with the Post Exchange sergeant to go into a huddle over the week's supplies for patients whose pay had not caught up with them.

Wenonah "Win" Wahler, Livingston, New Jersey, the other recreation girl, stepped in just then to write the name of the day's movie on the blackboard.

"How do you spell 'val-pak'?" asked a one-armed boy banging away on the typewriter.

Nancy Gatch, Washington, D. C., the unit's secretary, looked up from her filing to announce with consternation that she had run out of cards. Whereupon Jen decided on a shopping trip to town the next day for banking, supplies, and shopping errands for the patients.

A surgery major sent in for a coke for a wired jaw case who couldn't eat.

"I've written a song!" cried a patient, bursting in. He waved a sheet of paper. The girls smiled and said, "That's nice." He closed the door and with complete unselfconsciousness flooded the tiny room with his rich baritone, singing a lyric about Africa and Jersey moons.

Jack came back with the string. Nancy was called to the phone over at headquarters. The soldier who had brought the message, stopped to show a picture of his girl. It was explained to a bewildered patient, exploring on his first day out of bed, that this was not the PX, and that Red Cross did not sell anything. The Bobbsey twins came in with their signed loan papers. Talk was general, ranging from Radio City to the white sand of Florida.

Milly set off for the park with a music group.

Grausi, a French civilian helper, tried to tell Jen, with gestures, that he needed bigger screws for the desk chairs he was trying to fix.

Nancy's phone call turned out to be a cable for a man in one of Fran's wards. Fran shoved back her chair, applied lipstick briefly, tucked pencil, money order forms and brief service cards in her pocket and stopped to roll down her sleeves. Jen had said she looked like a laundress.

Why not? Red Cross girls in an Army hospital do about everything else for the patients.

Frances Bernhard, one of the Red Cross girls mentioned in the preceding narrative, wrote many letters to loved ones of patients at 12th General Hospital. As Americans and British had fought side by side, and occupied cots in the same hospital wards, her letters went to Great Britain as well as the United States. Her replies were numerous—letters of thanks and of entreaty, letters showing the anxiety and the courage of those who waited for their men to come home.

Among her collection, the following letters, their writers unidentified, were quoted in one of her monthly reports from the hospital:

Mrs. G.—— Whose Son Died

Dear Miss ——:

We received your letter of October 5th and we appreciate your writing to us very much. L—— never did get to come home. He died while in the hospital in Brooklyn, New York so I could not give him your good wishes. The Navy Department said he had a hemorrhage of the brain and he died while asleep. If you can tell us anything about him while in the hospital there we would appreciate it. God bless you, dear.

Sincerely yours,
Mrs. G——

An English Wife

My dear Friend:

I am writing to thank you for your kindness in letting me know the whereabouts and welfare of my beloved husband. I have been beside myself with worry. He is my whole concern. How much is he hurt? I would very much like to know. I would dearly love to see him as I could do a lot towards making him better, I know. If he were only in this country somewhere I could and would get to see him, but I know I will not have the lucky chance. I thank you from the bottom of my heart for the kindness of writing to me on his behalf. I know you have indeed made him happy and also myself and my children. Please may I ask you another favor for us. We need a written certificate from the doctor giving the time my husband entered the hospital as I keep his club paid here for him and then I can draw the club money for him.

You say he is a very fine person. He is, and to think he is so respected all those miles away is so wonderful. I am so very proud of him. Would you please show him this letter and also give him all my deepest love, and that I am always waiting his return. The children both send their daddy darling all their love and wish that he will be coming home soon. Goodnight and God bless you for the great kindness you have wrought.

Mrs. B——

The Father of Four Boys in the Service

Dear Madam:

I do thank you for writing to me for my son as I have been so very worried about him. As you say, it is hard, for I have one a prisoner in Japanese hands and then there was no news from "Johnny." You can imagine how I felt when I got your letter after six months with no word. I am very proud of him and my other three sons too. I do hope he continues to progress. Thank you very much. I am,

Yours sincerely,

Mr. R——

A Fiancée

Dear Miss ——:

Received your letter in which you wrote for my boy friend "Joe." It was so kind of you to take over for him and it made me the happiest girl in the world to hear from him after such a long time. His buddy told me his eyes were hurt. I want to thank you a million for making it possible to hear from him. I hope this finds you in the best of health. Give my love to "Joe" and God bless you both.

Sincerely yours,

Miss M——

An Anxious Father

Dear ——:

I am very much obliged to you for the pleasure you have given me and my family in writing this cheerful letter of my son "John." God bless you for it. You see, I knew that he was injured on the arms and it had me worried very much. How could he fit into society, the cost of living, supporting himself, his wife, and I hope some day his family. One of his buddies, Lt. M——, has returned to the United States and I saw him at the hospital. He told me that my boy was hit on the arms and chest. I think, like you, that that was an heroic deed of my boy, himself suffering terribly. He crawled up to this Lieutenant, cut his trousers and applied sulfanilimide to the shattered leg. To know that "John" expects to be able to write to me himself next week fills me with joy. His mother cried over the letter. Again thanking you and wishing you all the best in the world. God bless you. I remain,

Sincerely,

Mr. W——

A Brother in the Army

Dear Miss ——:

I was more than glad to hear that my brother is getting along fine. I appreciate your writing to me. I sure sweated the letter out. I know the location where he is at so I will try to get up to see him if possible, but I don't know when it will be so tell him to be very good until I get up to see him. I hope that you can stand his harmonica playing. I am glad you were able to find one for him, but I know he is not so good at it. Tell him that everything is fine where I am at. It is now time for all soldiers to be in bed so I will bring this to a close. Hoping to see you and my brother soon.

Sincerely,

J——

[P.S. He got here.]

The Mother of a Critically Ill Patient

Dear Miss ——:

I am writing to thank you for every kindness you have shown to my darling son. I also want to thank you for writing to me for him. I can't tell you how glad I was to get your letters. It was a great help to get letters from some one who had seen him. He is a very very dear son. I couldn't tell you how grieved I am that he is so badly hurt. I am sure he has begun to improve some now. I am sorry you wasn't allowed to tell me about the extent of his injuries. Thank you kindly for sending me the Surgeon General's address. He referred my letter to the Adjutant General. I hope he will tell me. Does my son get my letters? and the pictures I sent him. Please tell him to take care of himself, and get well. We love him and want him back. Thank you again. God bless you.

Mrs. S——

The Mother of a Patient Who Died in the Hospital

Dear Miss ——:

Received your letter and I can't write in words how glad I was to get it. You will never know how much better we all felt when we knew how good you all was to him. Yes, we were so in hopes there could be a mistake. We just could not give up until we got your letter and the nurse's letter which the War Department forwarded to us. I just wish I could meet you both and put my arms around your necks and thank you. It is so hard to give him up, but the Lord's will must be done and not ours. We surely appreciate everything that has been done. Thank you for sending me his Purple Heart. Please thank the doctors and nurses for me. If there is anything we can do for you here please write and tell me, or if there is anything you would like me to send you, candy or cake or anything, we would just love to do something for you. It will soon be one year since "Roy" went to camp. He didn't even get to come back on time. Again we thank you so much and I pray God will bless you in all your work.

Love,

Mrs. G——

A Wife

Dear Miss——:

It was indeed a pleasure receiving the money order which my husband, "T——" had you purchase to send to me, and your very gracious note accompanying the same. I'm very happy to know that he is coming along nicely and thankful to you for your kindness in visiting with my husband. I'm sure that something like you're doing brings many hours of sunshine and pleasure to my husband and many other boys, which they'll never forget.

To thank you would hardly describe my feelings. I'm very proud of my husband and proud to think that someone as nice as you has been so nice to us.

Sincerely,

Mrs. F——

The Mother of an Only Son

Dear Miss ——:

I received my son, Cpl. M——'s Purple Heart. I and his father are very proud of him. Not only of him, but of all the rest of you over there for you are all doing a grand job. We wish to thank you for your attention to our son. He has told us all about you. As you were so kind to write to us and let us know about our son, I am going to ask you for another favor. Do you think it could be arranged that M—— could come home for his convalescing period? We have a modern home with modern improvements. We are located 25 miles from a Veteran's Hospital. I have had some training as a nurse and I will give M—— all my time. We also have a very good doctor. Please let me know if this could be arranged. In any case, thanking you, I remain,

Mrs. C——

135

Dear Miss ——:

Thank you so much again for sending the letter for "F——." My father also sends his compliments and thank you. We think it is most kind of you. We are so glad and thank God he is in such good hands. I am sure he is a good boy. He is the baby of our family and we think the world of him. He's got a lovely nature (of course, he can be a young devil when he likes). I have had a lovely report of Major —— and yourself from Trooper "L——" who was a patient in your hospital. He was kind enough to write me when he arrived in England and told me all about "F——." I am expecting him to come any day. If, dear, you come to England, we would love to know you. Would you call us? There would always be a welcome for you. Thank you again and God bless you.

Mrs. P——

Later: the Same Mother:

We heard from the War Department that our "F——" passed away. We are all so broken-hearted about it. He fought so hard to come back to us as he had everything to live for and we all loved him so much. I have just come back from Cornwall where I have been with —— (his fiancée) to break the news. I am so sorry for her. It is so much worse when one is away from home and one's people. Your letter helped me. I understood that "F——" did not know he was dying and had a peaceful death. We sat here and imagined all sorts of things until your letter came. All we got from the War Office was his death certificate which nearly knocked us all silly for a time. Will you, dear, thank the doctors and nurses for all they did to keep "F——" with us. We thank God we knew everything possible was done for him to come back to us. As our prayers were not answered, God needed him most, but even that doesn't stop this dreadful heartache. Everybody that knew "F——" loved him. We did so want him back. Would you like a photograph of him? If so, I would love to send you one so that you can see what a nice face he had before he was burned. We will always make you welcome if you come to call.

If "F——" ever asked me to do anything or ever spoke about anything he would have liked done, would you let me know. I would be ever so grateful to you. He was my baby and I loved him so much, but I would never have liked him to come back an invalid. He would never have stood up to it. Please God he is happy. I do hope to get news where he is buried so I can get to see his grave as soon as possible. I suppose it sounds rather silly, but when I am

at our place by the sea on the cliffs, I feel I am much nearer "F——."
I suppose it is because his body is on the other side of the sea. We
all get funny ideas in our head sometimes, but I know you will understand. Thank you for all you have done for my "F——" and for
your kindness to me. God bless you and all the best of everything.

Mrs. P——

Chapter VIII

CHINA—BURMA—INDIA

"The American Red Cross has made an outstanding contribution to the high morale of the soldiers in the China Burma India Theater. Its ceaseless efforts put forth in conjunction with the Special Service work of the Army have helped to provide a wholesome diversion for the soldiers from their rigorous and exacting war duties. Throughout its work in hospitals, recreation centers, canteens, and other activities, the Red Cross has done much to fill the void in the lives of the fighting men who are thousands of miles from their homes and loved ones...."

—LIEUTENANT GENERAL JOSEPH W. STILWELL,
*Commanding General, United States Army
Forces in China, Burma and India.*

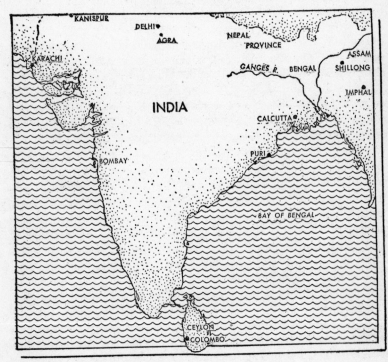

A GROUP OF EIGHT AMERICAN RED CROSS WORKERS—THE FIRST assigned to the China-Burma-India theater—arrived on May 16, 1942, at Karachi on the west coast of India.

They found Karachi overcrowded, rowdy, and boisterous—a town with a distinctive international flavor, yet reminiscent of the early American frontier. The U.S. Tenth Air Force—fighters, bombers and ground crews—shared the Karachi airport, largest in India, with the Royal Air Force. Army Services of Supply—engineers, port and quartermaster battalions, composed of mixed Negro and white troops—were also stationed in the ancient town. Mingling with American soldiers in Karachi's streets were American sailors and merchant seamen, and seamen of many United Nations, who had brought precious lend-lease cargoes safely through submarine-infested waters. Warehouses were jammed to the roof with the vital stuff (and with about 800 tons of American Red Cross China Relief stocks) intended for shipment over the Burma Road to hard-pressed China. And along the water front there was confusion, which the engineers and port battalions sought to clear. The docks were piled high with trucks, ammunition, small arms, artillery pieces, fuel, and other matériel, while out in the harbor lay scores of ships waiting to be unloaded, with additional war cargoes.

The congestion at Karachi (and at Bombay and other ports of western India) was the aftermath of Japan's lightning campaign in southeastern Asia. Within three months after Pearl Harbor, Hong Kong, Singapore, and the Netherlands Indies had fallen to the enemy. Thailand, having joined Japan's so-called "Greater East Asia Co-Prosperity Sphere," served as a springboard for the invasion of Burma in mid-January, 1942. Rangoon, Burma's chief port, the docks and warehouses of which were similarly overcrowded with China-bound stocks, was pounded repeatedly by Japanese planes. When it was finally abandoned by its British garrison early in March, 1942, Rangoon was a shambles. By a diversionary action, Lieutenant General Stilwell's Fifth and Sixth Chinese Armies saved this garrison from annihilation as it fought its way northward toward India through the Japanese lines.

From then on the story in Burma was one of continuous retreat for the British and Chinese forces and the few Americans who had come to work on the Burma Road. As the Allies grew weaker, the Japanese, reinforced and supplied by air, sea, and land, constantly increased in strength. They outmanned, outgunned, and outmaneuvered the Allied forces, whom General Stilwell himself characterized as "a piecemeal ragtag and bobtail affair." They employed the same tactics that had proved so successful in Malaya and the Netherlands Indies—infiltration and flanking movements well adapted to this rugged terrain. Moreover, they ruled the airways. The Flying Tigers and RAF squadrons fought heroically and took a heavy toll of Japanese formations but, with the odds against them, could not materially affect the outcome. In all Burma there was not a single antiaircraft gun, according to General Stilwell.

The retreating troops salvaged what supplies they could use and tried to destroy the remainder, but a not inconsiderable quantity fell into enemy hands. With the loss of Lashio at the head of the Burma Road on April 30, and of Mandalay several days later, Burma's doom was sealed. Fleeing British and Chinese troops and civilian refugees were pushed into a pocket in northwestern Burma. From there thousands of them were rescued by air in RAF and U.S. Army planes. For the rest, escape lay in plodding across the mountainous jungles into India, subsisting on food dropped by parachute from Allied planes.

General Stilwell, who had refused a plane, led one of the retreating columns out of Burma starting from Wuntho, on May 4. It was a mixed group of soldiers, nurses, and civilians—Americans, Britons, Burmese, Chinese, Indians, and Anglo-Indians. Among them was Dr. Gordon S. Seagrave of the American Baptist Mission, who subsequently became famous through his book, *Burma Surgeon*. Another was Major Frank D. Merrill, who was to return to northern Burma two years later and crack the Japanese positions there wide open with his fabulous "Merrill's Marauders."

At the end of a grueling twenty-day trek that brought him to Imphal in the India border country, General Stilwell flew into New Delhi. Wearing his old-fashioned campaign hat, khaki trousers, and a shirt without the three stars of his rank, he was still the redoubtable "Uncle Joe." Of the Burma campaign, he said:

"I claim we got a hell of a beating. We got run out of Burma and it is humiliating as hell. I think we ought to find out what caused it, go back, and retake it."

By June, India, Allied supply base for blockaded China, and base of operations for any offensive into Burma, was herself in imminent danger of invasion. Rommel's Afrika Korps had swept across the Libyan-Egyptian desert to threaten the Suez Canal and India's northern border. At the same time powerful Japanese forces were poised on her eastern border. Overhead enemy squadrons ranged far and wide bombing Calcutta and other mainland targets. The Andaman Islands off the Bay of Bengal were occupied, while in the bay itself a formidable Japanese task force had closed Calcutta and other East Indian ports to Allied shipping. The burden of supplying India's and China's needs was shifted to Karachi and other ports along the west coast.

This was the military situation, then, as the small American Red Cross staff tackled the staggering job that lay ahead.

This pioneer staff consisted of the following: field director—Porter C. Layne, Louisville, Kentucky; assistant field directors—Tim H. Kirk, Chicago, Illinois, and Richard B. Eldridge, New York City; hospital workers—Alice A. Todd, North Attleboro, Massachusetts; Jeannette Ross, Bloomington, Illinois; Beatrice M. Lynch, Mason City, Iowa; and Mrs. Lois Nickerson, Indianapolis, Indiana; secretary—Dorothy Ann Martin, Louisville, Kentucky.

While the rest of the staff set up shop in Karachi, Kirk, who later became assistant director of operations in the China-Burma-India theater, flew to Chungking for an interview with General Stilwell.

General Stilwell told Kirk the Army faced an acute morale problem that would become aggravated with expanding military operations. Well aware of the great need for Red Cross services, Stilwell suggested that Kirk visit as many of the Army posts and stations as possible, survey the needs, and report them to Red Cross National Headquarters in Washington.

Kirk's survey, and the specific requests of General Stilwell and his unit commanding officers, eventually led to the development of a sound Red Cross program closely integrated with the Army program and adapted to the peculiar needs of the China-Burma-India theater. But the path was rough and beset by innumerable obstacles and heartbreaks.

The major problems all related to the great distances to be covered. China-Burma-India was the largest theater of action in the global war. It stretched from the Arabian Sea on the west to the Bay of Bengal and the heart of Free China on the far east; from the Indian Ocean and Ceylon on the south, northward to 10,000 feet or more up into the Himalayas, and to the border of Asiatic Russia. Red Cross personnel and supplies had to come halfway around the world, and Red Cross installations at Army posts and stations were dispersed over an area greater than that of the United States. Communications were difficult; the mails were often slow, and the telephone of little use except locally. Transportation by rail was painfully slow, frequently involving transfer from standard to narrow gauge tracks; a train journey that in the States might have been made in a day required five days in India. Air travel, when available, often involved days of waiting at stopovers where backlogs necessarily took precedence.

The original staff at Karachi formed the nucleus of an organization that by August 31, 1944, numbered 532 trained, efficient workers, aided by volunteers and locally employed natives. It required perfect health, stamina, and intestinal fortitude to tackle the rugged assignments that fell to Red Cross workers, men and women, in this part of the world.

First of all, there was the climate:

One year ago [said Tim H. Kirk] if someone had tried to explain to me how hot it was in India, I would not have had the background to understand what they were talking about. For, until one has experienced the intensity of the heat in this country it is impossible to comprehend what heat means. This sun does not burn nor blister as it does in the States. But when one is in it for a few minutes he feels as though he has been inoculated with a lethargy serum which absolutely stifles ambition.

In contrast to the heat, there is one area held down by American troops where during the monsoon season more rain falls than on any other section of the world—between 400 and 500 inches. The huts in which the soldiers live are propped up on sticks anywhere from eighteen inches to eight feet off the rain-soaked earth. All leather goods mildew. Trunks and valises containing clothing and personal belongings are stacked on bricks off the floor to prevent mildew. Ants, crickets, termites, weevils and other pests find their way into valises no matter how securely locked. During the monsoon season the recreation problem is enormous. It is difficult to keep Red Cross clubs attractive because the floor is too damp for rugs and carpets, while chairs and other furniture fall apart as the lumber rots. And outdoor sports are impossible because the grounds are pools of water.

The heat, the rains, and the prevalence of tropical diseases resulted in nearly ten per cent of all Red Cross club workers being hospitalized at one time. Some clubs reported a higher percentage of malaria victims. Illness caused burdens to be shifted to the remaining staff workers, who ran chances of breaking under the added strain.

The burden of maintaining the spirit of America's fighting men in this theater fell heaviest on the Red Cross girls, who far outnumbered the men on the staff. In the fall of 1942 the Red Cross assigned four young women to clubs in Karachi, New Delhi, Assam, and China. They did their work so successfully that commanding officers of many other posts and stations clamored for Red Cross girls. National Headquarters assigned a steady stream of them to this theater, but the demand could not be filled adequately. One result was that Red Cross workers stretched themselves thin and sometimes overtaxed their strength. Yet they stuck to their jobs. One of them, Lillian Stevens, of Santa Monica, California, a hospital worker, had to be dragged out of Chakulia after she had lost twenty pounds. A rest brought her back on her feet, and as hospital consultant in crafts she made an outstanding record.

Walking about in GI shoes, mud-caked boots and coveralls, a Red Cross girl lost her individuality, though not necessarily her femininity. Wherever she served she was part of the military establishment, sharing the discomforts and privations of the soldiers. She washed out of an inverted helmet bowl and bathed under an open-air makeshift shower. Cosmetics taken for granted by American women—cold cream, lipstick, and rouge—were out of reach. Such civilian clothing as she was able to bring in her foot locker, hoarded for special occasions, showed the scars of war. Dresses could not hold up under the rock pounding and heavy charcoal ironing of the local *dhobi*, or laundryman. Her only girdle was chewed to tatters by crickets. She had to go stockingless—how could she wear something that long ago had succumbed to climate, ants, and various other vicious insects? She made her way about (when she could thumb a ride) in a jeep, weapons carrier, or Army truck. Powder room? Call it that if you will—that small, lantern-lit mud hut at the end of the pebbly lane. Except for the Saturday night dance at the Red Cross club, there was no night life in a jungle clearing in India. The darkness hid lurking danger in the form of a cobra, scorpion, or that deadliest of snakes, the banded krait, whose venom was known to cause death in a matter of minutes. And from the neighboring jungle came weird noises made by animals and tree life with names found only in the encyclopedias; and the rhythmic beat of head-hunters' drums.

A favorite GI quip was, "Who boosts Red Cross morale when *it* is low?" Red Cross workers smilingly met this question by pointing to the metal shield on their uniform which read: "Military Welfare." These young women had an important job to do in India. They knew that here, so very far from loved ones, the American soldiers were starved for home. Not just Seattle or Paducah, Wilkes-Barre or Raven Run, but any part of their beloved United States was home to them. It was the duty of the Red Cross girls to supply a touch of home—a breath of America. Merely being where a man back from the Hump could see an American girl's face was a substantial part of that job. It was not only the wonderful job done by Red Cross workers, but the manner in which they did it that over and over again called forth the praise of commanding officers.

"The progress the American Red Cross has made during the past year," wrote Major General Clayton L. Bissell, commanding the U.S. Tenth Air Force, "is truly miraculous, and possible only because of the untiring efforts of every man and woman in the organization. . . ."

And Brigadier General W. H. Holcombe, deputy commanding general of U.S. Army Services of Supply, wrote: "The Services of Supply, and all those engaged in its various activities, are deeply conscious of the generous help and cooperation which we receive from the members of the Red Cross. We greatly appreciate your assistance in this important task of maintaining a high standard of morale among our men."

From the very outset the Red Cross laid emphasis upon its work in the forward areas, where nearly two-thirds of its workers, mostly women, were assigned. Throughout these areas were clubs, canteens, and mobile units, as well as hospital workers and field directors. Wherever the American soldier was stationed, whether in the 125-degree heat of the plains at Agra, India, or at the almost inaccessible jungle air-warning outposts, or relaxing in the Army rest camps 10,000 feet up in the Himalayas, the Red Cross was at his side.

In India's ports of entry the Red Cross operated day rooms and reception centers for U.S. Navy, troop transport, and Merchant Marine personnel. As of September, 1943, the Red Cross had equipped 235 Army recreation centers which the organization had furnished and operated in various parts of the CBI. Some were set up in *bashas* and some in single or double tents. The majority had bamboo floors, the remainder brick, cement, slag, wood, or plain dirt floors.

In Calcutta the Red Cross maintained two luxurious clubs, one of them for Negro troops. Both provided lodging, meals, and entertainment to America soldiers on leave.

Leave-area clubs, so prominent a feature in other theaters, were a small part of the Red Cross program in the China-Burma-India. Few leaves were granted by the Army, and passes were discouraged because in all India there were only two or three cities which had facilities to satisfy soldiers on leave.

The emphasis was on "on-post clubs" to meet the Army's policy of keeping its personnel on their stations. Near-by villages offered no recreational outlets whatever, and generally were out of bounds anyway.

When building materials and equipment began arriving in sufficient quantities from the United States, Army Services of Supply built standard-type on-post club buildings and furnished the equipment. The Red Cross staffed them and operated them. Unlike the day rooms and recreation centers, these on-post clubs were substantial structures built of permanent materials. A typical club provided a game room equipped with tables for billiards and ping-pong, cards, dominoes, chess and checkers. The main room accommodated 250 soldiers, relaxed in easy chairs and sofas. This lounge with the comfortable appearance of home had a piano, radio set, and phonograph. There was also a library-and-writing room with good lighting, easy chairs, writing tables, books, magazines, and stationery. Wherever possible, floors were laid with rugs, and chintz curtains hung at the windows. Most of the clubs were located at or near airfields. After a long day in the jungle, or after a grueling mission over the Hump, the most treacherous air route in the world (between India and China), this little oasis in the jungle gave a man a real lift.

The GI's named the clubs themselves in contests. Some of the winning names were: "Monsoon Inn," "Tiger's Den," "The Hangar," "Java Jive," "The Last Resort," "Raider's Roost," "Sad Shack," "Gremlin Hall," "Duration Den," and "Tail Wind." The name of the on-post club at the Field Artillery Training Center, Kunming, China, was "Stable For Wheel Horses."

The soldiers took a real pride in the appearance of their clubs. GI artists helped with the color scheme and painted murals. And there were always soldiers who stayed behind after a dance to help rearrange the furniture, sweep the floor, or empty ash trays, so the club would look tidy until the native sweepers got to work.

Every on-post club had its snack bar where the boys sought a variation from the dull diet of canned meats and corned willy. Because of transportation difficulties, however, occasionally a snack bar could offer nothing more than corned willy. One ingenious Red Cross worker met the crisis in her canteen by running it through a meat grinder and mixing it with pickle, Worcestershire sauce, salt, and pepper. And the boys raved about the "pickled ham" sandwiches! Hamburgers, the most popular item on the menu, were

145

made out of bullock beef slaughtered and inspected by the U.S. Army Quartermaster Corps. This meat, the only kind available in a country where the cow was sacred, had to be beaten and pounded to make it edible at all. Wherever possible the Red Cross introduced such luxuries as chocolate, cake, and chicken sandwiches in its snack bars, canteens, and restaurants. Greens for sandwiches and salads were often grown in Red Cross victory gardens.

Running canteens in a land where food was scarce, native customs were strange, and cooking facilities difficult to obtain, engendered many headaches for the Red Cross staff. The Red Cross had a training school for canteen managers, workers, cooks, and bearers, who were taught how to prepare and serve American menus. The results were not always satisfactory. At one post the Red Cross girl obtained two field stoves from the Army and considered herself mighty lucky. The native cook's reaction was less enthusiastic. After putting up with them for two or three days, the cook went out into the garden and built himself a native oven, a pyramid-shaped affair of brick and sand with a sheet of tin for a door and using green wood for fuel. Frequently native cooks forgot their American Red Cross training and slipped back into native cooking habits with the result that their dishes always had that inevitable curry-rice flavor.

Some clubs tried to introduce native dishes as a novelty, but the GI's turned up their noses at them. That they really desired and craved American menus was evidenced by the interest they took in the club kitchens. This was true particularly of Army mess sergeants, who in their free hours helped Red Cross workers plan menus, supplied recipes, and offered tips to native cooks on how to bring out the flavor. In the China clubs, they taught Chinese cooks how to prepare chow mein and chop suey that in America had long passed for Chinese dishes.

Recreation programs at the on-post clubs varied with the climate in which they were located. For example, at "The Hangar," a club in the "dust bowl" area of Central India where the temperature would rise to 125 degrees, the troops had little desire for outdoor or indoor athletic activity. They preferred sedentary games, or just sitting near a fan or a "desert cooler" which brought the temperature down to 90 or 85 degrees, and sipping cool drinks in the snack bar.

Outdoor recreation was primarily the responsibility of the Special Services branch of the Army, but here, too, the Red Cross with its personnel trained as specialists in recreation and with its ability to buy recreation equipment on the Indian market, performed a valued service. By the summer of 1943 a pattern of Red Cross–Special Service co-operation was developed. In each area its mainspring was a Special Service officer's council composed of one noncommissioned officer from each unit in the area, the Special Service officer, the Red Cross field director, and the program director of the Red Cross on-post club. The field director was in a position to uncover specialized interests and latent talents. He brought them to the attention of the Special Service officer and the council, who used them to map the post's sports activities. Every form of sport, it was found, could be played in teams and tournaments. Leagues were organized, and keen interest in inter-area competition developed. Club program directors co-ordinated their activities with those of the council. The small organized games, such as ping-pong, were held at the club, and the awarding of prizes to winners was made a special event followed by a dance or an informal supper.

Many of the U.S. Army posts were ringed with jungles and mountains where wild game abounded. Red Cross field directors took advantage of this environment to arrange hunting parties. "Big game is available if you like," reported one field director from his post. "A native was killed and three injured by a leopard during the clearing of the site for the camp."

One Red Cross club attached to a bomber base sent out a weekly safari into the near-by jungles. The best hunting hours were found to be from dusk to dawn, as the big game did not emerge from their haunts before midnight or thereabouts. The safari used jeeps, scout cars, and trucks instead of the elephants of the maharajahs. The technique involved driving through the tangled brush and moving the spotlight slowly from side to side. The noise of the car startled the game, and the light caught their eyes as they looked up. That gave the hunters their target. Upon returning from the hunt, the GI's would stop at the Red Cross club for a cup of hot coffee.

An account of a big game hunt appeared in the *ARC Light*, a little paper of the American Red Cross in the CBI. Here it is:

Big game hunting in India may once have been the sport of Maharajahs. But the American GI's are rapidly "taking over." Six potential "Frank Bucks," Sergeant Robert Marlar, of Carlsbad, New Mexico; Pfc Joseph H. Beaman, Walstonburg, North Carolina; Sergeant Robert F. Hearell, Kilgore, Texas; S/Sergeant Wesley E. Davis, Okmulgee, Oklahoma; Sergeant Robert Jauman, Akron, Ohio; and Corporal Jeff Isbell, Houston, Texas, all members of a bomb squadron, spent 10 days hunting recently.

The group penetrated the Himalaya mountains to a height of 10,000 feet in search for game, living in native huts all the way, doing their own cooking and living off the animals they shot. That their table was well-stocked is proved by the account of their hunting prowess. They shot a 500-pound Himalayan bear, a 400-pound wild boar, a man-killing hyena, and a 600-pound deer. The hyena is thought to be one which had been terrorizing the neighborhood for some weeks, having killed several natives.

The safari, in addition to the GI's, included sixty-one beaters and bearers. These were supplied through the local Maharajah. All details of the hunt were arranged at the request of two American Red Cross field directors.

The head-hunter was a native called Nabi Akthar. When the group reached his native village, they were guests at a special feast, consisting of roast duck, rice pudding and sugar cane. The banquet took place on a platform surrounding the sacred Peepul tree in the center of town. A tribal drum dance was given as entertainment.

Panther squawls kept the party awake at night, and they killed one cobra that came into camp. There were many "flukes" during the trip, adding much to the fun. Once, on sighting a bear, one soldier became so excited he pumped thirty shots before he hit it. Another GI was so well camouflaged that a deer nearly ran him down.

Worst part of the trip, they agree, was the shave which a native gave them after the hunt was over. He took their eight-days' growth of beard off with a straight razor and no lather.

In appreciation of the good hunt, the boys are buying Akthar, who is stone-deaf, an amplifying device to improve his hearing.

Arranging social and entertainment events in each Red Cross on-post club was the responsibility of the program director aided by a committee of enlisted men.

Every club had its improvised acts. For their casts they drew upon talented GI's on the post, and for their songs, sketches, and jokes upon local doings and personalities. *Hump Happy*, a fast-moving two-act musical comedy that entertained in camps all over the CBI, grew out of programs at the "El Digaboo" club in Dibrugarh, Assam. Its cast of twelve were radio operators, mechanics, and office clerks who were relieved of duty. Because of the long distances, the *Hump Happy* cast traveled entirely by air, rehearsing en route in the cabin of their big DC-3.

"The Swing Patrol," another well-known band and entertainment unit on the CBI circuit, first blew its blues in the Red Cross KGA Hall, Karachi, in July, 1942. When they played for the troops, jitterbugs filled the aisles and tattooed the benches with rhythm. Captain Melvyn Douglas, the movie actor, accompanied "The Swing Patrol" as Special Service officer.

To bring good books to on-post clubs and other installations, the Red Cross set up a circulating library in Calcutta with Mrs. Anne-Morris Innes as librarian. It had thirty thousand books; some were purchased in India, some came over from the United States as gifts from the Victory Book campaign, and it included a valuable reference library received from Army Special Services. A list of titles was supplied to all clubs and hospitals. From this list the servicemen ordered their books. Their requests represented a remarkable range of interest and taste. Taking account of the climate and its effect on paper and binding, Mrs. Innes sent her books in specially-constructed steel trunks, each unit holding 150 books. Having built-in shelves which protected books from dust, dampness, worms, mold, and moths, the trunks served as book cases when set up in the club library rooms. The books themselves were shellacked to prolong their life, and when they came back from the field damaged, they were salvaged in a small bindery.

Magazines and newspapers were supplied by the Red Cross and Special Services.

Before the Army had accumulated enough building materials and equipment, it was sometimes necessary for Red Cross workers to build their own clubs from the ground up. And they met the challenge to their pioneering instincts admirably. Mary Jane Arnold, of Quincy, Illinois, was typical of these pioneers. Upon arrival at her station in the forward area of Assam, she found that her club existed on paper only. Cement and brick were lacking, and so were bricklayers. So she went house-hunting, and after four days acquired a battered old *basha*, whose roof thatch had been blown away and whose bamboo walls were losing their plaster.

From the Army Quartermaster's she obtained a pair of coveralls, and went to work. Having a rudimentary knowledge of designing, acquired at an art school and applied in designing hats for her millinery business in Quincy, Mary Jane Arnold drew plans for her Red Cross club. The hundred-foot shell was divided into three sections by arched partitions, one section for the snack bar, one for the library, and the third for the lounge. Native laborers did the heavy repair work under her supervision, and a couple of GI's whom she had drafted covered the ceiling with muslin to keep bugs and snakes from falling through the roof thatch, and sprayed the ceiling and walls with blue and white paint. The materials came from the Quartermaster's. And the furniture was hand-made by natives in the village.

Red Cross on-post club openings were gala events, as Elsa Adrienne Moore, of Portland, Oregon, one of the Red Cross club workers, tells:

The opening of a Red Cross on-post club in the wilds of India is a big thing, important enough for eight of us girls from "big city headquarters" to fly 300 miles to attend.

We loaded ourselves down with boxes of cakes from the warehouse, piled onto the springless benches of a lumbering six-by-six truck and were off for the airport in the heat of midday.

Out on the field our plane, Jeanie the Swine, spread her olive drab wings over the field, her nose in the air. The personal plane of the area's commanding officer, Jeanie was a wonder—equipped with a daybed, eight seats, icebox and lavatory.

It took an hour and a half, flying northeast at 7,000 feet, to reach the 6,000-foot concrete runway that marked our destination. An Army truck carried us to the club, which stood in the middle of the mud and brick barracks, looking for all the world like an Anne Hathaway cottage with its high chimney, tall-gabled roof and heavy rice-straw thatch. It had a building-length screened porch in front, from which opened the lounge, game room and a library. From the lounge, at the rear, opened the snack bar, with high stools, a counter and small tables. Off this were the pantry and kitchen.

Inside the club the boys were milling about. The family of the Maharajah of Cooch Behar had just arrived, also by plane. His sister was holding court in one end of the lounge, telling fortunes to impressed GI's. A bulking sergeant came up to her with an open book. "Would you mind signing your autograph, princess?" he said. The princess smiled and signed. Flowers from the palace gardens banked the tables.

At the tea not only GI's but post officers were present, taking advantage of the club's hospitality for perhaps the only time. The club is to be a strictly GI affair. That night at supper the mess hall held more women than ever before in its history.

The dance that followed was something never to be forgotten—thirteen girls and 300 men. We danced with ten or fifteen men in the course of one number.

During the evening the club was presented to the commanding officer, Major William Hinton, by Zenas Crawford, the Red

Cross field director resident on the post. The C.O. in turn gave the club to the enlisted men, represented by T/Sergeant Robert L. Gregory, of Omaha, Nebraska. The club name, invented by Sergeant John C. Buck of Owensboro, Kentucky, was also announced—*Teek Hai*, or Okay Club. But for us girls the evening meant music and more music and the continual swirl to Lieutenant Donovan B. Moore's orchestra. Like us, the orchestra had been flown in.

How does an on-post club opening look to one of the soldiers? The answer was supplied by Corporal R. H. Becker, attached to a bomb squadron in eastern India in a letter to his parents in Katonah, New York:

Dear Folks:

I wouldn't be at all surprised if most of the boys have had something to write home about the past week or so. A week ago Sunday evening was the grand opening of our new Red Cross recreation center here on the post, and take it from me, it really is something. For anyone who has been in India, it is hard to visualize such a place existing in the jungle. When I walked into the building it nearly took my breath away. We knew we were going to have a new club, but no one expected anything as grand as what we have.

It is complete in every detail—all for the comfort and pleasure of the enlisted men at this particular base. The main auditorium or lounge is decked out with nice Indian-made furniture, electric fans, radio, record player and table lamps—similar to a country club back home. There is also a reading and writing room with individual desk lamps; a fair-sized game room fully equipped; and last, but not least, a canteen and snack bar which is proving most popular. All in all it is a swell layout and something I feel sure is appreciated by every man on the post.

I personally feel that we fellows are greatly indebted to the American Red Cross for a grand place to spend our leisure hours. They are really a great organization and doing a swell job of keeping us up to snuff and raring to go.

Saturday night we had our first dance at the new club and it was a gala affair. Of course, there weren't enough gals to go around, but those who were present really got a good work out. I was fortunate in having a couple of nice dances with two of the Red Cross charmers stationed here. There are five of them and a more regular bunch of gals it would be hard to find anywhere. The feminine touch is just what the club needed to give it that homey atmosphere. In other words, it was just like a Saturday night dance at any club back home or just a wee bit of America right here in the heart of far away India.

Well, folks, I know I've written about nothing but the club, but right now that's the topic on everyone's tongue over here.

As Allied military operations in the CBI moved eastward toward the Burma front, the number of patients in American hospitals increased. Virtually every general, station, and evacuation hospital in the theater was staffed by Red Cross hospital workers supplementing the work of doctors and nurses with recreation and social work. Many of the Red Cross hospital teams arrived directly from the United States with the hospital units to which they were attached.

From "somewhere in India," Muriel B. Duncan, of Beverly Hills, California, a Red Cross hospital worker, sent this vignette:

It doesn't look in the least like a hospital; no gleaming white marble, no smooth green lawns, no parking lot for gas-rationed autos, no rubber-tired carts, no well-lighted operating theatre, no starchy-white uniforms—not even a sign reading, "Hospital —Quiet Please." Planes landing and taking off swoop low over the thatched roofs of the one-story wards like restless birds in ceaseless flight. The noise of the generators beats through the *basha* walls like the throbbing of some great heart and the jeeps and meat wagons [ambulances] rattling up the deeply-rutted roads sound as if they were loaded with empty tin cans.

But don't get me wrong, my friends—this *is* a hospital and what's more, it is a *heavenly hospital*. In army records it's listed as the Station Hospital. In army hearts, it's listed as a little bit of heaven.

A station hospital is usually in or near a combat area. The field hospital gives emergency treatment near the front and then those courageous flying nurses of the evacuation unit bring the wounded, broken or badly-burned boys back to the station hospital.

And the sheets are coarse here, so they'll stand up under the rock pounding of the *dhobis* and the blankets are the drab khaki of GI issue and the operating room is just a large bamboo hut with a thatch roof and doctors and nurses work with helmets and gas masks hanging nearby. But if you had been carried out of the mountains on the back of some guerilla with your broken legs uncared for for three days, or if some mischance sent you crashing to earth in a flaming ship or if that old devil appendix started raising Cain, brother, this place would look like an ivory palace to you.

And as you got better, the inevitable canned corned willy would taste like ambrosia and the awful water of the Lister bag would be as nectar and the tired-faced girls in army brown or Red Cross gray would look like angels.

And maybe you don't know how badly you're hurt and how awful you look. And as that Red Cross girl bends over your bed, her stomach is turning over inside her at the sight of your face with its lobster red burns and their ragged brown edges and that place where your eye should be. But she'll never let you know. She'll just say, "Is there anything you want, soldier?" And if you were that airman you'd say, "No. Just stay here and hold my hand awhile ma'am if you have time." And as you'd drift off to sleep, she'd hear you say, "Boy, is this heaven!" And this isn't just sentiment or emotion—this is the truth. That's just what you'd say—they all do.

From her station in India, Alice A. Todd, of North Attleboro, Massachusetts, another hospital worker, wrote co-workers at Red Cross National Headquarters. In the following excerpts from her letter, Miss Todd describes her surroundings:

Recreation here is rather difficult to manage for the patients. Some of the Indian types of entertainment seem rather slow to our boys. The Indian people are not as flexible as we are and conditions have to be pretty exact for them to cooperate.

Through the doorway the biggest elephant ever seen just lumbered into view with a swing of one hoof, then a hitch and a rhumba. He has now joined the rest of a small circus which is putting on a performance the Red Cross arranged for the patients this afternoon. Just beyond the circus group are several dozen native men, women and children. The men, in bright-colored turbans (pink predominates this week) are digging the foundation for a new ward, and the women, in flowing saris and full skirts of scarlet, gold, blue, red, orange, green, violet, yellow, purple, and combinations of these colors, are paddling back and forth, slowly and with dignity, poise and grace, balancing on their heads rocks which probably some four men hoisted and placed there.

In the foreground, groups of small children are playing and

one baby is swinging in a burlap hammock suspended from a pole. This is one solution of the problem of what to do with children while parents are at work. At one side two natives are filling their goat-skin bags with water before slinging them over their shoulders.

In back of this group is a long parade of patients en route to the circus—traveling by crutches, wheel chairs, walking, hobbling, but all eager to get there in their GI maroon bathrobes. Now there is a mingling of summer khaki, GI maroon, vivid saris, and the white of the nurses' uniforms. This is too good to miss. I believe they need a bit of Red Cross gray and I, for one, shall hasten to project myself into the scene for a little while.

It was interesting and, as usual, one of the most noticeable points about the show was the intensity of interest displayed by the patients. Added to this were several small boys and girls tenderly guarding smaller brothers and sisters, the latter group wearing only little blouses. All the children wear many earrings, nose beads, anklets, necklaces, and bracelets. It is a little horrifying to watch flies promenade over the noses and eyes of little children. Our friend the elephant, not content with the usual dust blowing, is scooping some up in his trunk and tossing it over his shoulder in a superstitious manner (mayhap he is wishing at the same time). Now a donkey cart and camel wagon are passing by.

Never do I fail to delight in the scenes here. En route to town we pass long camel caravans and sometimes we are fortunate enough to see across the desert a long line of camels, heavily-laden, silhouetted against the sky at dusk. A few days ago a British soldier, in a playful mood, turned the head camel in a caravan around so he would head back to town. The camel leader, asleep on the head camel, remained oblivious to this prank, and when last glimpsed the entire camel train was returning to town.

Then there are many colorful and dirty goat-herders and their flocks; these make a vivid impression upon both the eye and the nose.

Several days ago I had the pleasure of being a guest at a Parsee's wedding and invited some of the other Red Cross group also. Never have I seen such a splash of color—saris of every hue, with gold and silver trimming, jeweled adornments, and the men in white suits buttoned up to the neck and crowned with little round felt brimless hats. Never have I seen a more unusual ceremony nor heard English more beautifully spoken.

The bride and groom, each wearing garlands of flowers and carrying bouquets, were enthroned upon a flower-bedecked stage with the two mothers hovering anxiously in the background. The bride and groom were under constant fire of rice thrown at them steadily (they neither flinched nor ducked) for a period of twenty-five minutes by two chanting priests with voices pitched two and one-half tones apart. (I tried unsuccessfully for twenty-five minutes to determine which one was off key.) After the ceremony, the bride's sister had to bathe the groom's feet—then the bride and groom visited the Fire Temple. The Parsees are a very high-caste group who came down from Persia long ago to evade religious persecution, like our Pilgrim Fathers. (They probably came by camel caravan rather than by Mayflower. Sometimes I wonder if they were able to bring as many ancestors and furniture as our forefathers did.) They worship fire as the emblem of divinity. They comprise a very wealthy, well-educated group, merchants and professional people. All 1,500 guests were served light refreshments while all awaited a seat at the table under the tent where a real feast was served on palm leaves. Only a handful of military personnel were invited and they were all Americans. It was a very colorful and interesting experience. We were cordially greeted and had seats of honor.

All the little shops [in town] are interesting; each little alley has shops of one kind. The kitchenware, for instance, is easily located because tinwear hangs outside the door all up and down the alley. The next one is probably "tailors' row," all the sewing machines resting flat on the floor. Meandering around are sacred cows, goats, children, beggars, FLIES. On the sidewalks people brew tea and serve it to their broods; they sleep everywhere, sidewalks, doorsteps, building ledges—women sit on the sidewalk and do bead work on string attached to extended big toe; in fact, most of the functions of life take place on the sidewalks. One Sunday morning there were three natives sitting in a row not on the side of but in the street while three barbers trimmed their beards. It is thrilling to go to town and I never get tired of just looking.

The division of labor [caste system] has its amusing angle. For example, in the hotel one sweeps the floor, one dusts, one makes the beds, one scrubs the bathroom, etc. We refer to each as the lieutenant in charge of making beds, and so on. One day the slide bolt on the door refused to function. It was "finished." We reported it, and a little man, barefoot as they all are, in his flapping, draped, droopy drawers and long flapping shirt-tail, beturbaned, came with two big tools, products of the stone age. He hammered for half an hour. That accomplished naught. He departed and another one came with a little bag. Being the lieutenant in charge of removing the bolts, he removed the bolt. He was succeeded by the lieutenant in charge of cleaning the bathroom. You are right: privacy is obsolete in India.

We are adapting ourselves to the very limited means of transportation and in town never cease to delight in the klop, klop of the horse and *gharri* [carriages]—à la "Tales from Vienna Woods." I even rode one night eight miles through the desert "silvery moon and starlight" on camel back home from a party much to the delight of the entire camp and town. Nothing is sacred but cows and peacocks, so every move is known.

We are all on the alert because we know that some day we are going to need every resource we have to face what will come and meet the emergencies that may arise.

General Stilwell thought so highly of the morale value of Red Cross work in India that he requested Red Cross girls for China.

For the "Java Jive" club at Chungking, every stick of furniture, including a piano, and the three Red Cross girls to staff it, were flown in on the same plane.

"I don't believe it!" exclaimed a startled khaki-clad "grease monkey," as blond, petite Gerry Lennox, a former New York dancer, stepped from the plane. She was followed by Eleanor Liss,* of White Plains, New York, and Mrs. Alma B. Kerr, of Chicago, Illinois.

As the surprised and delighted GI's looked on, the three young women in their neat gray Red Cross uniforms went into headquarters for an interview with General Stilwell.

Then they rolled up their sleeves and set to work converting a former mess hall into an on-post club. And the boys pitched in to help them. When they unpacked the crates they were as happy as children around a Christmas tree. They found hand-made furniture, jute rugs, cotton curtains, games, party decorations, a piano, and the latest swing recordings of American name bands. The needle was started immediately. Chinese natives in passing rickshas were treated to the strange sight of husky American soldiers hanging curtains to Tommy Dorsey rhythms, and "cutting the rug" at the same time they were laying the jute rug on the floor.

In a matter of hours this became one of the most inviting Red Cross clubs "this side of the Hump." For their formal opening, the three proud Red Cross girls had as their guests some of the most distinguished persons in Chungking. Major General Thomas G. Hearn, Chief of Staff of the China-Burma-India Command, brought official greetings from General Stilwell. General Shang Chen extended a welcome in behalf of the Chinese Government. There were talks also by Captain M. W. Miles, U.S. Navy; Brigadier General William Bergin; and Colonel L. H. Chow, Chinese liaison officer with the U.S. Army. The keys to the club were presented to Yeoman 1/c Alexander G. Hardy, U.S.N., and Sergeant Joseph Lyons, the two men with the longest service in the theater.

Some of the boys then got out the instruments that had been flown in with the piano and furniture, and played for dancing. With the Red Cross girls were a number of Westernized Chinese girls who had attended American schools and could lead the conga

* Died of natural causes in India, June 8, 1944.

line, and even swing out to jitterbug rhythm. And of course the snack bar served good coffee with sugar and cream, and doughnuts, cake, and cookies, which were devoured by soldiers and sailors who had had no "stateside" pastry in nearly two years.

The Chungking club had many famous visitors. Mme. Sun Yat-sen, widow of the founder of the Republic of China, came one day to invite six servicemen and a Red Cross worker to tea at her home Sunday afternoons.

Former Vice-President Henry A. Wallace received a rare honor at this club during his mission to Chungking for the President in the spring of 1944. A signed document presented to him read as follows: "Greetings! Be it known that the undersigned Enlisted Men of the U.S. Army in Chungking do hereby confer upon HENRY A. WALLACE the honorary degree of GI with Magna Ding Hao! When properly presented at any Red Cross club, said Henry A. Wallace is entitled to any and all privileges of GI's."

What was it like—the life of a Red Cross girl in China? This question was answered by Guida Richey, hostess of a Kunming on-post club, in a letter to her family in Knoxville, Tennessee:

Dear Folks:

You asked about my life as a Red Cross girl in China, where it's natural to be one girl in a group of several hundred men. Well, it's all topsy-turvy, but it's fun!

I've learned to walk right into a GI mess hall and whistle right back at them without blinking an eye. I find myself classified as "she can jitterbug," and honestly wish I could be a wallflower. Every shift of hairdo, any change of dress is the topic of the day. And I remember how, at home, I used to be so pleased if my boy friend even noticed my new dress.

I can climb down into a slit trench with my helmet and gas-mask and gaze upwards with comparative calm at a fleet of silver zeroes and big Jap bombers. But, I still inwardly curse myself for getting a panicky feeling from tummy to toe when someone, in order to signal an air raid alert, sounds a gong I thought signaled only "Gas."

Traveling from place to place is via jeep, truck or weapons carrier, and sometimes the grand loan of a sedan and driver. Along the rocky, dusty road, we overtake bullock carts and the overladen miniature Chinese horses. When we drive through town, the townsfolk stare at a strange looking creature with hair that's yellow instead of black, eyes that are blue and don't bear the remotest resemblance to an almond. They are openly amused

158

at my substantial size 7's, in startling contrast to the women of "old China" teetering and tottering along on their incredibly tiny feet in gaily embroidered pixty-toes shoes.

Ever so often I come upon a line of rickshas totin' a bunch of self-conscious looking GI's instead of the sailors of "Join the Navy and See the World" posters. They "ups" with their thumbs and shout "Ting hao" [O.K.] to the tiniest tike or the lowliest coolie . . . then chuckle at the slit panty seats of the same tiny tots.

I share with the GI's the pangs of yearning for a glass of Grade A milk, and would almost trade my last bobby pin for a piece of chocolate. I can vaguely remember asparagus, roast beef, hot dogs and ice cream sodas. We all carry around a stack of bills that makes us look as rich as Croesus, but we don't have enough to pay the Chinese price for a good "stateside" fountain pen.

I wave and smile at every American lad I see (and wonder if when I get back home, my manner won't seem a trifle on the bold side). My bridge foursome is no longer "the girls," and I have learned that men gossip just as much as "the girls." I have complimented thousands of wives, sweethearts and children as their pictures are displayed by some rightfully proud husband, "feller" or father.

I've learned what it means to "sweat out" going home. I have talked to scores of men and women who walked out of Burma. My heart has ached for the boy whose brother wrote that "she" didn't wait for him, and for the men I know, and the men I don't know, who go away and never come back.

I have been surprised to learn the many purposes for which War Fund contributions to the American Red Cross go . . . for hamburgers instead of chop-suey in the Red Cross club for soldiers, for a lounge room where they can sit and read or play games, for a dance, where four American girls augmented by a few Chinese volunteers supply a little color and gaiety in the lives of several hundred soldiers.

Often I look back to the time when China and India were so far removed from my own horizon as to hardly be real. In those days, the contents of my mail box were a source of great interest, but not the key to my morale. Then, I didn't dream a house could be heated with charcoal, and that I'd learn to bank a fire better than the houseboy. I luxed my own then, and had never heard of an *amah* who knew the one English word "washee," and sprinkled clothes by "exploding" water through her teeth!

I dream of water faucets yielding crystal-pure liquid (I used to let some of the icy cold drops trickle through my mouth as I took a shower). Now, I don't dare drink anything that isn't boiled.

Now, "snafu," "sad sack," "chow," "ting hao" [O.K.], "poo hao" [no good], and "ching pao" [air raid], are all part of my lingo. I know what it means when a flier "hits the silk" (I even have a piece of the filmy stuff for a scarf). I can recognize a "fogey" or a "gold bricker." A November newspaper from my hometown is still a treat in March. My Easter bonnet is my American Red Cross overseas cap which no longer looks quite so jaunty (oh, for a crisp straw number with a flower and a veil). I glibly say "Golden Gate by '48" with the rest of them, and I'm as fit a member of the United States Chamber of Commerce as any overseas soldier and sailor. I dream of white tiles, candlelight that's just for beauty's sake, juke boxes, taxis and super highways, and of the day when "the hump" will once again be a camel's back, and not our lifeline. But, I'm as happy as I've ever been in my life, and I wouldn't trade places with any girl back home.

In 1944 virtually all the American bases in unoccupied China—Kunming, Chungking, Chengtu, Kweilin, among others—had Red Cross clubs. Kunming, terminus of the air supply route and of the Burma Road, had the first Red Cross installation in China. It was the "Victory Club," opened by Club Director Robert Drummond, on December 1, 1942. During 1943 a number of temporary recreation centers in Kunming were operated by Club Director Carl Edward Scofield, of Winsted, Connecticut. Late in the following year they were replaced by one on-post club of which Beatrice De Costas, of Bath, Maine, was director, and one off-post club directed by Flora Jane Coutts, of Newport, Vermont. The "Stateside Inn" at Kweilin, one of the largest clubs in the entire theater, was abandoned in the summer of 1944, shortly before the Fourteenth Air Force blew up its airfields and all the matériel and fuel that could not be evacuated. These measures were taken in the face of strong Japanese forces advancing on Kweilin, the great air base built by thousands of coolies.

A steady stream of Red Cross workers was flown into China to keep pace with expanding operations. To feed, equip, and provide facilities for these workers, the Army spent at the rate of ten dollars per pound for every item hauled by air over the Hump. Pianos, phonograph records, and miscellaneous equipment for Red Cross clubs that could not be purchased in China, together with the clothing and personal articles required by the club workers, were flown in like bombs and gasoline. Could there be stronger evidence than this of the value which the Army attached to the Red Cross program?

In many ways American servicemen were beneficiaries of the great prestige enjoyed by the American Red Cross in China, a prestige built up over a period of many years by the organization's China relief activities. For example, the name of the Red Cross was great enough to break down social customs centuries old. When the first Red Cross installations in Kunming were opened, dancing partners could not be obtained for Saturday night dances. As the number of young women (even among Westernized Chinese) who would dance with men, to say nothing of strange soldiers, was limited, the prospects for Saturday night dances were not very good. Club workers went right into the homes of the better Chinese families, and over teacups argued that American soldiers were just like their brothers and, furthermore, that the dances were sponsored by the American Red Cross. The first to break down were married women who agreed to come if their husbands gave permission, but the husbands insisted upon tagging along as chaperons. Unmarried girls would not come at all in the beginning.

Chinese peasants who in the early days of the war looked upon American soldiers with detached curiosity greeted them everywhere with enthusiasm in 1944. Grinning children gave them the "thumbs up" greeting and shouts of "Ting hao!"

A story illustrating the warm appreciation of the Chinese for American airmen was brought to one of the Red Cross clubs. The four airmen who "walked out" of their plane to be rescued by Chinese were: Lieutenant E. C. Gassner, of Nashville, Tennessee; Lieutenant Kenneth Snowden, of Wayne, Ohio; Sergeant R. H. Phillips, of Chattanooga, Tennessee; and Pfc E. W. Crews, of Monto, Virginia.

"They were really good to us," Snowden said of their Chinese rescuers.

Whenever the Americans tried to buy a souvenir, the Chinese refused payment. Their guide would point to the merchant and explain, "It is a present that he wishes to give from him for you."

Snowden showed a letter written in Chinese characters with an English translation, and signed by the magistrate, the secretary,

the Middle School principal and the doctor of the village C——.
The translation:

Dear Gentlemen:

We are pleased that at the dangerous you were all well and reached our Chinese inland. We so glad to see you and have the pleasure ask you to stay here some more days.

But we are very sorry cannot treat you more comfortable so we hope that you will excuse us.

Upon their departure, each man received a farewell gift, a carved marble inkwell for Chinese brush writing with the inscription: "Make fast the airplane to force our defence. We must fight to the enemies still them is bend their knees."

Said Snowden, "The Chinese sentence is not constructed like ours. What this means is, 'We must fight until the enemy bend their knees.' "

This typified the spirit of a China struggling against insuperable odds. Major General Claire L. Chennault's Fourteenth Air Force—the "forgotten airmen" of the war—fought side by side with the Chinese. Against a far more numerous Japanese air force, they defended almost the entire area of Free China, while dropping bombs on the Yangtze River and on many Japanese-held ports and bases, as well as stabbing tirelessly for the jugular of the Japanese military system—the sea routes between Japan and her conquered empire in the Pacific.

It was to serve these brave airmen who did so well with so little that the American Red Cross was in China. But there were also American Services of Supply units in China, and they too enjoyed Red Cross services.

With the powerful support of the Fourteenth Air Force, some of these American units accompanied twenty thousand American-trained and -equipped Chinese troops under Marshal Wei Li-huang across the Salween River on a one-hundred-mile front in mid-May, 1944. This full-fledged offensive was co-ordinated with the drive of Merrill's Marauders and Chinese columns under General Stilwell hammering at the Japanese in northern Burma from the Ledo Road. An immediate objective was a junction of the two drives. The long-range goal was the winning of a land route to bring heavy war equipment into China that would permit a military showdown with the Japanese Army.

The China-Burma-India Command became the Southeast Asia Command at the August, 1943, Quebec Conference between President Roosevelt and Prime Minister Churchill. Admiral Lord Louis Mountbatten was made Supreme Commander and Lieutenant General Stilwell second in command.

It was generally believed that large-scale amphibious operations against the Japanese in this theater would follow soon after the conference. Plans made at Quebec, however, did not materialize. Instead, the landing ships and craft originally allocated to the Southeast Command were used in the Anzio beach landings and subsequently in the invasion of France, according to Admiral Mountbatten.

Recasting their plans "on a less ambitious scale," in the Admiral's words, he and General Stilwell decided upon a campaign to drive the Japanese out of northern Burma and to reopen the Burma Road.

To provide a route for the supply of the Allied forces in this campaign, the Ledo Road was built in 1943-1944.

Starting at Ledo in northeastern Assam, India, the road runs through the Naga Hills in a generally southeasterly direction along the southern slope of the Himalayas. At the Burmese frontier it weaves in the same direction into the Hukawng Valley, held by the Japanese until they were dislodged by Merrill's Marauders. Through some of the world's densest jungles and across a series of mountain ranges, some of them a mile high, the Ledo Road dips, climbs, and zigzags to reduce the grade, follows old jungle paths here and there, and around ravines and mountain peaks narrows down from three lanes to a width barely enough for two jeeps to pass each other without sideswiping.

The barbaric beauty of the road was described by Stanley A. Haw, of Ottumwa, Iowa, one of the Red Cross field directors stationed there:

> The scenery is the finest I have ever seen. The country is steep and mountainous. The road runs like a ribbon around the tortuous hills. Everywhere is jungle green, with trees that are strange and new to me, many of them flowering. One that impressed me is a waxy-leafed magnolia type with great flaming flowers. All this colorful verdure contrasts with the brilliant earth. Usually the ground is sticky yellow clay, but at one point it is emerald green. And at a nearby pass it varies from deep purple to red. The hills themselves are strangely twisted and distorted in their stratification,

no two planes seeming to run in the same direction. The forests are alive with wild life. Besides the vermilion and yellow birds, and one blue and white which is my favorite, there is a variety of game—leopards, deer, and tigers.

I heard tigers at night but never saw one. The snakes also were interesting. Though I was on the road for many months, I only once saw a hooded cobra standing up and hissing at us as we drove by. Twice I saw 20-foot to 30-foot pythons. Both times they were brought in by GIs after they had been killed. The men gave the skins to some colored troops, and the Chinese took away the meat and ate it. Eating snake meat is a regular habit among groups of local porters [gharos], the men who carried most of the loads forward from the 44-mile mark into the jungle.

We had good food so we were not obliged to eat python. When we lacked meat, somebody went out and shot it, usually a deer or young buffalo. In the beginning it was a bit difficult, but now there is fresh meat at least three times a week on the road.

Building the Ledo Road through this savage land was one of the engineering marvels of the global war. Army bulldozers, trucks, jeeps, and rock crushers, transported 15,000 miles from the United States, did a wonderful job. But the human labor excited the most interest. The road was started in December, 1942, under command of Brigadier General John Arrowsmith, U.S. Army Engineers, and was carried to its farthest point in 1944 by Brigadier General Lewis A. Pick. Under them worked American and Chinese engineering units, aided by Asiatic civilian laborers, including gharos from upper Bengal and subjects of the Maharajah of Nepal. In advance of the road builders went units of a Chinese Army force, trained and equipped by the U.S. Army in India, who prevented interference from Japanese patrols.

Even before grading, surfacing, and drainage, U.S. Army motor convoys, driven by Negro soldiers, moved in a steady stream in both directions.

Among the U.S. Army units stationed at various points along the road, the 823rd and 45th Engineers, and the 45th and 21st Quartermaster's were composed entirely of Negroes, except for officers. American Negroes, who far outnumbered white soldiers on the road, made a proud record. Red Cross workers said that they were cool, brave, and patient under extremely adverse conditions. Inevitably there were serious accidents. Skidding in the slippery mud was common (except for small stretches of crushed-rock surface the Ledo was a dirt road). Some trucks failed to make the steep grade and overturned; some sideswiped each other. Occasionally a truck could not negotiate a hairpin curve, left the road and crashed into the bottomless gorge below.

For truck drivers, road builders, and maintenance crews the American Red Cross opened a roadside canteen at Ledo on June 1, 1943. Doughnuts, coffee, and quick-lunch snacks were served.

The idea was conceived by Margaret De Wolfe Erskine, of New York City, a recreation worker with the 20th General Hospital. Temporarily detached from the hospital, she set up a large EPI (Egypt-Palestine-India) desert tent about fifty feet off the road, and furnished it with cane furniture. Native boys of the neighborhood, working as bearers and waiters, were dressed in patriotic colors—white shirt, blue trousers, and red sash. On the first day seven hundred men were served. Later the number increased. Canteen hours were from 9 A.M. to 9 P.M. Closing time, however, was not the end of Miss Erskine's working day, as she spent an additional hour or two on book work and preparations for the next day's business. After four months, she was relieved by Star Giddy, of New York City.

The First Red Cross club in the Ledo area was opened at Margherita, six miles below Ledo, in June, 1943. A two-story dak bungalow, a type of roadhouse common in provincial India, was converted for the purpose. Serving twelve hundred soldiers a day, it was the largest Red Cross installation in Assam. Canteen and offices were on the first floor, clubrooms on the second. The settlement included *bashas* housing Red Cross staff quarters, kitchen, bakery, and tailor shop. There were three Dutch ovens in the yard. A clearing provided space for outdoor games, such as volley ball, horseshoe pitching and basketball.

Nathan H. Kaufman, of Pittsburgh, Pennsylvania, was the first director of the Margherita club. Assisting him in the beginning were the following young women, all temporarily borrowed from the 20th (University of Pennsylvania) General Hospital: Ruth Peterson, Peewaukee, Wisconsin; Bertha Carlson, Gary, Indiana; and Ann Townsend, Haverford, Pennsylvania.

Carl Edward Scofield, transferred from China, succeeded Kaufman as club director in January, 1944. He served during the period of Merrill's Marauders, when his aides were Dorothy H. Hubbell, New York City; Marion R. Broer, Northampton, Massachusetts; and Mary Brady, Woodmere, Long Island. Employed locally as canteen manager was Mrs. Joyce Matthews, an Englishwoman who, with her three small children, had hiked through the Burmese jungles to escape the Japanese forces; her husband, a railway official, had been killed by the Japanese in Rangoon. Mrs. Matthews trained six natives to cook and bake for the canteen.

The Margherita club inaugurated a flourishing Red Cross program along the Ledo Road. Clubs like "The Burma Basha" and "The Road Block"—names selected by the men themselves—consisted of cane-built *bashas*, constructed in a jungle clearing or set down on a mountaintop. Bright murals by GI artists, curtains made by Red Cross girls from damaged parachutes, and cane furniture woven by native craftsmen went a long way toward creating a touch of home.

The club at Tagap—Mile 85—was on one of the sites formerly occupied by Dr. Gordon S. Seagrave's Burma hospital. The one at Shingbwiyang—Mile 112—was in territory previously captured from the Japanese by Merrill's Marauders. The other principal clubs were at Loglai—Mile 56—and at Ting Kawk Sakan—Mile 135. Army supply depots and road maintenance camps were located at these points.

The first four girls to staff the Tagap club came from Ledo. It took them eleven hours to reach their destination, a distance of only eighty-six miles. It was an all-night ride, too, from 8 P.M. to 7 A.M. Such was traveling on the Ledo Road! Their command car led a convoy of four Army six-by-six trucks loaded with canteen supplies and equipment, including seven thousand pounds of flour, three thousand pounds of sugar, seven hundred pounds of coffee, ninety-five cases of canned milk, kitchenware, cooking utensils, and even cement and bricks for the construction of outdoor ovens. The four girls were Judy Fitch, Hudson, Ohio; Star Giddy, New York City; Maxine Robertson, Portland, Oregon; and Mary Elizabeth Rogan, Cincinnati, Ohio.

By the summer of 1944 there were four field directors evenly distributed along the road—Stanley A. Haw; Keith Berkner, Rochester, Minnesota; Earl Lewis, Clarks Summit, Pennsylvania; and Daniel L. Brace, Washburn, Wisconsin. Their presence on the road brought out in servicemen all those things that they wanted to talk about, get done, or have done; personal problems that neither the company commander nor the post chaplain could do much about as they required communication with the United States. Even here, 15,000 miles from the United States, Red Cross field directors kept open the line of communication between the servicemen and their loved ones.

Berkner was the pioneer field director on the road, his station being at rear echelon headquarters, Ledo. He set up a free mending service for officers' and enlisted men's uniforms. Such minor repairs as patching and sewing on buttons were made by several native tailors who brought their own Singer sewing machines (1915 model) with them. In March, 1944, 721 garments were repaired.

His "drop-bundle" plan was another popular feature. Small detachments of the Tenth Air Force were stationed at isolated posts in the jungle for which they had volunteered for six-month periods. As they were from ten days to three weeks by pack train from the nearest Army supply depot, their K rations and ammunition were dropped to them by parachute on a scheduled air-drop service. They did not, however, receive Army PX items, such as sweets and comfort articles, in this way. At the request of Major General Clayton L. Bissell, then commander of the Tenth Air Force, Berkner prepared a monthly "drop-bundle" containing these articles. The first drop was on November 1, 1943. On the afternoon preceding Christmas Eve, fifteen hundred individually wrapped Christmas gift packages were dropped to the men with the compliments of the American Red Cross. This service was greatly appreciated, as the ships bearing Christmas packages from the United States had not arrived on time. Occasionally Red Cross bundles fell outside the air-drop area and were picked up by Naga hillmen. Even so, eventually the articles found their way to the GI's by the barter route.

The promise of the Ledo Road as a supply route came to fruition early in 1944, when Merrill's Marauders suddenly descended upon it on their way to capture Myitkyina, principal Japanese base in northern Burma.

The Marauders shrouded their movements in utmost secrecy, as the success of their "extremely dangerous and hazardous mission" in enemy-held territory depended upon the element of surprise. To the Japanese-like tactics of infiltration and flanking movement they added "Marauder Magic," a bag of jungle tricks which confounded the enemy.

They started their spectacular march of 750 miles from Ningbyen on the morning of February 24, 1944. Their backs bent under the weight of heavy packs, their guns oiled and loaded, their spirits high, they marched up the Ledo Road into the Hukawng Valley for their preliminary operations.

At the base of the Ledo Road, during one of their brief rest periods, they had Red Cross doughnuts. Field Director Berkner had come by in a command car that moonless night, and delighted at the sight of American combat troops, the first in Assam, he offered to serve doughnuts and coffee. The beverage was ruled out because there was no time to unpack canteens. With the help of Pfc John Cassidy, of East Canton, Ohio, and Pfc John Gundy, of Warren,

Ohio, canteen detail, Berkner went down the line passing out doughnuts.

The next evening base headquarters requested more doughnuts. A Red Cross clubmobile from the Margherita club, staffed by Audrey Edmonds, of Falls Church, Virginia, and Judy Astie, of Freeport, Pennsylvania, and driven by Corporal Robert Geiger, overtook the Marauders some twenty miles up the road. So surprised were they to see Red Cross girls that one of them exclaimed "—— ——, is the Red Cross here too?"

The girls served doughnuts and cookies. Ordinarily, they sang and danced for the units they visited, but on this occasion they had to dispense with entertainment because of the secrecy surrounding the Marauders' movements.

Merrill's Marauders represented twenty-five nationalities, some with Mayflower ancestors, some who were recent German refugees. The original unit was comprised of three thousand hand-picked men, all volunteers. They came out of the Army jungle schools in Panama and Trinidad and out of the Buna, Munda, and Guadalcanal campaigns in the Southwest Pacific. Their forty-year-old leader, Brigadier General Frank D. Merrill, had entered West Point from the ranks in the regular army back in the twenties.

The Marauders faced a nature as implacable in its way as the wily, ruthless military foe. To survive they lived as jungle creatures and fought as demons. They had need of the jungle lore acquired from Kachin tribesmen and American missionaries. While they received supplies by air-drop, often combat teams were cut off from food and fresh water for days at a time and were forced to live off the jungle. They ate roots, ferns, grass, and bamboo shoots, and obtained water from bamboo trees and dysentery-threatening streams. They fell victim to malaria, dysentery, dengue fever, typhus, and other diseases. At one time twenty-five per cent of the sick suffered from an incurable type of typhus.

And as they marched they were made aware of the insidious presence of Japanese by the fire that come from unseen guns directed by perfectly camouflaged observers.

They scaled cloud-banked precipices, and blasted cliffs to make a trail. Often they followed paths known only to their Kachin guides. Rains made the trails treacherous with a top layer of slithery mud and dead vegetation. Pack mules and horses weakened and fell off the trail, sometimes into the misty abyss below. Marauders plodded on, cutting their way through the tall leech- and rat-infested *kunai* grass, fording streams, fighting Japanese, digging foxholes or graves for their fallen comrades.

Wounded were more in fear of being lost in the thick undergrowth than of pain. No wounded were left behind; but at Nhpum Ga, where the Second Battalion was trapped for ten terrible days, the sick and wounded could not be evacuated in time and suffered and died in their foxholes. Casualties were first treated by doctors of the two portable hospitals that accompanied the Marauders, one a U.S. Army portable hospital, the other a section of Lieutenant Colonel Gordon S. Seagrave's field hospital staffed by Americans and Asiatics. Casualties were evacuated by small American planes landing on river sand bars or on improvised air strips. More than a hundred of them were thus taken out in less than a day, the little planes sneaking through cloud-banked mountain passes and scraping treetops to avoid detection by the enemy.

Merrill's Marauders were an American counterpart of the late Brigadier General Charles Orde Wingate's Chindits, who made swift lightning attacks against Japanese communications and supply lines in Burma without accepting battle. The Marauders, on the other hand, did not restrict themselves to bushwacking but deliberately picked fights. Their mission was to move behind the Japanese, throw up road blocks, and pin them down while General Stilwell's Chinese columns attacked in strength from the north.

While the main force of Marauders was in the jungle, a number of them drifted back into the Red Cross roadside canteen at Ledo for coffee and doughnuts.

"Boy, what wouldn't I have given for one of these sinkers back there!" exclaimed one of them.

Field Director Berkner promptly offered to supply enough doughnuts for the entire outfit if proper clearance could be obtained. The men promised to request the necessary permission. What followed is told in Berkner's May, 1944, monthly narrative report:

Some days later, the request was granted and then men reported back. Miss Julia Mueller and Pfc Gundy who operate the Ledo canteen immediately went to work, and that evening six thousand doughnuts were in the hands of the supply officer of Merrill 5307 Comp. Prov. Unit. The next morning Red Cross doughnuts were dropped to Merrill's men on the front lines in Burma.

Sufficient time has elapsed so that these men are gradually drifting back to headquarters of the rear echelon and to the 14th Evacuation Hospital which serves them. At both of these places comments are frequently heard regarding the surprise and pleasure these men experienced when after months of eating only canned rations they suddenly found Red Cross doughnuts out in the Burma jungles.

The Marauders were in the field a hundred days, during which they fought five major engagements and thirty-two skirmishes, according to General Merrill. By capturing (with the aid of Chinese troops) the Myitkyina airfield on May 17, 1944, they won their main objective. This and the subsequent taking of the town of Myitkyina, rail and road junction on the upper Irrawaddy River, marked the end of the first phase of General Stilwell's campaign to drive the Japanese out of Burma and reopen a land supply route to China.

The Marauders' ranks were steadily cut down by disease, wounds, and exhaustion until they were a fraction of their original strength. Several days after the capture of the Myitkyina airfield, the surviving Marauders were flown back to Ledo, the rear base, for rest and recuperation. Red Cross workers said their faces were seared with fatigue. Seeing them made the workers feel that nothing they could do for these heroic jungle fighters was quite good enough.

The 14th Evacuation Hospital, of *basha* construction (thatch roof and bamboo matting for walls) was set up to take care of Marauder patients; the overflow were taken to the 20th General Hospital, and to the 73rd "Evac" up the road.

General Merrill was a patient at the 20th General, where Red Cross workers aided doctors and nurses in making his stay as pleasant as possible. One of them, Ruth Royce, of Arlington, Virginia, a recreation worker, in her monthly report told what she was able to do for him:

A time ago a young Lieutenant came in for books for our dear friend, General Merrill who was a patient in the hospital. He was quite flustered as to what to suggest so I picked out a selection of good novels and a few mystery stories and short stories, a few up-to-date magazines, and enclosed a note asking him "What do great Generals read?"—and that if he is like his grand boys of 5307 he will digest the Ellery Queen horrors with glee, but I was sending him a tempting literary list and he could send for what he liked as we had an excellent selection.

A week went by and then I received the following note:

My dear Miss Royce,
I enjoyed the books you sent me very much indeed. I must be slightly different from the rest of my gang since I enjoyed "Winged Citadel" more than anything else. If you have any other books not too deep on problems, still avoiding . . . junk writers,

170

would you loan me a couple? My aide, Lt. Higgins, will take care that they come back to you and when they let me roam around a bit I'll come in and thank you personally.

FRANK MERRILL

For General Merrill's fellow patients at the 20th General—seriously ill Marauders—the Red Cross staff gave essential service in an emergency, as indicated in the following letter from the hospital's Lieutenant Colonel Francis C. Wood, Army Medical Corps:

> I wish to thank all the Red Cross girls for their very efficient and timely help in feeding, fanning, and taking care of the sick typhus patients during the recent emergency. Without this help more of these patients would have died, and many would have been much less comfortable. It was heartening to see your girls during the excessive heat, giving their time and energy (and all they had!) to handle a very serious emergency.

The Red Cross staff at the time consisted of Ruth Peterson, assistant field director, to whom the letter was addressed; Elizabeth M. Gaynor, of Conshohocken, Pennsylvania, and Nell M. Carl, of Oklahoma City, Oklahoma, social workers; Bertha Carlson, Margaret DeWolfe Erskine, Ruth Royce, and Amelia Cox, of New York City, all hospital recreation workers, Ann Townsend, of Haverford, Pennsylvania, and Lucille Funkey, of Cedar Rapids, Iowa, secretaries.

The 14th Evacuation Hospital departed from standard practice in that patients were detained longer than the customary period. Attached to the hospital was a rest camp for able-bodied though tense, haggard, and weary Marauders. Cheering them posed a terrific problem for the Red Cross hospital staff: Ruth Horine, of New York City, assistant field director; Mrs. Mary Sylvander, of Jamaica, Long Island, social worker; Ruth Weythman, of Monitor, Washington, Margaret Dinwoodey, of Seattle, Washington, Madeline Lemere, of Colorado Springs, Colorado, and Sarah Edge, of Downingtown, Pennsylvania, all recreation workers; Freda Peterson, of Spartanburg, South Carolina, secretary; and Leona Thomey, of St. Cloud, Minnesota, staff aide.

In her May, 1944, report, Miss Weythman recorded:

> With the help of two of the able-bodied Marauders we had a bingo game for an hour one evening. Nestle's chocolate bars made very acceptable prizes. This is the nearest we have come so far to having a party. They enjoyed that activity enough to do it again.

171

With infinite patience and intelligent handling the Red Cross workers gradually succeeded in cracking the shell into which these tough infantrymen seemed to have withdrawn when they returned from Myitkyina.

For convalescent patients there was a comprehensive program of recreation under medical supervision—games of all kinds, sings, movies provided by Special Services, and entertainment by local talent and visiting celebrities from Hollywood and Broadway.

In the Ledo Road hospitals, as in many other hospitals in the China-Burma-India theater, handicrafts formed an integral part of recreation. They were taught by Red Cross recreation workers who had been trained in jungle crafts at the special school maintained by the Indian Red Cross in Calcutta.

The program at the 20th General was in charge of Bertha Carlson; 73rd Evacuation, of Virginia Alice Hanson, of Wauwatosa, Wisconsin; 14th Evacuation, of Ruth Weythman.

To supplement their own work, the girls enlisted native craftsmen from near-by jungle villages who passed on their skills to the hospitalized Marauders. They belonged to the Naga hill people who called themselves "American Baptist Christians," converts of missionaries from the United States. The Marauders got along well with them, even to picking up a smattering of their dialect.

Making beads from jungle seeds, weaving baskets and mats from local grasses, crude silk weaving, embroidering, and leather tooling—these were the native jungle crafts which absorbed the leisure hours of convalescent Marauders. And in the process they mellowed.

On May 20 Field Director Berkner was requested by base headquarters to set up a club for the Marauders within three days. Though the club was ready on May 23 there were no Marauders to enjoy it. A misunderstood order of General Stilwell for reinforcements had resulted in able-bodied and convalescent Marauders alike being flown back to defend the Myitkyina airfield against Japanese counterattacks. The boys felt in no condition for active service. In fact, they were under the impression that after a rest they would be returned to the United States on leave. The whole unit exploded into that "Marauder incident," which received widespread publicity in the United States. By June 1, however, they were nearly all back from Myitkyina, ready to enjoy the Red Cross club set up exclusively for them.

The special pains taken to make this club inviting for them were described in their May, 1944, report by the club workers: (Miss) Norris McClellan, Baton Rouge, Louisiana; Wren Barbe, Fairmont, West Virginia; and Mary Elizabeth Rogan, Glendale, Ohio:

It amounted almost to a "Command Performance" when the Army, at the personal request of General Frank D. Merrill, asked the Red Cross to set up in three days a club for the Marauders returning from combat duty in Burma. It was to be a temporary setup and would have first priority until completed—they said!

It was ready to operate within ten days, not three, but by that time the Army had forgotten all about first priority, and there were no men around to use the club!

But this is the story. To assemble a staff, the assistant club director was pulled out of Jorhat, the assistant program director out of Mohanbari, one staff assistant out of Tagap and the second staff assistant who never arrived and was replaced, out of Shillong. The assistant club director began work on May 24, the assistant program director on May 26, and the staff assistant having arrived on May 23, drew a bit of bad luck and spent her first five days in the hospital.

Four *bashas*, two large and two small ones, forming a quadrangle in the corner of two "street" intersections, were turned over to be used as the club. They had been standing neglected and unused for months, so it was a matter of literally "starting from the ground up" to renovate them. The rotten bamboo matting had to be slashed into pieces and removed from the floors, leaning walls had to be straightened and propped, leaking thatch on the roofs needed repairing and the sliding bamboo shutters on the windows had to be rehung.

That is to say nothing as to the condition of the acre or two of surrounding grounds composing the "compound." They were ribbed with ditches and slit trenches, shellacked with stinking muck, littered with debris and garnished with unsightly piles of trash.

It was a tired, dejected ghost town—and to make it completely desolate, it was raining.

One of the smaller *bashas* was well under way as a kitchen when the American Red Cross staff arrived. It was roofed with corrugated tin, a concrete floor was being laid, and it was already amazingly well equipped. One end of the kitchen was partitioned off as a supply room, which was stocked as soon as the shelves were built in it.

All of the *bashas* except the kitchen were immediately mosquito-proofed with hessian cloth [burlap] and netting, and all were wired for electricity.

One of the two larger *bashas* was speedily transformed into a library and writing room. This was to be a strictly "quiet room" with reading material, writing desks and lounging chairs. Surprisingly, the curtain and cushion material which came with the furniture was actually good-looking against the brown of the hessian cloth. To offset the monotony of brown walls and ceiling the upright and horizontal bamboo poles which support the *basha* were painted white. About four feet from the ground a strip of some six inches was painted red, and the rest of the pole down to the ground was painted black. Shades for the ceiling lights were made from the huge Indian bamboo hats painted white on the underside and trimmed with red and black.

The finishing touch which made the "quiet room" cozy, though rustic, was a gay runner of carpet down the center. By pure chance it was appropriately striped with red, black, green and tan. Men of the outfit had been drifting in and out of the library and writing room constantly since work had first been started on it, but they settled down to using it earnestly immediately upon its completion on May 29.

As in the case of the quiet room, all of the club *bashas* were utilized in the same transitory sort of way from the first moment of Red Cross activity in them. The other of the two small *bashas* was the next to be completed, by June 7, and was made into a game room. The second of the two larger *bashas* became the canteen and lounging room, not entirely completed, but sufficiently ready for use by June 11.

Every opportunity possible was used to put color where there was drabness. The bamboo poles in the game room turned a deep brilliant red under the painter's brushes. Instead of curtains in that room wooden valances were used above the windows and they were painted red also. Red and green furniture intended for use on the porch was taken inside. Even the green ping-pong table was an innocent accomplice to the color scheme. The dirt floor was covered with dark reddish brown sawdust which is not only satisfactory for utility purposes, but actually adds to the looks of the whole room. The ping-pong table is constantly in use and other quieter table games are equally popular.

The color scheme in the canteen room turned out to be yellow and black. The bamboo poles are yellow, with a base of black for some four feet above the ground. Wooden valances were again used instead of curtains, and striped diagonally yellow and black. The pencil-sized bamboo strips around the windows were finished in yellow. The piano was rejuvenated in black with the piece of woven bamboo which covers the back painted yellow.

A further description of the canteen would not be complete nor just without mention of the two carpenters who made it that way. They were borrowed from a neighboring outfit—Sergeant Robert M. Stribling and Private Pearl P. Little. They built the canteen counter with both open shelves and with drawers on which they put hand-hammered handles. They covered the front of the counter with woven bamboo and decorated the center section by bending slender bamboo "cord" to form the words "American Red Cross" and the CBI shield underneath.

A strip of colorful carpet, cushions, and sawdust on the floor finish off the room.

A concrete floor seemed advisable for sanitary reasons in the canteen as well as in the kitchen, and for a time the Army dangled the probability of it within tantalizing reach. However, it did not work out and the sawdust has been quite satisfactory.

In contrast to the "quiet room" the canteen might be called the "rumpus room." The piano, radio and victrola are all in there. That is where the noisy visiting goes on. Fellows gather around the piano, in the end of the room opposite the canteen counter, for informal entertainment and music. The room is long enough so that entirely unassociated activities can go on in either end without interfering with each other.

Operation of the club would have been impossible without the contribution of certain scarce commodities by outsiders. Paint, lumber, carpenters, and the loan of a jeep were outstanding examples. Again and again this statement was made by fellows from other outfits when approached for assistance: "We'll do everything we can to help. Nothing is too good for Merrill's men."

There was a dramatic moment on the afternoon of June 17 when the 5307 Red Cross club almost closed up before it opened. Contrary to all orthodox procedure, it never did open formally. Because of troop movements the "ghost town" was alternately alive and dead. The club could have been officially opened, and the canteen in use, ten days or so sooner than it was, except that the only men around to use it were a few stray hospital patients. That condition prevailed until the decision was finally made to turn the whole club—minus canteen operations—over to the hospital Red Cross. For fully one-half an hour, that is the way the situation stood. Then came the message that another conference had been held and that the club was to open as per original plans!

In view of the circumstances—more complicated than can be discussed in a report—it seemed foolish to try to have the formal opening which was scheduled for the following day. It seemed foolish to have a formal opening at all. So on June 19 the canteen started serving food at scheduled hours, and the 5307 Club spoke of itself thereafter as being "open."

In the meantime the ghost town became suddenly alive again and the club facilities are now being used to capacity.

In hanging verbal plaques the first one goes to the canteen manager of the club for the Marauders. He is British, speaks Hindustani fluently, and his name is Horace Kingham. He can "put his hand" to almost anything, and has proved it. A band arrived to play at the club one evening minus its pianist, so Horace, after having spent the day in the kitchen, stepped from behind the counter where he was serving, washed the doughnut grease from his hands, and played the piano with the band for the rest of the evening!

Special Services deserves one of the plaques. Base Special Services loaned a radio and provided the lumber and plans for an outside stage which the carpenters constructed. The 18th Special Services should have a plaque of its own for meritorious service. Without any fanfare or ceremony its enlisted men in charge of athletics arrived one day at the club and set up a badminton court, volley-ball court, horse-shoe pits and basket-ball, baseballs, bats, and gloves, softballs, a punching bag, ping-pong sets and a piano tuner!

They have been equally helpful as a liaison for suggesting and providing entertainment. In the less than two weeks that the club has been "open" the following entertainments have been brought to it: a rhumba band and a magician, a semi-swing band, a mixed unit with singer, guitarist, boogie-woogie pianist and comedians, and the B-Kit of radio broadcast transcriptions of "Command Performances." This B-Kit has been booked for two nights a week for the 5307 Club.

During the period while the ghost town was really a ghost town, a quartet of musicians flew from Jorhat to play for the Marauders. Since there was no one but hospital patients, the entertainment was turned over to the hospital Red Cross.

A ping-pong tournament has been run off in anticipation of the coming of a U.S. national ranking player who will have the 5307 on his itinerary when he arrives. That event was to have been the last week of June, but had to be postponed because the champ was behind schedule. Another "was to have been" is the reappearance of the rhumba band for June 30 when the Public Relations planned to take some pictures for publicity. That, too, is on the calendar for the future.

The staff agrees that it has never had more pleasure working with a group of fellows. Having had nothing the past months but battle, death and disease they are grateful merely for being alive. Though the Enlisted Men's Committee as such needs further developing, the enlisted men's functional committee has operated superbly. They handle eagerly and capably many of the routine tasks. They are fellows who asked to be assigned to the club, have worked untiringly and demand nothing in return. Because it was fun and because it was necessary, the American Red Cross staff began with its own hands each job as it came along, whether manual or mental labor—but it was never long until a GI volunteered for it and insisted on assisting or taking it over if possible. These same men have been flatteringly reluctant to leave on furlough when given a chance (or told to) and have actively resisted going. The esprit de corps among those who assist at the club and among all of the 5307 is a heart-warming inspiration.

Under "Plans for the Future" should be included in bold-face type the arrangement for free tailoring and pressing service for the Marauders as soon as satisfactory native labor can be located. A number of interviews have already been held. Under the same heading come several other much-longed-for and much-worked-on items. The walks connecting the four buildings of the club should be covered. . . . The two end sections of the canteen bar will eventually be decorated interestingly and attractively as well as having the Marauders' insignia painted on the back of the piano. . . . The men are showing sign of initiative in self-entertainment, in addition to using the recreational facilities provided for them, which means the utilizing of more local talent. . . . Because of the great interest in the athletic equipment sent to the men by Special Services the possibility of having a flood light placed outside to illuminate the badminton courts is under consideration. The canteen expects to furnish refreshments for the hospital Red Cross on special occasions. . . . These are extras, beyond the line of duty. Within the line of duty there is still much to be done, incidentally!

There are three accomplishments which the staff considers nothing less than major achievements for the month. Each deserves more space in this niche of honorable mention, but for lack of time and space will be disposed of in the same paragraph. They are—First, the refrigerator; second, a Jeep, permanently assigned; third, but far from least, after having pled and waited for one month—a LADIES LATRINE!

This has been a full month. It has been a month short in time, but long in experience. Its headaches have been comparatively few, its heartaches poignant, and its privileges supreme.

As was originally intended, the 5307 Club is for 5307 only, and so far there has been no serious implication that there would be trouble with outsiders disregarding that rule. However, there has been an occasional Negro dropping by, and a few white men from other outfits. When an M.P.—one of the Marauders—was asked his opinion on the matter of putting the intruders out or allowing them to stay, he looked up earnestly into the eyes of the enquirer and expressed the sentiments of "the toughest infantry unit" of the CBI. He replied, "Ma'am, I couldn't put those fellows out of here. This is just like my home. All along the Road [Ledo] other fellows welcomed us into their clubs. And as for the colored fellows, why their band met us on the Road when we were weary and discouraged, and gave us heart to go on. I just couldn't put 'em out!"

What can you do with boys like that but love them?

Marauders responded wholeheartedly to this program. One of the more articulate among them was First Lieutenant Logan E. Weston, of New Bedford, Pennsylvania. Known as the "fighting preacher" because of his ministerial studies, Lieutenant Weston was commanding officer of General Merrill's I. and R. (intelligence and reconnaissance platoon) that moved well ahead of the main body of Marauders charting Japanese positions and strength and signaling back the information.

Lieutenant Weston returned to the United States in September, 1944, and went to Fairmont, West Virginia, where he expressed his thanks to the parents and local Red Cross chapter of one of the Red Cross girls at the Marauders' club—Wren Barbe.

To share his gratitude with the world, Lieutenant Weston wrote a tribute to Miss Barbe and her club associates, Norris McClellan and Mary Elizabeth Rogan. Here are some excerpts:

Numerous remarks have been made about Merrill's fabulous Marauders in action against the Japs in northern Burma. Little or nothing, however, has been said about the activity behind the American lines.

While the Marauders were battling jungle, monsoons, tropical fevers, and forcing Japs southward, they were little aware of the fact that a similar battle was being waged by faithful and devoted Red Cross workers at the rest camp back in Assam.

178

Evacuation from Burma by plane landed members of the Marauders unit in a forward hospital base. From there, convalescing patients were sent to a rest area in which the Red Cross had established a club. The three workers selected for this station were first, volunteers, second, carefully picked. They were without question just as fabulous as were the Marauders.

These noble girls brave the same tropical diseases as do the soldiers. They are exposed to the reptiles, rodents, insects, malaria and numerous other maladies. It is not long before they realize that they are the first white women in this area, and that the natives have little idea about our methods. What a cost these true Americans pay! But they do so joyfully, in modest tones. They say they are just doing their bit to win the war. The thought for self-concern or comfort never enters the minds of these modern frontierswomen. Not unlike our nation's famous pioneers, they gladly accepted hardship and danger in volunteering for this forward base. They knew the Japs were just over the next hill, in a position to endanger their station at any time.

The Marauders, though tough because of necessity, are human. Under the hard and crusty outer shell, lies a pliable heart of flesh. The knowing dread of the wounded is that they fear the future. They are afraid of being a detriment and liability to loved ones when they return. They do not want sympathy, they want confidence. You and I can profit by the example set before us by these Red Cross workers, and help our buddies regain that confidence.

Finally, about the "Marauders' sweetheart," Miss Wren Barbe, of Fairmont, West Virginia, one of the three picked women. Despite her endless tasks she is always ready to greet the soldier with a beautiful smile, and listen to his tale of woe. Forgetting her own home comforts, loved ones and perplexing troubles, she patiently listens to his troubles. She offers cheery suggestions to help him recover from the blow of being jilted by the "one and only," or perhaps to help him recover from the loneliness that grips one's heart upon receiving news of the departure of loved ones. There are many other heartaches experienced by the soldier who has been long overseas, but perhaps the two mentioned are most commonly experienced.

For these, and many other morale boosters, we pay this tribute to our American Red Cross, and the "sweetheart of the Marauders":

"You have nobly performed a very difficult task, and have stayed with it. You have brought our homes and loved ones to us when we were unable to go to them. We have not been sojourners in a strange land, because you have brought our glorious America with all its joy and privileges right up to our front lines. You have represented all we hold dear and precious. Sweetheart of the Marauders, we salute you and realize that the battle you are fighting is not without the shedding of sacrificial blood, neither do we want you to think your work is in vain. You did not have to make those sacrifices, but we are glad you chose to do so. In so doing, you have strengthened our lines tremendously. Our hats are off to you and our hope for you is a speedy return to your normal way of life. Until then, God grant you health, prosperity, happiness, and in all things, God's best."

Chapter IX

SUPPLY LINES

AMONG THE UNSUNG HEROES OF WORLD WAR II ARE THE AMERICAN soldiers, sailors, and Coast Guardsmen who have manned Allied supply lines around the globe. Far more than in previous wars, the success or failure of battles has hung on them. Supply has been the key to Allied success.

Almost forgotten in the excitement of war news were these servicemen in sectors removed from the fighting fronts—under the hot, enervating sun of the Persian desert, in the humid Amazonian jungle, in the fog-hung Aleutian Islands, and far up north in the Arctic regions. They stood watch over bases, observed weather conditions, kept open radio communications, and moved the supplies. Cut off from civilization, enduring the extreme rigors of climate, struggling with heartbreaking terrain, they felt themselves marking time—"sweating out the war" was the GI phrase. They suffered the tedium of waiting, the pangs of homesickness and separation from their families, and the discomforts of isolation. And for these sacrifices there was no excitement nor glory of battle as a compensation; yet in the over-all military picture their services were indispensable.

Their plight made a particularly strong appeal to the American Red Cross. To serve them in the remotest outposts—yes, even on a post near the North Pole—went sympathetic and understanding Red Cross workers.

By keeping open the channels of communication between them and their families, by solving personal problems and problems induced or accentuated by monotony, they contributed greatly to the troops' spirit.

On their posts, Red Cross workers met the needs as they arose, whether it was giving chapter-made woolen mufflers, sweaters, and face masks to soldiers walking guard in the icy winds high on Newfoundland's cliffs, adding a home touch with curtains at windows in bare barracks, or bringing the latest motion picture to isolated men who had not seen movies for many months.

Some of their best work lay in the intelligent manner in which they guided the men to self-help. They unearthed skills and channeled them into recreational activities—amateur shows, concerts, and arts and crafts. And as they could draw on the resources of an organization with millions of volunteer workers, they were able to supply both tools and materials that enabled servicemen to make the best use of their skills.

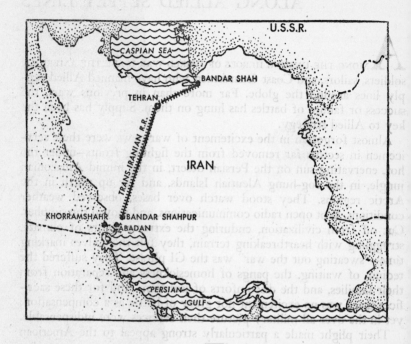

Persian Gulf Service Command

Soon after the arrival of the first United States Army service and supply battalions in December, 1942, the American Red Cross moved into the Persian Gulf Service Command. The command was established to relieve the British Army of the major responsibility for moving and protecting war supplies through Iran to Russia. This supply route was developed by the Allies as an alternative to the costly North Atlantic line through Norway's North Cape to Murmansk and Archangel.

A full year of extensive construction by United States Army engineers (and earlier by the British Army) had prepared the way for the Persian Gulf Service Command. Docks and jetties were built, harbor channels dredged and huge cranes installed. The construction program embraced truck and plane assembly plants, new highways and the improvement of old roads, airfields, and the overhauling and re-equipment of the Trans-Iranian Railway.

The port battalion at Khorramshahr and other Persian Gulf ports in American hands unloaded thousands of ships carrying lend-lease tanks, planes, spare parts, food, clothing, medicine, and innumerable other items that materially aided the Red Army in driving the Germans from Russia. Negro and white troops sorted the supplies and got them to the supply dumps. Loaded trucks were moved in convoy by both Negro and white soldier-drivers to Tehran and other transfer points where Russian drivers took over. Motor convoys went at full speed across the desert to escape the temperature of 145 degrees or more. The mountains to the north gave relief, but their tortuous, narrow roads increased driving hazards.

Stationed along the convoy route were road maintenance gangs, truck repair crews, and Military Police patrols. Their camps were isolated in a country as primitive as in the days of Omar Khayyam. By means of clubmobiles, snack bars staffed by Red Cross girls at the larger posts, hospital workers, and field directors, the American Red Cross gave them good coverage.

But there was one group of men—the small detachments stationed along the Trans-Iranian Railway—whose need for Red Cross services for a time furrowed many brows. Ordinarily their remote outposts might have been reached by clubmobiles, but the latter were ruled out because no highway paralleled the railroad.

The problem was finally solved by the operation of a "train-mobile," an idea conceived in the summer of 1943 by Douglas Gunter, of Richmond, Virginia, then American Red Cross Area Administrator in Iran. When Gunter first proposed that a caboose and freight car, staffed by a Red Cross man and two Red Cross girls, be placed on the railroad, the military authorities demurred. "It's a swell idea," commented one Army officer, "but girls?—no! That's a rough, hot, dusty ride even when made occasionally, and you're thinking of setting up a regular schedule? You'll never be able to go through with it."

Major General Donald H. Connolly, commanding officer, and Colonel Paul F. Yount, director of the Trans-Iranian Railway, finally gave the trainmobile their blessing. Army carpenters converted a crude caboose into comfortable quarters for the two Red Cross girls—blond, vivacious Anne L. "Lil" Hackworth, of Seattle, and dark-haired Marie "Rickey" St. Martin, of Baltimore. Their caboose had two bunks, two chairs, a table and lamp, wardrobe closets and a shower. Assistant Field Director Edwin L. "Bud" Abbott, of Lawton, Michigan, had his bunk and office at one end of the "glorified box car" which had been fixed up as a comfortable snack bar.

It was one of the most exciting events in Iran when on August 14, 1943, the Red Cross trainmobile made its maiden trip from Tehran down to Khorramshahr on the gulf, stopping at all the posts along the railroad.

Some months later Polly von Seht, of Scandia, Minnesota, American Red Cross correspondent in the Middle East, took the same ride.

This unique freight car [wrote Polly von Seht] is more than just a trainmobile to the hundreds of soldiers stationed along the railroad. To them it's a touch of home.

Picture all the grime, soot, and dirt that is a counterpart of any railroad—lonely railroad stops where American soldiers are sweating it out, operating and maintaining the most important railway supply line in the world. Imagine miles and miles of desert where hot winds blow, and the dust whirls with a temper all its own . . . long stretches of steel track that wind through precarious mountain passes, tunnels and bridges (in one stretch of 131 miles there are 132 tunnels). Add these up, and the result is about as exciting as Einstein's theory. It's so drab, in fact, you'll think American soldiers stationed in Persia are doing the most unexciting work in any theater, and under the most trying circumstances.

But step inside this box car for a moment. Three Red Cross workers try to make you feel this tiny club is your home. Edwin L. Abbott is busy turning the handle of an ice cream freezer and at the same time keeping one eye on the coffee pot that's sending off an aroma reminiscent of back home in Mother's kitchen. Over there at the window Lillian Hackworth is murmuring "15-2, 15-4," while she plays cribbage with a corporal from Minnesota. A gramophone is grinding out "Blues in the Night," and Rickey St. Martin is showing a sergeant in greasy fatigue clothes the latest jitterbug step she learned before she left the States in May, 1943.

The walls of the car are painted a light cream. Red and white checkered curtains flutter at the sooty windows. There's linoleum on the floor that matches the covering on the snack bar counter across the width of the car. On this counter is set a huge basket of fresh doughnuts. GI Joe and his buddy are taken right back to Main Street where they used to dunk sinkers at the Greasy Spoon, while a third soldier scans through a month-old edition of the *New York Times* to see what the Brooklyn Dodgers are doing. There's a large crude bookcase lined with detective and Western stories. A big blond private encased in a dirty sweatshirt mutters to himself, "Wonder why people back home keep thinking we're a bunch of morons? Wish they'd send books where we didn't have to figure out who killed the canary and why . . ."

So it goes until the Red Cross trainmobile pulls out of this tiny station and moves on to the next. The GIs know the exact time of its arrival there; being railroad men, they've telegraphed ahead. The fellows are right there when the trainmobile pulls in. Night may have fallen over the desert by this time. Bud Abbott prepares the "little theater" for a showing of "Madame Curie." The soldiers in this forsaken spot rarely see movies, and they're only too willing to help Bud set up the 16-mm. projector and screen supplied by Army Special Services. "This is great," says one soldier. "Ice cream and movies—just like home."

The end of a day's run on the rails doesn't add up to a cool shower and bed for Bud Abbott or these Red Cross girls. Maybe Lil and Rickey suddenly decide to beat up a batch of fudge, while Bud grinds away at the freezer for tomorrow's club callers. And if they're railed for the night anywhere near a big Army camp they make it a point to go over to the recreation center where Lil beats out a bit of boogie-woogie. Rickey dances with some 300 GIs who welcome a chance to dance with an American girl, regardless of the oppressive heat.

Pushing southward toward the Persian Gulf the Red Cross trainmobile runs into soaring temperatures. On most desert posts it averages from 130 to 150 degrees in daytime. The days are unbearable and the nights one long pool of perspiration. It's a country of sweat—honest soldiers' sweat. The fatigue clothes on the backs of GIs are covered with huge splotches of white, caused by excessive perspiration and salt release from the body.

Throughout this area, ice cream is a godsend to the soldiers. And the sight of a pretty Red Cross girl does something to lift even the lowest spirits.

Caribbean Area

The three principal American Red Cross stations in the Caribbean area were the Panama Canal Zone, Puerto Rico, and Trinidad. As old-line Army posts, Puerto Rico and Panama had field-director coverage long before World War II. Trinidad was one of the British islands leased by the United States in a destroyer deal before Pearl Harbor. Linked with other British bases, Dutch islands, Cuba, and United States insular possessions, Trinidad was vital in an impregnable chain of defense.

There were seventy-eight Red Cross workers on duty here with nine stations having resident workers and the others covered on an itinerant basis. Altogether the Red Cross was represented at Aruba and Curaçao (Netherlands West Indies), the Galapagos Islands, Ecuador, Peru, Cuba, including Guantanamo Bay, Great Exuma, and the Bahamas, all three Guianas, Antigua (Leeward Islands), Haiti, Jamaica, two posts in the Virgin Islands, Barbados, and Santa Lucia in the Windwards, in addition to Puerto Rico, the Panama Canal Zone, and Trinidad.

Eight hospitals, four in the Canal Zone, two in Puerto Rico, and two in Trinidad, had Red Cross hospital recreation programs, and some also had Red Cross social workers and secretaries.

An exhausting climate and inactivity, twin foes of morale, were reflected in the heavy case load. Red Cross communications into and out of this area averaged 8,000 per month. With Army Special Services providing a recreation program and USO responsible for off-post activities, the Red Cross stressed welfare service rather than clubs in the Caribbean area.

Field Director Alva E. Neal of Gallipolis, Ohio, arrived at Trinidad even before Pearl Harbor—in June, 1941. D. C. Poshusta of Mason City, Iowa, landed with Army units at Aruba, Dutch West

Indies, on February 11, 1942, the same day that Orry C. Walz of Dorrance, Kansas, went ashore at Curaçao, Dutch West Indies, and Claudius B. Webster of New York City came to Dutch and British Guiana in April, 1942.

During the height of the submarine warfare in the Caribbean Sea —1942 and 1943—Red Cross field directors spent much of their time looking after survivors of the many United Nations' ships sunk by German U-boats. For security reasons, not much publicity was given these sinkings, but the loss in shipping, cargoes and lives was very large.

Puerto Rico unquestionably cared for more submarine victims than any other island in the Caribbean. The American Red Cross chapter in San Juan performed an extraordinarily fine service in providing food, clothing, shelter, and medical aid.

Next to Puerto Rico, Trinidad probably was called upon most frequently to aid survivors of torpedoed ships. There being no Red Cross chapter on the island, Field Director Alva E. Neal took on Red Cross activities himself. The following excerpts from Neal's report for the period June 15–October 15, 1942, indicate the scope of his work.

Care of survivors has been a great task in the Trinidad sector. At one time (July 1942) more than 1100 survivors were on the island and in the sector. Red Cross stood ready to do its share in relieving the needs of these men who were victims of war's depredations. No agency but the Red Cross was prepared to meet the immediate needs of these men upon their arrival ashore, especially those who were landed within the jurisdiction of the leased areas. Many of these men were landed without a single article of clothing on their bodies. No bath had been taken, no shave, no water to drink, no food to eat for many days.

We were notified either by Army or Navy depending upon the receiving service, and comfort articles, cigarettes, and clothing sufficient to meet the immediate need were provided.

On July 27, fifty-six survivors were equipped from Red Cross clothing stores in the short period of forty-five minutes.

On August 8th another group of forty-seven Latvian seamen were completely equipped with clothing in less than an hour.

On September 5th, twenty-eight Panamanian and Brazilian seamen were outfitted through our facilities.

These and many more small groups were cared for by Red Cross, and many letters of thanks and appreciation were received.

During July a survivors' camp was set up by the Army, and

upon several occasions 200-300 survivors were housed there at one time. These survivors were quartered and fed from Army facilities. American seamen's living expenses were borne by the steamship company or the Maritime Commission's insurance division, and those of Allied seamen by their consular service. Clothing could not be purchased locally due to no supply being available in Trinidad stores.

No survivor case has been brought to the attention of the Red Cross where a need existed but what some service has been rendered.

We have provided complete outfits of clothing, individual garments, writing paper, stamps, cigarettes and matches; informed families of the safety and welfare of their husband, brother, uncle, cousin; asked chapters to extend service to families of stranded seamen; given seamen counsel, advice; cheered them on to better things; secured new jobs for them on Army Quartermaster boats to enable them to return to their homes; helped several to find work-away trips on commercial lines back to their ports of embarkation.

These and many other services have been rendered these victims of war's adversity.

Brazil

Brazil's neighborly co-operation in permitting the use of its coast led to the development of one of the Allies' most important aerial supply arteries—the South Atlantic line.

The great Parnamerim Field at Natal on Brazil's bulge was still under construction when, in November, 1942, Albert Meyers of Brooklyn, the first American Red Cross field director, arrived. With the aid of Bernice Goetz of Cleveland, a welfare secretary who came three months later, Meyers covered a vast territory extending from Belem at the mouth of the Amazon River southward across the jungles to Bahia. By 1944, twenty-four Red Cross girls and men ran thirteen stations in this same area—Belem, Natal, Recife, and Bahia, the main bases along the coast, and smaller radio, antiaircraft, and weather observation outposts hacked out of the Amazonian jungle.

The Red Cross area office was on Parnamerim Field, headquarters of the Air Transport Command's South Atlantic Division. Parnamerim was the chief airport of an airline that started at Miami and used the following bases in the Caribbean and the South Atlantic as principal stopovers; Borinquen Field, Puerto Rico; Waller

Field, Trinidad; Atkinson Field, British Guiana; Val de Cans Field, Belem; Parnamerim Field, Natal; and Ascension Island. From Natal to Bathurst, Africa, and from Ascension to Accra on the African Gold Coast, planes made connections with the trans-African military air route which, with branches, linked the Middle East, India, China, and Russia with England and the United States in a remarkably unifying network.

Through Natal passed a constant air traffic bound for the major war theaters. Many of the pilots of the Ninth Air Force who gave such extraordinary tactical support to the British Eighth Army in the Libyan desert and in North Africa made a stopover at Natal. So did the airmen who ferried the lend-lease bombers which gave General Montgomery timely air superiority at El Alamein; the B-25's and Douglas A-20's which contributed to smashing Russian victories in 1942 and 1943; and the planes that brought victory to American arms in North Africa, Sicily, Italy; and, too, the bombers that helped General Stilwell recapture Myitkyina in northern Burma. In addition to planes ferried under their own power, the Air Transport Command's huge transports carried plane engines, spare parts, V-mail, blood plasma, medical supplies and other high-priority items.

Transient air crews and passengers often were grounded on Parnamerim Field for periods ranging from one to five or more days. As they were confined to post with commercial amusements beyond reach, the commanding officer, Major General Robert L. Walsh, ordered the opening of two dayrooms, one for enlisted men, the other for officers.

The dayrooms were beautifully furnished with funds supplied by the "War Emergency Comité," a group of patriotic American citizens resident in Rio de Janeiro. This group similarly furnished and equipped other dayrooms and Navy recreation centers along the Brazilian coast. As a branch of the Brazilian Red Cross, members of the group gave valued assistance to American Red Cross workers in the South Atlantic throughout the war.

At General Walsh's request, American Red Cross girls operated the dayrooms at Natal. Under direction of Madeleine Schmid of Detroit, they held club programs and arranged beach picnics, sailings, and fishing trips, which helped make the transients' stay a pleasant one. Assisting Miss Schmid were Dorothea Winding of Miami Beach, Florida; Cora P. Menefee of Denver, Colorado; Mary Alice Huddle of Winnetka, Illinois; Frances McGill of Albuquerque, New Mexico; and Marguerite Boom of Grand Rapids, Michigan.

Distinguished transients were put up overnight in a special barracks on the field. As part of her duties Bernice Goetz welcomed and made comfortable a host of well-known people, including Prince Bernhard of the Netherlands, Mme. Chiang Kai-shek, Major General Claire L. Chennault, Ambassador Joseph C. Grew, Major General Patrick J. Hurley, H. V. Kaltenborn, Maxim Litvinoff, Captain Eddie Rickenbacker, and Lowell Thomas.

With the end of the North African campaign in the spring of 1943, Natal felt the beginning of a returning tide of American soldiers—the wounded being evacuated by air to hospitals in the United States. In an ever-swelling stream they poured through Natal, coming from North Africa, Sicily, Italy, and the China-Burma-India theater.

This rapid method of evacuation provided by the Air Transport Command spared many wounded heroes the ordeal of a several weeks' run through mine-infested waters. The South Atlantic was one of the air routes used for evacuation of the wounded, and Natal was one of the principal stopovers for hospital planes. Red Cross worker Dorothy Craig of Traverse City, Michigan, met these planes. She distributed reading material, cigarettes and candy, served coffee and took messages for transmission to the men's families, a service given by Red Cross workers all along the South Atlantic line.

Though air evacuation took far less time than by ship, experience showed that patients required some diversion in the hospital planes. The American Red Cross met the need with the "Red Cross Air-Evacuation Kit," a counterpart of the comfort kit supplied to sea-going patients. "We nurses have found the flight kit a success," reported Lieutenant M. Elizabeth Binkley of Montclair, New Jersey, an air evacuation nurse. "It's amazing how quickly the time goes for the men now. Some of them play cards together; some are well enough to read the magazine that is included. Our patients who are well enough to sit up appreciate the addition of the rubber air cushion to the uncomfortable aluminum 'bucket' seats, while the handing out of such things as lemon drops, chewing gum and wafer cookies has been an antidote for air sickness."

Ascension Island

Ascension Island, it is said, was originally selected by the British Government as the place of Napoleon's exile after Waterloo. Deciding it was too lonely, even for Napoleon, they took him instead to St. Helena, seven hundred miles to the southeast, where the French Emperor ended his days.

Several thousand Yanks stationed on Ascension in World War II experienced the loneliness of this volcanic rock in the South Atlantic, midway between the bulge of Brazil and the African Gold Coast. Before the war some seventy-five British subjects attached to a cable station and a few St. Helenese natives lived on the island with its Green Mountain, one hundred lower hills, and forty-eight craters. Only rarely, perhaps once a year, did a ship anchor there.

In 1942 Ascension suddenly became the scene of secret, bustling activity. U.S. Army engineers landed, surveyed, and performed. They built a 7,000-foot runway unlike any in the world. Across the middle is a hump of volcanic rock that could not be blasted. The engineers built gun emplacements facing the sea, and task forces that followed were ready for any eventuality—to attack Nazi subs, naval or air forces. When the huge airbase at Natal, Brazil, was completed, supplies and men and planes touched upon this pin-point island which shortened the distance of transatlantic flights. Ferry pilots and bomber crews having trouble with engines or bad weather marveled at their safe haven, familiarly called "the Rock."

The garrison was split up into small units living in tent colonies on the rocky hillsides. Except for some scrub on Green Mountain and a lone scrawny tree bending to the trade winds along the beach, Ascension was barren. Its smallness—five by seven miles—gave the GI's a sense of confinement, and their isolation depressed them. Preying on their minds also was the deadly routine—the daily ration of one gallon of water for drinking and washing; the sameness of the horizon and the vast expanse of sea surrounding them; the unrelieved rhythm of the pounding surf, and the constant trade winds.

It took a man with imagination to know how to maintain the spirit and interest in life of soldiers in this situation. And in Gerald Bannigan, of Orange, New Jersey, the American Red Cross had such a man. "Jerry and his Jeep" meant Red Cross in capital letters. Bannigan learned how best to help the enlisted men by living with them.

To satisfy their hunger for green things, he distributed flower and vegetable seeds that the men planted in volcanic ash irrigated with their rationed water. Victory gardens included Chinese morning glories and six-foot tomato plants.

"Color is what we need," said Field Director Bannigan. Through the Red Cross field office on the Brazilian mainland he purchased curtain material—soft pastel shades of green, mauve, and yellow for dayrooms, and gay tropical prints of parrots and flowers for mess halls. The same Red Cross workers also bought for him comfortable furniture hand-woven from native reeds and grasses.

The Italian game of *bocce* was admirably suited to the island terrain. Bannigan ordered wooden *bocce* balls made by native Brazilian cabinetmakers.

Then, at the approach of the Ascension garrison's first Christmas, Bannigan took orders from the men who had no way of purchasing Christmas gifts for their loved ones back home. The Red Cross office at Natal filled the orders in the Brazilian coastal towns —hundreds of pairs of sheer silk stockings, Carmen Miranda dolls, alligator purses, rubber sheets and toys for babies, guitars and mouth organs. ATC crews, glad to be of assistance, flew the Christmas cargo to "the Rock" on their way to Africa. The greatest pleasure, that of wrapping and sending the gifts home, was saved for the men themselves.

Bannigan, a former athletic instructor, encouraged the construction of a baseball diamond. Enlisted men started the work with a convoy of nineteen trucks and a steam roller, bringing volcanic surfacing ash from a hilltop three miles distant.

Their officers entered wholeheartedly into the work, completing the diamond on a Sunday while the men had the afternoon off. A constant round of baseball, basketball, volley ball, tennis, and horseshoe pitching tournaments was scheduled. Enthusiasm was so great that electric lights were installed for night playing. A basketball court in the nose hangar provided diversion for transient pilots waiting for plane repairs.

The island was also a fisherman's paradise. Twelve fishing poles were available in the Red Cross office. On off-duty men fished from the cliffs for rock bass or sailed offshore for deep-sea fishing.

Though organized recreation took up most of his time, Bannigan never overlooked the importance of serving individual soldiers. During his tenure of more than a year, he raised the spirit of many a soldier by solving personal problems of one kind or another.

In one of his reports, he related the story of Henry, a young Chinese-American soldier—the only one of his race on Ascension— who had become depressed over the lack of Chinese newspapers and music and because he had no one to talk with in his native tongue. This nostalgia Bannigan promised to satisfy.

A few days later a transatlantic transport plane alighted on the island, and out of it stepped several passengers—prominent Chinese Government officials. Jerry speedily whisked the young Chinese soldier to the airfield where he had the morale-raising satisfaction of conversing in his native tongue.

Meanwhile, Bannigan had written to the "War Emergency Comité" of Rio de Janeiro explaining his problem, and in time a parcel containing twenty copies of a Chinese newspaper and three phonograph records arrived. Two of the records were commercial and bore Cantonese sing song melodies. The third was a transcription made in Rio by a young Chinese pianist whose greeting in Chinese preceded a piano selection.

"They say that the Chinese are not demonstrative," wrote Bannigan, "but I wish that I could have taken pictures of Henry when he opened the package. And when he sat listening to 'his records' he was in his own Shangri La once more."

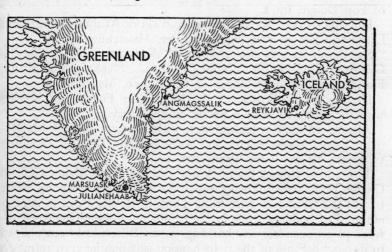

Iceland

In the great battle of the Alantic, the Allied bases on Iceland, Greenland, and Newfoundland played a vital role. United States troops occupied them in 1941 to prevent their capture by the Germans and to afford added protection to the Allied sea and air supply route across the North Atlantic to Britain, military base of the European theater of operations, and Russia.

Iceland, particularly, situated in the northern arc of the air service, was a strategic point. Submarine warfare surged around it. United States troops landed there in August, 1941, and soon after, the Iceland Base Command put through an urgent request for

American Red Cross services. A group of Red Cross workers reached Iceland late in January, 1942, in a convoy with many enlisted men. The British occupation forces, who were being relieved, were still on the island. Many of them were survivors of the historic Dunkirk retreat, resting from their ordeal while they kept a weather eye out for the enemy.

The pioneer group consisted of the following: Field Directors Charles McDonald of Binghamton, New York; Lake F. Russell of Atlanta, Georgia; and Assistant Field Director Frank H. Hagen of Monroe City, Missouri.

Recreation workers were Jane Goodell and Ethel Hague Rea, both of New York City; Betsy Lane Quinlan of Waynesville, North Carolina; Doris Thain of Birmingham, Alabama; and Mary Dolliver of Fort Dodge, Iowa.

Hospital workers were Ettienne Baldwin of Atlanta, Georgia and Elizabeth Clark of Framingham Centre, Massachusetts.

Secretaries were Nancy Duncan of Washington, D. C.; Camelia Greethan of Alexandria, Virginia; Helen Lee Stephenson of Miami, Florida; and Margaret Singer of Uniontown, Maryland.

Dr. George K. Strode, of the Rockefeller Foundation, arrived with the group to make a public health survey.

Already on duty in Iceland were Field Director John P. McDermott, Salem, Massachusetts, and Assistant Field Director Dryhurst G. Evans, Wilkes-Barre, Pennsylvania.

The entire United States Army garrison from Major General Charles H. Bonesteel down through the ranks made a sincere effort to win the Icelanders' friendship. Though the army was in desperate need of building space in the beginning, General Bonesteel refused to commandeer any buildings as the British had been obliged to do; and because of the tight housing situation he even refrained from renting property, not wishing to inconvenience the native population.

The American Red Cross staff developed a close co-operative working arrangement with the Icelandic Red Cross, which contributed to the growth of a wholesome relationship between the civilian population and United States armed forces. An example was the annual Christmas party arranged by American Red Cross workers.

Last year [wrote a Red Cross girl] our recreation hall rang with Icelandic folk songs of a children's chorus around the first balsam tree, towering ten feet high, they had ever seen. Nor had the majority of them ever seen a movie before. Each [Yank] enlisted man led a young child up to the tree for an apple and an orange, which were so rare, they were eaten skins and all. Their enthusiasm grew and they would not leave until they had their traditional Christmas dance.

As they danced they sang in Icelandic, and their khakied hosts replied in English. In the background a dim light filtered through a stained glass window made of oiled brown paper by an artistic soldier. Symbolically it portrayed a soldier standing guard on a hill overlooking huts, fjords and mountains. Behind him, the Northern lights flickered like the rebirth of the Christmas spirit in the children's eyes.

General Bonesteel's policy regarding Icelandic buildings, while admirable from a public relations standpoint, necessarily was a self-imposed hardship, and Red Cross workers suffered with the rest. The eleven girls in the group were packed into two small Nissen huts, each furnished with a stove, a coal bucket, and cots. The girls hung curtains at the windows and turned dry-goods boxes into dressing tables, but they were too crowded to feel exactly comfortable.

And they felt somewhat disappointed as their club program, so desperately needed for morale, was delayed until the Army could build clubhouses. At that time the troops had no means of recreation at all. The Red Cross girls were requested by the military authorities to make the best of the situation, so they carried recreation right into the camps scattered about the bleak island.

Traveling in twos and threes, using any type of conveyance available, even open boats in rough seas, the girls visited various camps every evening—the only time the troops were free. They held community sings, concerts, amateur shows, games and contests in any space available. Camp mess halls, day huts, and large Nissen huts housing trucks and equipment were all pressed into use until a temporary Red Cross recreation center was opened in schoolrooms donated by the Icelandic Government in June, 1942. A week after the center opened, military police reported that trouble with the soldiers in Reykjavik had dropped seventy-five per cent. The first permanent Red Cross club, acquired from the British who had used it as an officers' club, opened its doors on September 16, 1942. Subsequently, the Red Cross program was expanded until a staff of thirty-four workers covered three on-post clubs, housed in barrel-roofed Nissen huts and two hospitals in the Reykjavik and Keflavik sectors. Seven additional workers served the Army Transport Command at air strips.

Iceland's dreary climate created unusual problems. Such things as trees and flowers that were commonplace in the United States became of major importance to American servicemen. Red Cross clubs, therefore, were often decorated with hand-made colored tree leaves. One worker sent an urgent plea to National Headquarters for a small tree, even if dead, to serve as a stage prop for an amateur theatrical.

When the Arctic winds blew, all transportation, trucks and planes, was grounded by official orders, and nobody ventured out of barracks. The weather was subject to extraordinary changes. Often within fifteen minutes it changed from smiling blue skies to violent rain, hail, snow, rainbow and blue sky again. In winter when perpetual night replaced the round-the-clock daylight, and Arctic winds were particularly sharp, the troops found it difficult to keep warm, especially on the outposts.

The Icelandic summer, though brief, was pleasant, and Red Cross workers took full advantage of it by arranging hikes and picnics. Fields and mountains were beautiful with grass and flowers—but no trees. For a period of weeks GI's enjoyed the spectacle of twenty-four hours of continuous daylight, even though it interfered with their sleep.

During 1942 and 1943 thousands of American soldiers in Iceland waited for orders to proceed to camps in the British Isles. After Normandy some of these same men, now wounded in action, returned to Iceland in hospital planes for a few hours' stop en route to hospitals in the United States. Occasionally, when a plane landed and a Red Cross girl boarded it with a cheerful "Hi, fellows! Are you hungry?" she found a bandaged soldier with whom she had danced or played checkers only a few months before.

One patient, surprised to find Red Cross service right in the plane, exclaimed, "Now I'm convinced that if we'd gotten off our course and landed at the North Pole, we'd have found a Red Cross girl sitting on it with a smile, a cup of coffee, and news from home."

A wounded soldier in one of the ambulance planes mentioned to a Red Cross girl that he had a brother in Iceland with an Army engineering unit, whom he had not seen for three years. A telephone call to the Red Cross field director in the camp brought the brothers together. The casualty, though seriously wounded, had time to tell some of his experiences, while his brother offered the latest news of Mom and Dad, before the plane took off on the last leg of its journey to the United States.

Several days later came a tragic sequel to this reunion: the wounded brother had died shortly after his arrival at the hospital.

"It was tough having to deliver such disheartening news," wrote the Red Cross field director. "But the serviceman took it on the chin. He just looked away a minute, swallowed hard, and then said, 'It meant a lot when Red Cross took the trouble to find me so I could talk with my brother when he came through on the litter plane. Now it means everything.'"

Newfoundland

From Iceland en route home, hospital plane loads of patients landed on the large U.S. Army landing field at Stephenville on Newfoundland's western coast. No matter what time of day or night they arrived, an American Red Cross girl was on the field to greet them. The girls were Assistant Program Director Beatrice Massman of Buffalo, New York, and Staff Assistants Ruth Kellogg of New York City and Vivian Steinhoff of Caldwell, New Jersey.

Baseball-minded GI's referred to Newfoundland as "first base," the first of the British bases in the Atlantic occupied by United States troops, the advance contingent arriving on January 20, 1941. This island advanced the American defense line by more than a thousand miles eastward in the North Atlantic. From the great United States base at St. John's and the British airport at Cobb's Camp northwest of it, squadrons kept vigil over the island and the waters far out to sea. Warships steamed out of the long, sheltered harbors to patrol the sea lanes giving protection to the convoys bound for Britain. Newfoundland, one-third of the way to North Ireland bases from New York on the great circle route, was the jumping-off place for American-made bombers flying across the North Atlantic for delivery to Great Britain.

Canadian forces and the local native militia shared with the United States garrison the responsibility of guarding Newfoundland. Along St. John's cobblestoned Water Street, the town's Broadway, near the water front, as elsewhere on the island, Americans, Canadians and "Newfies" fraternized freely and met in friendly athletic competition.

The morale problem was far easier in Newfoundland than in Iceland, as American soldiers and sailors had less adjustment to make. Good for a laugh anywhere was the recollection that when the first United States troops arrived they expected to see Eskimos, while the Newfoundlanders mistook the parka-clothed GI's for Eskimos. Amusing to the Americans were some of the place names: Main Topsail, Cow Head, Blow-me-down, Come By Chance, Joe Batt's Arm, Seldom Come By, Heart's Content, and Tickle Harbor.

American servicemen were frequent guests at tea in Newfoundland homes and participated in local celebrations held in the fishermen's villages high on the cliffs along the jagged coast. Some married local girls and had families.

The American Red Cross work in Newfoundland was chiefly an on-post activity. Camp, club, and hospital personnel were concentrated at St. John's, Army base headquarters, where Lucille Mick of Austin, Texas, directed the club; at the Army and Navy base at Argentia, on the southern coast, where Betty Fleck of Huntingdon, Pennsylvania, was club director; at the Army base at Gander where Helen Reichenbach of Anchorage, Kentucky, was in charge; and at Stephenville. The Red Cross also staffed two "alert buildings" for transient airmen grounded by fog.

Armed with a portable movie projector, screen and films, Assistant Field Directors W. H. Higgs of Barre, Vermont, and Jacob Horst of Reading, Pennsylvania, visited remote outposts.

Greenland

As a convenient stepping stone for planes flying between the United States, Canada, and Europe, Greenland was an important Allied base. Its value was even greater as the "cradle of European weather."

Weather data from Greenland was of vital military importance to the whole European theater of operations. High and low pressure areas moving across Greenland in a general southeasterly direction gave accurate indications of what weather could be expected in England and on the European continent. The Royal Air Force and the United States Army Air Forces based in Britain plotted their aerial war strategy against Fortress Europe from weather information gathered by United States and Canadian troops stationed in this Danish colony.

Attaching high value to Greenland, the Germans early in the war planted several meteorological units there. The battle to freeze them out began in the spring of 1941 when the United States Government assumed its protection as essential to the security of the Western Hemisphere. From time to time German weather outposts were ferreted out and destroyed. In the fall of 1944, the crew of a U.S. Coast Guard cutter landed on one of these outposts, captured three German officers and nine soldiers and seized their meteorological equipment, radio transmitters, and firearms.

In June, 1941, a joint landing was made in Greenland by United States and Canadian troops, and a group of military bases was established along the coasts.

"Was Eric the Red color blind when he named this place?" wrote one Red Cross field director, arriving among Greenland's gaunt mountains and endless snow. Research revealed that it really had been green when the Danes first cultivated it, but changing ocean currents had left little to interest the newcomer except the vast glacial icecap and spectacular northern lights. There is not a single city in all Greenland, and only one town of any size, Godthaab, the capital, where the first United States consulate was established in May, 1940.

Snow-, ice-, and weather-bound, the few American Red Cross stations in Greenland had little contact with the outside world. In the season when the winds raced like the Valkyries and the land was locked in ice, they had no contact with each other. The scattered units of United States servicemen were entirely dependent upon themselves for whatever semblance of normal living they were able to maintain. This tested the ingenuity of the Red Cross workers assigned to them. Punishing hours on skis, snowshoes, or icebreakers were required for field directors to reach the small groups of men at outlying posts.

At one station a short distance from Julianehaab, Red Cross Field Director Robert T. Barrett of Atlanta, Georgia, received an appeal for a life-size poster of a woman from a group of isolated soldiers who had not seen a living female in almost two years. Barrett wrote National Headquarters that they wanted "a paper doll they could call their own," so that they might not forget what an American girl looked like.

For a long time no Red Cross girls were assigned to Greenland due to the extreme conditions there. In response to Field Director Barrett's frequent requests, however, National Headquarters finally sent four in the company of Army nurses, the group arriving on January 20, 1944.

The Post Executive officer [reported Barrett] called me that morning saying, "Bob, your girls will be here in five minutes." I was so excited, not having seen nor talked to a lady in nearly five months, that I jumped into the car, and went tearing up to the Post headquarters to let them know about the new arrivals. In my confused state, I had not taken time to consider that the message from the Executive Officer had originated at the post. The Commanding Officer thoroughly enjoyed my lack of composure.

The girls, all recreation workers, were Margaret Gallagher of Temple, Texas; Frances Nell Dunkirk of Zeeland, Michigan; Martha L. Franklin of Los Angeles; and Emily Climo of Wakefield, Massachusetts. The latter two were assigned to the hospital.

Red Cross business boomed overnight. After overcoming their initial shyness, the men flocked into the Red Cross club and the hospital dayroom. The result was that Red Cross supplies were soon exhausted, and back to Washington went a cable requesting "15 barrels of doughnut flour and fifteen boxes of shortening—soonest possible."

The Red Cross girls made their influence felt in many ways which added up to improved spirits. For one thing, the men were more conscious of their personal appearance even though the girls did not expect it of them. The bare Nissen huts in which the men lived needed brightening up; the girls gave them a homelike touch with drapes and curtains obtained from Red Cross chapter volunteers in the United States. They were called upon to change buttons, patch elbows, and sew chevrons. Together with the field directors, Walter Smith of Skokie, Illinois, Charles W. Moran of Niagara Falls, and Barrett, they distributed chapter-made sweaters, socks and other Arctic equipment.

The Red Cross club on this station was located near the ruins of a settlement founded some nine hundred years ago by Eric the Red, father of Leif Ericsson, thought to have been the first white man to discover the American mainland. The club building, erected by the Army, faced the runway where planes landed and took off against a backdrop of snow-capped mountains and an iceberg-dotted fjord. Soldiers, airmen, truck drivers and Coast Guardsmen, blue with cold, relaxed before the fire and had doughnuts and coffee.

The station hospital took care of patients with only minor injuries. This made possible greater participation in the hospital recreation program. Local Eskimos requiring hospitalization were also admitted to this Army hospital. One of them, Semoiya by name, had lost an arm in an accident. The hospital staff made a papier-mâché form for a wooden arm with an iron hook built by soldiers of the ordnance unit. For the straps, the Red Cross furnished the only suitable piece of soft leather, saved from billiard cue tips. Semoiya, who knew not a word of English, was taught to sing "Pistol-Packin' Mama," and the ward was convulsed in laughter each time he sang it.

The most northerly American Red Cross installation in the world, a lonely United States Army base located along Greenland's northern coast not far from the North Pole, was covered by Field Director James Bruskin of Philadelphia, for eleven months—from October, 1943, to September, 1944.

Our entire world [wrote Bruskin] consists of a space half-a-mile in area. The wildest, most rugged mountains you can imagine tumble right into camp, clearly making our boundaries. While the rest of the bases in Greenland have landing fields and air transportation, we are solely dependent upon water transportation through the fjord which knifes through the mountains. On a clear cold night the sky puts on a show that would stun a Hollywood producer—Northern Lights plus the Arctic moon.

The Army established this base, according to Bruskin, chiefly for weather observation purposes, though there was plenty of anti-aircraft protection to harass any German planes from Norway flying over the territory.

To reach this remote base from the United States, Field Director Bruskin flew to Julianehaab, and from there sailed in a freighter for four days. The nearest Red Cross station was more than nine hundred miles away, with no overland routes whatsoever to it. During the long winter months when the water was one solid mass of ice, the post was completely isolated from the world except for radio. Bruskin tells the story of a young soldier, a replacement, who, upon arrival in camp, picked up a telephone in a shack and called for "long distance" to talk with his family in the United States. It was only a camp telephone, however, with a wire no more than a mile and a half long.

During one period of nine long weeks the post was without mail delivery service, which greatly depressed the men. Bruskin, having free access to Army communications, radioed messages to their families and replies came back the same way usually within four days. The men never forgot this emergency Red Cross service. Morale picked up tremendously when the Army, despite extremely hazardous flying weather, established a regular mail delivery service that brought first class mail by parachute dropped from low-flying planes. But mail from home, arriving in accumulated lots, seemed to bring at least one problem for every man. A round of letter writing and radiogramming began for Bruskin as soon as the letters had been digested. This was the experience of many other Red Cross field directors in Greenland and elsewhere.

Detached from the base were a number of six-man teams who manned remote weather and radio outposts. In winter or summer Bruskin served them regularly. To reach them during the winter meant traveling in snow shoes and by dog sled across the snow fields, often in a freezing gale.

From October 1 to March 1, when the temperature dropped from twenty to forty degrees below zero, the post was shrouded in perpetual darkness.

Many of the soldiers were young enough—eighteen to twenty—to squeeze some fun out of their strange experience. Bruskin promoted Eskimo crafts, including ivory carving, and other recreational activity to keep them busy during their off-duty hours. A popular sport was skiing, though some of the boys landed in the station hospital with broken bones. One of their hobbies was growing beards, the shape and length of which led to good-natured competition. Some boys were from Wilkes-Barre, Pennsylvania, and upon learning that Bruskin had come from the same state they felt closer to him.

Christmas trees [wrote Bruskin] are as rare up here as bathing suits, but that didn't stop us from having one. Our tree was a two-by-four cut down to size and nailed to a supporting platform. Green camouflage paint, liberally sprayed on the branches, gave it a very real effect. Tinsel and icicles were cut out of tin cans, and some burned-out light bulbs painted red, blue and green made very satisfactory Christmas balls. The large star on top of the tree was cut out of the heavy tinfoil tenderly wrapped around our dehydrated potatoes. It was a beautiful tree and I know that even Joyce Kilmer would have forgiven me.

Problems brought on by the overlong winter were solved with the coming of a season near enough like spring to permit outdoor expeditions. For one thing, Bruskin was now able to visit the weather and radio outposts by crash boats instead of by mushing. Sixteen men at a time accompanied him by crash boat up the fjord to see the immense aquamarine expanse of the ice-cap and watch icebergs break off amid thundering roars and float out to sea. Crayons and paints went along with the men and many excellent sketches were made.

From June to the latter part of July the sun was overhead daily until midnight, and the GI's understood why Greenland is called the "Land of the Midnight Sun."

The most exciting occurrence on Bruskin's post came in July when three of the Red Cross girls from the southern coast arrived to entertain the boys. The bearded GI's were in the highest spirits dancing with the girls.

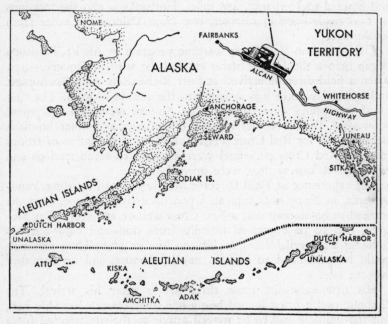

Alaska

Before the war the American Red Cross was represented in Alaska by ten active chapters. To cover the Territory's 580,000 square miles, only a small portion of which was settled, required the same stamina and courage displayed by the pioneers. Chapter chairmen, most of them seasoned frontiersmen, used not only radio, airplanes, coastal steamers, and fishing boats to maintain Red Cross services, but also, in the manner of sourdoughs, pack animals and dog sleds.

Pioneering instincts and ruggedness were likewise demanded of Red Cross field directors and girls who came to Alaska in the days after Pearl Harbor when the Territory was being developed as a vital outpost of the Pacific coastal defenses. On the mainland they faced severe cold except along the coastal strip to the south, from Cordova to Ketchikan, which the Army calls the "Banana Belt." There on the wet, heavily wooded islands and shore of the "Inside Passage" it is rarely zero. Primitive transportation was another serious handicap in a country of such vast distances as Alaska. There are only two railroads—Skagway to Whitehorse, 110 miles, and Seward to Fairbanks, 476 miles. Fairbanks is also the terminus of two roads open in summer, one from Valdez, the other from Anchorage.

The American Red Cross wartime program in Alaska Territory began before the United States entered the war—in January, 1941, when a field director arrived at Fort Richardson, near Anchorage, and a social worker was assigned to the station hospital. The first comfort supplies were received that August, recreation equipment soon after. By November outpost dispensaries and other hospitals began to ask for Red Cross services. Following the influx of troops in 1942, Red Cross personnel were assigned to seven stations and to other stations as they were opened.

The experience of Field Director Morris Gross of Reading, Pennsylvania, in Nome was typical. Upon his arrival in June, 1942, he learned to his dismay that a Red Cross welfare and recreation program had to be contrived literally from thin—and cold—air. No building was available for a club, no lumber or building materials could be purchased to build a new clubhouse, and no furniture was for sale.

His first assistance came three weeks after his arrival. The Catholic parish priest loaned him a one-story church assembly hall, but the building had to be moved a mile to the site selected for a Red Cross club. Townspeople, the Army, and civil engineers all helped in the moving. Both the building and the caterpillar tractors hauling it, however, bogged in the thawing summer tundra, and it took six more caterpillars to pull them out of the mire.

The problem of furniture came up next. Nome's stores had none for sale, and transportation difficulties precluded its being imported from the outside. Gross equipped his club piecemeal, obtaining a chair from one family, a table from another, a rocker from a third, and so on, until the club was completely furnished. From the family of a deceased Red Cross chapter chairman, he obtained the gift of a library and bookcases.

When the Nome Red Cross club finally opened its doors its usefulness was measured by the fact that it was the only public place in town, outside of the saloons, where soldiers could spend a companionable evening. By organizing the women of Nome and giving them a share in programs—there were decoration, hostess, dance, and other committees—Gross developed a fine community project around the club.

A young soldier, a musician in civilian life, gave him a hand in organizing a string band. Before Hollywood films started coming in, moving pictures made by Nome's amateurs were projected on the club screen.

When Gross left Nome in February, 1943, to be promoted to Red Cross training supervisor at Fort Lewis, Washington, he was replaced by a staff of six people—a club director, an assistant, two recreation workers, a hospital worker, and a secretary.

A challenge of a different kind was met by several other Red Cross field directors in 1942. Scattered over the vast expanse of Alaska were many remote outposts where men had not seen a motion picture in a great while. Though supplying them with films involved extreme difficulties of climate and terrain, the American Red Cross undertook the program at the request of the Army.

Priorities permitted the purchase of projectors and films within a week. Army and Navy co-operation resulted in a one-day clearance of the shipment northward from Seattle. Each pack consisted of a 16-mm. projector, reels of film, a generator capable of generating 120 volts, and a 100-foot cable.

The program was inaugurated in Kodiak in September, 1942. No floodlights accompanied this premiere, though the gathering was a brilliant one. Among those attending were General Charles E. Corlett and his staff, American Red Cross Resident Supervisor Carey Maupin and Fred F. Kislingbury, Pacific Area director of the Red Cross Hospital Motion Picture Service. An improvised hook-up set up by Red Cross workers broadcast word of the new program to the farthest outposts.

Distribution of the portable movie equipment began the next day. By dog-sled teams and jeeps, over roads and trails, some steep, some snow-packed, slushy or icy, and in all kinds of weather, Red Cross field directors carried Hollywood's latest productions to the isolated units. So often did these servicemen see films prior to their regular release dates, that one motion picture producer was moved to remark, "Hollywood might adopt a new publicity slogan: 'This picture was shown first to troops in Alaska.'" By a coincidence, Field Director Maurice L. Boyd showed "Holiday Inn" at South Beach, an outpost of Fort Raymond, on Christmas Eve, 1942. This is the picture in which Bing Crosby sings "White Christmas."

For the soldiers stationed on Montague Island where the rough seas made navigation difficult, Field Director Boyd had the Army drop the films by parachute. Army and Navy planes also transported the portable equipment over the longer distances, such as the 1500-mile hop from Kodiak to the Aleutian Islands.

The movies were showed in Quonset huts, mess halls, storehouses, barracks, hospital wards, and dayrooms, from Anchorage to the rocky tip of the Aleutian chain. Typical setting was a mess hall with the kitchen serving as a projection room. An audience of Minnesotans who hadn't seen a movie in ten months cheered Cesar Romero in "The Lucky Cisco Kid." In recreation centers of station hospitals, patients hobbled in on crutches, or, wrapped in warm robes, were wheeled in. They watched the pictures in silence, but when the lights were switched on again, their faces were inspiring.

At one lonely outpost—an air-rescue station—after the showing of a Sonja Henie picture, a soldier exclaimed spontaneously: "That's the first time we've heard a woman's voice in fourteen months."

In 1944 there were twenty-six American Red Cross installations (exclusive of Red Cross chapters) in the Alaska Territory, staffed by 144 workers, of whom seventy-eight were women. With Area headquarters at Fort Richardson, near Anchorage, American Red Cross operations stretched for more than four thousand miles, from Edmonton, Alberta, to the most westerly islands of the Aleutian archipelago.

In close co-operation with Army Special Services and Navy Welfare and Recreation, the Red Cross program embraced athletics, arts and crafts, community singing, dances, gardening, gold panning, parties, picnics, discussion groups, and even miniature golf.

Beautiful Ski Chalet, a branch of the Kodiak club and located in a secluded valley near Pyramid Mountain, was a popular retreat. Away from the routine of Army posts and Navy bases, the Chalet gave soldiers and sailors an opportunity to enjoy the homelike atmosphere of the lounge, music room, library, and snack bar. Louise Roloff, of Golden, Colorado, a recreation worker, swung a machete in the thick alder woods up the mountain slope to make nature trails along which wild flowers were labeled with gaily printed signs. Trail blazes also marked the way to hidden lakes and mountaintops. The bottoms and tops of coffee cans painted orange were nailed to posts along the trails to guide hikers who might get lost in the fog.

Skiing was the main winter program, with slopes for beginners and "schuss" hills for the advanced skiers. After ski races down the tallest mountain, steak fries were held for parties of four to sixty men. Groups of thirty-five to fifty men off Navy vessels were also entertained at the Chalet. For men cramped aboard ship the hike to Spectator Point, or a ball game at near-by "Swampy Acres" Stadium, with a home-cooked meal at the Chalet was a memorable event. Jeannette Griswold of Hanford, California, assistant program director, and Miss Roloff helped Captain John Hayes of Salt Lake City, post ski officer, in the promotion of winter sports. A popular item on the Ski Chalet's menu was the reindeer-burger, cousin of the home-town hamburger, made of ground reindeer meat.

At Whitehorse, halfway point on the Alcan Highway, the American Red Cross club was installed in an old log stable formerly used by the Northwest Canadian Mounted Police. The stable was remodeled and a wing added. On its floor, which once echoed the hoofbeats of the Northwest Mounted Police horses, Red Cross girls and other young American women danced with GI's. In the former oat bin a snack bar served coffee and doughnuts. What was formerly the hayloft became a dark room for camera enthusiasts, a workshop for arts and crafts, and the office of Field Director David T. deVarona of San Diego, California.

Whitehorse, made famous by Jack London's writings and the glamour of Yukon's gold rush, still had many buildings of log construction. Only a half-block away from the Red Cross club was the log church in which Robert W. Service, well-known Northwest poet used to worship.

And, here in the Arctic, the Red Cross served ice cream from a five-gallon, hand-operated freezer that once supplied the same dessert to Admiral Richard E. Byrd and his men on one of the Byrd antarctic expeditions.

During construction of the Alcan Highway in 1942 the American Red Cross staffed temporary recreation centers which the Army had built. They were appreciated by the thousands of engineering troops, Negro and white, who, with the aid of civilian workers, fought cold and loneliness, as well as one of the toughest terrains in the world, to build this sixteen-hundred-mile military supply route. And when the highway was opened to Army traffic in November, 1942, the Red Cross remained to serve the soldier truck drivers and military patrols.

The Alcan Highway starts at Dawson Creek, British Columbia railhead, and runs northwestward, winding around high mountains, spanning gorges, pushing through swamps and immense forests, until it ends at Fairbanks, Alaska. It parallels the Alaskan air lines. Red Cross on-post clubs along the Alcan Highway were located at Dawson Creek, Fort Nelson, Watson Lake, Whitehorse, and Fairbanks. In addition, there was a big club in Edmonton, and for a period, one at Big Delta. Karl W. Ernst of Akron, Ohio, supervised Red Cross installations along the highway.

Aleutian Islands

The air route through Alaska and the Aleutians is the shortest path to Japan from the United States. Attu, the westernmost island, lies only seven hundred miles from the Japanese base at Paramushiro.

In June, 1942, Japanese air forces made two daylight air attacks on Dutch Harbor. In the same month Kiska, 650 miles from this American naval and air base, and Attu, about 275 miles to the northwest of Kiska, were occupied by enemy forces.

To meet this threat, the United States immediately started an accelerated construction program in the Aleutians, including the building of two advance air bases on Adak and Amchitka Islands. The latter made it easier for the United States Eleventh Air Force to give effective tactical support to the amphibious troops who retook Attu in May, 1943.

On the night of August 14-15, 1943, a mighty United States amphibious task force arrived off Kiska. After a preliminary shelling and bombing, American and Canadian troops went ashore. They were surprised to find Kiska abandoned by the enemy. A team of four Red Cross field directors, who landed on the beaches, served coffee and cigarettes to the tired, hungry American and Canadian troops unloading supplies. The team consisted of Edwin Muchow of Marriemont, Ohio; Marion Thomas of Gainsville, Georgia; David T. deVarona of San Diego; and Matthew Howard of Beverly Hills, California.

With the Japanese driven off the Aleutians, the Eleventh Air Force built new bases, including one on Attu, developed others, and improved its supply lines. Thousands of American troops manned these bases all along the chain, and they did not like their surroundings.

Of volcanic origin, the Aleutians are barren except for tundra, a grass mat overlying swamplands, and low shrubs. West of Kodiak there is not a tree in sight. Troops on Attu became so homesick for a tree that the camouflage section built one and dubbed it "Attu National Forest."

Peculiar to the Aleutians are the Williwa winds. They are nearly always accompanied by rain and fog which seem literally to boil out of the atmosphere suddenly and without warning. Flying was extremely hazardous in this weather, and so was ground activity. Men literally crawled on their hands and knees to get from one point in camp to another. In winter they wore Arctic fur-lined parka and hood all day and even in summer they wore Arctic field jackets. The islands were under constant fog, reducing visibility to about fifty feet.

Consequently, the troops spent most of their spare time indoors. In their Quonset huts they played blackjack and poker, read books or magazines, or wrote letters. Letters were extremely important in this dreary environment. From one Army post alone, 20,000 letters a day were posted by the soldiers, and sent out by ship or air when the weather permitted. The Army and Navy did everything possible to improve mail service. Every letter a soldier received was shared by all his buddies. "That makes 'em last longer," remarked one man.

All Army and Navy installations in the Aleutians were covered by American Red Cross field directors and assistant field directors who concentrated upon the solution of servicemen's personal problems. Hundreds of letters and radio messages went out from Red Cross huts to home-town chapters all over the United States on behalf of these isolated men.

For a long while the Army considered the Aleutians too wild and rugged for Red Cross girls. But when Edith Newman of Troy, New York, an assistant field director assigned to Adak, bore up well under the hardships, the Army requested more like her. By the fall of 1944 there were nine Red Cross girls on the islands with ten additional ones requested. Elizabeth Bates of Highland Park, Michigan, a hospital recreation worker, served on a tiny island, one of the most westerly in the chain.

In the following narrative, Helen Cadwalader of Baltimore, Red Cross staff assistant, describes the bleak Aleutians as she and her fellow Red Cross workers experienced it:

We stepped out of the army transport plane that flew us down from the mainland, at 4 P.M. on an early January day. Wrapped up like sausages in sweaters, ski-pants and clumsy parkas, we still clung to our uniform caps with Red Cross emblems. After a

209

month of travel, we were at our final destination. Home—for a year.

"Girls, by golly—three of them!" The soldiers stared.

We took our first look around. Could this be that dismal Aleution area we'd been warned about so gloomily? Why, it was beautiful!

The sun was about to set, and over the huge, craggy peaks hung a gold haze. Pink clouds drifted across the wide sweep of treeless tundra. In the background was a sheet of deep purple water, with sparkling whitecaps. We glanced at each other. Wonderful, our winks said happily.

We were driven over jolting roads in a muddy command car to the station hospital, where we were to live with the nurses. "Sorry the roof blew off this car, but we had a storm the other night," said our driver. We huddled deeper into our hoods and shook a bit. You couldn't get around it; it was cold.

The hospital was a sprawling array of Quonset huts well dug into the ground, and connected by long enclosed ramps, or wooden walkways. Snow had drifted in ankle-deep in our ramp, and we had to tug to get our hut door open. Inside, it was bare and cold, but sunny with yellow paint. Beds, a couple of rough chests and tables, tin shelves with hanging space beneath, two stoves and—a venerable push-pedal organ!

I sat down on an empty crate and played "Chopsticks." It sounded wheezy and mournful. Marian stopped unpacking and laughed.

A day or two later, the Special Service officer came to drive us to the main Army post and show us the service club in which we were to work as hostesses. It proved to be a sizeable log building with a big rough stone fireplace at one end, a hallway and tiny music room at the other. And it was crowded with men.

"Hello," we said, a trifle shy before hundreds of eyes that refused to meet ours. The eyes goggled at us as if their owners thought we weren't looking, but turned suddenly away if we glanced in their direction.

Someone turned on the juke box, and the braver boys asked us to dance. They stammered, and even blushed. Dancing, you could feel them trembling all over.

"It's been two years since I've danced," they apologized over and over. "And in these heavy leather boots . . . and on a concrete floor . . ." We girls weren't finding it easy, either. They couldn't tell if we stepped on their toes, but we were not that fortunate.

The days began to fly. First, we wanted to make our club attractive. Curtains had been ordered four months earlier; so had a complete floor of dark red tile, to cover the dusty concrete. But—they were "on the dock at Seattle." Shipping priorities gave scant recognition to a recreational fixture, and we simply had to wait.

Gradually we began to absorb Army life in its details and to get the men sorted out—their names, their homes, their families, their branch of service, their company problems.

And always the ferocious weather, and the monotony. Cold, snow, sleet, rain, mud, and more snow. Williwas that lift you off your feet, knock you down and slide you yards across the ice. Pitch black nights when, if your flashlight fails, you drop abruptly into foxholes where you'd have sworn there were none.

We racked our brains eternally to think of something to interest or amuse these weary Aleutian soldiers. We held ping-pong tournaments, singles and doubles; a pool tournament; chess, checkers, bridge contests. We held talent shows, encouraged jam sessions among the musicians. And nightly, we smiled until our faces cracked, danced till our feet ached, admired sweethearts' photographs, listened to troubles, offered shoulders to weep on, romped and enthused and joked to the din of the juke box and the rattle of bowling balls and the howl of the wind outside.

What little spare time we had was devoted to laundry, letter-writing, and trying to get our stoves to burn without exploding and throwing soot all over our clothes. We had a full day off every Monday, and when the weather was tolerable, a group of us would tramp miles out over the tundra hummocks, or visit the boys at the outposts, or climb to the radar station on the mountain, or shoot ptarmigan, squirrels and ducks. Monday, too, was our day to see a movie—the early show, usually followed by "hog hips and cackleberries" [ham and eggs] gaily cooked up in the nearest messhall.

But there wasn't much time left for ourselves. The boys at the paint shop were giving a party; would the girls come? How about supper with the quartermaster boys on Tuesday? And the Navy base Wednesday? And the finance office boys want us to drop in after work Thursday night.

GI Joe, looking hurt because we would consult our calendar and name a day two weeks off as our first free day, would remark: "You gals have the best go on the post. All you do is play—and get paid for it!"

Little he knew how exhausting our "playing" could be.

Eventually, spring came to the Arctic, galoshes could be discarded, and the roads improved. Softball games began to blossom after chow time in the long, light evenings; the sun began to meet itself coming and going in its quick swing around the top of the world.

Slowly, changes began to take place on the post. New faces appeared, as the long-awaited replacements arrived and took over for the men going back to the States. The slang and the jokes in the service club changed, as did the phonograph records, and "Mairzy Doats" was heard more often, "Paper Doll" became part of the past.

Going down to see the boats pull out was an exciting but somewhat forlorn experience. There are your friends, grinning blissfully and hanging over the rail. "See you in Times Square!" "Look me up at the Paladium in L. A.!" "Michigan, here I come!"

You're glad, for their sakes. But you know that the club won't be the same. Not without Sammy, and Al, and Miguel. Good-by, Pop ... good-by to you, Little Ugly ... and Speed, and Alabam', and Shorty.

Oh, well, someday it'll be your turn!

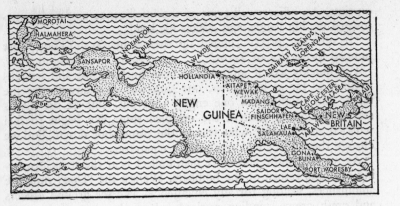

Chapter X

NEW GUINEA TO THE PHILIPPINES—
ISLAND HOPPING WITH MACARTHUR

W E PULL OUR TRUCK UP NEXT TO THE AMBULANCES ALONG
the strip. No one objects. In fact, they expect us. There are always four or five ambulances and several jeeps parked in a line
off the runway. We play only a small part at this big air base, but
the cold drinks are welcomed by men returning after hard-hitting
combat hours in the air.

As we stop our car and stretch our legs after the long drive
over muddy, rutted roads, the men waiting on the line stop and
stare at us. We are still somewhat of a novelty up here, dressed
in khaki shirts and culottes and army boots. We are used to being
an oddity, so we pay no attention. Besides, we are excited about
the mission. The tension of waiting for the planes to come in
is great.

As we wait we can hear the radio in the intelligence tent
crackling. Now we hear code, then a voice from a plane breaking in. Then rasping static.

Soon a captain we know and several lieutenants saunter over
and lean against our truck to pass the time of day and kid with
us. We ask if we are on time or if there has been any change
in the ETA (estimated time of arrival). We are told we are right

on time. An officer walks out of the intelligence tent and comes toward us. He laughs and shakes his head.

"It sure got pretty rugged up there," he says. "They were jumped by plenty of Zeros."

We quickly ask if anyone has been hurt or lost and he tells us that, as far as he knows, one ship was shot down over the target and another had one engine shot out. One of the planes stayed behind to protect the crippled ship. We begin to feel worried and wonder who was in the plane shot down. But we change the subject and reach for a cigarette.

As we talk, more and more men collect near the strip, "sweating out" the return of the bombers. We see the "Doc" near the ambulances, waiting for any emergency. We see ground officers and crash crews standing restlessly along the strip. Some wear khaki shirts and long trousers, others only shorts or dirty fatigue pants with tanned and sunburned chests and arms bare.

Now and then a dog darts out and is chased back. The sun is high and beats down on the brown dry earth and metal runway. Everybody is marking time, smoking and talking and staring into the sky. Fighter planes fly by in formation, then some transport planes, but all eyes are searching for the bombers.

In the distance a persistent droning becomes louder and we see four specks against the clouds. The watchers, with hands shading eyes, grow tense as the bombers draw near and peel off to circle the field. Landings are tricky after planes have gone through bursts of ack-ack and battled enemy fighters.

The planes look large and graceful against the strong blue sky as they circle in the traffic pattern. The sunlight builds silver whirls of the propellers. The first plane banks and floats in on its flaps, wheels feeling for the ground. The rubber hits the metal strip with a grunt and the plane rumbles down the runway with motors roaring. Someone near you draws in his breath.

"Look at those holes!" he says.

You stare in fascination at the holes in the side of the plane. The captain turns to you and tells you that when the four planes have landed you can cross the runway and start making the rounds with cold drinks. He says he will have a sergeant show you to the revetments where the planes are parked.

Another plane lands and taxies by with the top turret rolled back and the gunner standing up, hands clasped together waving them to indicate a victory. Everybody yells and waves.

"Hey!" someone shouts, "this one's coming in with a red light." Everyone crowds close to the runway to see. They know

214

what that signal means—wounded or dead aboard. And men start to follow, some running, others slowly, a bit hesitant.

You, too, walk slowly in the direction of the ambulance, hoping not to get too close. It's your closest touch with war. The plane turns off the strip and pulls up beside the ambulance. You see several men disappear into the belly of the ship and reappear carrying a limp, bloody body in their arms which they place gently on a stretcher. Presently the ambulance pulls away, and once again the crowd turns back to watch the planes landing.

"Was it bad?" you ask.

"Yeah, plenty!" someone answers. "One 20-millimeter shell burst in the ship and got one of the waist gunners. Nice kid, too—just had a baby last week. That stuff sure is tough on the wives."

You feel sort of sick and say helplessly: "That's awful," and you hang your head and look steadily at a pebble on the ground. Then you slowly walk back to the crowd watching arrival of more of the bombers.

Now another plane comes in, the gun turret shot away. Lucky gunner just got a scratch. You think, as that plane goes by, how strange is fate. One burst of a shell in a large ship hits a boy and kills him. And here is a gunner protected only by a plexi-glass turret. It is blown off and he escapes with a scratch.

You think of the time a captain you know, flying a Liberator, crashed in the water and went under 30 feet, hitting a coral reef. He and the navigator managed to get out, but the rest of the crewmen were killed. Or the same sort of accident where another Liberator, shot down, crashed in the sea, killing the pilot and co-pilot, while the others got free.

As you stand there, lost in thought, the M.P.'s start to push the crowd back. A ship is coming in with a yellow light. It is the crippled plane with one engine shot out. The yellow light means it needs plenty of extra room to land. All the men with vehicles start the motors and back up a hundred yards. The plane lands, swerves to one side. The crowd tenses. But the pilot steadies the plane and with everyone cheering he taxies safely down the runway.

Now the first formation is in and it is time for us to start work. We rush into our truck and speed down the runway to the revetment area. We pull into one revetment at the same time the intelligence section jeep arrives. We drive to the side of the plane while ground-crew men begin clearing the guns.

We wait at a discreet distance while the men get out of the

plane and go over to the intelligence officer. They are a motley-looking crew. Most of them wear long khaki "zoot suits," long, drab coverall affairs. They all have guns slung on shoulder holsters. They carry barracks bags full of emergency stuff for forced jungle landings, parachutes, knives, first-aid equipment. The pilot carries a businesslike briefcase. They drop their heavy gear on the ground and crowd around the jeep. They all seem to be talking at once. After the interrogation is over they turn and, seeing us, let out a yell.

"Come and get it, boys. The Red Cross gals are here." By this time we have started to ladle out ice cold drinks and open packages of cookies. As we serve the boys and look at them, safe on the ground, it seems completely unbelievable to us that they can fly a machine as monstrous and big as the one before us. They are all young kids, mostly younger than we are. To hear them talk of the raid or the Jap Zeros is like hearing a bunch of college boys discuss a football scrimmage.

"I'll be damned, but I never saw those Zeros," one will say. "The first I noticed of that Zeke that shot at me was when I saw the tracer bullets coming right at me. Boy, what a feeling! I thought that was IT for sure, but I pushed her away down and came up on the other side. And when I came up a P-38 had closed in. Boy, I don't know what we'd do without those pea-shooters. That fighter of ours came right in and gave a burst and wham, did that Zeke go up in flames! We were shooting like mad at another off our other side, but it streaked off! Aw, they sure won't fight when it's dead loss on their side." Then he shakes his head and makes a sucking noise with his mouth. "One got Sam's motor!"

"Yeah, I know," is the quick reply, "but his cannon blew the Jap right up. What's one motor against a dead ship?"

One of the boys walks over and asks: "Say, who went down over the target? I am pretty sure it was one of our ships."

"Boy, those Red Cross gals are strictly on the ball; I've never been so thirsty in all my life."

"Well, it was as rough today as I'd ever like to see it," a short, curly-headed gunner says.

"You ain't just a woofin! Something burst right outside our ship and shook us up so bad I thought we'd been hit," said the co-pilot.

"Listen to him talk," says the pilot. "You ought to see that Joe when we go over the target. He pulls his steel helmet down over his eyes so he can't see the ack-ack bursts!"

216

"Nuts! I always keep watching you out of the corner of my eye. When the ack-ack blows your head off I want to be ready to take over."

They laugh because they think that kind of talk is very funny. One of them chimes in and says: "You know, I think the Japs are getting mad at us." He slaps his thigh and holds out his cup for a refill.

They keep on kidding about what has happened or they chide us about our graceless army boots or tell us what dopes they think we are for coming up here of our own free will. Then the mess truck comes along and they hop on and we speed to the next revetment.

Perhaps this is the plane that had the casualty and the whole atmosphere is different. The men don't kid, but take their drinks and cookies and keep saying: "One burst of ack-ack. Boy, he was a good kid!"

We stand off at a distance and never enter into the conversation. We can't mourn for him. We didn't know him. We have no right. All we can do is feel depressed and awful and stand there.

Finally we pull away and go to the next plane. This one has the holes in it but no casualties. Their bombs did a good job. Here the men are full of wisecracks and joke about the stupid Japs and ack-ack and kid us. We get out and look over their ship. It is a twin-engined medium bomber with the head of a shark painted on the nose and the body of a luscious female nude painted on the other side. Running under the nude are holes from the ack-ack. Looking at the ship makes us realize what the boys have been through and we can't believe they can joke like that when such a short time ago—well, it had been rough up there.

We pull out and continue our rounds. Now, finally, we have one more revetment to visit. As we drive in we see some of the maintenance crew standing around under a tent built on the side next to the high bank of the revetment. We pull up and stop and call out, "Where's the ship?"

A GI gets up from a cot on which he had been sitting. He comes out from under the tent and looks at us.

"Are you kidding?" he calls.

"What do you mean?" we answer.

"Not much, except you won't see that ship around again. It's a dead duck."

You stop a minute, realizing how stupid you are. Your heart

contracts, your stomach feels like a piece of lead. "You mean . . . But of course you must . . . This was the plane shot down."

"Yeah," the GI answers bitterly.

You're frightened, but you ask, "Who was flying it?"

"Captain ——."

"Pete! Why, he wasn't supposed to fly today. Not Pete! They couldn't get him. No, I can't believe it. He could fly too well. No . . ."

You can't talk any more. You press your foot on the starter and stare at the empty revetment.

"What is the matter with her?" you hear someone exclaim. And someone who knows answers: "Shut up, you fool! She had a date with him tonight!"

—From "We Meet the Missions," by Annette Robin of New York City, staff assistant in New Guinea, in the *Red Cross Courier*.

The first unit of Red Cross hospital workers arriving in northern New Guinea created quite a stir in GI ranks. They were: Doris Daniels, Bowling Green, Kentucky; Mary Buckley, Scranton, Pennsylvania; and Betty Pasternack, New Rochelle, New York. Attached to an evacuation hospital, they were flown over the "hump"—the formidable Owen Stanley Range—together with a group of Army nurses. All were dressed in culottes and long-sleeved khaki shirts with dark jeep hats covering blonde, brown, and black hair.

As the girls climbed into trucks that were to carry them through endless clouds of thick dust, a jeep full of Navy officers stopped short in front of them. The men gazed silently at the group of Red Cross girls and Army nurses. After a moment or two, one of them found voice to exclaim: "White women! White women!"

As the khaki-clad girls bounced over the narrow, bumpy road, soldiers all along the way cheered and whistled, and as the girls smiled and waved, there was more cheering and whistling.

In New Guinea nothing stood still except perhaps the jungle air. This was a war of movement, with advance positions constantly being moved forward. As soon as the Japanese were blasted out of a coastal position or pushed back a couple of thousand yards from the beach, a defense perimeter was established.

Then came the backbreaking task of subduing this part of the jungle. The heat and dampness were conducive to slow motion and listlessness, but there was a job to be done, and everybody worked, even the fuzzy-wuzzies who performed much of the heavy labor under white men's direction. And the Red Cross personnel kept up the pace set by the Army.

Camp sites were cleared amid scrubby bush, *kunai* grass, banyan trees, and tangled vines, with row upon row of tents winding far into the dark interior. Engineering outfits, manning bulldozers and working with tar in the blazing tropical sun, built roads, some following native paths the GI's only a few days before had wrested from the enemy. Starting from scratch, in a matter of days, a whole new station came into being—mess halls, office space, warehouses, docks, hospitals, and Red Cross clubs and canteens. And simultaneously with all this building activity, training pursued its usual intensive and rugged course—amphibious warfare demanded it.

Even though the jungle was cleared, and a semblance of civilization created, New Guinea was by no means ideal for white women. The Army, once it permitted them in a secured forward area, could guarantee Red Cross girls protection from the Japanese, but neither the Army nor any other agency could shelter them from the hardships and discomforts inherent in the jungle. These they had to share with the GI's who had the added job of fighting the wily, ruthless foe. The jungle often was so dense one could hardly see ten yards ahead. It rained steadily—in sheets, almost horizontally. Clothes, particularly shoes, rotted quickly. Besides the rains, there were the oppressive heat, dust, mud, mosquitoes and insects which did not distinguish between a male and a female ankle. There, too, were horrible jungle noises at night and indescribable jungle odors. Red Cross girls, as well as GI's, suffered from bad colds, ear infections, boils, and skin infections as a result of the "wet." They dosed themselves against malaria, typhus, jungle rot, and other tropical diseases. And atabrine-yellow complexion was the hallmark of service on New Guinea.

Out of the jungle blossomed clubs, canteens, and hospital recreation rooms showing the influence of Red Cross girls. In July, 1944, there were on New Guinea and neighboring islands thirty-two on-post clubs, seven canteens, and eleven clubmobiles, and many others were being planned. A Red Cross club, usually a hut of native construction, stood along a road where, because of heavy troop traffic, its services reached the most men. The names of some became well-known among thousands of troops: "Shangri La," "The Circus Tent," "The Bomb Dump," "47th Heaven." Many closed down when the units they once served moved to more advanced areas. On special occasions and holidays these clubs were decorated with palms and staghorns, a parasitical growth with large green leaves. Red Cross girls in white blouses and GI slacks added the feminine touch.

Canteens serving food generally were located on air strips. These huts appeared as if by magic, served their purpose while the strip functioned, then closed their doors for good. Their customers were restricted to the transient personnel passing through the base or "sweating out" transportation—passengers and the crews of fighting planes and transports. The larger bases had several canteens serviced from a central kitchen where a food production line functioned from early morning till late afternoon, turning out sandwiches, doughnuts, coffee, fruit juice, and cookies. Many lunches were made up daily for the crews taking off on long flights; they included coffee or fruit juice kept in the plane's thermos jug.

Red Cross hospital service in the Southwest Pacific theater kept pace with the movement of hospitals to the advanced areas. In July, 1944, there were 232 American Red Cross girls giving service in both Army and Navy hospitals and aboard hospital ships plying the coastal waters of New Guinea. Fully seventy-five per cent of them worked in New Guinea's muck and mire. Their many activities had a single purpose: to help patients get the best possible benefit from the excellent care provided by the medical corps. Working long hours, they carried out this purpose by assisting patients to solve their personal and family problems, and bringing relaxation from the tedium of hospital life with handicraft and recreation approved by doctors. They transformed crude buildings into comfortable recreation spots where patients could while away many a lonely hour by reading, writing, playing ping-pong, and from time to time enjoying special programs. These recreation huts were made inviting by canvas chairs painted in bright colors, a piano, and flower vases made of large biscuit tins painted white.

Even off-duty hours were strenuous, as Stephanie Spector, of the Bronx, staff assistant, informs us:

As soon as night settles, the New Guinea army comes a-calling. The droves of jeeps up and down the battered hill smack of downtown traffic. White-starched shirts are pressed, the leggings fastened trimly, perfume is sprinkled across clean if not latest-styled coiffures, and sometimes a rebel green bow. They dance at noncommissioned officers' clubs. They dance at the Allied officers' clubs, on ships, and of course, in Red Cross clubs. They sit soaking and dripping on rainy nights out in the open, feet cemented in the mud, watching a Red Cross movie with the fellows. Once a Frank Sinatra picture was showing in the neighborhood, and some practical GI's set out hospital cots for the girls to swoon on.

And then there were the Red Cross clubmobile girls about whom one of them, Ellin Brooke, of Philadelphia, wrote:

This strange island of New Guinea . . . If we are not being smothered with dust, we are plowing through the mud; sometimes we have both. It's the only place I've ever been in where you can wade through mud to your knees and have dust in your eyes. When the bridge goes out, we ford the river. We try to "hit the road" no matter what the circumstances. When we get hot, wet and tired, covered with grime and dust, the face and words of one little private standing there looking up at us comes back: "Lady . . . this is the first really good thing I've had to eat in two days . . . and oh, lady, this is the first *cold* drink I've had in . . . well, I don't know when."

In the over-all picture of defeating Japan, there were sound, even urgent, military reasons for the campaign to recover the Philippine Islands. There was also a moral reason as General MacArthur pointed out:

". . . The American flag flew over the Philippines before the war. It is our duty and obligation and a matter of national honor to liberate the Filipinos as quickly as possible. American prestige in the entire Orient is at stake."

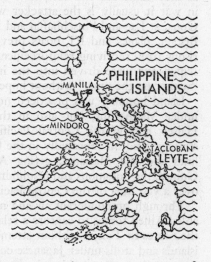

This quotation helps to explain General MacArthur's single-mindedness in the New Guinea campaign. His eyes and the eyes of all participating military and naval forces were ever turned toward the Philippines. The long, hard way started at Melbourne, MacArthur's first headquarters in southern Australia; led northward through Queensland to Port Moresby on the southern coast of Papua; pushed through mud and blood across the Owen Stanley Range to Buna and Gona where the Papuan campaign came to an end in the closing weeks of 1942. From there the road wound to Lae and Salamaua where the New Guinea campaign began—then stretched all along New Guinea's coast with side expeditions to New Britain and the Admiralty Islands.

The demonstrated ability of General Kenney's Allied air forces and Admiral Kincaid's Seventh U.S. Fleet to control the waters north of New Guinea was of incalculable value. With the Japanese thus cut off from reinforcements and supplies, MacArthur was spared the ordeal of laboring through the length of New Guinea's jungled interior (approximately fifteen hundred miles). Along the coast, he carried one Japanese stronghold after another by amphibious operations.

His strategy of "landing where they ain't" won a succession of victories with a minimum of casualties. The Japanese on New Britain thought an invading force would have great difficulty in landing on a certain stretch of coast and so concentrated their main strength elsewhere. But the First Marines attacked at the more difficult spot, and won their beachhead. On the Halmaheras, flank point for the invasion of the Philippines, the Japanese had built up a formidable force of crack troops. MacArthur simply put his troops ashore a short distance to the north on Morotai Island where the invasion was much easier. MacArthur never made a direct attack against a heavily fortified position when he could land his troops behind the Japanese lines. He made the Japanese attack, mowing them down as they came on, and each time they lost heavily in casualties, for in war it usually is the attacker who pays the cost. At Buna and Gona, at Lae and Finschhafen and farther up the coast, and in New Britain, planes and PT boats prevented beleaguered Japanese garrisons from receiving reinforcements and supplies. Those troops not wiped out were driven into the interior of the jungle and left to "wither on the vine," without hope of escape.

Island hopping was practiced not only in the Southwest Pacific under MacArthur, but also in the South Pacific under Admiral Halsey and in the Central Pacific under Admiral Nimitz. This strategy paid off repeatedly in the Gilberts, the Marshalls, the Carolines and the Marianas, giving Allied forces control over New Guinea, the Solomons and neighboring islands, the Bismarck Sea, and over a vast area of the Central Pacific.

Through preponderant air and naval strength, island hopping enabled Allied forces to capture a relatively few key island bases along the routes to Tokyo without attempting to touch hundreds of other islands and atolls under Japanese control. For the most part the hops were made in terms of hundreds of miles. Major strong points such as Truk and Rabaul were by-passed, subjected to repeated poundings from the air, and sealed off from all physical contact with the Japanese mainland or other sources of supply.

A not inconsiderable share of glory for the New Guinea victory belongs to a little-known outfit, the Second Engineer Special Brigade. "MacArthur's Amphibs," as the GI's called them, operated hundreds of landing barges, many of which they themselves had assembled in a specially built plant at Cairns, Australia. Their craft included the fifty-foot LCM (Landing Craft Mechanized) carrying 100 men; the thirty-six-foot LCVP (Landing Craft Vehicle and Personnel), the amphibious duck, and an amphibious tank called the Buffalo capable of carrying fifty men over coral reefs, sand, hell, and high water.

They did not handle the larger LST's (Landing Ship Tank) and LCIL's (Landing Craft Infantry Large). These were operated exclusively by the Navy in transporting invasion troops and tanks over long distances, as was done when Vella Lavella in the Solomons, Rendova, Guam, Kiska and many other Japanese-held islands in the Pacific were invaded.

The men of the Second Engineer Special Brigade were specially trained in amphibious warfare. These amphibian soldiers not only put the troops on the beach but also brought in their supplies and took part in the initial fight to secure a beachhead. In all the major landings since June, 1943, the SESB have won many awards for valor, including the Congressional Medal of Honor.

The American Red Cross covered MacArthur's Amphibs as well as all other outfits. In July, 1943, there were 387 field directors in the Southwest Pacific theater, and more were on the way.

Covering Red Cross activities in New Guinea in the fall of 1943 were Robert E. Lewis of Philadelphia, director of Red Cross public information service in the theater, and Harry E. Poague of Minneapolis, Red Cross photographer. In line of duty both were instantly killed in an airplane crash at Port Moresby on November 26, 1943. To succeed Bob Lewis, a fellow Philadelphian and close friend, Lewis H. Bowen, gave up his position as Red Cross national publicity director. Poague was succeeded by Richard Day of Kirkwood, Missouri, who received a Silver Star for an act of gallantry at the time of the amphibious landing at Wakde.

Through the months a general pattern of Red Cross service was developed in the New Guinea campaign. Four or five field directors were assigned to each division. Some landed with assault troops on D-Day; others, depending on the wishes of individual commanding officers, went in after the initial landing. Upon wading ashore, the field directors set up beach canteens.

Over and over again the timely distribution of Red Cross supplies proved essential. It was appreciated particularly in the vast spaces of the Pacific where the constant movement of combat troops in their unending drive, over long distances and through difficult jungle, necessitated Army shipments streamlined as to food, ammunition, and military supplies.

These priorities often delayed Army gratuitous issue during the early days or weeks of an operation. And the American Red Cross was able to meet emergencies because it moved its own supplies in fairly small quantities stowed away in PT boats, LST's, LCM's, and other craft, in spaces not otherwise occupied by the Army. Field directors accompanying a unit into a forward area carried along a large variety of items, the little necessities that fighting men need when the day's fighting is over, such as tooth paste, razors, shaving cream, toothbrushes, combs, and most essential, canteen supplies for quick lunches.

Red Cross men found tactical moving a grueling business. There were agonizing days of preparation and loading. Supplies had to be secured for any eventuality. Each move meant packing, water-proofing, and marking plainly for quick identification. Boxes had to be reduced to a size that could be carried by one man, at most by two men. And aboard humid and overcrowded transports and equipment-carrying barges there were sleepless nights. Units embarked from one coastal jungle and after several days at sea disembarked at another. This process went on week after week, month after month, in MacArthur's inexorable drive to redeem his pledge to the Filipinos: "I shall return."

A graphic description of one of these amphibious operations based on personal experience was contained in a narrative report from New Guinea by Red Cross Field Director Dudley F. Unkefer, of Johnson City, Tennessee:

> Preliminary preparations over, we boarded our ship in the heat of the day, and were soon to learn that this same heat never abated one degree, day or night, in the hot hold of that blacked-out vessel.
>
> We sailed for what seemed an indeterminable length of time to wake up very early one morning to an excited hush and the announcement that this was *the* day. Our few belongings were quickly assembled and packed, a good breakfast quickly swallowed, and a last minute check made of equipment.
>
> In the thick murk of the early tropical dawn, our convoy moved cautiously shoreward. A subdued excitement fell over the troops as land, strange land, loomed up ahead. Out of the skies came echelon after echelon of dive bombers. Warships maneuvered into position, and another invasion was on. Peeling off and plummeting out of the heavens came the planes with a shrill

whistle and a roar. Then the distant thunder of deck guns began. The softening-up of enemy resistance had started. Tracers streaked across the water, a red glow followed the impact of each bomb and shell, debris flew skyward.

Now our time had come. Barges lowered away. Men watched with tense faces and taut bodies. We scrambled overboard, down landing nets into the waiting barges. We shoved off. The water seemed alive with craft as we headed towards the beach. A beautiful palm-lined black sand beach, reminding me of a colorful "Travel-talk" movie of these Pacific islands. The barges grated on the sand, ramps lowered away, and soldiers plunged into the jungle.

As they pushed forward a relaxation of the tenseness in the body overcame one like a wave of comfort. A few scattered shots were fired but each felt that the beachhead was secured and the climax had passed.

As the sun crept skyward the beach became a very busy place. Supplies rolled in, barges broached and wrecked in the heavy surf, men sweated in the hurry of their tasks. Fortunately for us, the fifth barge to touch the beach with supplies carried a pile of boxes, each marked with the familiar red cross. We retrieved them from the depot into which they had been dumped and in 160 minutes after the first soldier had touched the beach, cocoa and cookies were being dispensed to men.

Two hundred and forty gallons of cocoa and innumerable cases of cookies disappeared into hungry GI's. Emergency dry rations were carried, but few that day stopped long enough to prepare them.

Darkness and torrential downpour ushered in the night. Men slipped into jungle hammocks, excitement subsided, and idle thoughts were all that was left of the day's doings.

Once the assault troops landed and knocked out enemy shore positions, the enormous task of unloading supplies and equipment from the landing craft and storing them in safe places began. This was the most complicated phase of an amphibious operation, handled for the Army by the trained men of the shore party and including the Navy's beach battalion, if a joint Army-Navy operation. When troops were put ashore for a campaign against a fanatical Japanese garrison, everything needed in the fight had to be delivered right behind them as they advanced inland.

Red Cross field directors mingled with the crowd on the beach and, once they retrieved their supplies, followed the main body of troops pushing into the interior. Tropical rains made the battle areas vast quagmires. Jeeps, the pack mules of the jungle, often had to be pushed through bogs with caterpillar tractors. Each day found troops scattered in the jungle, and each day the Red Cross men found an opportunity to bring cookies or fruit cake, cold lemonade or fruit juices to sweating GI's during a lull in the fighting. Primitive communication made it very difficult for them to reach the widely dispersed men and units, but they never gave up.

For troops waiting to go into action and for troops who had been pulled out of the lines for a rest, Red Cross field directors provided simple recreation. Large ward tents with sawdust spread on the earthen floor served as Red Cross recreation centers. Tents often were pitched in an area hacked out of a dense tangle of eucalyptus, paupau, mango and coconut trees connected by twisting vines and meshed with jungle undergrowth.

Inside one of these Red Cross tents, men, sweat pouring from face and shoulders, their trousers and heavy GI boots mud-caked, fought off swarms of strange insects flying into their eyes, buzzing around their ears, and taking root in their sweaty hair. Some sat on canvas chairs or bamboo benches listening to a phonograph playing nostalgic popular tunes from home, such as "Take Me Back to Where I Come From." Some were grouped around split-bamboo-pole tables reading old newspapers and magazines or writing letters. Some were at the crude snack bar in a corner munching on fruit cake and drinking cold lemonade. And still others were playing ping-pong, the steady click-click of the balls being heard above the drowsy chatter, the tinny phonograph music, the continuous artillery barrage, and the rhythmic pounding of the surf. A peaceful scene? Yes, in a way. But it was not wholly free of tension, as comrades were dying not many yards beyond. The ever-present threat of the enemy was never lost to their minds. His entrenchments were but a stone's throw away. Often his attacking planes were overhead.

Writing from one of these combat zones in New Guinea where his barge had just evacuated wounded soldiers, a field director said:

As we landed [on the beach] three ambulances backed down the bank to the water's edge and onto the ramp of the rolling barge. Litters with wounded were quickly carried into the barge. Shorn of all clothing and possessions, the only thing these wounded clutched to their sides was a brilliant blue Red Cross convalescent kit with the familiar words, "A Gift of the American Red Cross."

226

Because of the shortage of Army personnel and supplies, it was not always feasible for the military to provide adequately for the comfort and welfare of the wounded in the midst of battle. On these occasions, medical attention in its strictest sense absorbed all the time and energy of the Medical Corps personnel. The attention that the American Red Cross was able to give to the physical comfort of these unfortunate boys thus met a very essential need.

In combat zones too "hot" even for the brave Army nurses and Red Cross hospital women, Red Cross field directors gave friendly personal services to the wounded. They met casualties as they were brought into clearing stations direct from the battlefield and stayed at their side when they were removed to the portable hospital, and later to the evacuation ship. They distributed cigarettes and replaced personal articles lost in battle. They also aided the overworked medical officers in the field hospitals by wielding a fan for hours over an operating table or holding a candle for a surgeon performing an emergency operation in the night.

Equally important to morale were welfare services for the able-bodied in forward areas. In the midst of battle the full weight of communication between the serviceman and the outside world fell on the Red Cross field directors. There were no APO's in foxholes. Cases began to pile up soon after the first phase of an invasion was completed, and the troops settled down to a more routine Army life. The soldiers had not heard from their families, who at the same time were filled with anxiety about their men. Generally, a field director had a detachment of soldiers assigned to keep an eye on the recreation tent and other activities while he tried to handle the individual problems as expeditiously as he could without secretarial help. Daily the total of those problems mounted until they consumed most of his working hours. In the year ending June 30, 1944, about 100,000 domestic problems, involving help from local Red Cross chapters all over America, were handled by field directors in the Southwest Pacific. Traffic went both ways on this Red Cross bridge. Over the desks and through the hearts of Red Cross field directors in this theater passed thousands of cases initiated in the United States where the home chapter brought problems to the attention of the overseas field directors so they could talk with the men involved. In the same twelve-month period, field directors made emergency loans to approximately five thousand servicemen. Money, however, was not always necessary. The majority of the cases grew out of a lack of mail from either the soldier or his family. Piled on top of human frailties were the many disappointing factors of wartime communications that made a fertile breeding ground for worry and fear over loved ones.

Satisfaction in being able to serve these American heroes far from home, even in a small way, was the incentive that drove these Red Cross field directors on and on. Each day brought its own compensation, as one New Guinea field director found:

> I received through the mail a letter, and a Christmas package addressed to the field director. The letter, from a mother of a soldier who died in the New Guinea campaign a year ago, requested that the gift be given to a soldier who perhaps had received little or nothing at Christmas time. The package was delivered to the soldier's old company, and typical of GI philosophy, the gift was distributed to the entire squad of which the deceased soldier was formerly a member.

The time came when Red Cross recreation specialists arrived to take over a field director's recreation and canteen tent. Later Red Cross girls appeared. The area had been firmly established and signs of "civilization" were creeping up on it. This was a hint to the field director that he ought to be thinking about moving out, for he was a pioneer. He then began laying plans for getting his supplies ready for the next amphibious landing.

Field directors assigned to amphibian task forces were picked men. First of all, they had to be in the best physical condition as the going was tough. Being entirely on their own without supervision, they were required to have a thorough knowledge of Red Cross policy and procedures. Other qualifications included a willingness to do manual labor and share hardships; emotional stability, initiative, resourcefulness, and energy.

To list the landings made by Red Cross field directors during the New Guinea campaign would be the same as summarizing the assaults the Southwest Pacific amphibian and infantry troops made on Japanese strongholds since 1942: New Guinea—Lae, Salamaua, Wau, Finschhafen, Saidor, Aitape, Hollandia, Wakde, Biak, Noemfoor, and Sansafor; New Britain—Arawe, Cape Gloucester and Talasea; and Bougainville, the Admiralties and Morotai.

In July, 1944, Field Director Harold Templeman, of Cedar Rapids, Iowa, having trained with his men, made the jump with the paratroops at Noemfoor. Before jumping he tossed out seven bundles of Red Cross supplies so that he could begin operations immediately after landing.

Field Director John Taylor, of New York City, a World War I

veteran, accompanied the Australian and American troops who captured Salamaua, Japanese air and naval base, on September 12, 1943. He described his experience in the following letter:

Greetings from Salamaua! As you know it was captured Saturday night by isolated units. Early Sunday morning, on the first barges in, and in advance of the main body of troops, Leon Lewis [Norwich, Connecticut] and I had achieved priorities to take along a battalion cook, a one-burner gasoline stove, twenty-five gallons of water, coffee, sugar, canned milk, and a large tin of "Nice" biscuits, plus a case of cigarettes.

We landed on the Salamaua isthmus and established ourselves along the beach road so that all the troops would pass us. We made coffee all day long, seventy gallons of it, gave out cigarettes and the sweet biscuits, put out our fire when it got dark, curled up on the beach on a tarpaulin with a wet Jap blanket over us and their marine uniforms for a pillow.

Now I will start back. As you know, we set up our tents in Tambu Bay. We, or at least I, since Leo had to go back and get supplies, got into these ridges to see the battalions, a lung-breaking job.

Friday I was told to be ready with coffee and doughnuts to get to the units moving down from the ridges and in toward our objective. I got ninety dozen doughnuts fried and forty gallons of coffee. The coffee I lost in the difficult landings we had to make; we saved the doughnuts, lost everything else and almost our lives. Got ahead of the troops, stood on a jungle path surrounded with booby traps, litter and dead Japs and gave out our doughnuts to every infantryman passing. I lost our excellent "Kooie" can and two thermal units which had been given me, when the rowboat with a putt-putt, in which we were making the landing over reefs in treacherous surf, upset our boat just after we had taken off the doughnuts.

Later in the day, in the dark, we almost lost our skipper when he was caught underneath the rowboat as we capsized on our home beach, caught by two great waves. I had a wonderful ride for about thirty feet on top of the wave which picked me out of the boat and carried me in until it broke. Then I got swept out to sea again, landing up against the boat in time to grab the skipper who never expected to see me.

Previously in the week our tent had been badly riddled with shrapnel. Our installation is very near batteries that pounded the Japs all day long and all night through. Every afternoon between

229

2:00 and 4:30 he retaliated. Tuesday the Jap got mad and threw in everything, wide of his battery objective, and we got the works. Ten duds around our tents, one shell burst over it, one tree-burst to one side and one sand-burst on the other.

However, the duds increased and then everything was silent. Men came rushing down the road to dig us out or to throw the already dug earth over us for the final time. But we were in excellent shape though covered with gook. I had just started taking my pail bath and got into the trench very naked, so that everything in the way of dirt flying around us stuck to me.

We have had exemplary co-operation from the Army. Nothing has been too much trouble for those high up and those low down to do for us. We have gotten to the essential places first, so that we are now the gag, "the Army can't get you there but the Red Cross can." You should have seen the expression on the faces of the men, when, just coming down from the ridges and walking along, very dirty, without having eaten, they saw us with hot coffee and something to eat. You should have seen the expression on Colonel Archie Roosevelt's face when, having directed the first landing barge in, he saw two Red Cross men jump out with a stove between them and a cook carrying his precious tire pump and gasoline at their side.

In February, 1944, Lewis H. Bowen of Philadelphia and Arlington, Virginia, director of Red Cross public information service in the Southwest Pacific, visited two field directors in the Admiralty Islands to get their story of the Saidor landing in which they had participated on January 2, 1944. Their tent was pitched in the headquarters area at Yamai, Admiralties, less than one-half mile from the northernmost fighting front. Bowen, who was accompanied by Red Cross Photographer Richard Day, stayed long enough to witness a fresh local victory—the capture of Cape Iris. Their hosts were Field Directors Harry L. Stryker of Cleveland and Otto L. Petri of Milwaukee, attached to the 32nd Division of Buna campaign fame. Bowen reported:

We wouldn't have traded our last day and night at Yamai for any other experience.

Following up a successful flanking attack the previous day, two companies of the regiment on the other side of the river had pushed their way up to Teteri village, exactly opposite Yamai across the inlet. Holding the line there for the night, they waited while the three-inch guns and the 105's behind us blasted every living thing off the cape, aided by an afternoon bombing attack carried out by Aussie-piloted medium bombers.

Everyone smelled victory in the air, for that had been the mission—to take and to hold Cape Iris. The tenseness lifted noticeably. Colonel Bradley, truly beloved by all his men, came to dinner from the front lines, where he spent most of every day, to announce victory. The cape was ours. The enemy was retreating up the coast on the double quick. No blackout tonight! But there was no cheering, just light conversation, smiles from one man to his neighbor, a few whistles.

Earlier in the day seventy-five men, including the colonel himself, had received notices to pack up the next day to go home.

Victory and home! No wonder the "feel" of the camp changed.

Suddenly, from the woods at our right came a startling crash of martial music. Out of the jungle road marched the complete regimental band, tubas and all, playing the "French National," the colonel's favorite victory song. When they reached the clearing, four abreast, they made a snappy turn to the left and marched by the Red Cross tent, eyes straight ahead.

Dressed in the ubiquitous green coveralls, the vizors of their jungle caps turned upward, and wearing brown music bags over their right shoulders, they looked for all the world like a Civil War band on the town square. Even to the small fife player bringing up the rear with two steps to his colleagues' one.

Headlamps on jeeps, unused for six long weeks, provided light for the musicians. Across the inlet, the cape which every previous night had been swallowed by darkness, was dotted with the moving lights of trucks and jeeps carrying supplies and fresh men to the forward troops on Iris point, at the tip of the cape.

Lights were the order of the night. But practically everyone was too tired, with the excitement of Victory Day behind them, to take advantage of the luxury. After we chased the spiders, lizards and assorted insects out of our cots, tucked ourselves in the mosquito netting, all of us noticed the strange summer night's quietness. Crickets chirped. Bullfrogs croaked. All much the same as at home in July.

When the First Marine Division invaded Cape Gloucester, New Britain, the day after Christmas, 1943, two Red Cross field directors landed with comfort and recreation supplies in the second wave. They were Clarence R. Anderson, of Livingston, Montana, and Philip Layton, of Fort Morgan, Colorado.

While Layton remained on the beach operating a canteen and

directing newly arrived Red Cross field men who quickly pitched recreation tents, Anderson, a former school superintendent, went back and forth on an LST with casualties.

After the Gloucester show, Major General W. H. Rupertus, commanding the First Marine Division, wrote the following to Red Cross officials:

"The field directors . . . have, through their untiring efforts and commendable co-operation in all the morale and recreational activities of the First Marine Division, made for themselves a position not contemplated in any tables of organization, but realized now as being one that is a major factor in the welfare of the organization. . . ."

General Rupertus must have thought of services such as those described in the following narrative report by Field Director Clarence R. Anderson:

Pursuant to orders Mr. Weiner [Morris Weiner, Brooklyn] and I proceeded to Cape Sudest where we reported to Phil Layton, who had been attached to the 7th Marines for some months. As a combat team had been formed, including the 7th, 11th, and 17th, and several other units of operations, we divided ourselves among them. I moved in with the 17th.

We were part of a great invasion fleet of LST's, corvettes, cruisers and destroyers. Before dawn on December 26 we approached Jap-held islands and the beach of New Britain where we were to land.

The warships opened up with a bombardment that stretched for miles and blasted everything along the coast. It was a rare sight. Then bombers came in and unloaded their bombs. By then it was way past dawn but a curtain of smoke obscured the beach for miles. Marines from LCT's landed first, meeting resistance in only one place. Up to this time there had been no Jap resistance save a few shots from coastal guns. We ran in and beached fifty minutes later. Our Marines had already contacted the Japs a few hundred yards back and we could see one action over Target Hill. The beach was a mess; broken trees, mud, swamps and water made it almost impossible to unload the ships. Around two o'clock, before we had completely unloaded all cargo, we were ordered to pull out and "26" took our place on the beach. We were not out over fifteen minutes when Jap fighters and bombers came. I saw some Zeros (seven), one Jap bomber, and two of our own shot down. The LST next to us lost seven wounded and two dead caused by a bomb alongside. A destroyer was also hit. We got some machine-gun spray in our side. The action was intense with dog-fights, falling planes, parachutes, and so forth.

As we were ordered off the beach so soon, we only had eight evacuees with us, so it was an easy matter to attend to their needs. We arrived at Cape Sudest late on December 27, and beached December 28. We were loaded up once again. Incidentally, the canteen set up on the beach at Cape Sudest serving cold drinks was one of the best things the Red Cross has done. Thousands of troops embarking there were served.

We pulled off the beach again that evening. On this trip we hit a storm after APO 322 but managed to beach the morning of December 30. Bombers were laying their eggs just a few hundred yards in. We unloaded and took on twenty-five wounded and started back, hitting the same storm until we had passed 322. I had more to do this trip, but had everything that was needed. Two serious operations were performed on shipboard. Most of my time was spent with the patients. We arrived at Buna and anchored at 10:30 P.M. on New Year's Eve. We beached at Cape Sudest the next morning.

After seeing the wounded off, I sent for more supplies. These arrived just before the ship sailed again, carrying a very dangerous cargo, but not so many troops. During this trip we ran into another storm and had a hard time, getting to the beach on the morning of January 5. I spent several hours on the beach. I was prepared to stay in Gloucester, but after finding out we were to evacuate 250 wounded, I decided to stay on the ship.

Around 4 P.M. we were shelled by Jap guns from around the point and had to pull out at once. And now began one of the most unique trips ever imagined. About 100 wounded were placed in quarters below decks and 150 in the tank deck. Remember, the ship had just discharged a huge cargo. Decks were muddy, dirty, and wet. Rain began coming down in sheets, leaking through, and we ran into a terrible storm that rocked and tossed the ship. Nearly all the patients were brought onto the ship on stretchers, naked with only a blanket, and with very few personal belongings. For the next forty-three hours everyone, doctors, corpsmen, crew, and myself, worked like Trojans with just a few hours of sleep. I was not supplied with enough kits for 256 men, so I broke them open and used each article where needed. In this way I had nearly everything needed. I ran short of reading material but managed to keep what I had going around. Handkerchiefs, wash cloths, ditty bags, and tooth brushes—I could have used more.

Besides these material things, I did every imaginable service to the wounded, from bedpans to helping with intravenous feeding, talking to them, answering them. The rocking and pitching of the ship was scaring many.

One boy with a bullet through his eye and into his brain had to be strapped down. I came to him and put my hand on his chest.

"Please, fellow," he said, "take my straps off, take my bandage off."

I talked to him awhile and finally got the bandage up over his good eye. He looked at me, and asked who I was, and I told him.

"Please, Red Cross," he said, "keep your hand on me ... stay with me."

I held my hand there for forty minutes until he went under with morphine.

As I started down the line, hands went up all over the deck and wounded men made touching pleas for help with such remarks as, "Please, a glass [tin pan] of water, juice, candy, cigarettes"; "wash my face a little"; "give me a book, tooth brush, razor, handkerchiefs, gum"; "get me a bedpan or duck"; "please ask the doctor for morphine."

I was fortunate in being able to help—can't take time to tell you about all the cases. One nearly died from shock and gangrene in the arm, but American Red Cross plasma and whole-blood transfusions from the crew saved him. The smell of wounded was terrible, worse even than jungle smell, as they had lain in the front line in water, swamp, mud and rain for eleven days.

Anyhow, we arrived back at Sudest at 2 A.M., January 7, and moved down to "503," but did not get beached and unloaded until around 2 P.M. Then we came back to Sudest, anchored, and have been taking on water and supplies and repairing engines. We had been on rationed water for three days and no fresh water showers; clothing was a problem, but we had fine food and plenty of juices.

I believe the next few trips are going to be quite dangerous, from reports we have had. I intend to have some supplies sent to Gloucester and some aboard the ship. The needs up there [at Cape Gloucester] are terrific. Boys have to throw away even personal gear in going through swamps and quicksand, in lying in rain for days. It is the most terrible condition for fighting and living, I believe, of any place in the world. They need plenty of kits, clean clothes, and reading material. A canteen in the first days, serving cold and hot drinks, is a godsend. To see Red Cross men up this far doing a service has turned every officer and man in its

234

favor. Doctors, corpsmen, crew, and captain of this ship have come to me personally and expressed their appreciation.

After Gloucester, Saidor, and the Admiralties there were still other amphibious landings—Hollandia, which was developed into a great jumping-off base for the Philippines, and Biak, Noemfoor, Sansafor, and Morotai.

And then came October 20, 1944. The day of the invasion of Leyte Island in the Philippines! The climax of two and one-half years of heart-breaking work, of gathering strength in men and arms, of training and organization, and of island hopping. This was the biggest show of all for General MacArthur's Allied forces, and, on a proportionate scale, the biggest single operation of the American Red Cross in the Southwest Pacific theater.

Forty Red Cross field directors, many of them veterans of previous hops, landed on Leyte on A-Day. The first two—Howard Larsen, of Baldwin, Long Island, and his team-mate, George Leech, of Cleveland—waded ashore only one hour after the first troops. Unarmed as usual, with their supplies loaded high on a jeep-and-trailer, they were pinned down for more than hour by enemy sniper fire. Two hours later their Leyte *cabaña*, set up in a coconut grove just back from the beach, was serving hot coffee with canned milk and sugar and cookies.

Officers and enlisted men arriving on the beach in succeeding waves expressed enthusiastic surprise at finding the two Red Cross men ready to serve them.

All day long two queues passed by the Red Cross canteen—one of American soldiers, the other of Filipino men and women with babies and children, on their way from near-by *barios* to a camp set up for them by Lieutenant General Walter Krueger's U.S. Sixth Army. Children received milk and cookies, adults coffee and smokes. One patriarchal farmer hitched his scraggly water buffalo and calf to the Red Cross trailer before getting into line.

General MacArthur shook hands with Larsen and Leech as he congratulated them for being of service so soon after H-Hour. By a coincidence Larsen served in France during World War I with the Rainbow Division commanded by General MacArthur.

A large swamp separated the main hospital from the scene of action, making stretcher-bearing extremely difficult. This natural obstacle forced medical officers to do more emergency work on the beaches than otherwise might have been necessary. They had the aid of two precious Red Cross products from the home front: surgical dressings and blood plasma. Neatly rolled and carefully packed by untiring hands in Red Cross chapters all over America, thousands of surgical dressings went into action immediately. Clearing companies, evacuation sections, portable hospitals, evacuation hospitals and LST's offshore were amply supplied. Medical officers said the first dressing packages bore labels of the following Red Cross chapters: California—Oakland, San Francisco, Los Angeles, Pasadena, and Santa Cruz; Michigan—Calumet-Keweenaw, Torch Lake branch; Texas—Anderson County, Harris County; and South Carolina—Rock Hill.

Prompt use of blood plasma in hundreds of cases undoubtedly saved the lives of many wounded soldiers, according to Major William Buckland, of Wilkes-Barre, commanding the medical company of the Second Engineer Special Brigade. Medical corpsmen continued giving plasma transfusions on an alligator, LVT (Landing Vehicle Tracked), that finally carried the wounded across the swamp to the hospital.

On Armistice Eve, the American Red Cross opened its first service club in the Philippines. Located in the center of Tacloban, Leyte's capital, it was named for the late President Manuel Quezon. The latter's portrait was presented by President Sergio Osmeña during the opening ceremonies.

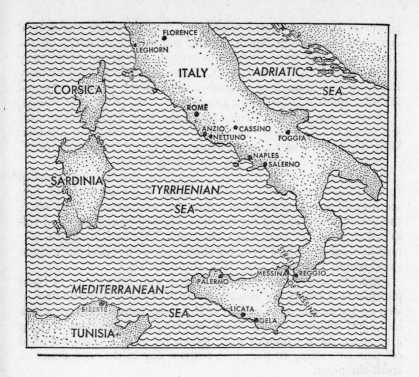

Chapter XI

GLORY AND DEATH IN SICILY—ITALY

EARLY IN JULY, 1943, TWO AMERICAN RED CROSS FIELD DIRECTORS, James P. Shaw and Russell Bullard, stood amid the rubble of bombed-out Bizerte, Tunisia, discussing the impending invasion of Sicily.

"When are you going in, Jim?" asked Bullard.

"Early—with the CP [command post]."

A common interest in youth had drawn them together when they first met as trainees at Red Cross National Headquarters in the fall of 1942 (Shaw had been director of the Neighborhood House in Erie, Pennsylvania, and Bullard a high-school athletic director in Lake Worth, Florida). They later took their practice work together at Fort Dix, shared a cabin on the ship taking the Second Armored Division to North Africa, and were tent mates on the Moroccan desert until amphibious training operations temporarily separated them in February, 1943, Shaw going to the 30th Infantry Regiment and Bullard to a combat team of the Second Armored Division. Shortly before the invasion they were reunited in Bizerte.

"Look," said Bullard. "You and I have been buddies ever since we joined the Red Cross. We ought to go into this thing together. Why don't you wait and come along with me on D-Day plus one?"

"Sorry, Russ, I can't . . . have my sailing orders."

After an intensive aerial attack, American, British, and Canadian forces landed on Sicily's southern shore on the morning of July 10, 1943. In attacking here and not on the northwestern coast where the enemy had prepared for invasion, General Eisenhower had followed the rule of "land where they ain't." While this tactical surprise saved many Allied lives, the landings were not effected without some enemy resistance, especially from the air.

Field Director James P. Shaw landed with his unit at H-Hour plus one near Licata, the first American Red Cross representative to step on Italian soil in World War II. Under constant enemy attack he moved gingerly on the beach, stopping here and there to light a cigarette for a wounded man, loosen his gear, or take his mind off pain by talking to him. In a foxhole dug in the sand dunes he spent the night.

The next morning he ventured out for some coffee and medical supplies. He was walking along the beach with Captain George M. Peckham, of Oakland, California, assistant regimental surgeon of the 30th Infantry Regiment, when a formation of enemy bombers swooped down from the near-by mountains. Allied ack-ack opened up immediately, and the two men took cover under a bulldozer.

Offshore, directly in front of them, an LST was maneuvering for debarkation position to unload its troops and a cargo of ammunition. An enemy dive bomber scored a direct hit on the ship, exploding the ammunition in its hold. Amid flame, smoke, and splattering debris, soldiers clambered down the side of the burning ship and plunged into the choppy waters. A strong crosscurrent made getting ashore extremely hazardous, especially for the wounded.

Shaw and Peckham immediately left the comparative security of their bulldozer shelter and waded out to help. During the action, a life raft had been lowered with two wounded men on it. As it splashed into the water, other soldiers clung to it. Shaw swam out to the raft while Captain Peckham went back for a rope. Shaw lashed it to the raft and all were towed safely in.

Without pause, the lanky, sandy-haired Red Cross worker returned again and again to the sinking ship to assist other men. "All of these acts," read a War Department citation awarding him the Silver Star, the first Red Cross man in World War II so honored, "were performed at the risk of his own life due to attacking enemy planes, the explosion of ammunition on the damaged craft, and the turbulent and treacherous water."

A chance encounter on the beach with the surgeon of Bullard's command established the fact that Shaw's fellow Red Cross worker was last seen aboard the sinking LST before the explosion. In the hope of finding his friend, Shaw carefully checked all the wounded in the clearing stations along the beach. But Bullard was not among them. He was never seen alive again, and the presumption was that he went down with the LST. Carried on official rolls for a year and a day as missing in action, he was officially declared dead on July 12, 1944.

It took only thirty-eight days for the Allied armies to complete the conquest of Sicily. Then General Patton's U.S. Seventh Army and General Montgomery's British Eighth Army swept across the Straits of Messina for the slow, costly, and difficult march up the Italian peninsula.

The first amphibious landing on the Italian mainland was made from an invasion fleet covering 1,000 square miles of the Tyrrhenian Sea at Salerno on September 9, 1943. There Lieutenant General Mark Clark's U.S. Fifth Army met stiff resistance from German armored divisions and artillery. The ensuing battle, savage and costly, finally ended with an Allied victory on September 16, the day the Italian Government surrendered its fleet under the armistice terms.

On October 1, twenty-two days after the initial Salerno assault, the Fifth Army captured Naples, and within a few hours the American Red Cross established there its first service club on the continent of Europe. Harry G. Boyte, of Charlotte, North Carolina, field director with the 82nd (All-American) Airborne Division, entered the city with these troops as Naples was taken. Snipers' bullets pinged off his jeep-and-trailer as he cruised about the city looking for a suitable building for his Red Cross club. Eventually, Boyte chose the Fascist Art Gallery with its marble floors in the Piazzi Carita on the Via Roma.

That night, accompanied by the sound of German artillery, a

gang of Italian laborers hired by Field Director Boyte worked to convert the place into a Red Cross club for GI's pouring into Naples. The city's utilities having been wrecked by the Germans, the laborers worked by candlelight and hauled water in buckets from the Bay of Naples. By sunrise Boyte was ready for business except for odds and ends to be picked up in town. One essential was a piano. For five dollars a month he rented a grand piano that had been hidden from the Germans in a music store basement.

By noon American soldiers were swarming through the doors. With German artillery still echoing in the hills behind Naples, they wrote letters home, sang lustily around the piano, munched on apples Boyte had discovered, played checkers, ping-pong, and read home-town newspapers. Several days later, while the club was having its first dance—local girls who had been carefully screened by G-2 were the doughboys' partners—the Naples post office next door was blown up by a time bomb planted by the Germans before their retreat.

Being a field director, Boyte operated the club only long enough for the regular club workers to take over—about two weeks after the opening. Meanwhile he had the help of members of his divisional clubmobile staff whom he had brought from Sicily in a C-47 several days after Naples' fall: Staff Assistants Janet Chatten of Evanston, Illinois, and Betty Coleman of Oklahoma City; and Assistant Field Director Louis R. Spealler of Philadelphia.

As military operations moved from North Africa into Sicily, covered Corsica and Sardinia, and pushed up the Italian mainland, the American Red Cross not only kept up with the troops but contrived to make its services increasingly mobile. This, however, was accomplished not without heartbreaks, the result of demoralized transportation, inadequate supplies and too few workers to meet the demands of a gigantic invasion.

Advance Red Cross groups, composed of field directors and hospital workers, went along with the troops. Several landed in Italy during the first perilous days, while many others followed later. In the landings they experienced the same perils as the troops—torpedoes, shells, bombs, and strafing. With the combat units they hit the dirt, holed up in the earth, slept on the ground, ate cold rations. Red Cross field men attached either to parachute units or to airborne infantry were flown in as soon as landing fields were secured. Unarmed, field directors went into and out of battle zones with the divisions to which they were attached. American Red Cross Delegate William E. Stevenson flew in from his headquarters in Algiers, North Africa, to direct Red Cross field operations.

Early in the invasion, Red Cross men in charge of clubmobile units landed with their vehicles and immediately began making and distributing doughnuts to the dispersed units. Soon afterward, when the area became somewhat safer, two clubmobile girls joined each unit.

As soon as Sicily was conquered, North Africa was transformed into a rest and hospital zone, and most of its service clubs were closed down. And even before the guns had ceased firing in Sicily, that island was covered with the same pattern of Red Cross services that had been developed in North Africa. Later it was carried over to the Italian mainland.

Red Cross workers came in through new headquarters in Italy and promptly established clubs in Naples, Rome, Florence, Leghorn, and other large cities within Allied-held territory. Red Cross workers moved with the troops from one combat zone to another, and Red Cross hospital girls were not far behind with their hospital units. And the ubiquitous clubmobile girls were everywhere along the front. As of June 1, 1944, the American Red Cross staff in the Mediterranean theater of war numbered more than 1,000, of whom 72 per cent were women and 28 per cent men. In addition, there were approximately 2,500 native civilian employees. The Red Cross operated ninety-three club units, including twenty-seven enlisted men's clubs, twelve officers' clubs, two Navy clubs, and nineteen Army rest homes. Among the most attractive and picturesquely situated of these rest homes were those for United States airmen on the romantic island of Capri.

In Italy, as in every other theater of war, supply was one of the most serious problems faced by American Red Cross workers. Sometimes they were able to supplement inadequate stocks by purchases in the local markets, from the Army Quartermaster's, or from Navy ships lying offshore. Not infrequently, in desperation they resorted to scrounging. But there was one Red Cross hospital recreation worker—Mary T. Buffum, former Shushan, New York, schoolteacher—who had an original approach to the problem. As described by her roommate, Frances Waterbury of Bedford, Ohio, also a hospital recreation worker, it was as follows:

This is the story of a bedroll.

And when Uncle Joe is boring his grand-nephews with how he made the landing at Salerno, Aunt Mary can well tell how she fought the war with a bedroll.

There are bedrolls and bedrolls—but there are, probably fortunately for the Army, few bedrolls like the one which belongs to Mary T. Buffum, American Red Cross hospital recreation worker in Italy.

Like people, bedrolls come in all shapes and sizes, but Buff's bedroll is one of those things of indescribable shape and size. The contents are even more indescribable. When the General Hospital shut up shop in North Africa after a busy time during and following the Tunisian and Sicilian campaigns, and climbed aboard ship for Italy, Buff's bedroll came in for its usual ridicule.

As the bedrolls were lowered to the hold, crashing and banging against the side of the shafts, the nurses stood and cheered as Buff's "carry-all," rivaling the circumference of a huge vino barrel, passed in review.

Buff's active mind and her well-stocked bedroll make an almost unbeatable recreational combination. If it's a long train ride while the unit is moving, she has guessing games and riddles to shorten the journey. If it's a jittery flier who has come back from a mission from which many of his buddies haven't, she's got a hammering and sawing job in the craftroom to keep him busy; if it's a serious burn case, where the patient is completely immobilized, she's got just the quiz game to play on the ward where "this side" of the room vies with "that side."

When it came time to celebrate Christmas with the patients in the hospital, Buff unrolled her bedroll. Out came some red cambric and some green yarn, and for weeks the nurses helped sew Christmas stockings. "What can we do to help you with your Christmas program?" they'd all volunteered.

Birthdays, like Christmas, are special occasions which have not been forgotten. Birthday-cake candles seem to come in the bedroll, and if little cakes aren't available to put the candles on, then Buff can figure out some way to dress up a precious candy bar to look like a small birthday cake.

With spring coming, the psychiatric ward decided it wanted a garden. "Did Miss Buffum have some seeds?" came the request to the Red Cross day rooms. The rest of the Red Cross staff gasped at such a question. Mary Buffum just dug into the bedroll and came up with some Morning Glory and Nasturtium seeds.

How the bedroll comes by its contents is in itself a marvel. At mail call there are always packages for Mary T. Buffum. Mary's mother, Mary's sister, Mary's former co-workers, the neighbors, and friends, are always sending packages. Everyone always gathers around to see what's in the packages. There are all sorts of things. And as Buff opens the boxes unimaginative individuals inwardly snicker. "What in the world can ever be done with those scraps of wallpaper?" And yet when February 14 comes around and patients want to make valentines for their best girls, the wallpaper incredibly fills the need.

The bedroll is often stocked locally, too. If there's a Red Cross dance in town, and Mary has finally been talked into going to get away from her Red Cross work for a few hours, she is most likely to be found not on the dance floor, but off in a corner talking animatedly to someone who she has discovered is stationed at a salvage depot where there are pieces of plexiglass, scrap aluminum, micarda and other such handicraft materials.

No inventory has ever been taken, but at various times the bedroll has been known to hold (besides the essential clothing and personal articles) such things as scraps of yarn, pins, beads, construction paper, scissors, hammer, nails, tacks, maps, crossword puzzles, pictures of all sorts, books, magazines, paint, paste, glue, a folding chair, a weaving loom, tea, bouillion cubes, a sterno stove, cooking utensils and popcorn.

Maybe it's an exaggeration to say that Mary Buffum is winning this war with her bedroll; maybe it's going too far to say that here is the biggest bedroll on the Allied side, but certainly Mary and her bedroll have brought lots of comforts, and many pleasant surprises and "saved the day" on many different occasions. The hundreds of boys who came in from the Tunisian campaign, the men who came in off the hospital ships from Salerno, the fliers who have "just made it back" from their missions—all these who have known Miss Buffum during their stay at the 26th General Hospital, have found their stay less monotonous, less "time wasted" because of the program she has organized and kept going to fill their wants and needs. And many have written back after they've gone on, and told her so.

The story of the bedroll is an interesting one; its contents are fascinating. Many have benefited by it, but there are a few people who, yet unaware of these facts, have come to look upon Mary Buffum's bedroll as a "cross to be borne." These few are the Red Cross girls who live in the same room with her, but who must, for lack of space, retreat when the bedroll is unrolled, and must, alas, when it is again rolled, help roll it!

To meet the demands of wind, mud, and cold along the Italian front, Red Cross girls indulged their individual tastes in clothing.

The result was that Johnny Doughboy saw many original variations of the regulation GI uniform.

Most rugged women's teams at the front were Red Cross clubmobile girls who drove open weapons carriers through every kind of weather. When they dropped into some muddy infantry bivouac calling, "Hey, doughnuts! Come and get 'em," soldiers saw them wearing khaki woolen GI pants and shirts covered by a tan poplin field jacket. What the GI's did not see was their gray woolen underwear, cut off at the knee, that they had bought in the men's section of the Army Post Exchange.

Though otherwise GI in uniform, nearly all clubmobile girls wore an officer's khaki raincoat. With its good shoulders, wide slouch belt, button-in wool lining and detachable hood, it was found to be ideal for driving through rain or dust and splashing through mud. Tan knitted caps, GI version of the campus beanie, and gloves to match, completed the clubmobile girls' outfit, except for the shoes.

As learned by some Red Cross girls who got trench foot, footwear was very important. Mud in Italy was distinguished for its remarkable qualities both of depth and stickiness. As a result, the girls discarded regulation oxfords for anything from galoshes and GI field shoes to fleece-lined flying boots and knee-high Navy rubber boots. One hospital worker wore puttees over her galoshes because the mud was too deep for her rubbers. Many girls had additional leather flaps sewn on the tops of their GI field shoes.

Feminine individualism among clubmobile workers was as much a part of the Army as the competitive spirit among divisions. The Red Cross clubmobile girls serving the 36th Division wore skirts whenever they could because the men liked to see them that way. But the Third Division thought their Red Cross girls cute in strictly GI outfits. Girls of the 34th Division varied their GI uniforms with skirts, strapping puttees over their shoes and stockings, while an armored formation group stuck to regulation issue gray slacks despite mud splatters. Fleece-lined leather jackets marked a clubmobile team as strictly air force. Each girl wore the insignia of her own Army unit on her field jacket.

Probably the most unique outfit was worn by Betty "Butch" Jones of Oklahoma City, when she left for a forward area high in the mountains to serve doughnuts and coffee to combat troops. Up there it was cold, windy, muddy, and with German shells falling, dangerous. Miss Jones, a staff assistant assigned to clubmobiles, prepared for all contingencies. It took two buxom Italian women to push, snap, and button her into an outfit that consisted of the following items of clothing: a suit of heavy, long GI underwear; snuggies and a vest bought in Oklahoma City; a feminine looking slip "for appearance"; a pair of Mack Sennett-like heavy, khaki-colored stockings hand-knit in Rome by the grandmother of another Red Cross girl; a pair of rayon stockings brought from Oklahoma; a pair of wool socks; fleece-lined, fur-topped "clubmobile boots" over a pair of regulation shoes; men's GI garters; a knit sweater; a regulation nurse's blouse; a regulation Red Cross winter uniform of jacket and skirt; a wool scarf bought in Italy; a uniform topcoat, an officer's raincoat, and woolen GI mittens. Topping all was a "hat" fashioned from the woolen knit cap worn by soldiers inside their steel helmets, trimmed with little white flowers; and finally, over it a GI steel helmet.

The rugged outdoor life sharpened Red Cross girls' appetites. While they ate with slight regard to waistlines, slender girls usually gained weight and the buxom ones lost it.

Though doing physical work that would have taxed the strength of the hardiest American pioneer woman, these Red Cross girls did not neglect their femininity. They kept precious soaps and cosmetics in field packs, ammunition cases, and C-ration boxes beside their cots. Lipsticks and nail polish were not overlooked. There were, in addition, some improvisations. Lemon powder, saved from rations, made a good lemon rinse. Shaving-cream lather was used as a shampoo. Roommates paired up, heated water in GI cans, and gave each other helmet shampoos.

Red Cross clubmobile girls often turned up where they were least expected. On Christmas Day, 1943, a doughboy in a foxhole up in the rain-soaked mountains was about to open a can of C-rations for his Christmas dinner. Suddenly he looked up to find Isabella Hughes of Baltimore, Red Cross clubmobile girl, crouching on the edge of his foxhole, a box of doughnuts in one hand and a pot of steaming coffee in the other. "Good Lord, sweetheart!" he exclaimed. "What in hell are you doing *here?*"

Italy's roads—muddy, bumpy, and mountainous—furrowed the brow of many a pretty head. The clubmobile, though a sturdy machine, often proved unequal to these roads. On the mountains the girls had to drive Army weapons carriers, and on some of the more precipitous slopes even weapons carriers were useless. Then the Army resorted to mules and donkeys for the delivery of essential supplies to forward combat units. To reach these men the Red Cross used the same animals, the girls calling them the "donkeymobile."

On one occasion, two clubmobile girls—Margaret Decker of

Towaco, New Jersey, and Gladys Currie of Greenwich, Connecticut—planned to take doughnuts and coffee to a certain unit on a mountain peak. No road, only a mule track, led to their position. The Army offered to get the girls there if they were brave enough to ride donkey-back for several miles up the steep mountain slope. The girls accepted the offer with alacrity. Red Cross Field Director Murray Nace of Lynbrook, New York, went along. Each was assigned a donkey as a mount, while the doughnuts were loaded on a mule. Reaching the spot where the combat troops waited, the girls were surprised to find them shaved and washed. Their coming had been heralded by an official military notice posted on the camp bulletin board. The boys were so excited at seeing the two Red Cross girls on this dangerous mountain peak that, after coffee and doughnuts, they formed a ring on the ground and had their pretty visitors sit in the center. The ping of mortar and the whine and crashing of shells charged the air as the group took time out from the war to talk.

The coolness and courage of Red Cross personnel in Italy won the admiration of the whole Army from General Mark W. Clark down to the humblest buck private. And so when the Rangers issued an official citation to Lois N. Berney of Fallon, Nevada, a clubmobile worker, it was commonly accepted as a form of recognition for the entire Red Cross personnel in the theater. Miss Berney, a former secretary to Harry Hopkins, served the Rangers during the North African campaign and again in the violent Venafro sector on the Italian front. The citation, signed by Major (later Lieutenant Colonel) Roy A. Murray, Jr., commanding officer of the 4th Battalion, read as follows:

During the most inclement weather my men have had to endure since the beginning of the Italian campaign, Miss Lois Berney, Red Cross field representative, was present at my forward command post on November 17, 1943, and distributed coffee and doughnuts to all my men. Our bivouac area is about one mile from our forward outposts, and is subject to harassing artillery fire; and on the above-mentioned date the enemy shell fire fell close by during her visit.

Miss Berney remained unconcerned and her smile and cheerful word for each man as he came to her and received his rations was indeed an excellent morale builder. She cheered up my men and successfully changed a tense atmosphere into one of cheerfulness.

All the officers and men of my command express their gratitude and thanks to Miss Berney, and desire that she be recognized as a real and true American Red Cross girl who has afforded them good cheer by her visits to them in Africa and here at the fighting front.

In transmitting this citation, General Clark, commander of the U.S. Fifth Army, wrote as follows:

I take great pleasure in forwarding this letter of commendation of the splendid performance by Miss Lois Berney, American Red Cross. This represents a fine example of the courageous, energetic and cheerful manner in which personnel of the American Red Cross are daily performing their tasks in the Fifth Army under what are often extremely trying and hazardous conditions. I desire to add my praise of Miss Berney for her actions on this occasion.

Coming from the American Rangers, this citation represented a high distinction as they were considered to be one of the toughest outfits in the Army, and a Red Cross girl serving them necessarily performed her work under fire.

The pick of United States Army training camps in Northern Ireland, these young fighting men, whose average age was twenty-five, received their specialized training in the British commando school. Specialists in night fighting, house-to-house combat, and mountain warfare, they preferred the use of the bayonet for its silence, though expert with the rifle and many other weapons. They got their baptism of fire in the Dieppe raid. Together with the British Commandos, the American Rangers were the shock troops of the Allied forces storming Hitler's Fortress Europe. Led by Colonel William O. Darby of Fort Smith, Arkansas, founder and commanding officer, the Rangers were in the vanguard of the amphibious landings in North Africa, Sicily, and Italy, distinguishing themselves at Kasserine Pass and El Guettar, at Gela, Sicily, on the Salerno beachhead, and in the bloody mountain fighting that led finally to the capture of Naples. Their only defeat and tragic climax came on the Anzio beachhead—but of this later.

While Miss Berney was the Rangers' No. 1 Red Cross girl, Gordon Jackson of Fort Thomas, Kentucky, was their Red Cross field director. He was known as the Rangers' Jackson ever since he joined them on the Italian front in October, 1943. On a warm afternoon in June, 1944, thousands of troops passed in review at Camp Butner, North Carolina, before a small group of Rangers home from war—less than ten percent of the original 2,000. The remainder were still overseas, some in Army hospitals, some in German prisoner-of-war camps, and many were dead. On the reviewing stand also were Wendell Willkie, Josephus Daniels, and Governor J. Melville Broughton of North Carolina. They, too, were honoring the Rangers. Sitting with the heroes was a prematurely gray, handsome man of forty—the Rangers' Jackson. He was sharing their tribute as he had shared their tribulations in the Venafro sector and on the Anzio beachhead. Like them he was wearing a citation device on his right breast, as he was included when the President cited the 4th Ranger Battalion.

How Gordon Jackson earned this distinction was told by Randy Fort of Tuscaloosa, Alabama, an American Red Cross staff correspondent on the Italian front.

When Jackson joined up, many a tough Ranger wondered at the advisability of having his outfit encumbered by a civilian.

Early in November, 1943, two Ranger battalions, the 1st and 4th, moved up to the front, but their Red Cross man didn't. He was a whole day behind. The remaining Ranger battalion in Italy, the 3rd, was not yet to move up, and Jack had arranged a party for them.

On the second day, however, Jack, driving his jeep-and-trailer loaded with supplies, caught up with the two forward battalions. Officially, he was attached to the 1st, which was under Colonel Darby's direct command. And it was then that the Rangers learned about Jackson.

His own battalion, the 1st, was bivouacked on The Hill, a spot of hell and death just above the town of Venafro, a favorite shelling target of the Germans. To most Americans, The Hill would be a mountain. Actually a series of irregular peaks, it was a rugged piece of earth, the more so because Jerry inhabited its other slope.

The Hill was very rocky, yet mud tugged at everything. Its trees were shattered by shell and smaller shot. A deep foxhole adjoined each tent.

To reach the Rangers' bivouac, one first had to negotiate Shell Lane and Shrapnel Junction. Shell Lane, a level stretch of good road, led into Venafro. As vehicles plunged into it from either direction, their occupants gambled their lives. Jerry couldn't see the Lane, but he had it under range, and any old time he could send some heavy stuff over it. Sometimes drivers made it; sometimes, they didn't.

248

Shrapnel Junction was smack in the middle of Venafro, and traffic streaked through from all directions. Jerry also had it in his sights. And you had to pass the Junction, with its vigorously gesturing MP's, to get to The Hill.

Jack came to the bivouac hot on the tail of his Rangers, and there he stayed with them for more than a month, except for frequent trips to Naples and other rear-area points to replenish supplies, run errands for the men or perform other chores. Each round trip meant running the Lane and the Junction twice.

"Jack was our medium, between the line and civilization," says Captain Joseph N. Fineberg, Ranger officer from Philadelphia. "If there was anything we needed in the rear—*we* couldn't leave the line—he got it for us."

On one occasion, there on The Hill, Jack received an inquiry from the States. A girl in the West hadn't heard for some time from her man in the 1st Rangers. Although he formerly had written often, the press of fighting had restricted his writing. She was worried. Jack set out to make a routine check that he might cable her that the soldier was well. As he walked down The Hill toward the boy's tent, he saw the fellow talking with some friends.

"Hey, Buddy," Jack yelled and waved.

"Buddy" started to wave back. Just then came the whistle of an incoming shell. Jack dived for a hole, and made it. "Buddy" dived, and didn't. That afternoon the Red Cross man helped bury the boy. He could not answer the girl's frantic message, for only the War Department may report men killed.

Perhaps his most appreciated service was setting up in and around Venafro five "rest rooms" or "drying rooms" for men just off the line. Up to that time, men with two or three days' continuous contact with the enemy would come out of the line, wet, muddy, bitterly cold, exhausted. Bolting down food and coffee at the mess tent, they would strip off their soggy, dirty clothing, lie down on the cold ground in their pup tents and try to sleep.

Jack spotted five rooms—one was a little church—in Venafro. He cleaned them up, installed a few little comforts, arranged for a charcoal fire in each, and turned them over to the Rangers.

Several of these rooms were bombed out as enemy artillery "zeroed in," but Jack promptly established other centers.

"Jack materially helped keep our men in good health," says Lieutenant Colonel Roy A. Murray, Jr., commanding officer of the 4th Rangers. "We had seventeen continuous days of heavy rain there at Venafro, and the men were pretty miserable until he set up these drying rooms."

Although attached to the 1st Ranger Battalion, the Red Cross man also served the 3rd and 4th Battalions. As all were on the line, it called for daily shuttling back and forth among the scattered units in his jeep-and-trailer.

With Christmas approaching, the Rangers decided they wanted to send out Christmas cards, war or no war, Hill or no Hill. The job was Jackson's.

A soldier-artist made a sketch of Hitler and Tojo retreating and a recumbent Mussolini trying to get away from the Rangers. Followed the business of having a stencil cut, locating mimeographing facilities and paper, finding unattached labor, having censoring done and mailing the "cards," which were on V-mail sheets.

This meant many a round trip to Naples and to Fifth Army headquarters at Caserta, wheedling and cutting through red tape. But the Christmas greetings, four to a man, were in the mails in time to reach the States on schedule.

After long, bitter weeks on The Hill, the Rangers finally were pulled out of the line just before Christmas, and Jack decided their good fortune should be celebrated appropriately. The Rangers then were resting at the seaside town of Lucrino, north of Naples.

The field man obtained a twenty-foot Christmas tree from a Red Cross club in Naples. He bought some tree trimmings in the big Italian city, and also used ribbons and bright-colored bits saved from Christmas packages. Everybody helped trim the tree.

The boys also built a big table, fifteen feet by seven feet. Jack located ten additional sidewalk tables on which he placed cigars, cigarettes, all the candy he could find, and hundreds of pounds of oranges, tangerines, apples and nuts.

Also there were several cakes from unopened packages of men who had not come down The Hill alive.

"We knew they'd want it that way," Jack explains.

A temporary altar was erected in the place that had been taken over as a Red Cross dayroom. The Christmas program opened with a midnight Mass on Christmas Eve.

Following the Mass, open house was held around the tree all through the night. A Protestant Christmas service took place in the morning.

The service over, a six-piece Italian orchestra played the remainder of the day and through the evening. In the course of the afternoon two Red Cross girls appeared with 3,000 cookies.

After a month's rest, the three Ranger battalions received their new orders: they were to spearhead another amphibious landing, this time on the Anzio-Nettuno beaches about thirty miles south of Rome.

Field Director Gordon Jackson sought to go along, but the Rangers would not hear of it. Yes, they admitted, Jackson had proved in the hot Venafro. sector that he could take it, but what was the use of an unarmed civilian sticking his neck out needlessly? "You stay around here in Naples two or three weeks, till we ease things up a bit there," they said.

But for the impatient Jackson this was too long a wait. Forty-eight hours after D-Day (January 22, 1944) the Red Cross man and his jeep-and-trailer were on an ammunition-laden LST sailing for the Anzio beachhead. To say the Rangers were surprised to see him is an understatement. For three days they had been on the beachhead fighting under remorseless enemy fire, on scanty rations and without sleep or rest. And here was their Red Cross man Jackson, weeks before he was expected, bringing cigarettes, chewing gum, smoking tobacco, candy, and such toilet articles as towels, razors and blades, toothbrushes, tooth paste and shaving cream. But even more important than these were twenty-five sacks of Ranger mail that he had contrived to bring from Naples. Eyes bloodshot, grimy, and stubble bearded, the Rangers were speechless with gratitude.

The mail from home—the first in weeks—gave the Rangers that extra lift that enabled them to go on fighting day after day and night after night. On their sixth sleepless night they were ordered to take Cisterna, a key mountain village held by a garrison of German paratroopers. The 1st and 3rd Battalions marched off into the blackness of that bitterly cold night of January 28, 1944, singing "Pistol Packin' Mama." They were to terrorize the garrison with special Ranger tactics long enough for the 4th Battalion to come up a gravel road, while the infantry closed in on Cisterna from two sides.

This, essentially, was the plan, but something went wrong. There were far more Germans in Cisterna than supposed. The 1st and 3rd Battalions found themselves encircled by paratroopers using automatic weapons and panzer grenadiers with tanks and 88's. Rushing to their assistance, the 4th Battalion ran into unexpectedly heavy enemy fire and lost many men and officers. And the infantry could not break through either on the left or the right of Cisterna to relieve the 1st and 3rd. Trapped within the Germans' ring of steel they faced hopeless odds. Their last cryptic radio telephone message was their epitaph: "They're closing in, but they won't get us cheap."

The 4th reformed its ranks and again attacked, this time cracking the German ring. While breaking up what might have developed into a German counterthrust, the attack came too late to save the 1st and 3rd; out of 800 a mere handful came back.

The Germans enjoyed a great advantage in that their guns were emplaced in the hills overlooking the beaches. There was scarcely a square inch on the crowded and busy Anzio-Nettuno beachhead that was not under observation of enemy posts, or within the range of enemy guns. And they fired at will day and night. LST's were unloaded at the waterfront, and trucks, jeeps, and Red Cross club-mobiles moved back and forth in the pitted streets and roads of the wrecked little seaside towns of Anzio and Nettuno almost in defiance of whining and crashing shells. Now and then the Army laid down thick smoke screens to conceal particular movements, but generally its attitude seemed to be, "The hell with them."

The Anzio beachhead was a nightmare of sound—the sound of artillery, mortar, and machine-gun fire, the sound of bombings, strafings, earth-jarring explosions, and of terrific outbursts of Allied antiaircraft fire.

There were virtually no rear areas here. Everybody was at the front. Every human being, even the unarmed Army nurses and Red Cross girls, was on the firing line in this tight little sector. It was a steel trap from which there was no escaping. The tension that came from knowing that the terrible, ruthless enemy was looking down upon you from the hills, that he was making a target of you every moment of the day and night—this tension was indescribable.

Nowhere was the violence reflected with greater accuracy than in the Army tent hospitals near the front. The nurses and Red Cross girls in the receiving tents could tell you from day to day whether the fighting was light or heavy by the number of casualties admitted. Unfortunately, heavy days were far more numerous. The 16th Evacuation Hospital, for example, with 750 beds, often operated beyond its capacity, according to Captain Ella G. Leitzke, of Chassell, Michigan, the hospital's head nurse. On some busy days, she said, her hospital admitted between 175 and 200 soldiers, and on one black day 467 battle casualties were received.

And the 16th Evacuation was not the only hospital on the Anzio beachhead. There was a whole hospital zone where a number of Army hospitals were grouped together. This gigantic city of tents with thousands of beds was laid out in the middle of the whole sector, just below the town of Nettuno near the water front. In accordance with international agreements they were out in the open and in plain view. To identify them as hospitals, the tents were marked with large red crosses, and in one field a huge red cross had been laid out in gravel and brick. Whether plastered with mud in winter, or hazy with dust in spring and summer, these red crosses were visible for miles from the air.

Hospitals, like the infantry, were underground, with only the upper parts of the ward tents showing above the surface. The tents were reached from the road by steps. Sandbag parapets were placed against the side walls. The tents were poorly ventilated because the side flaps could not be turned up, and dingy, with electric lights burning all day. On rainy days the effect was depressing. And how it rained! Doctors, nurses, Red Cross girls, and patients all joined in mocking the phrase, "Sunny Italy." Hospital staffs laid walks with boards or rocks, but they still had to slog through knee-deep mud.

Red Cross hospital workers tried to relieve the monotony, drabness, and grimness of the Anzio existence for the GI's. Each hospital had its own Red Cross recreation center consisting of one or two ward tents pitched partly underground like the rest of the hospital. The Red Cross girls hunted around the Italian neighborhood for comfortable furniture to make the tents inviting. The tents were brightened with flowers and gaily colored Italian pottery bowls filled with Red Cross cigarettes, matches, candy, V-mail and Red Cross stationery to which the boys helped themselves as needed. Two or three times a week there were movies, the Red Cross providing screens and projectors, Army Special Services the films. The Special Service officer at each hospital handled live entertainment, but relied on the Red Cross recreation worker to find talented patients. One original skit, written and produced by convalescent patients calling themselves the "Anzio Foxhole Club" poked fun at familiar situations and personalities. There was no lack of artistic, theatrical, and musical talent at Anzio. There were other things in the Red Cross "rec" tent—phonograph music, games, books, and magazines. A popular feature was the registration board where men put down their names, units, and home towns, resulting in happy reunions.

The patients of the 38th Evacuation had red and white roses to wear on Mother's Day, because the three Red Cross hospital workers—Lucy Brooke, of Englewood, New Jersey; Mrs. William E. Stevenson, of Stamford, Connecticut; and Frances Engeman, of Flemington, New Jersey—had gathered the flowers outside the hospital area.

Maryles Nahl of Oakland, California, the first Red Cross girl to land on the Anzio beach, planted a vegetable garden of onions, carrots, Swiss chard, radishes, and lettuce beside her tent from seeds sent by her mother. It had to be laboriously transplanted when enemy shellings came too close.

Existence, however, was pretty grim for the Red Cross hospital workers. There was work to be done from early morning till late at night. As much as the nurses desired to do little extra things for their patients they just didn't have the time. They and the doctors cared for the patients' medical needs. The Red Cross girls looked after the extras. They did not shrink at the sight of wounds, nor waste time pitying the men. They kidded them, laughed with them, and mothered them to hasten their recovery.

When the routine chores were done, Red Cross girls helped nurses feed the wounded who could not feed themselves. Captain Leitzke tells of this in her hospital:

You should see a ward of men with arm wounds. You would see them feeding each other, in high glee at their mutual awkwardness. Also you would probably see a couple of the nurses, and a Red Cross worker or two in the middle of it, ladling out the chow to those who were too awkward. We had quite a time one evening with our arm injuries when it turned out that all the men were right-handed, and had been injured in their right arms. The Red Cross girls really did a feeding job that time!

Battle-shocked patients, abnormally sensitive to bombings and shellings, posed a difficult problem for Red Cross girls whenever enemy planes were overhead. Lucy Brooke of the 38th Evacuation recalled one horrible night when German planes were over the hospital area at the very moment that it was being shelled.

I had one tent as my responsibility, and was very busy going from cot to cot talking with the boys and, incidentally, trying to ignore the fireworks myself. Finally, I found several boys who wanted to sing, so we tuned up.

A chaplain, Captain Delmar Dyerson, who was a patient in a near-by tent, heard us and came over to join us. With Captain Dyerson playing the accordion, more and more joined us until the singing was loud enough to drown out the noise outside.

Actually, we sang for several hours. During this time I became very much interested in one boy who suffered from a severe case of battle-shock. He had been with us several days, saying nothing and staring into space with glazed eyes.

When the raid started he squatted on his heels in a corner of the tent, trembling. For some time, even after the singing had started, he took no notice of anyone in the tent.

The singing had been on for some time when the soldier stood up and slowly edged over toward our group, the glazed expression gradually leaving his eyes. The whole thing was like something out of a book. It sounds hardly true, but when the captain started playing the National Anthem on his accordion the battle-shocked boy started to sing. As the last words rang out, he was singing just as strong and loud as any of the rest of us.

One of the hospitals on the Anzio beachhead was the 95th Evacuation where Esther Richards, of San Francisco, was the Red Cross hospital social worker. A native of North Platte, Nebraska, Miss Richards was educated at the University of California and Columbia University. As a graduate nurse she served in World War I. From 1920 to 1932 she was with the U.S. Veterans Bureau, and from 1937 until she joined the American Red Cross for overseas service she was a social worker on the staff of the San Francisco Public Welfare Department. In this capacity she aided civilian evacuees from Hawaii after Pearl Harbor.

As a Red Cross hospital social worker, Miss Richards arrived with her hospital unit in North Africa in July, 1943, on the way to service on the Italian front. Thirty-six hours after D-Day (September 9, 1943) at the time of the amphibious landing at Salerno, her hospital ship was struck offshore by a bomb and had to be abandoned. The blow came as she was asleep in her cabin. The concussion threw her out of bed. Her eye and forehead were cut and her back injured. Crawling on hands and knees through the debris of crashing walls, she found a hole through which she escaped from her cabin. Struggling to the deck, she found a rope ladder and climbed down safely into a lifeboat. She was shipped back to a hospital in North Africa.

From her hospital cot, she wrote Red Cross National Headquarters,

The weather has been very severe in this locality. Work is carried on in driving rainstorms and thick mud ruts, following storms. New Year's Day was ushered in with a freak wind and rain storm which blew down the Red Cross tent and office.

To a fellow Red Cross worker, Esther Richards confided that she was haunted by a premonition of death. The worker tried to take her mind off thoughts of death, but Miss Richards said she could not shake them off.

Nevertheless, so all-pervading was her sense of duty toward the wounded and sick GI's that as soon as she had recovered from her back injuries, she insisted upon being shipped immediately to the Anzio beachhead, then the hottest fighting front in Western Europe. Only a few days after her arrival at Anzio, her hospital, the 95th Evacuation, was bombed and shelled.

At the 95th Evacuation she shared Red Cross responsibilities with a recreation worker. In addition to her technical duties, such as helping doctors prepare patients' medical histories, she proved helpful in other ways. To hospitalized soldiers alarmed over the reactions of their mothers, wives, or sweethearts with respect to their loss of a leg, an arm, or other serious injury, she was a tower of strength. Miss Richards wrote home for many of them. Many tried to spare their loved ones' feelings by glossing over their injuries. But she counseled against it. The folks will have to know sooner or later, she would say, and it was best that they be prepared for the inevitable. Sometimes she enlisted the help of Home Service workers in local Red Cross chapters to interpret a man's condition to his family so that they would receive him with understanding, not pity. The patients themselves were inspired with self-confidence and hope for the future. She dwelt on the miracles of modern plastic surgery and orthopedics, and if they were destined to be discharged for disability, she explained the extensive benefits offered by federal and state governments—pensions, vocational training, and opportunities for future employment in civilian life.

One day, just as the Germans launched a counterattack apparently aimed at wiping out the entire Anzio beachhead, Miss Richards, already overburdened with her own duties, took over for the Red Cross recreation worker, who had become ill. However, with the battle raging only a short distance away, she spent most of her time with the wounded in the receiving tent. As one man was carried out to the surgery tent, his place was taken by another casualty brought by ambulance from the clearing station in the front lines. Tired, grimy, and bloody, the wounded heroes lay on stretchers, some receiving blood plasma, some undergoing emergency operations, some waiting for the busy doctors and nurses to reach them. Moving among the wounded was Miss Richards, tender, compassionate, and completely understanding. The American Red Cross patch on her sleeve inspired the waiting men to turn to her for small favors—a drink of water, a cigarette, a stick of gum. Some asked questions. Talking helped a man forget pain, and so Miss Richards talked with as many men as she could. She was in the receiving tent performing her duties in midafternoon, February 7, when a lone German plane swooped low over the hospital and dropped antipersonnel bombs on the tents. One of the bombs struck a corner of her tent splattering shrapnel. Miss Richards, critically wounded, was rushed to the surgery tent. While every effort was made to save her life, she died on the operating table. Two fellow Red Cross workers were with her to the end.

Two nurses were among the others killed that afternoon. Finally brought down, the German pilot said that he had jettisoned the bombs to escape two Spitfires on his tail.

Esther Richards was the first American Red Cross woman in World War II to be killed in action. Secretary of War Henry Stimson confirmed this in a letter awarding her the Purple Heart posthumously.

On March 6, 1944, in an impressive ceremony held in the rotunda of the city hall, the City of San Francisco presented to members of her family a memorial resolution adopted by the Board of Supervisors.

The Italian Government's War Cross of Military Valor has also been awarded to Miss Richards posthumously. The citation reads as follows:

This heroic Red Cross worker, heedless of the enemy's extremely violent fire, gave proof of a high sense of duty and of contempt for danger. She sacrificed her young life for the ideals of civilization and for the liberation of Rome.

The American Red Cross suffered more casualties in Sicily and Italy than in any other theater. Most of the deaths have been due to accidental airplane crashes. In one plane a field director and six Red Cross girls were killed with military personnel. In addition, three field men on their way to the China–Burma–India theater were lost when their ship was torpedoed and sunk in the Mediterranean.

Chapter XII

IN GREAT BRITAIN
PREPARING FOR D-DAY

I N GREAT BRITAIN, THE AMERICAN EXPEDITIONARY FORCES WERE widely dispersed. In groups varying from a few hundred men or less at isolated outposts to many thousands undergoing invasion training in camps, the great majority were stationed in rural areas. Many of the posts were five or more miles from the nearest town or village.

How the American Red Cross solved the complicated problem of properly serving the scattered units forms one of the fascinating stories of the war. Because of space limitations only a suggestion of the kaleidoscope can be given here.

With headquarters in London, Red Cross services were spread out over the United Kingdom in a series of concentric circles until not a single American serviceman or woman was overlooked. The Red Cross emblem was carried into the remotest reaches where motor roads turned to muddy tracks and telephone wires were un-known—even to the wild and desolate moors beyond which the At-lantic shows its teeth. There American soldiers carried on in the wind and rain, and there the Red Cross came to them.

Side by side with traditional Red Cross services in Great Britain—field, hospital, and club—preparations for invasion were carried on. Like the Army, which plans its transportation and supply problems far in advance of a major campaign, the Red Cross had to work and plan to hold its appointed place in military operations. Men of wide experience were putting in countless hours in the planning and exe-cution of the smallest details. A heaping stock pile of supplies needed on D-Day and for some time after—millions of pounds of doughnut flour, vast quantities of towels, toothbrushes, tooth paste, shaving cream, candy and gum, playing cards, matches, many millions of cigarettes, and other items to be distributed free to the GI's—was being accumulated. To handle these supplies required thousands of cases, properly marked and packed, and hundreds of employees marking and packing them. Vast warehousing space had to be found to segregate the material. Red Cross supply officers in Britain and on the continent would follow the cargo movement through ports and overland to final destinations. Cargoes first assembled in New

York, Boston, and other ports would end up in forward areas where Red Cross workers distributed them directly to the combat troops.

Mobility, watchword of the Army, was also the key to this vast and all-embracing Red Cross pre-invasion program. Hundreds of motor vehicles were being assembled to serve as clubmobiles, trucks, soup kitchens, vans, trailers, and mobile generators.

As of July 31, 1944, there were 38,298 paid and volunteer workers serving the troops in Great Britain and Western Europe under the American Red Cross flag. The backbone of this service was provided by more than 2,700 professional Red Cross workers from the United States. Building up a staff and recruiting local labor, paid and volunteer, were in themselves tremendous tasks.

No wonder the lights burned late every night in Grosvenor Square, ETO headquarters of the American Red Cross.

The driving force behind this huge organization was a volunteer, Harvey D. Gibson, American Red Cross commissioner to Great Britain and Western Europe. President of the Manufacturers' Trust Company in New York, he was on leave from his bank to serve the Red Cross overseas. Mr. Gibson's Red Cross career was long and distinguished. In World War I he was a member of the War Council, and also Red Cross commissioner to France in 1918 and to Europe in 1919.

Mr. Gibson assumed his World War II duties in September, 1942, shortly after his arrival from the United States. He succeeded William E. Stevenson, Red Cross delegate to Great Britain who, after serving from the spring until November, 1942, left for North Africa to become Red Cross delegate to that theater. Preceding Mr. Stevenson as Red Cross delegate to Great Britain, Bernard S. Carter had come to London before Pearl Harbor.

American Red Cross Military and Naval Welfare Service in the United Kingdom was inaugurated by Supervisor Robert C. Lewis, veteran Red Crosser who, during the week of December 3-10, 1941, started a program for servicemen attached to the United States Embassy.

With the arrival of American troops in Northern Ireland, announced late in January, 1942, and of the first contingent of American Red Cross workers, announced March 5, the Military and Naval Welfare Service made good progress. This pioneer Red Cross group consisted of John S. Disosway* of San Antonio, Texas, field director; Elmer A. Quist of Minneapolis, and Thomas Ford McHale of

* Mr. Disosway died of natural causes while on duty in England May 25, 1943.

Olyphant, Pennsylvania, assistant field directors; Thomas W. Irving of Rockford, Illinois, recreation director; Jean P. Napier of Emory University, Georgia, and Elsie Davies of Wilkes-Barre, medical social workers; Nancy M. Jones of Nevada City, California, and Miriam L. Spaulding of Lowell, Massachusetts, recreation workers; Marjorie H. Stein of Chevy Chase, Maryland, and Helen H. Cantrell of Strafford, Pennsylvania, secretaries. Supervisor Robert C. Lewis was in charge.

The first major task undertaken by Commissioner Gibson and his staff was of a social nature. The Army was starting its policy of giving each soldier an eight-day furlough every five or six months. Great Britain was a very busy place in wartime with hotels in the larger cities taxed to capacity. As these were the very places the soldiers would rush to from their isolated stations, it was obvious that something definite had to be done to provide sleeping accommodations for them while on furlough. To meet this need, the Red Cross was requested by General Eisenhower to establish service clubs for them in the cities.

The first two service clubs in a Red Cross chain that soon covered the United Kingdom were formally opened on the same date: May 6, 1942. One was the Eagle Club in London used in pre-Pearl Harbor days by Americans serving with the British forces. The other was located in Londonderry, Northern Ireland. This club generally took precedence over the Eagle Club as it was the first entirely organized by the American Red Cross. The third club was opened in Glasgow, Scotland, on June 28, 1942. American troops in London celebrated the Fourth of July, 1942, by attending the opening of the Washington Club. Formerly the Washington Hotel, this old building was modernized and adapted to the special needs of the Red Cross, becoming a model for future service clubs. There were clubs for officers as well as for enlisted men. Even the women —Wacs, Army nurses, ferry pilots, and Red Cross workers on leave—had a club of their own in London. A number of clubs were located near large concentrations of Negro troops and were staffed by Negro professional Red Cross workers from the United States.

At the peak of the program in Great Britain more than 2,000 Red Cross staff workers were on duty in 265 service clubs. They were assisted by nearly 13,000 British volunteers and nearly 10,000 paid employees.

A man leaving camp on an eight-day furlough received, along with his pass and travel warrant, a card that reserved for him a bed at a Red Cross club on a certain day in the city to which he was traveling. Soldiers on leave were not required to use the Red Cross club, but virtually all did so. What actually happened was that upon arriving at their destination the men checked in at the Red Cross club, dumped their kit in their bedrooms, changed their dollars into English currency, and rushed out to kick up their heels.

The American dishes served in Red Cross clubs had an irresistible appeal to homesick GI's on leave. The kitchens were manned by chefs and assistants whom the Red Cross had specially trained in American cooking and in the preparation of American dishes. Despite Britain's drastic rationing restrictions, they were able to turn out many a surprise that reminded a soldier of Mom's cooking, and the verdict of most GI's was that the Red Cross clubs had the "best grub in town." In compliance with the request of the War Department, and in keeping with the practice of Allied service clubs in Great Britain, Red Cross clubs made a small charge for food and lodging. Charges, however, were below cost, the deficit being made up by the Red Cross. The price for a bed and breakfast was fixed at 2s 6d, or 50 cents in United States currency. For a regular dinner the charge was only one shilling, or twenty cents. A dinner consisted of plenty of bread, one main dish of fish or meat, with at least one vegetable in addition to potatoes, plenty of gravy, and dessert; dessert generally was pie, pudding, or waffles, often with real maple syrup.

These clubs provided everything else that a soldier could hope for in his wildest dreams—a cafeteria, snack bars, check rooms, hot and cold showers, barber shop, tailor shop, shoeshine parlor, and game, recreation, reading and writing, and first-aid rooms. One of the greatest attractions was a large map of the United States labeled, *Is there someone here from your home town? Watch the flags.* The map was dotted with tiny red flags with the name and home address of the American soldiers using the club at the moment. This device led to many pleasant reunions of friends and relatives. And one of the busiest spots was the information bureau, where all questions were answered. Here were distributed complimentary tickets to commercial theaters, cinemas, and concerts; and arrangements were made for sight-seeing tours and overnight and week-end visits with British families. The clubs also held dances, free movies, concerts, and theatrical productions by local amateur and professional actors and actresses.

Of the clubs, the best known was Rainbow Corner, off Piccadilly Circus in London. It was a clearing house for all the others in the European theater of operations. Ideas spread from it in widening circles. One of them, the art and handicraft displays of American servicemen, aroused so much public interest that it was sent on tour. As a traveling exhibit it was seen by more than a half-million people.

Rainbow Corner was also the place where servicemen arriving on leave were assigned rooms in the other Red Cross clubs in London, and where all difficulties were ironed out, usually by a house committee of servicemen. When Rainbow Corner was opened the key was thrown away. Its doors were never closed, service continuing around the clock. No matter what hour of the day or night a man arrived in London he found a staff on duty ready to welcome him. This club was also the largest Red Cross recreation center. There was something doing there every night—shows, movies, dances, prize fights, wrestling matches, and all sorts of athletic tournaments with prizes. The Red Cross went to extraordinary lengths to provide entertainment.

One of the many volunteer workers at Rainbow Corner was sitting behind her desk one day when a GI grinned: "Where do you come from in the States?"

"I'm just one of those Omaha, Nebraska, girls," she replied with a chuckle.

The volunteer was Lady Cavendish, Adele Astaire.

This charming American woman who, with her brother Fred as a dancing partner, once danced herself into the hearts of two continents, made a unique place for herself at Rainbow Corner. If the juke box happened to be playing a lively tune she might step out on the floor with one of the GI's. For the most part, however, she stuck to her job penning letters to addresses all over the United States. Far from formal, her letters gave a friendly report to mothers, wives, and sweethearts of their loved ones with whom Adele had talked at Rainbow Corner.

"What I like most about my job," said Adele, "is the return in dividends I am getting in the form of letters from America. This type of fan mail is genuine and to be treasured. Most of the mothers and wives call me 'Dear Adele' and their letters are so warm and friendly that they almost make me feel one of the family."

From one mother: "Dear Adele: Pardon my informal salutation but I feel as if I know you."

From another mother: "I was so thrilled with your letter that I had everyone read it, even the Parish Priest."

From a young wife: "The papers say your brother, Fred, is going across to entertain the boys. Three cheers for the Astaire family."

From a sergeant's wife: "It's women like you who are helping we women at home to carry on."

From a young woman: "As you know, Adele, my Tony is a very wonderful person. Please tell him that I love him truly, sincerely and forever."

From another young woman: "Your letter reassured me a lot. It is true that girls at home become just a bit worried knowing that their men are meeting lovely girls elsewhere—but I don't mean you, Adele."

Now and then a tragic note crept into Adele's fan mail. From a mother: "Thank you for your kind letter written for my son. Yesterday we received a telegram telling us of his death in action . . ."

Without volunteers like Adele Astaire, together with some British paid workers, the service clubs could not have been operated. British workers spent between twenty and forty hours a week performing such chores as washing dishes, peeling potatoes, making beds, serving in the canteen, and answering questions at the information desk. With many, the hours they gave to the Red Cross represented time left over from regular war jobs and housework. They stood patiently in line for rations, squeezed their shopping into crowded lunch hours, spent one night a week fire-watching from blackout till dawn—compulsory for all men and women between fifteen and fifty-five years—and worked in the Red Cross clubs.

Englishmen also volunteered to serve with the American Red Cross. One girl supervisor in a club outside London was surprised when a certain man came to volunteer his services. He explained politely that he would have to confine his activities to the evening as he was busy in a war plant all day.

"After a long day like that," asked the girl, "why do you want to work at a Red Cross club?"

"I've got to!" the man said grimly. "It's the only way I can see anything of my wife."

The volunteers represented a cross-section of the British population, titled women working alongside women of all classes. Like the paid workers, they too combined Red Cross work with housework and war work.

Volunteer nurses from the British Red Cross and St. John's took care of minor ailments in the first-aid rooms of the American Red Cross clubs. One of them, a veteran of the London blitz, found that her patients, suffering from minor cuts, headaches, and blackout bumps, seemed more interested in her accounts of the blitz than in anything else. She concluded from their remarks that they were sorry they had missed the excitement of the blitz.

One volunteer spent her mornings on a WVS (Women's Volunteer Services) tea car, her afternoons at an American Red Cross club snack bar.

Some gave up their leisure to take GI's sight-seeing. In London, a volunteer named E. J. Cormack was known as the "doughboy's guide to London." After spending six days a week working in a war plant his idea of Sabbath rest was showing the sights of London to groups of American soldiers.

There were so many offers from British families to entertain Yanks in their homes that a hospitality exchange with a supervisor was set up in each Red Cross club to clear invitations. More than 100,000 men a month were guests of British homes. "Such hospitality makes it a pleasure to be a stranger," wrote one greatful GI epitomizing the sentiments of his comrades. Mrs. Harris, chief potato peeler in one of the clubs, laughed every time she recalled her first experience as a hostess to two certain GI's. Invited for supper, the two soldiers stayed three days. They helped her in the kitchen, learned to brew English tea, washed the dishes, and performed other chores. In every respect except one they were perfect gentlemen: they left Mrs. Harris' cupboard completely bare. Yet she did not seem to mind. In fact, she invited them out a second time, and a third. "They've been coming back ever since," she laughed. "Well, you know, the Yanks need us, what with being away from home and all."

An American Red Cross club in Scotland devised a plan for bringing together American soldiers and British civilians with common interests. At a club-sponsored dinner, local farmers, lawyers, teachers, newspapermen, and representatives of other occupations were invited to meet their counterparts in khaki. This led to Americans being invited to inspect farms, newspaper offices, schools, and other places with which their British parallels were connected.

And so the exchange of ideas and information between Americans in uniform and British civilians widened the horizons of both peoples, promoting Anglo-American understanding and friendship.

By far the majority of the United States troops in Great Britain were stationed a good way from Red Cross service clubs. A large proportion of them were members of the Eighth Air Force, later joined by the Ninth Air Force, who were pounding the roof of Fortress Europe. Restricted to their stations, flyers and ground crews were unable to take advantage of the service clubs except when on leave. Yet their need for recreation was urgent. So the American Red Cross was requested by the USAAF to undertake the operation of a network of recreation centers to cover these rural installations. For groups of 500 or more men, the Red Cross established "aeroclubs" on airfields or camp clubs for other military units. The terms were applied to differentiate them from service clubs, but in every respect except beds they offered all the facilities of the service clubs. Each was staffed by a Red Cross field director and two Red Cross girls—a club director and a staff assistant, plus British paid and volunteer workers. At the peak, in the fall of 1944, there were 100 of these aero- and camp clubs. Many of the recreation centers were buildings taken over from the British Canteen Service after the Royal Air Force had moved on. Virtually overnight the Red Cross girls transformed them into attractive homelike centers. Furniture being scarce in wartime Britain, the girls supplemented the available pieces with some ingenious ones of their own. Couches, for instance, were fashioned out of Army cots padded with GI mattresses and covered with cretonne. The smart taste of Red Cross girls was reflected in the interior decorations. Matching chairs and settees and coffee tables were grouped cozily before a brick fireplace in one lounge. The tang of burning logs seasoned the atmosphere of this room where men sat around in flying jackets or fatigues reading or listening quietly to the phonograph. There were also a library and writing room, a game room, and a snack bar. Planned entertainment was held several nights a week.

Another Red Cross service to the American airmen based on Great Britain was staffing rest homes. The USAAF took over beautiful large country estates for airmen who, having had too much combat flying, were in need of a rest and a change of scene. Two Red Cross girls with outstanding qualifications took over each of the rest homes and endeavored to run them as if they were their own homes.

How effectively they did their job was told in the *Red Cross Courier* by Captain David Wright, psychiatric consultant for the Eighth Air Force, after six weeks' observation at Coombe House "somewhere in England."

Here are excerpts of his article:

Many of us—including the fliers themselves—did not believe in the beginning that rest homes could actually accomplish that job. Even after the Red Cross agreed to come into rest homes to create a more homelike, less military atmosphere, I was skeptical. I did not believe that the Red Cross's young women workers, for all their good intentions, could reach the men effectively enough to help them. Flying men are quick to recognize a forced hostess attitude; they hate the feeling of "somebody's being kind to us." We knew that a too-sympathetic attitude with these men was something they very much did not want, and one which would consequently have little if any effect.

That is why now, less than five months after Red Cross began shaping a new rest home pattern, the results in terms of rehabilitating fliers are to me impressive and surprising. Certainly I am now convinced that none of it would have been possible without Red Cross, which has established the character of the homes as homes, and has performed the management job of running them as such.

I can say now that rest homes are saving lives—and badly needed airmen—by returning men to combat as more efficient fliers. That efficiency has been developed by making them individuals again—men with a feeling of stability and a renewed sense of belonging to a world they knew before, in which familiar things and people still exist for them.

It is hard to tell you just how Red Cross women are accomplishing this. I found many intangibles. The girls make each newcomer feel himself a welcome addition to the household. The atmosphere of so many things "just like home" reawakens a feeling of some real security for him—the comfort of a chair by an open fire, games to play in the living room (if he wants to), home-cooked food by candlelight, and good, natural, happy companionship. He finds he is accepted as an individual on his own merits as a human being; he gets into civilian clothes and becomes just "Tex."

To reach the boys in the mudholes—those scattered detachments untouched by service clubs and aeroclubs—the clubmobile was born. The first "club on wheels," a hastily converted half-ton truck, chugged its way into the world on October 26, 1942. Its crew consisted of Mrs. Hope Simpson of London, England; Mrs. Joan Banker Reardon of Cranford, New Jersey, and Miss Camilla Moss of New York City. They toured the airfields of East Anglia dispensing coffee and doughnuts.

In the beginning not all the top executives of the American Red Cross in Great Britain were agreed as to the wisdom of a clubmobile program. Some held that doughnuts could not be made on the run. Commissioner Harvey D. Gibson was not among the skeptics. He had envisioned the role to be played in World War II by this humble brown object of sweetened dough—the morale-building importance of hot coffee and doughnuts to fighting men who had been subsisting on cold rations. He also sensed the symbolism involved. The doughnut was not just diet. Served by cheerful Red Cross girls, it was also ammunition, ammunition for the heart and spirit.

So when the time came to make the decision, Mr. Gibson said, "I think we should order these twenty trucks." They were ordered, and the term "clubmobile" joined the company of "jeep" and a host of other new terms in the nomenclature of World War II. From

Britain the idea spread to the other war theaters. On the first anniversary of the clubmobile, some one hundred clubmobilers and guests held a dinner in London honoring Harvey D. Gibson as "The Father of Clubmobile."

The clubmobile went through several stages of experimentation before the exact type was determined. For a long time the backbone of the service was provided by forty single-deck buses acquired through the British Ministry of Transportation from a discontinued London bus company—the Green Line. Their detachable clubmobile equipment made it possible to turn them into ambulances upon two hours' notice. The crew consisted of a male driver, locally employed, and three Red Cross girl staff assistants. The front two-thirds of the clubmobile body contained the equipment for making and serving doughnuts and coffee with plenty of space left over for the storage of magazines, writing paper, chewing gum and cigarettes, all of which were distributed free. The rear third became a miniature clubroom with books, newspapers, a phonograph and loud speaker. This section also held three folding bunks in which the girls could sleep when they were unable to get back to their base at night. The country was divided into clubmobile areas, each one with a base from which the service fanned out. At each base living accommodations with storage facilities were secured for clubmobile crews. Usually it was a small house known as a clubmobile center.

Isolated detachments too far apart to be reached from a fixed clubmobile base were covered by roving clubmobiles. They made a series of one-night stands and were on the road for as long as two weeks at a time. At night they slept in the cabin of their clubmobile.

How one Red Cross girl felt after a trip to a camp off the beaten track was told in her article, "H'yah, Mud's the Name," in the clubmobilers' informal mimeographed publication, *The Sinker:*

> You arrive nattily enclosed in mud, an armored combat helmet, a field jacket and a GI raincoat. You find the men looking tired, muddy, and cold. Even before you give yourself away by clambering female-fashion out of the jeep, they yell, "Hey, a woman" and flock around to talk to *you*, politely ignoring your edibles. You serve and they say everything tastes swell and gee, gum too, thanks, as though they'd never seen it on the clubmobile, and they build *your* morale something terrific. By now you are clothed in shiny satin, so you make sure your tiara is on straight, and step daintily back into your brougham. On the way back to the clubmobile you decide that this is the Army—the decent top kick, the major who carried the coffee urn through the mud for his men,

that you like 'em, everyone; that you'll write a book about 'em called "Bless Them All," that you suddenly trust their skills and their integrity, and that mud, like cabbages, can be beautiful.

Another worker, one of the "Clubmobile Rangers," included this illuminating paragraph in her report:

It was worth every trouble to watch the GI's under those heavy packs dance down the platform to the tune of our clubmobile records, to see a smile of anticipation lighten that heavy, hungry look, and to hear one boy who hadn't eaten for 14 hours explode with "Thank God for the American Red Cross!"

Clubmobile Rangers, who covered railroad stations in Great Britain, and later in France, were on one of the most grueling endurance jobs of the American Red Cross in World War II. One group covered the railroad station of an important English port through which passed many thousands of American soldiers. Grim and silent, with heavy packs, they marched endlessly through the town from ship to waiting troop train.

The Rangers served coffee and doughnuts in the comparatively few minutes between the soldiers' arrival at the railroad station and their departure through the drizzle of a fogbound dawn to some undisclosed destination. The boys responded to this unexpected service with surprised delight and gratitude.

The Rangers, hand picked for this special branch of the service, asked no questions, and only their clubmobile captain knew in advance the number of men to be served and the time of their arrival. They worked on twelve-hour shifts, skipping breakfast, lunch, and even dinner until a particular operation was over. They were awakened at weird hours, often in the middle of the night, and quickly got into their heavy GI underwear, battle dress, boots, sweaters, coats, and inevitably, raincoats (it always rained!). They served in the near-open, protected only by a badly bombed roof that threw its somber latticework silhouette against the dark sky. Up and down the platform the Rangers moved trolley pushmobiles weighing anywhere from 300 to 400 pounds when loaded. Each held 750 doughnuts and urns containing 400 cups of coffee. Grease-spotted, rain-soaked, hair plastered to their cheeks, dragging their feet, they were all but exhausted when they stumbled into bed at the end of an operation. Glamour? Hardly.

Service clubs, aeroclubs, camp clubs, and clubmobiles—seemingly they were everywhere in the United Kingdom. Still there were some outposts untouched. So, again at the request of the Army, the American Red Cross spread another chain of recreation centers. This time they were called "Donut Dugouts," restricted to the remotest backwoods country. They were not, as the name might imply, improvised sandbagged huts, heated with smoky little stoves and blankets hung across the doors to keep out the weather. On the contrary, Donut Dugouts were established in the best village buildings available within walking distance of American camps.

One of the first to be opened was situated in a quaint little market town surrounded by miles of lonely moors on which wandering gypsies pitched their tents and hauled their jaunty caravans. Into this story-book village drove little Mrs. Hope Simpson, clubmobile supervisor, a few days before Christmas, 1943. She looked as though the wind from the moors might blow her out to sea, but she was far stronger than she appeared. Her experienced eye soon selected a small unused shop on the narrow main street as most suitable for a Donut Dugout. Even before obtaining a room in the picturesque little hotel, she telegraphed her clubmobile crew in London to "get crackin'."

The villagers stared curiously as the procession arrived. First rolled a giant clubmobile, equipped with a machine capable of turning out 5,000 doughnuts daily, and large coffee urns. Then came the smaller cars loaded with the crew's personal baggage, a phonograph and piles of records, tonneaus of books, cases of cigarettes, gum, soft drinks, and various other things.

Early the next day clouds of dust swirled into the cobblestone street as busy brooms and mops freshened up the little shop. Trucks from the British Ministry of Works drew up to unload comfortable chairs and settees and tables, even a Christmas tree. Willing GI's from the near-by camp swept, washed, cleaned, and painted as they never had done in their own homes back in Podunk or Riverdale.

Then the official opening date was set and invitations to the ceremony broadcast by word of mouth across the melancholy moors. . . . The Yanks had taken over still another English village!

Nor was the Navy neglected. Navy personnel were always as welcome in Red Cross service clubs as soldiers—in Great Britain as in any other war theater. In seaport towns men of the armed guard on merchant ships flocked to them as soon as they landed. The Londonderry club, the first in the United Kingdom, catered to Coast Guardsmen, sailors, and Marines. In Glasgow the Shore Patrol was billeted in the American Red Cross club.

It was not until early in 1944, however, when the Navy made known the presence of large numbers of its personnel who had arrived secretly to participate in the Normandy invasion, that the Red Cross established its "fleet clubs" in Great Britain. They were distinctively "Navy," where floors were decks and walls bulkheads and the talk had the tang of the sea.

When the time finally approached for the amphibious assault on the continent, the Red Cross emblem followed the invading forces right into the channel embarkation ports. The last food consumed by the men before embarking for France was Red Cross coffee and doughnuts. At first, for security reasons, only Army personnel handled the refreshments. On the sixth day after D-Day, however, the Red Cross girls took over. They worked so efficiently that when the Army added hot meals to the send-off the girls were asked to supervise the business end of the chow line.

American Red Cross workers—field directors and girls—were themselves part of the invasion forces. As there was still much work to be done in Britain, not all Red Cross girls were lucky enough to win assignments to the continent. For those staying behind, parting brought pangs of sorrow. They were saying good-by, perhaps for the last time, to outfits they had come to know so well through the months.

Isobel Millier, of El Monte, California, was among the girls remaining in England. When she poured out her heart to her mother, little did she know that she was expressing the feelings of so many of her sister Red Cross workers.

Her letter (as printed in *This Week Magazine*):

Dear Mom:

For the first time in many months I cried this morning—in front of about a thousand men. My boys have gone. At five o'clock this morning I stood at the No. 1 guard post, a coat over my pink pajamas and my hair flying, and tears streamed down my face as I waved good-by and returned the salutes of each man. No mother ever felt worse when her sons went out to do battle.

This, of course, is the day we've been waiting for—packed and ready for days now, just waiting word. If God was ever good, He was last night when He made me decide not to stay overnight at the Red Cross station at a near-by camp where I had gone to a party. I haven't been away for weeks, fearing that if I turned my back I'd come home and find them gone.

I just had a feeling last night that I better get home, and sure enough about two-thirty this morning I began to hear suspicious noises. Any similarity my boys might have had to the Arabs who folded their tents and quietly stole away was purely coincidental, because they made so much noise wisecracking, laughing and shouting, that I thought they were playing football on the hill.

Well, to make a long story short, they were leaving. So a little after four I got up, put on my coat and slippers and wandered down by the motor pool. It was still dark and it was some time before anyone saw me.

'Hiya, Isobel, coming with us?"

"Hey! You're out of uniform."

"See you in Paris."

"How about a date in Los Angeles next summer?"

Then I wandered up and down through the vehicles, shaking hands, kidding, patting boys on the shoulder and quipping back and forth.

"Be a good boy, Junior. Mind your sergeant."

"Sergeant, make Junior wash behind his ears."

"Hurry up and get things organized, fellows, so I can follow with the doughnuts."

"Good luck, soldier."

After that it was about time to start pulling out, and I went over to where the convoy was forming. The three commanding officers were standing in a circle, all ready to jump in their vehicles and give the word to start rolling. I guess that was the beginning of morale building for this Red Cross girl, because when I approached them, they all stood at attention and gave me a snappy salute. I just couldn't seem to get out any words and finally the Colonel put his arm around my shoulder and said:

"Well, Issy, I wondered if you were going to come and see us off."

Then they began to thank me for doing what I've had more fun doing than anything else in my life. That was where I stopped being a calm, cool and efficient Red Crosser and started being just a lonely little girl whose whole family was leaving her behind.

Then the zero minute came and the Colonel jumped in his half-track and, with one motion of his hand, started the forward movement for which these boys had been waiting for three long years. This was it!

Well, I guess I stood there for two hours waving good-by—one lone girl in pink pajamas, smiling but with tears streaming down her face. When the last vehicle rolled past, I had collected twelve kittens, several dogs, two mother cats, about twenty bicycles and an assortment of telephone numbers and last-minute messages which I'd promised to deliver to various lady-loves. I guess I must have been about the most forlorn person in the ETO when I turned to go back to bed, and all day today I've felt as though a tank had run over me.

I wish everyone at home could have stood with me this morning in the cold gray dawn and watched those men go out to fight. Maybe if they had been there with me, we wouldn't be likely to have another war very soon.

Everyone's been forlorn today and I've had a time comforting my little dog, "Doughnuts." My old black cat, "Mrs. Greenberg," has wandered around the club just meowing her heart out. And my cook and cleaning women have been in tears all day. We're supposed to cheer up the boys. I wonder who cheers up the Red Cross worker!

Love,
Isobel

P.S.—Nothing new to report. Could use a couple pairs of stockings.

Chapter XIII

ON TO BERLIN!

T HE DAY CHERBOURG FELL INTO AMERICAN HANDS, TWO GRIMY paratroopers picked their way warily through its rubble-littered streets. They finally stopped in front of a well-preserved building to stare curiously at a German sign reading: *"Kameradschafthaus."*

"This must be the place that old Frenchman said was a Jerry officers' club," observed one of the troopers. Then his tired, bearded face relaxed into a wide grin. "Look at this, Joe," he said, pointing his pistol at a hastily scrawled note nailed to a boarded-up window. The note:

> "This building reserved for an American Red Cross
> Club by Floyd Gates, Field Director."

Floyd H. Gates of Dayton, Ohio, the first Red Cross worker in France, having landed H-Hour plus forty, was staking out the first Red Cross service club on French soil. Defying snipers' bullets, and within hearing of artillery fire and house-to-house combat, Gates had made the rounds of the city with an officer of the French underground in search of a suitable building for a club. The one he selected was formerly a department store with ample floor space for club purposes. There was also a bit of irony to his choice. Until a few days before this had been a comfortable German Army officers' club, and soon, with appropriate changes, it would become the "Club Victoire," home of enlisted men.

The club opened its doors at 6:30 P.M. July 20, 1944. A grinning crowd of GI's clapped and cheered all through the opening ceremony. Louisa Farrand of New York City, club director, took charge of the program. The Mayor of Cherbourg presented the tricolor flag of France, which ceremoniously joined the Stars and Stripes and the Union Jack as the band played "The Marseillaise."

The big moment was reserved for Commissioner Gibson, who flew over from London. As Commissioner to Europe in 1919, he formally closed the last American Red Cross installation in France of World War I. Now a quarter of a century later he was opening this war's first club on French soil.

In a matter of days after the initial landings on the beaches of Normandy, Red Cross Deputy Commissioner Don S. Momand, of New York City, assumed direction of American Red Cross operations on the continent, with temporary headquarters in Cherbourg, and later, permanent headquarters in Paris.

Clubmobiles, cinemobiles, trailer kitchens, and trucks carrying hundreds of tons of supplies and equipment rolled off LST's, and despite many difficulties, were quickly woven into the pattern of military operations. This mobility enabled Red Cross workers to do more with less and faster. With each new advance of the American forces, new clubs were set up in stores, under tents, in apple orchards, former prison camps, in the wing of a palace, and in many other improvised places. Barracks were brightened up, and bombed-out hangars swept with bulldozer "brooms." Doughnuts were served in whitewashed barns, grand hotels, and chateaux. By autumn, three permanent service clubs had been set up in liberated Paris, one of them named for the famous London Rainbow Corner. The second American Red Cross doughnut served in Paris after liberation went to Ernie Pyle who remarked, "I never liked doughnuts, but this Red Cross variety has changed my taste." The first doughnut had gone to an anonymous ack-ack gunner in the Place d'Alma. Herbert S. Casey of Wayne, Pennsylvania, headquarters field representative in charge of five Red Cross clubmobile groups, had served both.

As in every amphibious landing, field directors were the first Red Cross workers to land in Normandy. During the many months of intensive training in Britain, they had roughed it with the GI's in almost every phase of simulated warfare, and were prepared for any eventuality.

Among field directors arriving after Floyd H. Gates in the vanguard of the Allied invasion forces were: Byron Wallace of Washington, Indiana; John Butler of Wilkes-Barre; Joseph N. Trice of Richmond, Virginia; and Charles L. Skarren, Jr., of Washington, D.C.

After them additional field directors came pouring in with their Army units, all under supervision of William L. Prince of Concord, New Hampshire, and W. Birch Douglass of Richmond, Virginia, director and deputy director respectively of the Red Cross Field Service. Within the first month they were 100 strong, with more joining their ranks daily.

Attached to each regiment and combat team, they kept up with the swiftly moving units—adjusting, improvising, and overcoming the difficult problems of supply, transportation, and communications to discharge their basic Red Cross responsibilities. In their improvised offices on the landing beaches and along the main highway across the Cherbourg Peninsula, they issued comfort articles to soldiers in transit and took personal messages which they relayed to the soldiers' home-town Red Cross chapters.

On August 15, 1944—D-Day for the United States Seventh Army invading southern France—other Red Cross field directors, drawn from the Mediterranean theater of operations, landed with their troops. One of them, David T. deVarona, a veteran of the Alcan Highway and the Aleutians, parachuted with his airborne task force, landing on a steep hillside not far behind the Seventh Army lines. The next day more than a dozen parachutes bearing his supplies, including 5,000 doughnuts intended for his unit, were dropped after him. Luck and the winds of misfortune were against him that day, as every parachute drifted well inside the German lines. Said de Varona: "That was undoubtedly the first time the American Red Cross has actually served doughnuts directly to the enemy."

Unarmed, these Red Cross field directors stuck close to their units under all circumstances, moving from foxhole to foxhole, as the Allied armies swept across France toward Germany. In World War I it was a long trek from the support trenches to the nearest "hut" in which the soldiers might find such comfort articles as were handed to them under fire by Red Cross field directors in World War II.

The experience of Field Director Charles L. Skarren, Jr., who was in the battle for Cherbourg, was typical:

We crossed the channel in tank carriers, and I was with my 9th Infantry Division, the boys who saw so much fighting in Africa and Sicily. We made a safe passage and the beaches were fairly free when we arrived. We advanced in to the back country and saw many dead Germans and a great deal of destruction in the towns. We were part of the force which was then cutting the Cherbourg Peninsula. I followed close to my unit, and, with my jeep and trailer, carried supplies to make up for lost kits, such as toilet articles, and the usual cigarettes, gum, and so on. On the return trips I lent a hand at anything from carrying our dead to helping carry bags of mail. The roads were constantly being blown up ahead of us and each trip was more or less of a nightmare.

Once I drove five miles into enemy territory in search of my unit. Whether the Germans saw the words, "American Red Cross" on my jeep or not I cannot say, but I was not fired on. I ran into one of our patrols and when I told them where I'd been, one of them said, "Boy, you're born lucky. You've had your hand in the lion's mouth."

The first American Red Cross hospital workers in France were Jean Dockhorn, of Baltimore, and Jascah Hart, of Syracuse. They arrived only four days after D-Day with nurses of the first evacuation hospital to establish itself on the Normandy beachhead.

Their effect on the men's spirits was electrifying, according to Eleanor C. Vincent, National Director, American Red Cross Hospital Service, who toured the combat zone.

One officer [wrote Miss Vincent in the *Red Cross Courier*] told me that, after four days under continuous fire, the men who had dug into the Normandy beachhead had become downhearted. Suddenly on D-Day plus four, one man shouted, "Wow! I hear a woman's voice!" The others listened and, unbelieving, heard a light feminine laugh. As the first American nurses and the Red Cross workers jumped from their landing barge and waded to shore, men jumped up all along the beach; they squared their shoulders, held their heads high and said, "If they can take it with a smile, so can we!"

Close upon the first two arrivals came other Red Cross hospital workers with field, evacuation, and general hospital units. Within the first three weeks there were thirty-eight of them, the only Red Cross girls in France. Besides visiting the wounded in the wards, the girls contrived to equip recreation tents in the rapidly moving hospitals, covering packing crates with Army blankets and scattering pillows made of brightly covered ditty bags stuffed with towels. The hospitals moved frequently with the fluid front that summer of 1944. They loaded up in the morning and were ready to receive patients in the new area that night. Sometimes they arrived before the bomb disposal squad, and before the bodies of fallen soldiers had been taken away.

Red Cross hospital workers and nurses helped French evacuees wounded in their own homes by booby traps planted by the retreating Germans. In one village a mother and a baby were the only ones left of a large family after the father had unwittingly stepped on a booby trap their first day home. Hospital staffs not only dressed their injuries but turned over extra food and clothing to the French Red Cross for refugees.

Early in the invasion, a hospital train loaded with wounded American soldiers waited four hours in the Cherbourg railroad yards for an overdue trans-channel hospital ship to carry the men back to England. The patients had not been fed since early morning, which worried the medical officers. A nurse and two GI corpsmen walked across town to see what could be done about tiding over the men until they could be fed aboard ship. At the Red Cross Club Victoire the trio enlisted the aid of Mrs. William J. Bland of Kansas City. Within an hour the wounded soldiers on the hospital train had coffee and doughnuts and were kidding the Red Cross girls serving them. This marked the beginning of a regular service in France under Mrs. Bland's direction. Not only coffee and doughnuts, but also cigarettes and candy were distributed on hospital trains terminating at the docks. Frequently, to expedite the transfer of the wounded from train to hospital, it was necessary to serve patients as they were being moved aboard LCT's or amphibious ducks. Red Cross workers traveling with the wounded to hospital ships anchored in mid-harbor called these amphibious landing craft "duckmobiles." One duckmobiler, Wilma Clizbe of Detroit, felt repaid a hundredfold when a man almost completely encased in a cast muttered, "We knew the Red Cross wouldn't let us down."

American Red Cross girls were also aboard the hospital ships evacuating wounded from France to England. They helped the medical aid men serving sorely needed food and hot drinks to patients just off the battlefield who had not eaten hot food for as long as twenty-four or forty-eight hours. The girls performed backbreaking jobs helping prepare food and liquids, working in the pantries alongside ward men, washing dishes, and carrying heavy trays of food into wards. Clad in air-force-blue battle dress, the girls would ride away from their quarters to the docks in jeeps or in trucks. They departed at all hours, turning up again several days later looking slightly less dapper than when they had left. This hospital ship operation was agonizing and dangerous, and the girls had to volunteer for it.

The first Red Cross girl to make this trip—Virginia Force of Kansas City—sailed from an English port bound for the Normandy beaches only six days after D-Day. Upon her return with a shipload of wounded, she was met by Red Cross officials eager to learn of her experience. She sat down with them, made her report, and went right back to her ship. By the time the next hospital ships were ready to sail, the Red Cross had placed two girls on each one and organized replacements to wait in the port, on a continuous shuttle service.

On the continent, the Red Cross hospital workers' life during the first two months of the invasion consisted of loosening tent ropes, tightening tent ropes, tugging at cases of cigarettes, hauling wood and water, and moving on an hour's notice. They were accustomed to guns on the other side of the hedge, to dividing their scant sleeping time between a tent and a trench. And none escaped action; one group was strafed by a German plane the pilot of which became a patient when shot out of the air. Anne Kathleen Cullen of Larchmont, New York, was killed in the bombing of an evacuation hospital in Belgium on December 20, 1944. Formerly a clubmobile worker, she was on duty in one of the hospital wards when the bombs fell.

On the scene day and night, helping out in any way called upon, these Red Cross girls knew the human side of the war. They got used to a lot of things, such as reaching into a pocket to pull out a soldier's wallet for him, and feeling pocket, wallet, and hand sticky with blood.

Said one of them, Kathleen Knight of Wellesley, Massachusetts: "Sometimes I want to stop and cry for every young arm that is amputated, for every young face that is burned, for every young man who dies. But I can't. There isn't time."

And then there were the Red Cross clubmobile girls.

"We want the clubmobiles!" reverberated throughout northern France the first few weeks of the invasion. "When are the clubmobiles coming?" assailed the ears of poor, harassed Red Cross field directors ever since D-Day.

As field directors, waylaid on every side, kept the wires humming for news of the girls, the clubmobilers themselves, together with their motorized equipment, were in England impatiently waiting for the "Go" signal from General Eisenhower.

Finally, in mid-July, word came through that B group, the first clubmobiles to arrive in France, had just docked. A visitor from Mars might have thought the war suddenly had ended the way the GI's reacted as the convoy of fifty-one vehicles, carrying sixty-four persons, including twenty-nine clubmobilers, rolled off the LST's ramp.

Scheduled to arrive first on French soil, Group A, made up of twenty-nine clubmobilers, had become tangled in the old game of "hurry and wait." They were held up in their concentration area in England for two weeks while Group B got in ahead of them.

Rolling on to the Normandy beachhead at 5 A.M. July 19, these A clubmobilers were serving doughnuts and coffee twenty-four hours later only three miles behind the front lines. As described by Staff Assistant Ann Newdick, of Boston, this is how it was done:

278

When American soldiers in France stared incredulously at eight gray clubmobiles lumbering across the beach, their cheers made the dusty convoy a triumphal procession and their whistles made the tired girls who were driving seem like glamorous movie stars.

It was D-Day for the doughgirls.

In the early light of dawn, the doughgirls stepped on starters and the clubmobiles rolled over the beach, their calm and sedate appearance utterly belying the excited feelings of their drivers.

The first MP peered into the cab. "My gosh! Women!" he said. "How many?" "Twenty-nine," said Kathleen Crocker [Boston, Massachusetts]. "Twenty-nine women! Twenty-nine women!"

That's the way it was everywhere along the road to the chateau where the girls were to be based—soldiers shouting, whistling and hollering for doughnuts until the girls began to wonder how the invasion had progressed that far without them.

"Le Chateau Sinker" has charm, the one characteristic of French chateaux, and nothing else. No furniture, no lights, no windows and, of course, no plumbing.

The harassed leader of the group, Red Cross Field Director Harry Ratliffe [San Antonio, Texas], gave the girls a few hours to unpack and then called a meeting. "The Army wants to know when you can start serving," said Harry. "They know you're tired and you need to get settled, but will a couple of days be enough?"

"The troops are ready for us now," said the clubmobile captain, Vicky Atkinson [Washington, D. C.]. "We could start the dough-nut machines now and work in shifts all night," said someone else. "Let's go out tomorrow."

Soon the meadow in which the cars were parked was bustling with girls hunting for things in the dark and tinkering with machinery. Nothing was where it should be in the tightly packed mass of equipment. Fuses blew. Doughnut machines were temper-amental. The girls cracked their shins on the crates scattered around in the dark.

But the familiar warm fragrance of doughnuts soon began to fill the night air and big boxes were crammed full and stacked away in readiness for the next day.

Their eagerness was rewarded just after midnight when four clubmobiles and four supply trucks started moving.

After driving for over two hours by "cat's eyes" (a pinprick headlight—more to warn approaching vehicles than to aid the driver's vision) they arrived at a rest area about three miles from the front lines where fighting men return for showers, clean clothes, letter writing, movies and whatever relaxation they can find so close to combat. Here the doughgirls served their wares for the first time in France and listened to the men talk—heard stories of forty days of fighting without even the break of the rest area.

Other clubmobile groups followed B and A in quick succession. By midsummer a fleet of eighty sleek gray clubmobiles, using the chassis of two-and-a-half-ton General Motors trucks, roamed the highways and byways of the combat areas in France, the number divided evenly between General Hodges' First Army and the Third Army of General Patton. To bring their service within reach of all branches of the invasion forces, they were organized into groups of eight, identified by a letter of the alphabet. Supplies for service, maintenance, and the personnel were carried in auxiliary trucks and trailers. Each lettered group contained twenty-nine pieces of rolling equipment and sufficient reserve to continue its program for fifteen days should it become detached from its base supply. Individual clubmobiles, staffed by three Red Cross girls, were named for the states and some cities; the remainder bore names such as Pathfinder, Magnolia, and Daniel Boone, of historic or symbolic appeal to American soldiers.

Each group had a male supervisor who, with Army G-I and Special Services, planned clubmobile itineraries. Field Representative Camilla Moss, of New York City, one of the Red Cross pioneers in the ETO, was liaison officer between Red Cross headquarters and the Army outfits to which clubmobiles were assigned.

These Red Cross clubmobile girls had one of the most extraordinary experiences of the war, performing an unprecedented service with enthusiasm and a contempt for personal danger that had the whole Army tossing its helmets into the air. They had a ringside seat at one of the greatest dramas of all times, moving with more freedom than many soldiers. Even war correspondents could not drive in and out of battle lines as they did every day. In and out of the rain and mud they moved with the headlines, from hedgerow to plain, from orchard to orchard, amid bomb craters, shell holes, and crumbled towns. To the boom of artillery and the whistle of shells they took their freshly made doughnuts and steaming coffee right to the GI's on highways, in hospitals, rest areas, gun sites, and even to the edge of foxholes.

An Army division paper headlined the story of six clubmobile girls who rolled into the division area in two clubmobiles—Sitting

Bull and Daniel Boone—calling to some GI's: "Where are the front-line doughboys?" It took some time to convince them that a club-mobile just wasn't T/E battle equipment like mortars, bullets, and bayonets, and that the alternate plan of smuggling one up with a quartermaster load of K-rations just wasn't covered by Army regulations on record.

The girls, however, did not admit defeat. After a huddle they announced that they would produce doughnuts for jeep delivery to front-line troops. Into the heaping boxes of doughnuts, they tucked dainty little notes which inquisitive GI's in the rear area were politely told were top-secret for front-line men only. "So if you find a doughnut batting around with your rations," the paper advised its readers, "remember it was sent up with loads of sweet thoughts from an American Red Cross girl who earnestly wishes she could come right up to your foxhole and sing out that familiar, 'How about some coffee and doughnuts?' "

The girls participating in this incident were: Virginia Sherwood, New York City; Katherine "Tatty" Spaatz, Washington, D. C.; Julia Townsend, New York City; Jeri Jean Ford, Long Beach, California; Louise Clayton, Minneapolis; and Frances Goodwin, Cincinnati, Ohio.

Said Mary Coleman, of Loveland, Ohio, clubmobiler of another group:

> The infantry retreated back to the high ground where we were serving. We were then right in the front lines. Shells started whistling, and when Ruth Gray [Old Town, Maine], heard someone shout, we all ducked. I was cutting candy but when I heard a rat-tat-tat like a machine gun, I didn't stop till I was under the truck, 'way down under my helmet—real small.
>
> At this point we looked up to see a plane spinning down on fire. The rat-tat-tat I heard was its machine gun set off by the fire. After the plane crashed in the field across the way, we looked up to see an American pilot busily cutting his parachute cords as he dangled from a tree. We helped him down, and his first remark on searching himself was, "My gosh, I've lost my pencil!"
>
> But his next remark was made to order: "Got any coffee?"

Supervisor W. Lloyd Davies, of Wilkes-Barre, took his Group G, consisting of thirty-one Red Cross girls, on a 220-mile trek across France to the front lines in August. At Chartres, only eighteen miles behind the front lines, Davies heard of a Bing Crosby show to be held in an aviation factory, and decided to attend. Leaving four girls to guard the clubmobiles, he escorted the remaining twenty-seven to the improvised theater. What followed is told by Mr. Davies:

When we reached the factory there were about 5,000 men crowding the place. They were sitting on their helmets or hanging from the rafters. Headed by Group Captain Maxine Preas [Knoxville, Tennessee] the girls filed in, and the boys swept a pathway for them to the very front row. And the cheers! I've never heard anything like it before or since. By the time Bing came on to sing "White Christmas" they must have all been hoarse, but they had plenty of welcome left for that popular fellow.

How did clubmobilers live? Mildred H. Broughton, of Newark, Ohio, a member of the "Yosemite" clubmobile, gives a close-up of camp life.

Tents were rigged, with six or eight to a tent; foxholes dug; camouflage strung up and over the top. Like those of the Army each tent is getting a name, those of the plush London hotels preferred.

Ours is the Grosvenor House. Instead of ringing for room service, we walk down a lane, very quiet at 6 A.M. to another field, edged on one end with mess tents, and scalloped with the chow line. This is really a Cook's Tour, from kettle to kettle, with a stop-over in the wheat, eating picnic fashion.

Few of us crawl inside our sleeping bags because you can't get out of them in a hurry. The first night we slept in our clothes. Then we decided to try pajamas again, but with coveralls on top for both warmth and protection. Most of us have light colored p'j's that have a phosphorous glow in a foxhole.

Before crawling in, you carefully place helmet and coat on the ground, with slippers in the middle; so, when the time comes, your feet feel for your shoes while each arm grabs helmet or coat. This is one time you pray your right hand knows what the left is doing. Then swish, you're through the flaps and sliding feet first into the hole, like Babe Ruth making home base. Then you hope that all you'll hear the rest of the night will be the tinkle of your tent-mates' dog tags as they roll over.

In place of a tile bathroom, we have something more individual than Chic Sales ever dreamed up. The walls are draped khaki, with a ceiling half canvas and half camouflage netting. The Army, too, believes in that theory of modern architecture of merging inner space with the great outdoors. The GI's painted it lavender, because they thought it would give a feminine touch. Outside, a neat blue and white sign reads: "Ladies Powder Room," or, "La Toilette des Dames."

The barber shop department has now been taken over by Anne Stuart [Lake Forest, Illinois]. Setting up shop beneath the trees, she cut swathes through the hair of a first sergeant. In return he painted a brilliant red and white barber pole on the front of her tin hat. The job not only satisfied the top kick, but also the Commanding Officer, who decided to be the next customer.

Probably no clubmobilers lived a more rigid, disciplined camp life than the thirty-one girls of Group L quartered at the great tented base "somewhere in France" where Lieutenant General George S. Patton had his headquarters, in the summer of 1944. One of the girls was Jean Gordon, of South Lincoln, Massachusetts, the general's niece.

Patton took a personal interest in the welfare of his charges. Between visits to the front lines he always stopped by their camp.

His courtesy and kindness notwithstanding, General Patton laid down rules and regulations that had the girls singing, "We're in the Army now" (though not within the general's hearing).

The girls had to be back at their camp before blackout time. After that they could not enter or leave their tented living area without calling the guard on duty and giving the password, which changed every night. They wondered who made up the ludicrous-sounding passwords that ranged from "black," "white," to "applesauce" and "dipsydoodle."

General Patton was not the only high-ranking officer who valued the clubmobilers' services to the troops. Lieutenant General Omar Bradley had them in mind when he wrote to Deputy Red Cross Commissioner Don S. Momand: "As we progress deeper into the continent we shall always be gratified to know that the Red Cross is with us, assisting our troops in the many ways they have come to depend upon you."

Some of the clubmobile teams were officially cited by commanding officers for their good work. One young woman, a group captain, Elizabeth Schuller, of Upper Montclair, New Jersey, received the Army's Bronze Star for her contribution "to the success of the 4th Infantry Division in battle." She was the first Red Cross woman in World War II to receive an Army award other than the Purple Heart. Major General R. O. Barton, commanding general of the division, cited Miss Schuller for being "materially instrumental in maintaining a high level of morale" among his troops.

In the triumphal entry through French towns draped with flags and alive with cheering people, the Red Cross clubmobile girls became arm-weary from returning salutations. They feared that a split in international relations might result if they failed to return a single bow or wave of the hand.

Staff Assistant Eliza King, of Georgetown, South Carolina, told how she and her sister clubmobilers felt about "the boys we serve":

Here we are in a combat zone, with the enemy sometimes twenty, sometimes twelve, sometimes two miles away, and yet it's far from being all thrills and excitement.

For those who do the actual fighting, it's a long-drawn-out nightmare. For thousands, it's boredom and loneliness. It's no place to go, nothing to do, no mail from home. It's choking dust or plodding mud. Now and then when enemy planes or artillery shells come close, it's sharp, human fear.

Our first group was a battalion of field artillery in the same fields for two weeks, with, for the most part, only each other to talk to. Soon after we arrived the order came to fire the guns, at a target they couldn't see. We went down and heard the final check-up before the "boom" of the guns, and on our way back noticed the soldiers were all shaving. I did much dancing in GI shoes that day.

Up closer towards the front are ack-ack crews who live right with their guns, retiring to individual foxholes, but otherwise hardly out of each other's sight. Most of them have been under shell fire and strafing, but they've got to stay right there, until they're sent back to a rest camp for three days' luxury of pup-tents, hot food, movies, news, and a radio. They are a quiet lot, who consider themselves lucky to be able to stretch out flat on the grass and know that for a brief time they can look up through green leaves without keeping constant vigil against death.

Ordnance groups have no complaints about not working. It's their job to keep the machines going; to go out and retrieve those that can't be driven back. We waited to give a cup of coffee to a sergeant who had gone out to bring in a dead tank. He brought a dead tanker, too. The medics had been busy that day.

Those medics! They and the combat soldiers form a mutual admiration society. They go out into the thick of the fighting, carrying litters, giving first aid. They get shot and they get killed, but when they talk, it's about the spirit of those they take care of.

One tank battalion we visited had just been pulled back out of the lines after about fifty days' continuous fighting. Their exhaustion was complete. One jokingly said, "Can't get us a furlough, can you?"

"How I wish we could," I answered. "But if it's any help to you, we are all proud of you."

Life is sweet to our fighting men who somehow manage to enjoy it, somehow manage to remain human beings. They laugh, they joke, their spirits are high, and they like France, because, as one very wisely observed, "It's on the way home."

The first American Red Cross clubmobile to serve coffee and doughnuts to United States troops in Germany was the Bearcat. Its five members, representing a reconnaissance squad, started a curb service in the village square at Roetgen, just seventy-two hours after United States armored units had captured the town.

Staffing the Bearcat were: Supervisor Hope Simpson, one of the three pioneer clubmobilers in the ETO; Ruth S. Boyle, Springfield, Pennsylvania; Dorothy Stout, Vicksburg, Mississippi; Helen G. Stockdale, Ravenna, Ohio; and Katherine Bruns, Syracuse. They were part of Group D, and attached to the First Army.

A report of the Bearcat's historic stand was made by Staff Assistant Katherine Doering, of Carrington, North Dakota, who accompanied the five girls.

The road to Roetgen had just been declared open the night before. According to an officer of a Military Police unit, the town itself formed part of a small pocket, the entering wedge into the "Fatherland." The front line curved around the town on all three sides, but the freed village was already two miles behind the lines.

As Miss Simpson expressed it, "We were told that the town was now perfectly safe, and that enlisted men would welcome doughnuts and coffee if we could get through. Before sending out the fleet to the many camps surounding the area, it was best to make the test run a day ahead of time."

Armored vehicles streamed back and forth along the intersection. They slowed down at the sight of the "Bearcat." Amazed GI's, dusty, tired, nerves high-geared from battle strain, clambered down to listen to the latest swing records and gulp down a hasty cup of real coffee. An incongruous scene, laughter, song and merriment, dimming the sharp crack of ack-ack and mellowing the grim boom of the 155-mm. guns thundering in the distance!

A carefully driven Army ambulance, headed for the nearest

evacuation hospital, pulled up for a few moments. Inside were six enlisted men, with hastily bandaged wounds. They were minor casualties but their faces gleamed pale from the dusky interior of their van. Eagerly they downed several cups of coffee apiece. As they munched their doughnuts, their faces lost that white strained look. Soon they were chattering as merrily as if they were sipping at some soda fountain back home. When the driver gave the signal for them to move on, they waved a reluctant good-by with the words, "Come see us soon!"

The few villagers who remained in the town stood quietly by watching the merry Yanks. "These people are different from the French and the Belgians who gave us such a terrific welcome as we passed through," said a member of a tank unit.

On the homeward trek, the huge clubmobile was stopped short by ack-ack from our guns firing at a German plane circling overhead.

"This is it! Take cover!" yelled American soldiers bivouacked at the road's edge. Hastily, the girls grabbed their helmets, and made a dash for the ditches only a few feet away. They watched as a lone German plane beat a fast retreat, over the green-foliaged horizon, back to the safer side of the Siegfried Line.

Thirty miles into Belgium, back at their headquarters, which seemed so still in comparison to their front line experience, these girls made plans to cook doughnuts at dawn for their second visit to U.S. troops in Germany.

By way of livening up their work, clubmobilers turned to minstrelsy, even to improvising their own songs.

There were Joan Walsh of Philadelphia, and her teammate, Elizabeth Krider of Richmond, Long Island, attached to an antiaircraft artillery brigade of the Seventh Army. Dressed in all the warm clothing they owned, Miss Walsh and Miss Krider ploughed through knee-deep mud in rubber boots, rotating among the various units of the brigade—from the boys who manned the gun positions supporting the infantry to the mechanics in the motor pool and the enlisted personnel at brigade headquarters. As the crowd dunked their doughnuts, Miss Walsh and Miss Krider would sing the following ditty:

> We're gonna be the donut dolls
> That you can call your own;
> The dolls that other outfits cannot steal.
> And when you sight us from afar
> In the general's "recon" car,

286

Forget the car—it's just our clubmobile!
We'll travel over field and over highway,
We'll hitch our little wagon to a star,
Though we may go away, we'll be back some other day—
We're the G.I. Johnny Doughboy's Donut Dolls!

Another popular team of Red Cross troubadours was made up of Rita Shaw of Paris, Maine, and Catherine Overstreet of Minneapolis. Both sang and played the piano, Miss Shaw specializing in popular tunes and her teammate in classical music. They were reported to be the first American Red Cross girls to have slept in Germany—on the Siegfried Line, no less (Date, September 17, 1944; hour of the first nod, 10:51). They were showing a movie to a signal group and unable to beat the blackout to their bivouac area across the border, spent the night curled up in their clubmobile. The Germans put on a terrifying show for them that night. "But our boys put on a better one the next day," they said. "We're living our best show!"

Germany was the fourth foreign country in which Miss Shaw and Miss Overstreet trouped together under the American Red Cross emblem. As recreation workers traveling in a jeep, they toured the lonely outposts in Iceland cheering up American soldiers. After more than a year in Iceland they chose to go on to England instead of returning home. They arrived in London in time to join a group of Red Cross girls receiving special training in the operation of the cinemobile, an American Red Cross innovation designed for use on the Western Front. Between classes in truck driving, movie projection, and other technical subjects, they entertained in Red Cross clubs. And when the cinemobiles started rolling toward France early in the invasion, they were in one of them.

Red Cross cinemobiles, bringing entertainment to men who otherwise would have had none so close to the front lines, were a spontaneous success on the continent. A rolling theater, built on a chassis of a one-and-one-half-ton General Motors truck, the cinemobile was complete with sound projections, portable screens and films, a portable stage, small piano, and public address system. Each truck was staffed by two Red Cross girls, one to play the piano, the other to lead in group singing. By early fall there were twelve cinemobiles in operation, divided evenly between the First Army and the Third Army.

The whole combat zone was a stage to these Red Cross minstrels. They drove wherever Army G–I and Special Services considered their services most needed. They entertained in many places—

tarpaulin-covered clearings deep in forests, in haylofts, hospital wards, and the courtyard of a chateau. Group G's Betty Walters, of Winona, Minnesota, and Judy Underdown, of Cornwall-on-the-Hudson, New York, put on a show in a village under fire, with "things popping all around" drowning out their song.

Cinemobile units averaged two or three shows a day, each lasting from one and a half to three hours. The girls never failed to receive collaboration from their audiences. Talented singers, musicians, and dancers among the GI's usually came forward with offerings of their own.

The fact that these Red Cross girls were not professional artists, but talented Red Cross girls who had volunteered to cheer them up in this way, made a strong appeal to the GI's. One engineers' unit was so eager to have Group L's Mary I. Austin, of Williamville, New York, and Loretta McLaughlin, of Sioux Falls, South Dakota, come back that they moved the side of a house so they could drive their cinemobile right in.

Once, in the midst of a tank battle on a near-by hill, an artillery-spotting Piper Cub plane swooped down on Group K's redheads, Ada Wattenmaker, of Charleroi, Pennsylvania, and Pauline Tompkins, of New York City, asking, "When's the next feature?" Then the plane circled back for a reply.

Group B's Evangeline C. Boner, of Minneapolis, and "Joni" Johnson, made up a song, "We're in the Cinemobile" with which they opened their shows. Driving into an area they let down their portable stage, rolled out the bantam piano and sang:

> Now my name is Joni,
>   And my name is Kay;
> Won't you gather 'round and listen, please,
>   To what we've got to say.
>
> We've got a little melody
>   That sums up most our job,
> We'll sing it to a boy or two
>   Or shout it to a mob.
>
> We sing a little, dance a little,
>   Beat out jazz and jive;
> And if you'll only encourage us,
>   We'd even harmonize.
>
> If you ever need us,
>   We'll be right here to say—
> We're 100 percent for every guy
>   That comes from the U.S.A.

From the saga of Group G, Clubmobiler Henri Barnhart composed a poem, "It's No Life for a Lady," which she recited to the troops. Hearing it, a GI in the line improvised a response in rhyme. Both poem and response landed in the October 15, 1944, issue of *Over Here*, the little Red Cross workers' paper published in Paris.

Miss Barnhart's poem:

"Blood, sweat and tears," said Churchill,
  "England soon shall know."
For clubmobilers in Zone V
  It's mud, rain and dough.

Fall out of bed at half past six
  And clutch a muddy legging;
No water in your canteen? ... Hell!
  And breakfast's gone a-begging.

The generator's thrown a shoe
  Your field stove's blown a gasket;
"Feed seven hundred at two P.M."
  Each doggoned day they'll ask it.

The scenery is lovely,
  And *Il pleut comme l'enfer*
I've fleas in both my blankets,
  And the French are in my hair.

It's no life for a lady,
  And it's no life for me.
What—you suggest I go home?
  NUTS! I'LL STICK WITH "G"!

The GI response:

Let's listen to this doughboy
  Who has just received your booking;
"You know," he says unto his friends,
  "Those girls are really cooking."

You're the finest of our country
  You're the best in any land;
Every soldier in the Army says:
  "The Red Cross girls are grand."

Chapter XIV

AT HIS SIDE

Relief to Prisoners of War

MANY THOUSANDS OF AMERICAN SOLDIERS AND SAILORS IN 1944 were in enemy hands in Germany and the Far East. As the war increased in intensity, others of their countrymen would join them to mark time in improvised compounds or permanent camps surrounded by barbed-wire fences and unscalable walls. Though out of the war, these prisoners nevertheless remained American military or naval men and retained their rank. As such they were still the concern of the United States Army and Navy. With change in status from fighting men to prisoners of war, they also became the concern of the American Red Cross, acting through the International Red Cross Committee, a neutral body, at Geneva, Switzerland. In the general world dim-out, the Red Cross shone as a precious light.

The Geneva Convention of 1929, signed and ratified by the United States Government, as by most of the other civilized countries, governed the treatment of war prisoners. The Japanese representative signed but his government did not ratify this convention. Nevertheless, after Pearl Harbor, it gave the United States Government "a commitment to apply the provisions of that convention to American prisoners of war and, insofar as adaptable, to civilian internees held by Japan," in the words of former Secretary of State Cordell Hull.

In general terms the Convention sets forth the rights and duties of soldiers who may be taken prisoner by the enemy. They may be interned in a town, fortress, or enclosed camp, but they cannot be imprisoned or held in unhealthy regions. They must be lodged in buildings or barracks affording all possible guarantee of hygiene and healthfulness.

Officer prisoners of war must receive the same pay as officers of the same rank in the armies of the enemy power. Private soldiers may be used as laborers outside the camps on work not directly connected with the war and must be paid for their labor. Both officers and men are allowed to correspond with friends and relatives and enjoy free postage. They may also receive parcels containing food, books, comfort articles, and many other things appearing on a prepared list supplied to the next of kin.

To deal with the authorities of the prison camp the men elect a "man of confidence," or a spokesman to act as their representative. While officers and men may only write a stipulated number of letters and cards a month, their spokesman, or elected representative may write as many as may be necessary for him to communicate with the agencies or organizations interested in the welfare of the prisoners.

The Convention also provides for the establishment of official information bureaus for the exchange of lists of prisoners among the belligerents. Provision is also made for the work of relief societies in the prisoner-of-war camps. And further provision is made for the representatives of the protecting powers to visit the camps and see that the rules of the Convention are carried out. In this connection also, delegates of the International Red Cross Committee have the right to visit camps to carry out the humanitarian work of the agency.

Through this international body the names of American prisoners are first transmitted to the United States. Its agents are charged with the responsibility of seeing that the prisoners actually received supplies shipped to them from this country.

Even before the United States entered the war, the American Red Cross was shipping relief supplies to prisoners in German-held European territory.

Since Pearl Harbor, the American Red Cross, in co-operation with the International Red Cross Committee, has provided the setup required for the shipment, distribution, and control of supplies for more than a million prisoners, including Americans.

The weekly eleven-pound Red Cross food packages for each American held by Germany, plus clothing and comfort articles, were paid for by the United States Army for its own men, by the Navy for naval prisoners, and by the President's Relief Fund for civilian internees. The American Red Cross provided out of its own funds the "capture" parcels and medical, dental, and orthopedic supplies, and garden seeds for American prisoners. Supplies shipped to United Nations' prisoners—Belgian, French, Greek, Netherlands, Norwegian, Polish, and Yugoslav—were financed by official agencies of United Nations. The volume shipped to Europe increased tremendously with the passing months, and by August 31, 1944, more than $101,000,000 worth of weekly food parcels, clothing, medicines and other permissible items had left American ports for prisoner-of-war camps.

Red Cross relief supplies, including next-of-kin packages and some prisoner-of-war mail, were shipped to Europe by the American and Canadian Red Cross societies on the Red Cross fleet. This fleet, in 1944, consisted of ten ships—the *Caritas I*, the *Caritas II*, and the *Henri Dunant*, owned, and the *Mangalore*, *Travancore*, and *Saivo*, chartered, by the International Red Cross Committee; and the *Malange*, *Lobito*, *Congo*, and *Finn*, under charter to the British Red Cross.

These transatlantic Red Cross ships, constantly plying between Philadelphia and European ports, traveling under safe conduct, along a designated course and brightly lighted at night, carrying supplies both ways for prisoners of war of all nationalities, were literally and symbolically ten beacons of continuing civilization.

Sailing under neutral flags with neutral crews, they carried medical, recreational, and clothing supplies provided by the United States War and Navy Departments and the Procurement Division of the Treasury Department, the American, British, and Canadian Red Cross societies, and organizations such as the YMCA and the National Catholic Welfare Conference. From the European terminal ports of the Red Cross fleet, the supplies were transshipped to Geneva for distribution through the International Red Cross Committee to the various camps.

In Geneva more than 5,000 persons, many of them volunteers, were employed by the International Red Cross Committee. Among other duties, they were responsible for getting these supplies to their destinations. The committee handled thousands of pieces of mail a day. It was also responsible for exchanging information between prisoners and civilian internees of belligerent nations, and tracing the whereabouts of civilians uprooted from their homes in the general dislocation of war. The Red Cross card index in Switzerland contained more than 16,000,000 names of displaced people.

Many letters from prisoners of war reaching the United States spoke in glowing terms of the eleven-pound Red Cross standard food packages received weekly. Although the Geneva Convention stipulates that all prisoners of war must be given the same food rations received by the detaining power's own base troops, the food served American prisoners, compared with American standards, was insufficient. These packages made the difference between a man going hungry and being fed adequately. The standard package was carefully designed by nutrition experts of the American Red Cross and the United States Army. The food articles for these packages were purchased by the United States Department of Agriculture and assembled and packed in Red Cross packaging centers in several cities. On the anniversary of Pearl Harbor, 1944, the centers produced their twenty-millionth package.

Cablegrams from the prisoner's family announcing a death or birth were routed to the interested parties by the American Red Cross through the International Red Cross Committee.

One cablegram to the United States from a camp in Germany, signed by twenty-one young Air Force lieutenants, carried the same message to their respective wives: "Now a prisoner of war. Has the baby come yet?"

Another contact with the outside world was the monthly *Red Cross News* put out by the American Red Cross. Copies of this specially printed paper containing noncontroversial and nonpolitical information were sent to each camp. Amusing or human-interest stories from each of the forty-eight states, sports items, and some of the better-known comic strips were featured in this unique publication. Articles that might be of interest to the prisoners without offending the German prison authorities were also included. Each edition must be approved by German censors before its distribution in camps.

Letters from next of kin in the United States must be mailed according to special instructions issued by the Post Office Department to avoid postmarkings such as "V for Victory" and "Buy War Savings Stamps and Bonds," which the German authorities find objectionable. Next-of-kin parcels are prepared in accordance with instructions issued by the Provost Marshal General for the same reasons, to prevent their being confiscated.

Relatives in the United States have been receiving mail regularly from their loved ones in German prisoner-of-war camps, though not as frequently as they desired. Mail from Japan was even less frequent than from Germany.

The American Red Cross endeavored in several ways to fill the gap left by these limitations on communications. In June, 1943, it started its monthly *Prisoners of War Bulletin* for the relatives of American prisoners of war and civilian internees. At that time, the late Norman H. Davis, Chairman of the American Red Cross, set forth the purpose of the new publication. It would serve, he said, "to give information, consistent with war conditions, about American prisoners of war and the methods for providing aid and comfort to them." Each month this publication has brought accurate, authoritative information and advice, in addition to comfort and consolation, to the families at home. Its pages carried interesting quotations from personal letters written by the prisoners in European and Far Eastern camps, camp notes, and detailed reports on the condition of the camps where Americans were imprisoned, together with photographs.

From month to month the Bulletin continued giving scraps of information which, when pieced together, gave relatives a fairly accurate though necessarily incomplete picture of the life led by their loved ones in war prisons. The August, 1944, issue printed a photostatic copy of a little camp paper, *Kriegie Times*, put out by the men confined in "Stalag Luft III." (American prisoners of war in Germany referred to themselves as "Kriegies"; it is an abbreviation of the German *"Kriegsgefangener,"* or war prisoner which the American and British found too hard to pronounce.) Located about ninety miles southeast of Berlin in the direction of Breslau, this camp for United States Air Force officers and noncommissioned officers was probably the best in Germany. International Red Cross delegates called it "a country club."

Headlined "American Senior Officer Pictures Life in Prison," the leading article by Delmar T. Spivey, Colonel, USAAF, gives a glimpse of the POW camp life in Stalag Luft III:

In the hope that our people at home may have a small insight into our prison life, we dedicate this issue of our camp newspaper, designed for home consumption. We hope you receive it and by so doing come into closer contact with us and our daily lives.

It is extremely difficult for us to keep abreast of your doings and with the trend of the times because of our complete isolation imposed by censorship, separation from all other than German news, and barbed wire and alert guards.

We strive to set up a model community designed to keep our bodies, minds, and souls healthy and alert, awaiting the day we can return to our own homes within our own land.

We think of you and thank all of you for your wonderful gifts to us—from individuals, and from the Red Cross, Y.M.C.A., and other charitable institutions,—and above all for your letters and prayers.

Those who detain us have not treated us badly, and have given us many small concessions which have made our incarceration lighter. The spirit of the Geneva Convention has been carried out and our treatment, in general, has been good. For this consideration we are grateful and know, that in return, the treatment of German prisoners at home is considerate.

We have our moments of loneliness and hunger for the companionship of home and home folks, but on the whole we laugh

and play most of the time. The rest of the time is spent in study-
ing, reading, working and hoping.

We shall hold firm to our faith in all of you and are ever assured of your love and consideration.

The picture was far less reassuring with respect to American prisoners of war and civilian internees held by the Japanese in the Far
East. The American forces on Bataan and Corregidor fought to the
last crumb of food, the last drop of water. Such heroism merited the
respect of the enemy. Instead of water and food, which were abun-
dant in the Philippines, and instead of medicines so plentiful in captured American military stores, the Japanese subjected these fallen
heroes to the unspeakable horrors of the "March of Death," according to the official Army-Navy revelations.

From the beginning of the war to late summer, 1944, the American Red Cross sent 194 cables to its own representative or to the
International Red Cross Committee in Geneva in an effort to get
supplies moving regularly to America prisoners of war and civilian
internees in the Far East.

The American Red Cross, working in co-operation with interested
departments of the United States Government, continued striving
through diplomatic and international Red Cross channels to open
such a route.

Without waiting for the end of these protracted negotiations, the
American Red Cross took advantage of the two sailings of the
diplomatic exchange ship, *Gripsholm*, during 1942 and 1943 to send
large cargoes of relief supplies for the imprisoned American na-
tionals (and the Canadian Red Cross did the same for its own
people).

The American Red Cross has in its possession receipts from several
of the camps for portions of the supplies delivered. The 1943 supplies were delivered to the Philippine internment camps before
Christmas, and to the Shanghai camps about Easter. While by no
means adequate, considering the long interval between shipments,
nevertheless they raised the morale of internees.

More than one-third of the 200,000 Allied soldiers and civilians
held by the Japanese were interned in the area north of the Philippines. In Japan proper, International Red Cross delegates were allowed to visit some camps and report on them. But many of them
have never been seen, their location remaining a mystery. The Japanese have also withheld information about most of the camps in
Korea and Formosa. Conditions in Hong Kong camps were found

unsatisfactory. Thousands of American and British civilian internees were in Shanghai area camps visited by International Red Cross delegates.

Nearly two-thirds of the prisoners of war and internees in 1944 were held in the southern area: the Philippines, Java, Borneo, Sumatra, Malaya, Thailand, and Burma. The Japanese would not reveal the location of the camps in these countries nor, with a few exceptions, even recognize a protecting power's right of access to them. In Malaya, an International Red Cross delegate was able to buy supplies locally for Allied prisoners, but was not permitted to distribute them himself. In Thailand, the Swiss Consul was recognized by the government, but was without authority as far as the Japanese authorities were concerned. Reports indicated that some mail and relief supplies from the 1943 *Gripsholm* trip had reached these prisoners.

In response to a statement by the Japanese Government that it might consent to receive supplies overland or by sea from Soviet territory, the American Red Cross in 1943 shipped to Vladivostok more than 2,000 tons of urgently needed food and medical supplies. After these stocks had lain in Soviet warehouses for a year, the Japanese agreed to send ships to Vladivostok to pick them up. Vladivostok being by then a naval base, the Russian Government suggested transferring the supplies to an equally accessible port, Nakhodka.

The Japanese Government at long last in the fall of 1944 dispatched the Japanese ship *Hakusan Maru* to this new port. The consignments consisted of about 300,000 eleven-pound food parcels packed by the American and Canadian Red Cross societies; 2,661 cases of drugs and medical supplies; 19,500 sets of clothing; 7,080 overcoats; 4,200 pairs of shoes; 125 cases of shoe-repair material; 21,000 sets of toilet articles; 1,000,000 cigarettes; and 299 cases of books and recreational and religious material shipped by the YMCA.

The *Hakusan Maru* made its first call at a Korean port and unloaded about 150 tons for the prisoners of war held in Korea and Manchuria. The vessel then proceeded to Kobe, where the remaining supplies were unloaded. The American Red Cross requested of the International Red Cross delegate supervising the forwarding of the supplies that they be distributed to United Nations', as well as American, prisoners of war and civilian internees in all Japanese-held areas.

A cable from Japan via Geneva in November, 1944, stated that the supplies would be distributed to prisoners of war in Japan proper and other localities as far south "as feasible."

Gift of Life: Blood Plasma

Somewhere in Italy, an Army ambulance came to a sudden stop in front of a clearing station. The American medical officer, a captain, and three corpsmen threw open the door and jumped in to work on the tall, grimy soldier lying on the bare floor covered with blood and dirt.

"Plasma." "Gauze." "Alcohol." "Bandages." The medical officer's orders were followed with the rapidity and efficiency of the operating room. The ambulance men explained that they had tried to administer plasma on the trip from the farther-front, but the road was too rough and the wounded man's veins too faint.

After quick, desperate efforts the officer finally injected the needle into the vein which was almost too thin to receive it; the plasma poured its life into the unconscious man. Calling for another plasma bottle, the doctor started another injection, with corpsmen holding the containers steadily.

As the medical men watched, the miracle happened. The wounded soldier remained unconscious, but his breathing strengthened and steadied while his paleness eased toward normal ruddiness.

The bottles emptied, the ambulance carried the patient toward its next stop, a clearing station farther back where facilities were better.

"I won't say positively that man will recover," said the doctor as the ambulance started rolling away. "He was badly wounded, and there may be injuries I couldn't find in that quick examination. But, you saw him when he got here and you saw him when he left. If he gets well, one thing saved him: plasma. Without it, he'd have been dead right now."

Out of the battle zones in every part of the world have come many stories such as this one from Italy, in which plasma from blood collected by the American Red Cross saved or helped save the lives of wounded soldiers and sailors. Plasma was the great savior of World War II. Time and again overseas Red Cross workers heard servicemen say, "When they're brought in, you'd swear they won't last to the clearing station. After the plasma, they're demanding a cigarette."

Little dramas such as this one described by Ivan H. (Cy) Peterman, war correspondent of the *Philadelphia Inquirer*, were enacted on all the battlefronts:

This happened one night in a field hospital eight miles from the front line in Tunisia. I was there, a patient myself, and saw it.

The soldier was brought in after lying two days and a night on a slope under command of German machine guns; they would let no medic near. He had a tourniquet and stopped the bleeding, but was in severe shock when picked up, and looked like a dying man when unloaded from the ambulance. They had given him plasma at once, but now they continued with whole blood transfusions donated by willing GI's from the near-by ordnance station.

All that night a Medical Major, who happened to know this man, fought to save his life. It was simply a case of will power, the Major's determination and the task of restoring the man's blood—and his strength through that blood.

It was an all-night battle; the Heinkels droned overhead, the wounded murmured in their sleep, a paralyzed artilleryman swore and fought his gun in delirium, a neurotic screamed in fear, a mine victim moved his hands across the blanket feeling for shattered legs, and down in front of me, alternately lifting him to an upright position, draining blood from a sucking wound, detouring it back into the veins, adding more blood—donated by unidentified citizens thousands of miles back home—that Major finally won his wrestle with death. In the morning color had returned to the dying man's face; 24 hours later he was on the way to recovery.

Blood plasma, running mate of sulfa drugs in beating battlefield deaths in this war, had saved another life.

Writing of the bloody battle for Cape Gloucester, New Britain, future historians undoubtedly will make note of a hill named "Plasma Ridge" by the United States Marines who fought there. Ordered to take the hill to clear out a Japanese pocket, the Marines fought bravely until ambushed by snipers and machine-gun nests. Wounded men and the few who had escaped injury were pinned down in hastily dug foxholes. Marine corpsmen, carefully shielding precious bottles of plasma, crawled forward on their stomachs. Their prompt use of plasma in the foxholes was credited with saving many lives that day.

Observed General Eisenhower: "The use of plasma quickly after a fighter is wounded, constitutes the most important single advance in surgical treatment of wounded in this war."

Ernie Pyle, writing from North Africa, told of urgent pleas by medical officers for more and more plasma. "Write lots about it, go clear overboard for it," they told him. "Say that plasma is the outstanding medical discovery of this war."

Plasma was human blood in action—the gift of life itself from the home front—wherever American boys fought and bled. Everywhere empty plasma bottles and discarded plasma cartons offered mute evidence of wounded men having been given a new lease on life. In the dingy first-aid stations right at the front, in the clearing sta-tions a short distance back, in the field hospitals, evacuation hos-pitals, and much farther back in the base hospitals, this precious lifesaver was at work.

One Medford, Massachusetts, sergeant torn by shrapnel in Tunisia said, "I'd have died without it." An Albany, Georgia, pharmacist's mate wounded during a South Pacific naval engagement declared, "There was hardly any hope for my living. I would have died from shock if it hadn't been for that plasma they gave us."

Men slashed by steel and shrapnel, shocked by concussion, and seared by flame, were saved by transfusions of blood from volun-teer donors in the United States; blood collected under the hu-manitarian symbol of the American Red Cross in a project that ranked as perhaps the most dramatic of all civilian wartime activi-ties.

During World War I many lives were lost because of the lack of suitable blood substitutes. Some attempts were made to preserve and use whole blood, but they were unsatisfactory. Nor were regular transfusions practical. To begin with, the donor and the recipient had to have the same type of blood and had to be brought together for the transfusions. This was impractical under combat conditions.

After that war, research workers discovered that plasma—the liquid part of the blood remaining after the red and white corpuscles had been removed—is an ideal blood substitute. It eliminates the necessity of matching the victim's blood type. Moreover, a method was developed whereby plasma could be dehydrated into a light, straw-colored powder that would keep for years without refrigera-tion. Rushed to front-line foxholes or stored aboard ship, it can be made available for immediate use by mixing it with distilled water.

The first dried human blood plasma was tested some months before Pearl Harbor by Captain E.A.M. Gendreau, Fleet Surgeon, stationed aboard the U.S.S. *Pennsylvania*. He had received from the Naval Medical School in Washington what appeared to be a strange package. Encased in a brown cardboard box about 7 by 7 by 4 inches in size were two tin containers. In one was a bottle filled with a light, flaky, straw-colored powder; in the other, a bottle of distilled water and an assortment of needles and rubber tubes.

Proceeding according to instructions, Captain Gendreau put the package through one of the toughest tests imaginable. Huge 14-inch guns roared into action, and after each barrage the package was carefully observed for possible damage. Navy dive bombers screamed earthward from terrific heights to see if the force would affect the package. It was thrown into landing barges, lugged ashore by Marines, fished from the surface, put under varying extremes of temperature. The package met every test.

No one then dreamed that a few years later the very same kit would be auctioned off on a network radio program to help sell war bonds for a United States at war; and few indeed imagined that before long duplicates of that simple brown package would become "the foremost livesaver of the war," according to the Surgeons General of the Army and Navy.

The Japanese attack on Pearl Harbor marked the first mass demonstration of the effectiveness of blood plasma in saving lives. On that tragic December day, 750 pints were used.

At the request of the Surgeons General of the Army and Navy, the Red Cross Blood Donor Service was inaugurated in February, 1941. Under the terms of the agreement, the Red Cross, at its own expense, established, maintained, and operated thirty-five fixed blood donor centers, and sixty-five mobile units regularly engaged in procuring blood from volunteer donors in 800 near-by communities. The blood was shipped to laboratories designated by the Army and Navy. Up to this point the entire cost was borne by the American National Red Cross and the chapters participating in the project, except in a few instances where, in view of the shortage of doctors, the Army and Navy assigned doctors to the centers to supplement the medical staffs employed by the Red Cross.

The National Research Council had charge of all the technical aspects of the service. Red Cross responsibility ended with the arrival of the blood at the laboratories in good condition. The Army and Navy made their own contracts with the laboratories, paid for the actual processing, and owned and controlled the finished products. Part of the blood was processed into dried plasma, part into serum albumin, another blood substitute.

The program started modestly with an Army-Navy request for only 15,000 pints of blood. The volume, however, increased tremendously after the entry of the United States into the war. At the end of 1942 a total of 1,300,000 pints had been delivered. A year later this had been increased to 5,700,000. By January 1, 1945, the total was approximately 11,000,000; almost one pint for every man and woman in the armed services. A statistically minded person in the Blood Donor Service calculated that in the three years since Pearl Harbor blood had been collected at the rate of six pints per minute.

Dramatic scenes were enacted at the fixed centers and the mobile units—mothers and fathers donating blood in the hope that their sons would never need it; or servicemen "repaying" the blood that saved their lives; whole plants turning out to donate in honor of a former fellow employee wounded in battle, as occurred in Milwaukee.

All over the country, individuals and groups were donating—rich and poor, industrial workers and business people, cabinet members, senators, and other high government officials, housewives, stenographers. Many became members of "Gallon Clubs" by donating every two months, required intervals between donations. Hundreds of business firms and organizations, government agencies, and labor unions assured the success of the program by sending in a regular number of donors each week. "At least one blood donor for every star in our service flag," became a group slogan in many stores, plants, and offices.

The basic reason for the success of the blood donor program was a widespread desire to make a personal contribution to the men at the front. Many people seemed to think that money was not enough. Donating a pint of blood was an emotional experience in which everybody shared alike, and the result of which was a gift of life itself to the wounded heroes of the nation.

One of the most touching stories to come out of Red Cross blood centers was reported from New York. A secretarial voice called to cancel the appointment of a businessman about to leave his office for the Center when a telegram from the War Department notified him that his son had been killed in action.

"No, don't cancel it," the bereaved father broke in. "My boy would want me to keep that appointment. That pint of blood can save someone else's son."

He came to the Center with the telegram clutched in his hand.

For the Merchant Seaman

"Everybody is familiar with the fine work the Red Cross is performing for the Army and Navy, but few people realize the wonderful job it's doing for the merchant seamen—the boys who get the stuff through in spite of the dangerous submarine hazard."

This statement was made by Captain William O'Brien, of San Francisco, at a South Central Pacific base where he represented the United States War Shipping Administration. He had just seen a ship limp into port, its officers and men having lost all their personal possessions.

"I was impressed by the way the Red Cross went into action. Even while the survivors were being tugged in, two Red Cross representatives and a launchful of supplies—cigars, cigarettes, candy bars, cookies of all varieties, playing cards, fruit juices—were speeding out to the ship.

"I know the men appreciated it tremendously," Captain O'Brien concluded, "for the merchant seaman, not being in uniform, is usually the last to get consideration."

At the height of the Axis submarine campaign in the Atlantic, the Caribbean Sea, and the Pacific, all the coastal Red Cross chapters, and those of the Panama Canal Zone and Puerto Rico, mobilized their resources to give emergency relief to merchant seamen and other survivors of torpedoed vessels. Awaiting survivors in port were warm and comfortable quarters, medical aid if needed, and a complete change of clothing. The rescued men received special survivors' kits containing clothing, woolens, cigarettes, and comfort articles, prepared by volunteers in Red Cross chapter work rooms. When stranded on some isolated spot or drifting in open boats awaiting rescue, torpedoed seamen received these kits from the air, dropped by United States Navy scouting blimps. In many cases, Red Cross first-aiders put out to sea to help bring survivors to safety through surging waters, and then set up first-aid quarters for treating those suffering from exposure.

The same type of service was given by Red Cross workers around the globe. The world-wide activities of the American Red Cross in World War II proved a boon to American merchant seamen. The latter may or may not have had a girl in every port, according to the traditional saying, but certainly they found American Red Cross workers wherever they docked—Glasgow, London, Southampton, Cherbourg, Marseille, Naples, Oran, Casablanca, Karachi, Bombay, Ceylon, Sydney, Auckland, Noumea, and many other Allied ports.

Joseph McDonald, of Buffalo, New York, second assistant engineer, learned about that. His vessel was discharging war cargo about a half-mile offshore during the Italian invasion when it was struck by a bomb. As the order came through to abandon ship, all hands hurried to the lifeboats, leaving behind everything but the clothes on their backs. When the survivors reached the North African mainland, they were met by American Red Cross workers who found temporary quarters for them, arranged for their meals, and supplied them with fresh clothing.

In its March 31, 1944, issue, the National Maritime Union's official organ, *The Pilot*, published a group picture and the stories of a crew whose ship was sunk, presumably in the Indian Ocean. After other crew members had described their experiences, one of them said:

We stayed in the lifeboats all night. About 1:30 the next day we were picked up by a corvette, manned by an Indian crew.

We were taken to a native camp of thatched huts. We lay on rope springs, each covered with one blanket. There were no mattresses. By that time we were half-starved to death. We were glad to wrap our faces around some food. They gave us corned beef, sardines and native beer which tasted as if it had been scraped off the bottom of a barrel.

Nine hours later we were on a train. After three days of travel we reached Ceylon. As we stepped off the train, the American Red Cross was there to meet us. They gave each of us two packs of cigarettes and some razor blades.

We spent the next few days in a British rest home, where we were treated fine. The Australian Red Cross gave us these gray uniforms, as well as shirts, shorts and shoes. They were really all right.

Many members of the National Maritime Union carried batches of the latest American newspapers and magazines to the farthest corners of the world. Upon arrival in a foreign port, they were met by American Red Cross workers who accepted the reading material for distribution among United States troops.

In the Seamen's Institute, New Orleans, the local Red Cross chapter gave first-aid training to some three hundred merchant seamen on the "installment plan." Classes were held from time to time on whichever days the boys returned to port.

A high percentage of merchant seamen gave blood regularly to the Red Cross blood donor centers on their brief shore leaves. When the ship *John D. Whidden* was commissioned on June 6, 1944, members of her crew concluded that the occasion called for a group blood donation. Twelve of the crew, National Maritime Union members, comprising all the men off watch at 6 P.M., made their donations in the Cleveland, Ohio, center on June 14. "The ship was commissioned on D-Day," they explained. "We're taking her to the east coast, and from there to the invasion area. We decided to do a little something for the boys already on the beachhead."

Many wartime seamen, when their ships tied up at Allied ports for a few days, made the American Red Cross service clubs their headquarters. They were given a clean bed (linen changed every night), good meals, and a homelike atmosphere complete with all the facilities available to servicemen. Also at their disposal was the American Red Cross field service. A sympathetic, understanding field director was available to help solve a personal problem, locate a friend, or if there was time, find out the condition of a sick relative, or whether the expected baby had arrived. If a man's draw had run out, he might even get an emergency loan to keep him for the rest of his shore leave.

Seaman Michael Trani, of Brooklyn, was one of the men who experienced the benefits of the Red Cross field service. At a North African port, Seaman Trani walked into the office of Red Cross Field Director Joseph B. Lippincott, of Somerset, Pennsylvania, to ask for information about his wife who was expecting a baby.

Lippincott dispatched an inquiry to Brooklyn, and the wait was on. This prospective father was a more pathetic case than other long-distance floor walkers whom Lippincott had aided. Again, and again, and again, Mike returned to the Red Cross office, each time more nervously anxious than before. "Any news today, eh?"

Then came Mike's last call: his ship was pulling out and what should he do?

Lippincott reassured him. "Listen in to — radio station at — period during the day, or have one of your shipmates listen in for you. As soon as the news comes from Brooklyn, we'll broadcast it to you on your ship."

The "stork report" came the very next day: "Son Michael Louis born. Both fine."

Lippincott immediately called the radio station and explained the situation to Captain Andre Baruch, former radio announcer, and now of Army Special Services.

"Did you say Trani?" asked Captain Baruch. "Not Mike Trani? Why, he lives next door to me in Brooklyn."

So Seaman Michael Trani received the news of his son's birth over his ship's radio at sea.

As a group, seamen are known for beaching in a port, resting a few days or nights, and then pulling out for another harbor, far distant, leaving their last port as but one more string of hazy memories—here today, gone tomorrow. This is why American Red Cross Club Director George Weir of New York City was surprised to receive the following letter signed by six members of the Seafarers' International Union of North America. Addressed to the Southampton Red Cross club, the letter read:

Friends:

Words can hardly express the feeling of gratitude we have for the many services rendered us by your organization.

You have made it possible for S.I.U. members of the crew of our ship to contact brothers, sons and friends of the armed forces stationed here in England, and this is a service which meant more than any words could express.

Through your efforts, it was made possible for these servicemen to visit our ship as guests of our fellow men and their respective relatives, and again, the good effect this had on morale could never be put in words.

May we then attempt to thank you by writing you this letter of deep and sincere appreciation so that you might be aware that we are truly appreciative.

We can assure you that any S.I.U. ship will do all in its power to show you their appreciation for your kind services.

American Red Cross Nursing Service

In World War I many nurses caring for sick and wounded servicemen wore the uniform and insignia of the American Red Cross. In World War II, this organization recruited graduate, registered nurses who were commissioned in the Army and Navy Nurse Corps.

On October 1, 1940, more than a year prior to America's entry into the war, the first member of the War Reserve of the American Red Cross Nursing Service was called to active duty by the Army Nurse Corps. She was Agnes C. Roesle, of Washington, D.C., who, after service at the Walter Reed Hospital, Washington, and at Camps Wheeler and Stoneman, sailed for duty in Australia and New Guinea.

Following in Miss Roesle's footsteps, more than 60,000 nurses joined the Army and Navy Nurse Corps. In all the war theaters they gave efficient, devoted, and often heroic service to the armed forces. Some sacrificed their lives.

However, nurses wearing the uniform of the American Red Cross performed many important duties on the home front, and some served in dangerous zones.

To meet the urgent need of nurses after the Pearl Harbor attack, the American Red Cross, at the request of General Delos C. Emmons, the military governor, recruited in the United States seventy-five nurses for emergency service in the Hawaiian Islands. Nurses with disaster experience were given preference, and only those ineligible for military duty were accepted. Upon arrival in Honolulu, the nurses were assigned by the local Office of Civilian Defense to stations on the different islands in the group. Wearing their Red Cross caps and insignia, and working under direction of the OCD, the nurses staffed emergency hospitals, first-aid stations, blood donor centers, and other emergency facilities set up for expected further Japanese attacks. In 1944, the danger to the Hawaiian Islands having passed, the Hawaiian unit of Red Cross nurses was disbanded. The opportunity was given to members of the unit to stay on individually, and many elected to do so. In a tribute to these nurses, the Hawaiian OCD stated: "Personally and professionally they have shown themselves to be of outstanding excellence and this community owes them a debt of gratitude that will never be paid."

Also outstanding was the group of Red Cross nurses who some months before Pearl Harbor, volunteered for duty in England with the American Red Cross–Harvard University Hospital, a 100-bed installation for the study and treatment of communicable diseases under wartime conditions. The Red Cross provided the nursing staff and Harvard University the medical staff, in addition to maintaining a public health unit for field and laboratory work in epidemiology.

Five acres of open field amid English poppies and bluebells near Salisbury in southern England were selected as the proposed hospital site. The American Red Cross undertook to build and equip a temporary or hut-type hospital, prefabricated in the United States, transported to England, and set up on foundations provided by the British Ministry of Health. Across the submarine-infested Atlantic, in the holds of more than seventy ships, went boxes and cases of brass pipe fittings, building materials, kitchen utensils, sets of hospital and laboratory equipment, surgical supplies, and medicines. When the project was finally set up it consisted of twenty-two green huts housing a complete public-health unit, as well as the hospital and laboratory.

To staff this unit, forty-eight Americans, including twenty-nine Red Cross nurses, sailed from Halifax in a British convoy in June, 1941. Because of the thick fog, which lasted five days, the ships found it hard to stay in convoy formation. On the seventh day, 400 miles from Greenland, one of the vessels, the S.S. *Vigrid*, limping behind because of engine trouble, was torpedoed by a German submarine and sunk.

Clad in warm clothing and wearing their lifebelts, ten nurses were lowered into lifeboats—two nurses in one boat, and four each in two other boats. With one group of four nurses were ten men from the passenger list and crew. As their boat rocked on the choppy waters, they were shocked to see a German submarine rise to the surface in front of them. A guttural voice shouted questions at them: How many ships were in the convoy? What were they carrying as cargo? What was their destination? No one answered and the submarine disappeared under water.

For twelve days and eleven nights, the four nurses and ten men drifted about in the open sea, cold and hungry. Their feet and hands were severely frostbitten, and despair was settling down on them, when they were finally picked up by an Allied ship that took them to Iceland. Ultimately they were transferred to the *Norfolk* and brought home, the first women victims of the Battle of the Atlantic to reach the United States. The young women were: Marion Blissett, Detroit, Michigan; Victoria Pelc, Auburn, New York; Lillian M. Pesnicak, Albany, New York; and Rachel St. Pierre, Newton Center, Massachusetts.

In another lifeboat, Margaret Somerville, of Catskill, New York, and Helen Jurewicz, of South Amboy, New Jersey, had harrowing experiences of their own. With them were the first mate, chief engineer, and five other members of the ship's crew. It was cold and raining when they were set adrift in heavy seas; the surface was littered with floating wreckage. Taking survey of the water and food supplies, the survivors agreed to the issue of two ounces of water twice a day, one biscuit a day, and small rations of meat as long as it lasted.

Recalling their experience, the two nurses said:

> We amused ourselves at first by describing in detail the meals we would eat when we reached home. But after the fourteenth day, when we failed to attract the attention of a passing ship, nobody troubled to talk. About that time the food supply gave out and we tried unsuccessfully to eat barnacles taken from wreckage. The only activity on board was using the distilling plant, with which we could make drinking water from the sea water—about a quart every four or five hours. The men rigged up a shelter for us two women, but it did not help much.
>
> On the nineteenth day we were drifting in complete despair. Nothing mattered any more. Suddenly the chief mate spotted a destroyer on the horizon, and since it was three o'clock in the morning, we had to send up flares. Our spirits came back in a rush. It was as if a magician's wand had been passed over us. We laughed, cried, sang, and danced, and celebrated by drinking all the remaining water.

The two young nurses were rushed to a London hospital where they soon recovered. Later they joined the staff of the Red Cross–Harvard University Hospital, for which they had volunteered.

The four Red Cross nurses in the remaining lifeboat were never found, and they are presumed to have given their lives in the performance of their duties. They were: Phyllis L. Evans, Everett, Massachusetts; Dorothy L. Koehn, Oshkosh, Wisconsin; Dorothy C. Morse, Boston, Massachusetts; and Nancy M. Pett, Detroit, Michigan.

The S.S. *Maasdam*, carrying sixteen Red Cross nurses and the hospital's housemother, Mrs. Ruth Breckenridge of Winston-Salem, North Carolina, in the same convoy, was also torpedoed. Mrs. Breckenridge and Maxine C. Loomis, of Putney, Vermont, were lost after a horrible experience in a leaky lifeboat.

The other girls were rescued by a tanker and taken to England. They were met by representatives of the British Ministry of Health and the British Red Cross, and were received by Queen Elizabeth.

Despite abnormal wartime conditions—overcrowded air-raid shelters, disruption of sanitary installations by German bombs, overwork, and undernourishment—no epidemics developed in England during the fifteen months that the American Red Cross–Harvard University Hospital functioned. The number of nurses on the staff grew to sixty-two. Wearing their attractive blue serge suits and brimmed felt hats, bearing American Red Cross insignia, the nurses accompanied staff doctors on public health investigations about the country. They were lionized everywhere. People stopped them in the streets, on buses, and in restaurants to greet them with friendly remarks such as "Hello, America," and "Thank you." Strangers invited them to tea and dinner. In the shops, clerks addressed them with "Sister," the common British term for hospital nurses.

In August, 1942, the buildings and equipment of the American Red Cross–Harvard University Hospital were taken over by the United States Army in Great Britain for use as an epidemiological unit in the field of preventive medicine.

Thirty of the unit's sixty-two nurses, released from duty by the Red Cross, volunteered for the Army Nurse Corps, and remained in the European theater of operations.

INDEX

Abbott, Mrs. A. W., 31
Abbott, Edwin L., 183, 184, 185
Accord, Vivian, 115
Accra, Africa, 189
Adak Island, 208, 209
Admiralty Islands, 221, 228, 230, 235
Afrika Korps, 83-4, 85, 114, 140
Agra, India, 144
Aiea, 9
Air forces, U.S.A., 49, 58, 84-96, 104, 109, 208, 119-24, 139, 144, 160, 162, 167, 189, 208, 264; Ferry Command, 85
Air Force Victorettes, 52
Air Transport Command, 188, 189, 190, 192
Aitape, 228
Akthar, Nabi, 148
Alaska, 203-8
Alaskan Chapter, 203-4
Alcan Highway, 204, 207-8
Aleutian Islands, 206, 208-12
Alexander, Gen. Harold, 114
Alexandria, Egypt, 84, 89, 96, 98
Algeria, 110, 118
Algiers, 109, 110-13, 116, 124, 125, 128, 241
Allen, Richard F., 44
Allenby Bridge, 97
Allied Club, Oran, 114, 115
Allin, W. S., Jr., 5
Aloha Tower, Honolulu, 3-4
Amazon River, 188
Amchatka Island, 208
American Baptist Christians, 132
American Field Service, 57
Ames, Rosemary, 114
Amphibian operations, 224-6
Anchorage, Alaska, 204, 206
Andaman Islands, 141
Anderson, Clarence R., 231-2; quoted, 232-5
Anderson County (Texas) Chapter, 236
ANGAU, 59
Antigua 186
Anzacs, 85
Anzio-Nettuno beachhead, 163, 247, 251-7
Arabian Sea, 141
Arabs, 96, 103-4, 108, 126
Arawe, 228
Archangel, Russia, 182

ARC Light, 147; quoted, 147-8
Argentia, Newfoundland, 198
Arizona, 15
Army, U. S., in Australia, 38-53
Army General Hospital No. 13, 34
Army General Hospitals: Australia, 34, 54; Burma, 170; Hawaii, 7-8; New Guinea, 61; North Africa, 128
Army Medical Corps, 60
Army Special Services, *see* Special Services
Arnold, Mary Jane, 149
Arrowsmith, Brig. Gen. John, 164
Aruba, 186
Ascension Island, 189-93
Ashley, C. W., 40
Assam, India, 143, 149, 163, 165, 178
Associated Press Bureau, Tokyo, 116
Astaire, Adele, 262-3
Astaire, Fred, 262
Astie, Judy, 168
Ataneo de Manila, 17
Atkinson Field, 189
Atkinson, Vicky, 279
Attu, 208-9
Auchinleck, Gen. Claude, 83-4
Auckland, New Zealand, 45, 49
Austin, Mary I., 288
Australia, 32-55, 62, 64, 66, 67, 69, 73, 74, 121, 305; American soldiers in, 39-49; Brisbane defense plan, 38-9; care of wounded, 53-4; clubs, Red Cross, 43-8; farmers, 50-1; food supply, 48; hospitals, 54; rest homes, 49, 50-3; recreation program, 40-1; social conditions in, 41-2; supplies, Red Cross, 36-7; volunteer workers, 47-8, 52-3; war base, 38-9, 42
Australian-American Association, 55
Australian Comforts Fund, 37, 45, 54-5
Australian Red Cross, 31, 32, 34, 37, 42-3, 54-5, 303
Australian Hiring Authority, 45, 50
Australia-New Guinea Administrative Unit, 59
Austria, 104
Axis strategy, 82-4

B.A.E.C. programs, 116, 117
Bahamas, 186
Bahia, Brazil, 188
Bailey, Charles E., 103
Bain, Ralph, 86, 103